The *Arab Spring*

Nijhoff Law Specials

VOLUME 82

The titles published in this series are listed at brill.com/nlsp

The *Arab Spring*

New Patterns for Democracy and International Law

Edited by

Carlo Panara and Gary Wilson

MARTINUS
NIJHOFF
PUBLISHERS

LEIDEN • BOSTON
2013

Library of Congress Cataloging-in-Publication Data

The Arab spring : new patterns for democracy and international law / Edited by Carlo Panara and Gary Wilson.
p. cm. — (Nijhoff law specials ; 82)
Includes index.
ISBN 978-90-04-23041-5 (pbk. : alk. paper) — ISBN 978-90-04-24341-5 (ebooks)
1. Conflict of laws—Public policy—Arab countries. 2. Arab Spring, 2010– 3. International law. 4. Democracy. 5. Democratization—Arab countries—History—21st century. 6. Revolutions—Arab countries—History—21st century. 7. Arab countries—Politics and government—21st century. I. Panara, Carlo. II. Wilson, Gary, Dr.

KMC128.5.A73 2013
909'.097492708312—dc23

2012039081

This publication has been typeset in the multilingual "Brill" typeface. With over 5,100 characters covering Latin, IPA, Greek, and Cyrillic, this typeface is especially suitable for use in the humanities. For more information, please see www.brill.com/brill-typeface.

ISSN 0924-4549
ISBN 978-90-04-23041-5 (paperback)
ISBN 978-90-04-24341-5 (e-book)

This book is printed on acid-free paper.

The *Arab Spring*

New Patterns for Democracy and International Law

Edited by

Carlo Panara and Gary Wilson

MARTINUS
NIJHOFF
PUBLISHERS

LEIDEN • BOSTON
2013

Library of Congress Cataloging-in-Publication Data

The Arab spring : new patterns for democracy and international law / Edited by Carlo Panara and Gary Wilson.
p. cm. — (Nijhoff law specials ; 82)
Includes index.
ISBN 978-90-04-23041-5 (pbk. : alk. paper) — ISBN 978-90-04-24341-5 (ebooks)
1. Conflict of laws—Public policy—Arab countries. 2. Arab Spring, 2010– 3. International law. 4. Democracy. 5. Democratization—Arab countries—History—21st century. 6. Revolutions—Arab countries—History—21st century. 7. Arab countries—Politics and government—21st century. I. Panara, Carlo. II. Wilson, Gary, Dr.

KMC128.5.A73 2013
909'.097492708312—dc23

2012039081

This publication has been typeset in the multilingual "Brill" typeface. With over 5,100 characters covering Latin, IPA, Greek, and Cyrillic, this typeface is especially suitable for use in the humanities. For more information, please see www.brill.com/brill-typeface.

ISSN 0924-4549
ISBN 978-90-04-23041-5 (paperback)
ISBN 978-90-04-24341-5 (e-book)

This book is printed on acid-free paper.

CONTENTS

LIST OF CONTRIBUTORS

Dr Carlo Panara—Senior Lecturer in EU/Public Law and Research Co-ordinator, School of Law, Liverpool John Moores University, UK. E-mail: C.Panara@ljmu.ac.uk.

Dr Gary Wilson—Senior Lecturer in Law, School of Law, Liverpool John Moores University, UK. E-mail: G.Wilson@ljmu.ac.uk.

Dr Tamás Ádány—Senior Lecturer in Public International Law, Faculty of Law, Department of Public International Law, Peter Pazmany Catholic University. E-mail: adany.tamas@jak.ppke.hu.

Dr Andrew Coleman—Senior Lecturer, Department of Business Law and Taxation, Monash University, Australia. E-mail: andrew.coleman@monash.edu.

Olga Jurasz—Lecturer in Law, School of Law, Open University, UK. E-mail: olga.jurasz@open.ac.uk.

Dr Jackson Maogoto—Senior Lecturer in International Law, School of Law, University of Manchester, UK. E-mail: Jackson.Magaoto@manchester.ac.uk.

Dr Abdullah Nawafleh—LLB in Law, Amman University (Amman-Jordan); LLM in International Law and Diplomacy, University of Derby (Derby-England); PhD in Law, University of Westminster (London-England). E-mail: a.nawafleh@gmail.com.

Prof Michèle Olivier—Reader, Law School, University of Hull, UK; Extra Ordinary Professor, Unit for Advanced Studies, University of Pretoria, South Africa. E-mail: Michele.olivier@hull.ac.uk.

Edward Phillips—Principal Lecturer in Law, Law School, University of Greenwich, London, UK. E-mail: E.P.Phillips@gre.ac.uk.

Dr Nirmala Pillay—Senior Lecturer in Law, School of Law, Liverpool John Moores University, UK. E-mail: N.Pillay@ljmu.ac.uk.

Dr Vasiliki Saranti—Lecturer, National Police Academy; Researcher, European Centre of Research and Training on Human Rights and Humanitarian Action, Panteion University, Athens, Greece. E-mail: vasiliki_sarandi@hotmail.com.

Dr James Summers—Lecturer in International Law, Law School, Lancaster University, UK. E-mail: j.summers@lancaster.ac.uk.

Dr Jure Vidmar—Leverhulme Early Career Fellow, Faculty of Law, University of Oxford. E-mail: jure.vidmar@iecl.ox.ac.uk.

Mohamed Youssef—Pro bono legal assistant, Defence Team for Saif Al-Islam Gaddafi, International Criminal Court. E-mail: mohamed.youssef@icc-cpi.int.

PREFACE

THE 'ARAB SPRING': CONSTITUTIONALISM AND INTERNATIONAL LAW

The socio-political phenomenon known as the 'Arab Spring' began in North Africa in December 2010. Since then, an extraordinary wave of protests has shaken all of the Arab world. One after another, the regimes in power in Tunisia, Egypt, Libya, and Yemen, were overthrown. With a differing degree of intensity, protests and demonstrations erupted and are still continuing in a number of Arab countries. Civil uprisings and brutal military repression are still ongoing in Syria.

Since the meltdown of the communist regimes in Eastern Europe in the late 1980s and early 1990s, the wave that is changing the Arab world is certainly one of the most momentous events in international politics. In relation to the fall of communism, the breakdown of an ideology and of its economic system, offered a sufficiently clear framework for comprehension. In the Arab Spring, the 'common thread' appears more difficult to find. The fact that the uprisings and protests took place in the same geographical region (North Africa and Middle East), and that the majority of the populations involved are Arab speaking Muslim, would be a too simplistic explanation for the 'Arab revolutions'. In the Arab Spring there is no single ideological framework which has been challenged and no two regimes were identical.

So far the Arab Spring has involved 17 Muslim countries in North Africa and Middle East, with an overall population of approximately 300 million people. Alone these figures explain the importance of the 'revolutions' and their impact on the international community. This is why Gary Wilson and I had the idea to organise a conference about this topic at Liverpool John Moores University (16 September 2011), and to edit a book emanating from the conference. Gary is an International Law expert and was concerned about the international law related aspects of the civil war in Libya, whilst I, given my constitutional and comparative law background, was very interested in the outcome of this emerging wave of 'Arab constitutionalism'.

During the recent events, the Arab world has become an original 'workshop', where new solutions and patterns for both international law and constitutionalism are taking shape. Once regime change in a number of Arab countries has taken place, or is in the process of taking place, the question of the possible outcome of the ongoing reforms is at the forefront. This aspect is addressed in Maogoto and Coleman's chapter (1), dealing with the question of what type of constitutionalism is best suited to the Arab countries after the revolutions.

Michèle Olivier (chapter 2) addresses another question closely linked to the previous one; whether existing international law, and particularly the African Union framework, affords a right to democracy. This question leads to another; that of the legitimacy of undemocratic regimes under existing international law. This second aspect is examined in Jure Vidmar's chapter (3), showing again that in the contemporary world constitutional and international law profiles are inextricably entangled.

The phenomenon known as the 'Arab Spring' entails a demand for freedom. Arab countries will need to reform themselves and to create more liberal, more accountable, and ultimately more democratic regimes. However, the 'revolutions' are likely to be doomed to failure, if they failed to address Arab masses' immediate concerns; unemployment, corruption, poverty. Abdullah Nawafleh (chapter 4) considers this specific aspect and makes a case for reforms creating an efficient legal environment, capable of favouring local and foreign investment.

The armed intervention in Libya is the focus of Gary Wilson's chapter (5). The co-editor of this volume argues that UN Security Council's resolution 1973, allowing armed intervention of Western powers in Libya, whilst being on paper aimed to protect civilians, in practice could be used as a 'smokescreen' for regime change. Once again, as with Vidmar's chapter (3), one can see how aspects of constitutional law (regime change, democratisation), are intertwined with international law.

An aspect that needed to be investigated is the role of women in the recent and ongoing revolutions. Olga Juresz (chapter 6) focuses on the tragedy of the rape of Libyan women by Gaddafi's forces as punishment for their anti-governmental activities.

A critical appraisal of the UN Security Council's resolution 1973 is the topic of Mohamed Youssef's (7), and of Vasiliki Saranti's chapters (8). Like in Wilson's chapter (5), the theme that arises is the full compliance of military intervention in Libya with the UN Charter. Youssef addresses the question of whether the resolution actually sides with one party of the conflict (the Libyan rebels), rather than being neutral and genuinely directed to protect civilians. Similarly to Wilson, Saranti questions

the real objective of Western military intervention, this possibly being the democratisation of Libya, rather than the protection of civilians.

In the aftermath of the 'Arab revolutions', Arab countries (are) and will be faced with the political and legal problem of the accountability of those responsible of the atrocities committed by the previous regimes. Tamas Adany (chapter 9) argues that due to the lack of ratification of the Rome Statute in a number of Arab countries, domestic courts, rather than the ICC, are the most effective place for prosecuting the authors of the atrocities.

North Africa and the Middle East are a fundamental part of the cradle of civilisation and their archaeological heritage is of incommensurable value. Edward Phillips (chapter 10) devotes his attention to the important aspect of the protection of this historical heritage from armed conflicts occurring in the context of the 'Arab Spring'.

The last two chapters focus on developments in two key areas. James Summers' chapter (11) deals with Palestinian self-determination. Although on the side of recent events, this issue is crucial for a full understanding of the equilibrium within the Arab world. Nirmala Pillay's chapter (12) focuses on perpetration of torture in Egypt until the removal from power of President Mubarak. Compliance with human rights and repudiation of torture will be among the most important tests for post-Mubarak Egypt.

Events in the region are still open to all possible outcomes and in the forthcoming years the Arab world is likely to remain a unique 'political laboratory'. This book is our contribution to a better understanding of the phenomenon called the 'Arab Spring' from a constitutional and international law perspective.

Carlo Panara
Liverpool, UK, June 2012

ACKNOWLEDGMENTS

Gary Wilson and I would like to thank all the conference speakers and the contributors to this volume. A special thanks goes to the publishers, Martinus Nijhoff, for believing in this project. A heartfelt thanks to our partners, children, friends, and colleagues, for having been able to endure us during the preparation of the conference and of the book; if our psychological balance has not been overly deteriorated by the work, it is due to them only.

CHAPTER ONE

CHANGING THE GUARD—THE PRICE OF DEMOCRACY: LESSONS FROM THE ARAB SPRING ON CONSTITUTIONALISM

Jackson Nyamuya Maogoto* & Andrew Coleman**

1. Introduction

In late 2010 the self-immolation of a Tunisian street vendor—Mohamed Bouzazi—unwittingly encapsulated the frustration of corruption and heavy-handed administrative structures by the vast bulk of Tunisia's populace.[1] What would have been an isolated act and a country specific phenomenon morphed into potent totemic symbolism for Arab citizenry in coming weeks long frustrated by living under modern fiefdoms. Civilian unrest on the streets rapidly toppled the Tunisia government generating a political earthquake across the Arab World in a groundbreaking regional citizenry political project.[2] The upheaval in Tunisia inspired civil uprisings, widespread protests, armed confrontation and even civil war that in weeks was consuming an ever increasing number of North African States and extending its reach into the heart of the Middle East. The political earthquake was of such a magnitude that it swept into Egypt, Morocco, Libya, and Algeria, rocked Bahrain, Jordan and Syria, with aftershocks felt in Saudi Arabia, Oman, Kuwait and Lebanon.[3]

Numerous factors led to the protests. On a balance they were anchored in basic common denominators and conditions: autocratic regimes, lack of representative institutions, flagrant inequities, corruption, nepotism and

* LLB (Hons) (Moi), LLM (Hons) (Cantab), LLM (UTS), PhD (Melb), GCertPPT (UoN); Senior Lecturer in Law, University of Manchester (UK).

** BA, LLB, LLM (Monash), PhD (Melb); Senior Lecturer in Law, Monash University (Australia).

1 Kurt Anderson, "The Protester" in *Time Magazine*, 26 December 2011/2 January 2012, 33.

2 See e.g. Adam Tarock, "Time for the Government to Fear the People", *The Australian Rationalist*, 88 (Spring 2011): 26; Noah J Feldman, (Reviewer) "Constitutions in a Nonconstitutional World: Arab Basic Laws and the Prospects for Accountable Government (Nathan J. Brown)", *International Journal of Constitutional Law*, (2003): 403.

3 See for example, Editorial, "The Arab Awakening, Revolution Spinning in the Wind" in *The Economist*, July 16, 2011, 41; Jack A. Goldstone, "Understanding the Revolutions of 2011, Weakness and Resilience in Middle Eastern Autocracies", *Foreign Affairs*, 90(5), (2011) 13.

cronyism against a background of rulers who had made it unofficial government policy to treat public resources as private goods. A generation of disillusioned youth was questioning through tangible action (violent and non violent) their relationship with those in power and the loss of dignity orchestrated by predatory regimes.[4] These events were a "... culmination of a century of Arab popular struggle for freedom and sovereignty."[5] Although the civil uprisings share many similarities they also differ as local conditions varied "... which accounts for strikingly different trajectories in Egypt, Tunisia, Libya, Bahrain, Yemen and elsewhere."[6] For example, in Tunisia following President Ben Ali's ouster and departure, a state of emergency was declared and a caretaker coalition government was created. In Egypt when Hosni Mubarak was finally forced out of presidential office the military dissolved the Egyptian Parliament, suspended the Constitution and partially lifted the nation's emergency laws that had been in force for thirty years promising to hold free, open elections.[7] Libya was to stand as a watershed frontier. Determined to prevent the fate of regimes elsewhere Qaddafi's government rolled out the police and military to crush protests. The deployment of the military and a rising death toll prompted the United Nations Security Council to take a formal stand through a rare concurrence by the permanent members of the Security Council to protect civilians.[8] A campaign to avert a humanitarian disaster morphed into a vigorous NATO led bombing campaign against the Qaddafi regime marking the first direct international intervention by Western liberal democratic States in the political unrest besieging governments across North Africa and the Middle East.[9]

---

[4] Suzy Hansen, "Egypt's Mean Queen" *Newsweek*, January 9/16 2012) 36, 41; Lisa Anderson, "Demystifying the Arab Spring", *Foreign Affairs*, 90(5) (2011): 3–4.

[5] Rami G. Khouri, "The Long Revolt", *The Wilson Quarterly* 35(2) (2011): 43; Tarock, "Time", 26; Jean-Pierre Filiu, *The Arab Revolution, Ten Lessons from the Democratic Uprising*, (Oxford: Oxford University Press, 2011) 16; Goldstone, "Understanding the Revolution", 8; Anderson, "Demystifying", 2–3.

[6] See e.g. International Crisis Group, 'Popular Protest in North African and the Middle East (II): Yemen between Reform and Revolution Middle East/North Africa Report No. 102', 10 March 2011, Introduction, 10 (document on file with author); Aryn Baker, 'Bahrain's Stillborn Revolution' *Time Magazine*, January 23, 2012, 22; Anderson, "Demystifying", 3.

[7] International Crisis Group, "Popular Protest", 1.

[8] Security Council 1973 (2011), United Nations S/RES/1973 (2011), adopted by the Security Council at its 6498th Meeting.

[9] With the exception of Saudi troops being sent across the causeway into Bahrain, however, in this instance the Saudi troops were sent as a display of force to reinforce the current regime, and only stayed for a brief moment.

The marginalization of important social, sectarian and/or ethnic groups lies at the heart of the Arab Spring. The greatest threat to post-Spring stability and self-identity of the citizenry in the Middle East is (and will remain) the uncertain role and metamorphosis of the security forces (primarily the military) and Islamist parties. The perception in the liberal West and elsewhere has long been that Islam is incompatible with democracy,[10] and that Arabs were/are the exception to the rest of the world in their rejection of tolerating liberal socio-political values.[11] This Chapter while taking into account the different trajectories encapsulated by the Arab Spring seeks to illustrate that constitutionalism informed by principled governance is *a process as well as a goal*. In particular it cautions against the pitfalls of implementing monolithic liberal preferences for a "corporatist" State as this can oust a normative agenda for local stake-holders in the quest for reformed and limited government.

2. Sovereign but Unstable—Hollowed Out Polities

It is imperative to note that the revolts that encapsulate the tenor of the Arab Spring are very different to the Arab nationalism of the 1950's and 1960's, which was anti-colonial in nature as well as a response to perceived *external aggression*.[12] The primary impetus of the Arab Spring was a response by large segments of the citizenry to *internal aggression* by their own governments premised on a desire to improve their political freedom and participation in governance. Aggrieved at being treated like serfs in contemporary States based on feudalistic systems of yester centuries, they sought a sense of dignity as citizens with freedom to make their own choices over attempts by regimes that had endeavoured to control the minutiae of their lives.[13] However, caution should be taken before confusing these desires with a craving for greater democratic "space".

Democracy may be one way of working towards these goals, but it is not necessarily *the goal*. It is conceivable that the above goals can be achieved

---

[10] Tarock, "Time", 26.

[11] As Filiu so eloquently describes this sentiment: "The Arabs were [portrayed as] the quintessential Other, lagging behind modernity and its countless rewards". Filiu. *The Arab Revolution*, 5.

[12] From the US, the West and Israel: Khouri, "The Long Revolt", 44.

[13] As noted by Khouri: 'Average people were willing to endure as long as they felt that the future held out hope of a better life for themselves of their children.' Khouri, "The Long Revolt", 44.

simply through the removal of dictators and changes made to transform the police State into a civic polity. Bahrain, Oman and Saudi Arabia seem to have witnessed "stillborn revolutions" due to tactical government moves towards what can only be termed as "reformist window dressing" as previously benign political murmurs manifested themselves on the streets and led hereditary absolute monarchs to yield some ground.[14] The problem with the situation in any of the States of the Arab Spring is that without systemic change the removal of one dictator may merely result in replacement with another, even a so-called *benevolent* one.[15] Benevolent dictatorships sound appealing because they theoretically combine efficiency and outcomes with benevolence, but the reality is much different. The spectres of tribalism and sectarianism when combined with any form of autocracy inevitably result in patronage, cronyism and discrimination, as regimes trade patronage for loyalty, thus leading to a divide and conquer mentality by the administration that plays one group off against another. The net effect of this is normally hollowing out societies through marginalization of important social, sectarian and/or ethnic groups whilst maintaining a façade of sovereignty and national cohesion.

It is the "sovereign but unstable hollowed out polities" that activists set their eyes on changing.[16] For example, whilst in Bahrain the monarchy initially was not in the crosshairs of activists, the feeling amongst the majority Shi'a population is that true reform of a skewered governance structure can be only achieved through some spectrum of democracy.[17] As noted by Lisa Anderson, Tunisia had enjoyed the best educational system in the Arab world, a well-organised labour movement, as well as a large middle class, and yet protesters still advocated for democracy.[18] Thus, the uprisings were more than just a demand for the removal of dictators responsible for the problems faced by the respective peoples of the Arab Spring. They were a rallying point for the reform of repressive governance structures dominated by hereditary or self-made political elites interested more in ruling rather than governing and thus administrative structures whose basis was consolidating rule and eviscerating dissent in any form through limitation of many civil and political rights.

---

14 See e.g. Baker, "Bahrain", 23.

15 Many of the dictators removed by the Arab Spring could be described as benevolent by some group.

16 Anderson, "Demystifying", 3; Goldstone, "Understanding the Revolution", 8.

17 See e.g. Baker, "Bahrain", 22.

18 Anderson, "Demystifying", 3. Goldstone describes the autocratic governments as "Sultanistic dictatorships": Goldstone, "Understanding the Revolution", 8.

The protesters that fuelled the Arab Spring in alleys, streets and public squares amidst deaths, disappearances, mass arrests, volleys of teargas canisters and live bullets by overzealous government security apparatus reached a significant conclusion, and a consequential epiphany which in the surreal political development of the Middle East was groundbreaking—fear and status quo was no longer an option and power corrupts, and absolute power corrupts absolutely.[19] First-hand experience of the darker side of "benevolent" patronage/dictatorship had thrived but also exposed a very real flaw in the polities system of benevolent patronage—power had to have limits, and the exercise of absolute authority needed a logical basis. A primary method to constrain power is to enshrine civil and political freedoms in a constitution.[20] However, even a well-crafted constitution can be merely a political alibi for government machinations and quasi legitimacy in the absence of an ethos of limited government and participatory rights.[21] It is imperative that the reform of political systems dwells on consensus and a realisation that constitutional frameworks should serve different purposes rather than necessarily mirror modularised checklists of best practice. Such an epiphany can often be at odds with the realities of a society, but more importantly faces a difficult challenge when the respective societies are essentially unstable hollowed out polities as noted above.

3. Socio-Political Ambiguities and Fractured Identities

Lessons to be derived from divided polities undergoing the pains of transition from autocracy to democracy or from civil strife to "rational" governance are extremely difficult and failure often results from seeking to develop simplistic patterns at odds with particularised settings. This potential failure is of great import regarding the Arab Spring, with its eclectic mixture of tribalism, historical struggles against external

---

[19] This is paraphrasing the famous comment made by Lord Acton (1834–1902) to Bishop Mandell Creighton: "Power tends to corrupt, and absolute power corrupts absolutely. Great men are almost always bad men."

[20] The authors are aware that much of the success of a constitution limiting power is dependent upon the people it governs and how they respect it. Nonetheless it is a good start. See Feldman, "Constitutions in a Nonconstitutional World", 391; Wayne Norman, *Negotiating Nationalism, Nation-Building, Federalism, and Secession in the Multinational State*, (Oxford Oxford University Press: 2006), 75–79.

[21] Donald S. Lutz, *The Origins of American Constitutionalism* (Indianapolis: Liberty Fund 1988), 16.

controls, resource allocation (primarily oil wealth), religion and artificial nationalism. Furthermore, the Arab Spring has taken place in the shadow of September 9/11 and the War against Terror paradigm—a volatile *realpolitik* issue often linked in analytical and conceptual thinking with Islamism.[22] While the Arab Spring and its general underpinnings are relatively easy to paint, the different societal and sectarian divides dictate particularised solutions. The victims of State policies have often experienced this along different spectra of ethnocentrism, discrimination, tribalism and political exclusion. Thus neither rights nor well-intentioned commitments to democracy and good governance will be sufficient (in isolation) to address the governance malaise in the Arab World. Political solutions will need to be resolved at their source in a manner that overcomes the many divisions that can be expected (and some that cannot) in societies fragmented along ethnic/tribal lines and religious sectarianism. Roger Hardy sums up the consequential trajectory exposed by the Arab Spring thus:

> Lesson 1: All politics is local
> While Arabs share the same grievances—over autocracy, corruption, the lack of jobs—the expression of these grievances plays out differently in each country ... In no two cases is the balance of forces identical.
>
> Lesson 2: Islam is part of the picture
> In origin, the Arab uprisings were nationalistic. They brought together different groups united by the demand that a hated dictator should go ... A split between a more reactionary Islamist old guard and a more open-minded younger generation is not inconceivable.
>
> Lesson 3: The West is not the driver
> Western powers, not least the Obama administration in Washington, have been slow to realise the limits of their influence. They are reacting to events, not driving them ... But everywhere the mood has changed. In city after city, the barrier of fear has been breached. In that sense, at least, there can be no going back.[23]

---

[22] Whilst the US and the West have vigorously denied their actions are a war against Islam, it has often been perceived this way, particularly by Islamic fundamentalists. (See Tarock, "Time", 33.) Thus, it is important to note that many fundamentalist groups such as the Muslim Brotherhood, and Salafists not only originate and exist in the regions affected by the Arab Spring, but have formed political parties seeking to participate in elections. Various Western commentators have noted this point with concern, see: Donald L. Horowitz, 'Writing the New Rules of the Game', *The Wilson Quarterly* 35 (2) (2011): 52–54; Eric Trager, 'The Unbreakable Muslim Brotherhood, Grim prospects for a Liberal Egypt', *Foreign Affairs*, 90(5) (Sept/Oct 2011): 124; Editorial, 'The Arab Awakening', 42.

[23] Roger Hardy, "What happened to the Arab Spring?", April 2011 available at http://www.bbc.co.uk/news/world-middle-east-13091091 (accessed 12 August 2011).

Hardy's three observations are significant. *All politics is local* infers that whilst there are similarities amongst the motivations of Tunisians, Egyptians, Libyans and other Arab countries under strife, this does not mean that they are willing to adopt a common approach to constitutional reform. For example, the Bahrainian "rebels" are a Shi'a based movement concerned but importantly irritated by a (minority) Sunni elite repressing them.[24] Furthermore, in Bahrain the rebels are not seeking to overthrow the monarchy, quite the opposite since the monarchy is revered by the overwhelming majority of the population.[25] Similarly but from the opposite angle, in Syria the opposition draws largely on its Sunni majority with a Shi'a minority in charge of the levers of power. But this is not the case in Tunisia, Egypt, or in Libya. Important is the question of whether Political Islam wants to forge a theocracy or secularism, or something in-between. Thus, Hardy's observation lesson takes on a crucial nuance: *Which Islam?* This question feeds back into his first observation, since it leads to another question: How will Sunni-dominated, wealthy States like Saudi Arabia perceive constitutional reform in Bahrain that may upset the perceived balance between these two sects of Islam? What will this mean for Saudi-Iranian rivalry on the back of the fact that, Iran is the dominant Shi'a State in the region and a bitter religious and political foe in geopolitical dominance?[26] Such *realpolitik* concerns may prompt the West with their vested interests in oil-production to seek to intervene, and thus Hardy's third observation is paramount: the West is not *and should not be* the driver.

The reality to be faced is that practical democracy on the ground in fractured States involves a multiplicity of discrete communities trying to reconcile their own histories and destinies from a multitude of historical experiences some often conflicting. These disparate forces are often engendered in diverse and occasionally opposing contexts.[27] There are several pathways that may be followed across a broad panorama from

---

[24] Baker, "Bahrain", 22. Filiu argues convincingly that fears of a Shi'a "crescent" and the "Iranian" or Persian "Bogeyman" has been deliberately exaggerated by Arab autocrats: Filiu, *The Arab Revolution*, 137 & 145; Baker, "Bahrain", 23.

[25] Baker, "Bahrain", 23. Thus whilst rebels want to end what they believe is a Sunni—apartheid style government, the idea of removing the monarchy is anathema. So the creation of a genuine constitutional monarchy with a democratically elected parliament (UK or European style) is not out of the question.

[26] Editorial, "Syria's Opposition, Gaining Ground", *The Economist*, December 17, 2011, 77; Baker, "Bahrain", 23.

[27] Nsongurua J. Udombana, 'Articulating The Right To Democratic Governance In Africa', *Michigan Journal of International Law*, 24 (2003): 1213 & 1283.

integrationism and consociationalism to accommodatism in addressing the chaotic political landscape spawned by the Arab Spring. This Chapter turns to sketch the general rubrics of these broad ideological umbrellas in the next sub-section followed by two illustrative case studies focusing on Libya and Egypt—two disparate examples which illustrate the pitfalls of modularised political/constitutional templates.

3.1. *Which Way—A Compass for Socio-Political Identity*

Integrationism seeks to construct a single overarching public identity. The underpinning pragmatism is that conflict results from group-based partisanship and hence the need to establish government that is impartial and eviscerates patronage and cronyism through rights based meritocracy. Accordingly parochial groupings (tribal, sectarian, religious etc.) should be actively discouraged in favour of cross-societal groupings. There is acknowledgment that identities are malleable and fluid hence the need to focus on a cross-sectional transformation. However, consociationalists think that in certain contexts these group identities can be resilient and durable.[28] This presents the key dilemma in the authors' opinion: How to manage such an untidy mosaic of seeking cosmopolitanism yet accommodate parochialism for ascriptive community identities—ethnic, sectarian, etc.?[29]

Accommodatism does offer a pathway that navigates the dangers of "corporatism", and thus "avoids privileging certain 'group' identities while remaining responsive to demographic shifts".[30] It is important in States with multiple societal identities since the framework seeks to embrace stakeholders in governance *and* government by involving pivotal segments of society (whether tribal, sectarian or religious) and a sense of proportionality that ousts public bastions of discrimination and patronage/cronyism. This is in light of the reality that corrosive political practices of marginalisation and exclusion are often based on religious, sectarian or religious groups or sub-groups.[31]

---

[28] *See generally* John McGarry, "Political Settlements in Northern Ireland and South Africa", *Political Studies* 46 (1998): 853.

[29] See e.g. John McGarry & Brendan O'Leary, "Iraq's Constitution of 2005: Liberal Consociation as Political Prescription", *International Journal of Constitutional Law*, 5 (2007): 670, 692.

[30] Ibid., 692.

[31] Ibid., 675–6.

Historical antecedents in the Arab World may well militate against accommodatism and point to centralized government as the preferred pathway to perform vital nation-building tasks.[32] The premise is that a collective appreciation of the State's administrative capacity would contribute to a "collective sense of identity that can rival or even replace sub-State, centrifugal political mobilization"[33] by promoting a "shared vision of the future."[34] However, it is cautionary that often the leading community and/or societal segment tends to seek to nationalize government and hence the State in its own image to the exclusion of *the other*.[35]

There are several thorny issues that need to be considered when discussing whether an integrationist or a consociationalist approach should be applied to the variegated manifestations and consequences of the Arab Spring across the region. The major issue with choosing either an integrationist or a consociationalist approach is how well either will deal with established elites,[36] and this in turn is dependent upon what role *the other*—that section of the citizenry (tribal, ethnic, religion, sectarian or a combination) that is not (politically) dominant—plays in expanding political "space" and a new emerging socio-political dispensation. At this juncture, the authors pose several rhetorical questions regarding *the other*, which they will grapple with as the rest of the Chapter unfolds. Do they want to eviscerate the elite or reform it? Do they wish to usurp power where they have wherewithal and become the new elite to correct historical asymmetry or genuinely seek a more egalitarian society? Just whose identity will dominate? Which approach will provide and promote human rights, the denial of which fuelled the Arab Spring? And finally, one which worries some Western commentators, is which approach will best enable each State, and its people, to come to terms with the inevitable central

---

32 Toby Dodge, "State Collapse and the Rise of Identity Politics", Markus E. Bouillon, David M. Malone & Ben Rowswell (eds) *Iraq: Preventing a New Generation of Conflict*, (Boulder Lynne Rienner Publishers: 2007) 35; Thomas Barfield, 'Afghanistan's Ethnic Puzzle, Decentralizing Power Before the US Withdrawal', 90 *Foreign Affairs* (2011) 54, 54.

33 Dodge, "State Collapse", 29.

34 Ibid., 35.

35 *See generally* Rogers Brubaker, *Nationalism Reframed: Nationhood and the National Question in the New Europe* (Cambridge University Press Cambridge 1996).

36 As one commentator has noted: "... democracy appears chronically dysfunctional when it comes to policies that impinge on the rich", Jeffrey A. Winters, 'Democracy and Oligarchy' in *The American Interest*, VII (2) (Nov/Dec 2011): 18. The point is that an elite established under an autocratic regime has the potential, during a period of democratic transition to morph the emerging democracy into a *plutocracy*, arguably something the uprisings of the Arab Spring were fighting to remove/prevent.

role of Islam as a pivotal religious but also socio-political game changer. The Chapter will do this by comparing Libya with Egypt.

3.2. *Libya: Imagined Nationhood? A "Clean Slate" for Political Re-construction*

In a world that recognises States and not societies, artificial heterogeneous States struggle (and are still struggling) with the task of nation-building as opposed to State—building in consolidating nascent national identity and the artificial edifice of territorial integrity. Of all the States involved in the Arab Spring Libya suffered the most traumatic change since the uprising grew into a full-blown civil war complete with international involvement culminating in the death of its former leader and key members of the political elite who exercised control over a modern state in the style of a medieval fiefdom. Libya, as a consequence of Libya's history, its very "creation" and 42 years of rule by Qaddafi, out of all the States in the Arab Spring is the one that requires "nation" rather than "State" building—Libya is a "clean slate".

For centuries Libya was always part of someone else's empire.[37] The modern polity was created by European powers as they dismantled firstly, the Ottoman and secondly, the Italian Empire after the end of World War II.[38] Traditionally Libya comprised three major provinces: Cyrencia with the major port of Benghazi, Tripolitania with the port of Tripoli, and Fezzan the southern interior. However, it is in many senses an artificial State cobbled together by external powers, primarily the West, and as such its citizens arguably lack a true-shared national consciousness.[39] The *native* inhabitants, the Berbers—a nomadic and fiercely independent people—are not organised into a single polity even within the confines of the iron ring of the State's territorial integrity imbued with the imprimatur and discourse of international law's dictum on territorial integrity along recognised borders. Rather as native inhabits they are shaped and adhere to first principles of societal organisation—the clan. This fealty is often dismissed as small minded ethno-centric nationalism and fails to recognise that allegiance to the clan is not simply a matter of familial ties but also a commitment to a unit that serves an important political

[37] John Wright, *Libya: a Modern History*, (London Croom Helm: 1982), 11.

[38] Henry Chapin Metz (ed), *Libya, a Country Study*, (4th ed) (US Government Washington DC, 1989) 33–37; Lisa Anderson, 'Qadhafi's Legacy: An Evaluation of a Political Experiment' in Dirk Vandewalle (ed) *Qadhafi's Libya, 1969–1994*, (New York St Martin's Press: 1995), 223–236, 224.

[39] Metz, "*Libya, a Country Study*", 33–37; Anderson, "Qadhafi's Legacy", 224.

and administrative role. This is important when one considers that often national government seeks to marginalize tribes and ethnic groupings by quirks of political realism divorced from natural and territorial entitlement by fact and existence. The *native/indigenous* Berbers are in many ways different to the "urbanised" inhabitants of the main cities—Tripoli or Benghazi.[40] This may appear a simplistic painting of Libya until we consider the challenges faced by the Transitional National Council (TNC) which jelled together as a seemingly co-ordinated civilian defence militia in opposition to, and in the course of the civil war to oust, Qaddafi.

Whilst the TNC members and the rebel groups knew what they wanted to get rid of—the Qaddafi regime and its convoluted governance/pseudo administrative framework[41]—the question and reality they faced once the regime fell was: Did they have any constructive ideas that transcended the demise of the Qaddafi regime to the pivot of the main grievance—a nuanced State building agenda? Could they *build a national consciousness* to replace a hollowed out political landscape and stunted government administrative framework? The squabbling over battle victories, where Qaddafi's body would repose, was emblematic as was the distribution of the political spoils with members of the TNC bargaining based more on the basis of regional sacrifices in blood in the course of the protracted civil war. The full extent of the problematic nature of these questions is revealed only when Qaddafi's legacy is fully understood.

Of all the leaders and States affected by the Arab Spring, indeed of all the autocratic States in the Middle East, Qaddafi's regime crudely epitomised the famous statement reputedly made by Louis XIV of France: "*L'Etat c'est moi*" (The State is me).[42] Qaddafi's autocratic and eccentric reign was a complete irony to the title he gave to the Libyan State: the Socialist People's Libyan Arab Jamahiriya (which conflated the terminology of State and people).[43] The "State of the Masses" was in reality Qaddafi's personalised vision that combined socialism, pan-Arab nationalism, tribal/ethnic values of collective consultation with anti-imperialism.[44] By dismantling

40 See Metz, *Libya, a Country Study*, 3–8, 64–68, & 73–78; generally Wright, *Libya*, 11 and the Map of Libya before the Preface, which also includes the area of Sirtica. Since the death of Qaddafi there has been resurgence in Berber identity and pride.

41 Editorial, "Closing in on Tripoli", *The Economist*, July 16, 2011, 48.

42 See e.g. Omar I. El Fathaly and Monte Palmer, 'Institutional Development in Qadhafi's Libya' in Vandewalle (ed) *Qadhafi's Libya*, 158.

43 See Metz, *Libya, a Country Study*, 177; Wright, *Libya*, 191; Vandewalle, *Qadhafi's Libya*, 1; Francois Burgat, "Qadhafi's Ideological Framework", Vandewalle (ed) *Qadhafi's Libya*, 51.

44 The establishment of the Jamahiriya State was the second stage of the "Libyan revolution"—rather than *coup d'etat*—began with the removal of the monarchy: Geoff

government institutions to make way for People's Congresses,[45] Qaddafi claimed to establish a polity that truly was *direct* people power in practice[46] while in reality dismantling manifestations of government institutions paved the way for Qaddafi's ambitions of unchallenged power and dominance.[47] Libya's fragmented birth into modern State offered Qaddafi a platform upon ascendance into power to politically re-engineer Libya's identity as a forward looking republic. Rather than create a utopia Qaddafi essentially created in reality a non-State.[48]

Arguably the singular removal of Qaddafi and his political cronies from power united the TNC and created their identity and unity of goals. However, can this identity and unity survive Qaddafi's death? Do the rebels in Libya see themselves as Libyans, or as anti-Qaddafists? If the latter this aspect withered in the climax that followed the dictator's death yielding in a few weeks to an anti-climax. Government institutions such as a legislative body can be built, even be stocked with delegates and representatives to create a federal model of sorts, but without a well-established *national consciousness or identity an integrationist approach will fail.*[49] It is highly questionable that an integrationist approach would work in Libya for the simple reason that 42 years of rule by Qaddafi eradicated an "overarching civic identity". In essence it is the "nation" rather than "State" that needs to be built in Libya.

Would accommodatism be more successful in Libya, would it create a national consciousness? If a liberal consociation model were adopted based on Libya's traditional regions, Cyrencia, Tripolitania, and Fezzan, it may at first glance generate the space and time necessary to enable a nuanced organic consciousness to develop considering that the underlying premise of a "liberalist" model is "self-determination", a notion "that

---

Simons (2nd ed), *Libya, the Struggle for Survival,* (London Macmillian Press: 1996): 209–10.

45 See Table 7.1 in Moncef Djaziri, 'Creating a new State: Libya's Political Institutions' in Dirk Vandewalle (ed) Qadhafi's Libya, 177–200, 191, & Wright, *Libya*, 192–196.

46 This vision was Qaddafi's 'Third international Theory, as expressed in his *Green Book Part One-The Solution to the Problem of Democracy*, published in 1976, and *Green Book Part Two-The Solution to the Economic Problem: Socialism*, published subsequently in 1978. Wright, *Libya*, 188–196; Fathaly and Palmer, "Institutional Development", 157–176.

47 Ibid., 160.

48 Editorial, 'Closing in on Tripoli', *The Economist*, July 16–22, 2011, 44–48. Also as noted by Wright: "... the survival of the system was considered doubtful without the continual personal guidance of ... [the] 'Brother Colonel'." Wright, *Libya*, 193.

49 This problem is exacerbated by any policy of sectarian privileges, which many integrationists argue is the problem in reconstructing a polity in Iraq: Mc Garry and O'Leary, "Iraq's Constitution", 672.

leaves it to local democratic constituencies to decide if they want to amalgamate into federal regions or not...".[50] In essence starting with a *confederation* rather than a federation similar to the one adopted in the 2005 constitution of Iraq to resolve contested spaces with the underlying logic that sectarianism across peoples and religions could and can be riveted together from an all encompassing constitutional framework.

However, such an accommodatist model raises the possibility that separate consciousnesses could develop, and therefore Libya "sub-dividing" into possibly three separate States.[51] This fear is mitigated by economic concerns heavily influenced by the main economic resource—oil wealth. It is concentrated in certain parts of the country. Resource allocation/distribution matters, as much as democracy, as demonstrated in other countries rocked by the Arab Spring. Tackling the distribution of oil wealth will perhaps influence which approach is taken in Libya. Integrationists criticise Iraq's 2005 Constitution, for being too weak because it is too decentralized. It is the authors' opinion that the Iraqi Constitution may not be an appropriate model in addressing the resource issue—an important part of Libya's future. A hasty appropriation into an ill-defined national framework may inflame rather than mollify loyalists who need to be artfully incorporated into a broad based government. Herein the transparency that was lacking previously under the Qaddafi regime becomes especially important in a new constitutional and administrative dispensation.

3.3. *Egypt: Islamism vs. Secularism: Muslim or Citizen?*

In contradistinction to Libya, Egypt's identity as a polity and a nation literally stretches back to the days of the Pharaohs. Egypt is a colossus that has cast both rays and shadows in the black and grey divide of North Africa and the Middle East—a firm foot in Africa by location and presence and a core member of the Arab World. Thus at first glance an integrationist approach may work in Egypt, but an integrationist approach in Egypt faces challenges from Political Islam and the military. The Egyptian military has retained a very privileged position for many years and it stands to lose many of these privileges if free and genuine elections lead to an

[50] See Editorial, "Closing in on Tripoli", *The Economist*, July 16–22, 2011, 48 & the interview by John Simpson with an un-named Libyan official, BBC News, Africa, 'Halt to Rebel Advance Creates Libyan Divide' available at the BBC website: http://www.bbc.co.uk/news/world-africa-12901820 (accessed 17 October 2011).

[51] McGarry and O'Leary argue that three federation units are fragile: McGarry and O'Leary, "Iraq's Constitution", 679.

independent minded and transparency driven civilian administration. Whilst the military nominally returned to their barracks, they are wary of civilian administrative structures that threaten their privileges—this was one of the primary reasons why it withdrew support for the Mubarak regime as civil protests in Egypt seen as transient persisted in the face of a regime's unaccommodating political intransigence. As violence mounted and the security forces clamped down even harder the military had to take a stand for or against the citizens demands or be seen for what it was—a pillar of the government's survival as its "praetorian" guard.[52] In an act of self-preservation it opted to let the Mubarak regime collapse.

Egypt is the spiritual homeland of the Muslim Brotherhood,[53] so it is Political Islam that potentially poses the greatest threat in the opinion of many Western commentators.[54] Not in the manner stereotyped by some Western commentators,[55] but because it threatens the national consciousness. Hence the question posed in the title of this Chapter's sub-section: Muslim or citizen? For integrationism to succeed it requires a single overarching public identity, either a pre-established one or one it constructs. However, the theory discounts religion as an organisational criterion, possibly because there is not one monolithic religion (without discrete parts to the sum). Multiple religions create parochialism, inhibiting the development of a national *overarching* consciousness, and leading to the problems of sectarianism manifest in different dynamics in the Arab world. Due to the existence of non-Muslims (especially Coptic Christians whose faith and pedigree (in existence) matches the Islamic faith), it is not possible to argue that all persons within Egypt are Muslims, but certainly they are all Egyptians. The question to be asked therefore is whether Political Islam will seek to promote Islam as the overarching identity rather than a nationalist one through the implementation of Shari'a law.

Islam does provide a consciousness that is overarching, and one that aims to transcend national borders. Arguably it can create a consciousness that extends across the States of the Arab Spring, and thus threaten the

---

[52] See e.g. Tarock, "Time", 29; Aaron David Miller, 'For America, an Arab Winter', in 35 (2) *The Wilson Quarterly* (2011), 36–42, 38; Jeff Martini and Julie Taylor, 'Commanding Democracy in Egypt' *Foreign Affairs*, 90(5) (2011): 127 onwards.

[53] More out of the fact that its leading thinkers emanated here rather than any other reason least the authors be seen as condensing vast and contested socio-political and religious events and history into convenient scholastic commentary.

[54] Trager, "Unbreakable", 122.

[55] See e.g. Editorial, "The Arab Awakening", 43; Trager, "Unbreakable", 115; Khouri, "The Long Revolt", 46; Editorial, "Moving Ahead" in *The Economist*, July 16–22, 2011, 44.

evolution of a distinct Egyptian (and Tunisian) consciousness, but again only if Hardy's question of "Which Islam" is resolved. Will it be a version of Islam that can balance religious mores with liberalism? Western commentators fear that Political Islam will inhibit political freedoms. Islamist parties conjure images of Sharia law, repression of liberalism, intolerance of many "Western" values and concepts, and security threats particularly towards Israel. There is some truth in these comments. Hazem Salah Abu Ismail, a Presidential candidate, and a leading Salafist cleric in Egypt when asked in November 2011 (a few months after the demise of the Mubarak regime) what he would do as president with the idea of a woman wearing a bikini on a beach replied she would be arrested.[56] The response in its simplicity had far deeper political resonance on other significant matters. Accordingly the success of the Islamic parties in first post-Arab Springs elections sent shivers down many spines in the West.[57] However it was Israeli Prime Minister Binyamin Netanyahu who gave voice to the fears when he labelled the Arab Spring a failure on the seemingly simple basis premised on the triumph of Islamist parties at the polls.[58] However, such comments are in the main scaremongering, with obvious vested interests touted as constructive comments, for the following reasons.

First and foremost, the act of forming political parties is an indication that Islamists have embraced some form of democracy. After Ismail's comment above the Al Nour Party (Islamist) were quick to distance themselves, labelling his comments as being unrepresentative. Subsequently, in reply to a question regarding the sale of alcohol in Egyptian hotels—an important issue in the crucial tourist industry—Mohamed Nour, a spokesman for the Al Nour Party, responded that he would be more concerned with resolving a more important question—delivery of clean drinking water to forty million Egyptians who don't have access to sanitary water.

Secondly, the success of the Islamist parties reflects a need to address popular dissatisfaction in the Arab Spring as States recently free from the

---

[56] Thomas L. Friedman, 'Political Islam Without Oil', *International Herald Tribune*, 12 Jan 2012, biyokulule on-line, http://www.biyokuule.com/view_content.php?articleid=4262 (accessed 28 February 2012).

[57] See e.g. John M. Owen, IV, "Why Islamism is Winning", *New York Times*, January 6 2012, NY Times on-line http://nytimes.com/201/why-islamism-is-winning.html (accessed 28 February 2012); Editorial, "Tunisia's General Election, Islamists to the Fore", in *The Economist*, October 29, 2011, 46.

[58] Netanyahu's criticism and claims of a failure of democracy reform due to the success of religious parties is somewhat ironic given the disproportional influence religious parties play in Israeli politics.

shackles of dictatorship embrace the notion of popular participation and governance, rather than an Islamic Renaissance.[59] The natural choice were the Islamist parties for the simple reason that Islamist groups such as the Muslim Brotherhood have existed for decades, are better organised, and are relatively free from tainted association with the former dictators that have (will?) be overthrown.[60] They also have (allegedly) large financial support from conservative States such as Saudi Arabia and Qatar.[61] By contrast secular parties really only formed *after* the Arab Spring, and have little or no sponsorship, and virtually no association or ownership within the general population. Thus it is highly likely that Islamist parties will be in the short and medium term significant political players but that does not guarantee that they will *always* be successful.

Thirdly, Egypt's economic concerns, rather than spiritual matters, appear to be high on the priority list for Islamist parties. Whilst some may question the veracity of such claims there is one hard cold truth that supports this argument—Egypt lacks oil. Oil wealth can save economies, but more importantly can enable a State and its elites to thumb their noses at the international community, and their own citizens. However in the absence of substantial oil wealth Egypt will be forced to deal with the international community. Ten percent of its economy and tens of thousands of jobs rely on tourism which in turn majorly relies on visits by millions of foreigners, crumbling infrastructure needs large amounts of external investment (loans and grants) so does its rather advanced light and heavy industrial base and emerging transnational companies. The newly elected officials of the Islamist parties cannot hope to survive if they put religious matters ahead of the economy. Previously Islamist groups such as the Muslim Brotherhood could snipe in comfort from the political sidelines: now they are in the line of civilian ire whose sacrifices are indelible. No longer will they be able to hide behind religious spirituality if they cannot deliver practical economic solutions. As Filiu states:

---

59 In Tunisia the Islamist party, Nahda, has won 88 seats in the 217 seat assembly: Editorial, "Tunisia's General Election, Islamists to the Fore", *The Economist*, October 29, 2011, 46; the Salafist Al Nour Party, an Islamic fundamentalist party, has polled over 60% in recent elections in Egypt, and the Muslim Brotherhood will win half of the seats in the lower house. Secular parties will only claim approximately 25% of all seats in the Egyptian parliament: Owen, "Why Islamism is Winning".

60 See e.g. Editorial, "Messy Politics, Perky Economics", *The Economist*, October 8, 2011, 55; Trager, "Unbreakable", 115; Martini & Taylor, "Commanding Democracy in Egypt", 133.

61 Owen, "Why Islamism is Winning".

"Islamists have to choose, after decades of having just to oppose, and that is a revolution within a revolution."[62] The potential for failure is heightened by the fact that groups like the Muslim Brotherhood have existed for many decades, and thus have had time to develop their theories about how to "cure" problems within Muslim societies, the same problems at the heart of the Arab Spring.

Fourthly, if there is one lesson the Islamist parties should have gleaned from the Arab Spring it is that citizens are wary of replacing one despot with another. Even those who identify themselves as Muslims first and citizens second, will not welcome a despotic theocracy, a fact that the Islamist parties acknowledge.[63] The Arab Spring was *not* a religious movement; none of the protests were motivated by religion.[64] The slogans that were shouted at rallies during the Arab Spring were not the religions slogans of the Muslim Brotherhood—"Islam is the solution", but were secular, and nationalistic: "Egypt or Mubarak", or "Egypt is born again" and "You are Egyptian, lift your head high".[65] It was *not* the Islamists that defeated the autocratic regimes: "... it was the liberals who delivered Egypt from authoritarianism. This, in turn, brought legitimacy to liberalism and generated the powerful feeling of nationalist awareness among Egyptians."[66] Consider that in 2001 surveys held in Egypt revealed only 8% of Egyptians considered themselves as Egyptians: 81% identified themselves as Muslims. After the Arab Spring these figures were as follows: 50% identified themselves as Egyptians, and 48% as Muslims.[67] Filiu has captured the moment by stating: "So Muslims are not only Muslims",[68] they are unemployed university graduates, taxi drivers, street vendors: *citizens*. Thus an integrationist approach will work in Egypt, as long as the Islamist parties do not derail the process by insisting on an overarching *Islamic* identity.

The issue of Muslim versus citizen is not restricted to Egypt alone, all States of the Arab Spring face a similar question, but Egypt's example

62 Filiu, *The Arab Revolution*, 29.

63 Friedman, "Political Islam Without Oil".

64 Bahrain may be the exception where rebels argue they are fighting a Sunni dictatorship, but even there the issue is not religion, it is abuse of power.

65 Filiu, *The Arab Revolution*, 23–27. It is unclear what such a survey would reveal if held in Libya.

66 Mansour Moaddel, 'What do Arabs Want?' *Joins.com*, 10 January 2012, biyokulule online, http://www.biyokuule.com/view_content.php?articleid=4262 (accessed 28 February 2012)

67 Ibid.

68 Filiu, *The Arab Revolution*, 27.

provides an important lesson for all.[69] Islam did not necessarily define the "identity" of the peoples of the Arab Spring, a point that both the West and hard-core fundamentalists need to reflect on.[70] And Islam will not continue to define the peoples of the Arab Spring, for if democracy is to evolve organically the peoples of the Arab Spring must see themselves as citizens first and Muslims second. This conclusion does not mean that Islam and democracy or Islam and liberal values are irreconcilable, quite the opposite.[71]

4. Which Building Block? Community or the Individual

Another key question that is caught up in this Chapter's discussion is: Which building block will constitutional reformists focus on—community or the individual? Put another way, how best to protect against the corruption of power? Will protecting the rights of an individual extend to protecting the community? Previously in the Arab World, religion was co-opted by autocratic depravity with constitutional preambles or amendments seeking to exploit and trumpet that Islam does not create an individualist culture and that society's goal should be protecting the *community* of believers. Has this been changed by the events of the Arab Spring? Tamim Ansary in his history of Islam, "Destiny Disrupted" summarises this dilemma rather poignantly:

> ...Western customs, legal systems, and democracy look like a project to atomize society down to the level of individual economic units making autonomous decisions based on rational self-interest. Ultimately, it seems, this would pit every man, woman, and child against every other, in a competition of all against all for material goods.
>
> What looks like, from one side, a campaign to secure greater rights for citizens irrespective of gender, looks from the other side, like powerful strangers inserting themselves into private affairs of families and undercutting people's ability to maintain their *communal* selves as familial and tribal networks. In short, what looks from one side like empowering each individual looks, from the other side, like disempowering whole communities.[72]

---

[69] Arguably the fact that Egypt's *national consciousness or* identity pre-dates its conversion to Islam is significant.

[70] Filiu, *The Arab Revolution*, 29.

[71] See e.g. Bobby Ghosh, 'Edrogen's Moment' in *Time Magazine*, November 28, 2011, 23.

[72] Tamim Ansary, *Destiny Disrupted, a History of the World through Islamic Eyes*, (New York Public Affairs: 2009), 353.

Borrowing on nuanced realities and factoring in the Arab Spring the authors aver that institutions of freedom *often* arise through political fragmentation rather than the favoured mode of autocracy—standardised conformity and compliance that punishes or excludes divergence. Autocracies inherently seek to impose rather than negotiate practices and/or models of political and social order. By ousting institutional experimentation the pathways for a restive society are often through extreme action by the citizenry and over reaction by the political elite. The Arab Spring is a classic example of the pitfalls of centralism and a governing monopoly which views any other centre of authority as competition. Heavy-handed use of police powers to constrain civic participation means that government becomes arrogant and calcifies. Increasing denial of basic freedoms means autocratic governments become incapable of reform as they focus on ever more malignant pathways in consolidating power and authority. This trend is captured aptly by Francois Fachini in his erudite analysis of religion, law and development. Looking at the strengths and weaknesses of the Arabian and Turkish empires he notes:

> ... monopoly creates a strong power which no longer has to learn from other States. It has no credible competitor. It becomes careless and limited. It is closed to experimentation of others and blocks on solutions which made its power. The monopoly thus blocks the spirit of innovation and change. It subjects the cities to its power and prevents them from becoming autonomous ...[73]

Drawing on the quote above and factoring in the events spawned by the Arab Spring, autocratic regimes are geared to conformity, which necessitates muzzling the citizenry's critique (or criticism) of government and governance. In the name of societal solidarity these regimes marginalise individual rights claims as destabilising societal stability whilst trumpeting the importance of nationalism though cynically it is to grant government *negative* legitimacy. This is facilitated by the political and ideological reality that nationalism is a flexible instrument that readily lends itself to the imperatives of government legitimacy, and by fragmentations caused by tribalism, religion, and wealth disparity.

Liberal democracy paradigms with their preference for a "corporatist" State by design or implementation often can also oust a normative agenda

[73] Francois Facchini, 'Religion, Law and Development: Islam And Christianity—Why Is it in Occident and not in the Orient That Man Invented the Institutions of Freedom? *European Journal of Law & Economics*, 29 (2010): 108.

for local stake-holders which shields its paternalistic conception—it is not always about a representative democracy *but* a representative government. Considering the different complexities across the countries subjected to the Arab Spring phenomenon, rule of law and the finer details on supporting administrative structures/forms should be negotiable. Otherwise a broad generalised meta-narrative on governance will stifle leeway in negotiation and implementation on the nature and limits of government and hence reform agendas within a particularised setting. As aptly enunciated by Steven Wheatley:

> Laws and regulations are legitimate to the extent that the processes of deliberation and substantive outcomes are consistent with the principles of deliberative democracy. There must be an inclusive process of democratic decision-making, with those who will be subject to the laws and regulations able to participate effectively in the process. In those deliberations, participants must put forward reasons that others may reasonably accept and reject proposals "on the basis that insufficiently good reasons have been offered for them": the requirement of public reason . . . This is particularly important when the impugned measure will have the effect of interfering with, or negating, the rights of subjects recognized within the legal order.[74]

The authors asked above whether the Arab Spring has changed the perception of individual or community and the answer is yes. Filiu succinctly captures the moment thus: ". . . the Arab world has changed, and there is no turning back."[75] The lesson learned is that using communities as the building block enables autocracy through "divide and conquer" tactics to maintain the status quo; it also leads to sectarian violence. The protesters saw themselves as citizens, whose community was best protected by sanctioning protection of individuals.

5. Constitutionalism & Identity—Accountability, Representation & Participation

Nathan Brown writing in 2001 on purposes for non-constitutional practices in the Arab World reflected on ideological signalling and the organization of State authority. He noted that non-constitutionalism held

---

74 Steven Wheatley, 'The Security Council, Democratic Legitimacy and Regime Change in Iraq', *European Journal of International Law*, 17(3) (2006), 546–7.

75 The full quote is: 'Most of the Islamist militants have not changed yet, the Arab world has changed, and there is no turning back.' Thus raising the point made earlier, Islamists can derail the process: Filiu, *The Arab Revolution*, 29.

some importance when Arab nationalism was vibrant as they coalesced into sovereign States, but presciently seemed to aver that as the political landscape progressively disillusioned the citizenry ideological purposes became anachronistic.[76] Brown reflecting on experiments in constitution writing in the early days of nascent Statehood in the Arab World noted that they were often driven "by an impulse toward internal rationalization and taxation rather than an intention to grant "any of the traditional liberal rights".[77] The primary goal being was "to strengthen the authority of the State in the face of internal rebellion, fiscal crisis, and external penetration".[78] Stretching this further, the authors opine that the task of nation building and consolidating nascent national identity and territorial integrity meant a crude appeal to nationalism as the pillar of *mutual cohesiveness*. The process of societal cohesion was effectively subsumed in a bigger narrative—nation building—which often provides a convenient avenue to stifle domestic consensus on local issues creating an uneasy co-existence of disparate groups. The project is then not so much informed by shared goals that derive from legal and formally prescribed responsibilities but an overwhelming reliance on police powers to attain compliance.[79]

To solve seemingly complex societal dynamics the solution was a coercive infusion of the corporate State—which sought to control, manipulate or sideline other centres of power (tribal, religious etc.). The tendency to accumulate and consolidate power through government machinery and patronage while refusing to accommodate local actors viewed as non-compliant is natural to autocratic minded rulers. The majority of constitutions in the Arab World created councils, parliaments and/or assemblies, but in no case was this body powerful enough to withstand the rapid assertion of power by the executive. The end run is that in the bulk of the Arab World, the constitution played no major role in the dynamics

---

[76] Nathan J. Brown, *Constitutions in a Nonconstitutional World: Arab Basic Laws and the Prospects for Accountable Government* (State University of New York Press, New York, 2002). See also the synthesis on this point by Feldman in a review of this book in Feldman, "Constitutions", 390–396.

[77] Brown, "*Constitutions in a Nonconstitutional World*": Feldman, "Constitutions", 393.

[78] Brown, *Constitutions in a Nonconstitutional World*, 33.

[79] James N. Rosenau, 'Governance, Order and Change in World Politics' in James N. Rosenau & Ernst-Otto Czempiel (eds), *Governance without Government: Order and Change in World Politics*, (Cambridge Cambridge University Press: 1992): 1.4.

of "*governance*" but rather supported "*rule*".[80] In sum their constitutions rather than limit power, enhanced it.

Far-reaching organic institutional reforms entail not an ever-increasing array of "corporatist" governmental bodies and constitutional amendments but an engagement with extant frameworks. One need only consider that in the early 1990s's a so-called "second wind of change" (the first wind was decolonisation and independence) swept through sub-Saharan Africa as citizenry shook off the shackles of virulent autocratic regimes steeped in many of the unsavoury practices identified above that generated the phenomenon of the Arab Spring. Constitutional reforms dominated political discourse as the transition from authoritarian to democratic rule gathered momentum underpinned by greater political awareness by citizenry on the imperatives of accountability, participation and representation. This tangent is echoed with regard to Arab constitutionalism by Noah J. Feldman's observation:

> To the extent that a written constitution aspires to embody rule-of-law principles by reducing norms of governance to a form recognizable as positive law, enforceable by and against government actors, it, too, would seem to be fundamentally defective if the law can be ignored by those it is intended to constrain. But of course there is a serious drawback associated with the insistence that the rule of law and true constitutionalism exist only where legal norms are applied consistently and across the board. It makes it far more difficult to develop a vocabulary for speaking of systems in which legal and constitutional rules affect government actors and their decisions without binding them absolutely.[81]

The weaknesses of parliaments and constitutional courts in Arab States suggests that it is not so much constitutional text as the underlying political reality of autocracy that stands in the way of limited government. It follows that what Arab States need in order to establish limited government is more basic than anything constitutional texts on their own can accomplish: they need an infusion of actual democratic accountability in order to supplant and eventually replace autocracy.

---

80 Libya was a classic example of this phenomenon.

81 Feldman, "Constitutions", 391.

6. Assistance or Interference?

The West's involvement with the demise of Qaddafi's regime in Libya is well known, and without this intervention the TNC would have been defeated and Qaddafi may well have completed his promised pogrom of revenge. Whatever may be their true motivation—oil or humanitarian concerns—the question remains: Will the West play upon their much-needed assistance in order to gain a seat at the table of constitutional reform, shaping a post-Qaddafi Libya, as well as the other States of the Arab Spring? The West's past involvement in the Middle East is not necessarily one that will curry them any favours at the constitutional reform table. They retain a great deal of political and economic influence overtly or covertly and it is an important clout. However, action may merely reinforce the not unfounded suspicion that they are only concerned with protecting their vested interests.[82] The Arab peoples should be forgiven their cynicism regarding Western influences since despite rhetoric towards creating democratic space, it has historically and in contemporary times supported the status quo, and even acted *against* the development of democracy where it would not be in the West's perceived national interests.

Traditionally the West prefers stability rather than democracy in this region.[83] Stability meant regimes supported implicitly or explicitly by the West with the United States at the helm. Control was seen as best achieved with "friendly" autocrats rather than a democracy where attitudes and policies may change with every election.[84] It was not the will of the Arab peoples that should govern, but the will of the West.[85] Qaddafi was an exception to this control of course, which won him the nickname "mad-dog".[86] For example Western support led by George Bush Jr. for Egyptian democracy suddenly disappeared when elections held in 2005 resulted in the Muslim Brotherhood garnering 60 seats in the Egyptian parliament.[87] Western States also supported the Ben Ali and Murbarak regimes to counter the rise of Islamic fundamentalism now entering the

---

82 Tarock, "Time", 33.

83 Chomsky, *Deterring Democracy*, 415, 419.

84 The former US ambassador to the UN, the US preferred autocracy, and not democracy. Kissinger developed this policy during the Nixon presidency: Tarock, "Time", 32–3.

85 Ibid. Thus these regimes might support the US in matters before the UN.

86 Tarock, "Time", 32.

87 Ibid., 33.

democratic stage.[88] Even during the events of the Arab Spring Israel's Netanyahu *actually* advocated continued support for Mubarak.[89]

With the success of Islamic fundamentalist parties in initial post-Arab Spring elections in Egypt and in Tunisia there will be a strong temptation for the West to intervene in some manner.[90] Emergent Arab democracies may indeed look very different to those found in the "core" Western States.[91] The uncertain quantitative and qualitative issue is how the Arab peoples grapple with secularism and Islam.[92] There may be a perception in the West that the Islamist parties will use these initial elections as a sort of political Trojan Horse,[93] enabling them to be *legitimately* appointed to positions of power, and once empowered convert the nascent democracies into theocracies.

It is argued here that the West must resist the urge to intervene, regardless of how benevolent their intentions may be. There is one lesson the West should have learned from Iraq—even liberators can outstay their welcome. The authors believe that if true stability and a genuine democratic polity were to develop it requires that it is "home-grown". While the authors are in no doubt of the need for reform, what is often lost is that the activities of the Western powers often disregard the social effects of their proposals or demands and frequently attempt to displace domestic organizations and institutions in the belief that they lack the ability to adapt themselves to "new" or alien socio-political dynamics. Often States are forced to recognize and implement Western demo-liberal ideologies and structures, but without dealing with problems that hinder adaptability to the general interests of the society in a given State hence the quandary of States striving to fashion themselves in the image of Western liberalism and too often failing. The authors do not doubt that shared and acknowledged values should converge on standards on common

---

[88] Goldstone, "Understanding the Revolution", 14. In fact a State Department Official once stated that they would prefer an "Iraqi Assad", to Saddam Hussein, because they would be predictable: Chomsky, *Deterring Democracy*, 415.

[89] Fareed Zakaria, 'The Real Threat in the Middle East' *Time Magazine*, January 23, 2012, 10.

[90] The West could intervene in a variety of manners, with the drafting and formulation of new constitutions, or by providing support to the liberal, non-religious political parties to overcome the organisational advantage Islamist parties currently retain.

[91] See e.g. Khouri, "The Long Revolt", 46.

[92] Mustapha Kamal Pasha, "Predatory Globalization and Democracy in the Islamic World", *Annals of the American Academy of Political and Social Science*, 581, (2002), 124–125.

[93] The reference here is to the mythical horse used in the siege of Troy.

calibration. The issue is the presupposition that one-size-fits-all, the basis of the metanarrative critique that underpins key aspects of this Chapter. While certainty is necessary, it should not oust discretion and flexibility. Even when the general ends are the same, there may be many means to achieve them. The failing occurs when demo-liberalism doctrines seek to negotiate exclusively on their terms when relating to systems whose fulcrum is different. It is difficult to alienate one system's pivot in a negotiation of attributes considering that governance is highly political in character and is heavily dependent on the society's underlying culture for its effectiveness.

Furthermore, the West in an attempt to protect their interests, or through misguided, conceited "assistance" have a history of making matters worse: the "blowback" theory.[94] For example, their action to counter fears of ethnic destabilization in Afghanistan was heavily influenced by what had transpired in the Balkans, rather than by actual events and the "Afghan reality".[95] Another example is the Bush Administration's increased pressure on Iran in the wake of September 9/11. This pressure caused a backlash against any idea that had "a Western aroma", and totally derailed an emerging and radical discussion in Iran that each generation should and had the right to interpret Shari'a law, something that had taken decades to develop, and heralded an awakening, the beginnings of discovering the nexus between Islamic and liberalist values. Instead of cultivating a dialogue that moderated fundamentalism, and perhaps beginning the process of building bridges between Islam and the West, the Bush Administration guaranteed the election of Ahmadinejad, and a return to conservatism.[96] Perhaps the best examples are Afghanistan and Iraq. Commentators are sceptical that the West's involvement in Afghanistan has resulted in a *permanent* democracy, or protection of liberalist values taking root in Afghanistan, that the Taliban or another Islamist theocracy will resurface.[97] Iraq's 2005 constitution has been heavily criticised

94 See for example Chalmers Johnson, *Blowback, the Cost and Consequences of American Empire*, (London Time Warner: 2000), 7.

95 Barfield, "Afghanistan's Ethnic Puzzle", 55–59.

96 Tamim Ansary, *Destiny Disrupted, a History of the World Through Islamic Eyes*, (New York Public Affairs: 2009), 355.

97 An example is Aryn Baker, who has stated that: 'The prospect (the withdrawal of international forces) is frightening: Afghanistan has the potential to be even more destabilizing for the region and the world than it was under the Taliban.' Although these reports may have a vested interest, they nonetheless send a chilling message. Baker, "Bahrain", 27.

for being too "weak" because it is too de-centralized, and fuelling sectarian resentment and violence.[98]

Sadly even where commentators recognise that Western actions may worsen the situation or lay seeds for future conflict (with the West or internally) commentators still use language such as: "If significant fissures do truly exist then the United States should hammer at them hard, cracking apart the bloc once and for all", or "Above all, the United States must distinguish clearly between friend and foe . . ."[99] The antagonistic tone of such writings does not bode well for "home-grown" democracy, or at minimum an objective assessment of the evolution of Arab democracy, and suggests that hoping for non-interference is already a lost cause. Perceptions of threats and interference may subvert a national consciousness, give strength to the evolution of Islam as an overarching *regional or supra-State* identity, which could bring about the West's worst fears, but more importantly signal the end of democratic reform.

7. Conclusion

Much has been written about the Arab Spring, and no doubt much more will be written, speculating about how this crucial moment will change our world. This Chapter has discussed different approaches to the construction of new constitutions for the States involved but the fulcrum is whether the tail of an ethos of constitutionalism is cultivated since it is this that imbues the text with meaning in operation. Regardless of which approach manifests itself, one point has been assumed, by all concerned: these States due to past experiences and dynastic patronage, need an ethos of principled constitutionalism. The advantage of the certainty that a constitution brings is something that we all assume will benefit these States. How the future of these States unfolds *will not* depend on whether an accommodationist approach is adopted or any other approach. No, the question that will resonate is much simpler: how will the "protesters" cope with power? Fareed Zakaria addresses this in his eloquent observation that: ". . . the danger in the Middle East is not that Islam corrupts but that power corrupts" and "[i]n fact, the growth of democracy in the Middle East is under

98 See the discussion of this point in McGarry & O'Leary, "Iraq's Constitution", 681.

99 Michael Scott Doran, "Doran Replies", *Foreign Affairs*, 90(5) (2011): 188.

substantial threat, but not from Islamic democrats. The threat arises from the lingering authoritarian impulse of those in power . . .'[100]

The weak who are now strong, the victims who are now powerful, what will they do? For those who have suffered for generations, who have experienced at first hand the very real consequences of being powerless in a society dominated by predatory elites and their torture chambers there may be a very real temptation to construct a constitution that protects their interests with any suffering of other causes and groups considered to be atonement. Will they give in to this very understandable temptation? Do they seek a constitutional structure that protects their own vested interests at the expense of *the other*? Do they become a new elite with all the potential for future strife this choice will bring? Or do they take the high road, a much more difficult one, and perhaps more uncertain one as well, and construct a constitution that seeks to protect all citizens, even if at a cost to themselves? Only time will provide the answer as the Arab Spring project evolves and stretches well into the future.

---

100 Zakaria, "The Real Threat", 10.

CHAPTER TWO

THE EMERGENCE OF A RIGHT TO DEMOCRACY—AN AFRICAN PERSPECTIVE

Michèle Olivier*

1. Introduction

The poor quality of governance, lack of democracy and inability of the rule of law to take root in Africa, have been longstanding causes for concern and are directly linked to the ills befalling the continent. In the post-Cold War era there is a growing perception amongst global and regional organisations that democracy is indeed the only acceptable system of legitimate domestic rule. Despite a common acceptance amongst both African leaders and civil society of the human rights encapsulating the core elements of democracy, African voices often call for a distinctly African understanding of democracy.

This chapter examines the commitment of the African Union (AU) and sub-regional organisations to democracy and the extent to which distinctly African legal instruments encapsulating democracy are evolving. To provide a background to the discussion, a short explanation will be given of the historical and cultural context of governance in Africa and how it was shaped by colonial and post-colonial attempts at governance. This will be followed by an analysis of the continental conventional and customary international framework in place relating to democratic governance. Against this background the impact of the pro-democratic protests of 2011 in North Africa (NA) will be assessed pointing out the significant differences between NA and Sub-Saharan Africa (SSA) despite a common commitment to African unity. Before narrowing down the discussion to Africa, it is necessary to start with a brief discussion on the broader context of democracy within international law. It will be indicated that Africa played an important role in placing democratic entitlement on the international agenda.

* Law School, University of Hull, UK and University of Pretoria, South Africa.

2. A Right to Democracy in International Law

The international law position that prevailed at the end of WWII was one of ideological neutrality, leaving it to the sole discretion of states to determine their systems of domestic governance.[1] When the United Nations (UN) was established in 1945, democracy was not considered to be a precondition to the maintenance of international peace and security, which was the primary goal of the organisation. However, the seeds of the development of democracy as a standard for legitimacy in international law already appear in the recognition of 'respect for the self-determination of peoples' as identified by article 1 of the UN Charter as a measure to strengthen international peace. The UN Charter attempts to build an international community based on fundamental human rights where self-determination (art 1(2)), sovereign equality (art 2(1)), territorial integrity (art 2(4)) and non-intervention in matters falling in the domestic jurisdiction of states (art 2(7)) were regarded as principles that would enhance international peace and security. The system of governance states opted for was considered as falling within the domestic jurisdiction of states, hence no mention is made of democracy or any other system of governance by the UN Charter. Instead the UN system of the time emphasises the importance of peace-loving states (art 4(1)) as a qualification for UN membership and civilized nations (art 381(c)) of the Statute of the International Court of Justice) as determinant of general principles of law that the International Court of Justice would apply to disputes that are submitted to it.

WWII saw African colonies fight in the armies of their colonial masters against an unknown enemy. When the UN was established, African states were still under colonial rule and did, therefore, not qualify for UN membership. Rising nationalism post WWII was, however, in the order of the day and stimulated African colonies to lobby for political independence. Repression of nationalism, be it tribal or continental (African) nationalism, in an effort to protect colonial interests led to tensions which destabilised not only states but whole regions, as neighbouring states often became involved supporting and harbouring national liberation movements. Thus the surge towards political independence spread like a wave across all of Africa. The struggle to free Africa from its colonial yoke gained momentum in the early sixties. The legality of these efforts was enhanced with

[1] Richard M. Burchill, "Introduction" in *Democracy and International Law*, ed. Richard M. Burchill (Aldershot, Hampshire: Ashgate Publishing, 2006), xx.

the adoption of the Declaration on the Granting of Independence to Colonial Countries and Peoples by the UN General Assembly in 1960 which not only underlines the important role of the UN in assisting the movement for independence but also outlawed colonialism.[2] As a result of decolonisation the UN experienced a huge increase in member states and the face of the international political landscape was forever changed.[3]

The Organization of African Unity (OAU) was established in 1963 as an expression of pan Africanism,[4] to lead the struggle against all forms of colonialism. In order to achieve political independence, sovereignty, territorial integrity, non-interference in internal affairs and independence were regarded as sacrosanct (art 2 and 3). The OAU Charter[5] epitomises the power of states to choose whatever system of governance they wish as long as it remains free from the interference of other states. Article 3(5), for example, condemns subversive activities on the part of neighbouring or any other states. OAU membership is unconditional and therefore open to all independent sovereign African states (art 4). With the exception of the recognition of the inalienable right of all people to control their own destiny and of freedom, equality, justice and dignity as essential to achieve the legitimate aspirations of the African peoples, no mention is made of either democracy or human rights.

The link between independence from colonial rule, human rights and democracy was soon established with the birth of multilateral protection of human rights. The Universal Declaration of Human Rights (UDHR), adopted in 1948,[6] does not make any direct reference to either democracy or self-determination but does imply a link between human rights and governance by making express mention in its Preamble that the protection of human rights by the rule of law should protect man from tyranny and oppression. Reference is made to political rights encapsulating core components of a democracy: freedom of opinion, expression (art 19), assembly and association (art 20) and the right to participate in government (art 21). Being a UN General Assembly resolution, the UDHR was not drafted with the intention of creating binding rights.[7] It did not purport to be more than a manifesto, a statement of ideas and a path-setting instrument. When the

[2] United Nations General Assembly Resolution 1514(XV), 14 December 1960.
[3] In 1960 alone, seventeen new UN members were admitted.
[4] See Preamble: "Desirous that all African states should henceforth unite . . .".
[5] Adopted in Addis Ababa, Ethiopia, 1963. Available at www.africa.org.
[6] 1948 UN DOC A/811.
[7] Thomas Buergenthal, *International Human Rights in a Nutshell* (Eagen: West Publishing, 1995), 33.

Covenant on Civil and Political Rights (ICCPR) was adopted in 1963, giving conventional status to the political rights referred to by the UDHR, the political context had changed. It coincided with the birth of the OAU and newly independent African states becoming UN members. Accordingly, the right to self-determination is recognised in common article 1 of the ICCPR and the International Covenant on Economic Social and Cultural Rights (ICESCR). Franck identifies self-determination as the historic root from which democratic entitlement grew, becoming the most dynamic concept in international relations after WWII, thus legitimising decolonisation in international law.[8]

Independent African states provided a stage in the rallying for political influence during the Cold War. The conflict between communism and capitalist western ideologies was conducted in a covert but very tangible way in developing states. The tools, tactics and strategies of the Cold War which included the granting of military and other aid to vulnerable states, propaganda, proxy wars and the fostering of communist revolutions and coups had a long lasting effect on the psyche of newly independent African states, stifling the possibility of developing legitimate systems of governance. With the demise of communism and the end of the Cold War in the late eighties, the insistence on democracy as domestic system of preference emerged. Powerful western states became insistent on attaching democratic and human rights conditionalities to trade, development assistance and other forms of cooperation with the developing world. Eminent international law scholars such as Franck and Fox accordingly detected in the 1990s an emerging global right to democracy[9] or "the right of people to be consulted and to participate in the process

---

[8] Thomas M. Franck, "The Emerging Right to Democratic Governance," *American Journal of International Law*, 86 (1992): 52. See also Gregory H. Fox, "The Right to Political Participation in International Law" in *Democratic Governance and International Law*, ed. G. H. Fox and B. R. Roth, (Cambridge: Cambridge University Press, 2000): 48–90.

[9] Thomas M. Franck "The Emerging Right to Democratic Governance," *American Journal of International Law*, 86 (1992): 46–91; Tomas M. Franck, "Legitimacy and Democratic Entitlement" in *Democratic Governance and International Law*, ed G. H. Fox and B. R. Roth, (Cambridge: Cambridge University Press, 2000): 25; Gregory H. Fox and Brad R. Roth "Democracy and International Law," *Review of International Studies*, 27 (2001): 327–52; Gregory H. Fox, "The International Protection of the Right to Democracy," *Max Planck Encyclopaedia of International Law*, March 2008 available at http://www.mpepil.com; Mikulas Fabry, "The Right to Democracy in International Law: A Classic Liberal Reassessment," *Millennium: Journal of International Studies* vol. 37 No. 3 (2009): 724; Ronald Rich "Bringing Democracy into International law," *Journal of Democracy*, vol. 12 No. 3 (July 2001): 20–34, Same Varayudej "A Right to Democracy in International Law: Its Implications for Asia," *Annual Survey of International & Comparative Law*, vol. 12, Issue1 (2006): 1–18.

by which political values are reconciled and choices made." International law commentators remain reluctant to regard this claim to 'democratic entitlement' as a fully-fledged and enforceable international law right, particularly in the light of inconsistent state practice.[10]

The developing world, particularly African states, has long been sceptical of the way in which the powerful states (and the so-called Bretton Woods institutions) use democracy (structural change) as a bargaining chip to achieve self-serving political goals.[11] The absence of such a double agenda by Russia and China has made Africa a compliant recipient for development assistance from these states. Foreign investment not burdened by moral requirements and unequal power arrangements has considerable appeal to Africa who wishes, as will be pointed out in the following discussion, to embrace democracy on its own terms and time scale. An internationally agreed concept of democracy would only enjoy credibility in Africa if it is flexible enough to accommodate local conditions and value systems. Such a relativist interpretation of universal norms has been suggested in the past with respect to the interpretation of human rights in the developing world.[12] If international law supports democracy confined to a minimal content,[13] it limits the possibility for abuse through international manipulation, and leaves scope for the development of regional practice. It is against this background that the question is asked to what extent African states contribute to the possible establishment of a right to democracy within the continent specifically against the background of the on-going events in NA challenging autocratic governance.

3. Governance in an African Context: A Historic Overview

At the outset it is necessary to establish whether it is correct to refer to Africa as a monolithic unit for purposes of the present discussion. This

---

[10] Richard Burchill, "Cooperation and Conflict in the Promotion and Protection of Democracy by European Regional Organizations," in *Cooperation or Conflict*, ed D. G. Galbreath and C. Gebhard (Ashgate, 2010): 61; Susan Marx, "The End of History? Reflections on Some International Legal Theses," *European Journal of International Law*, 3 (2010): 49–77; Gerry J. Simpson, "Imagined Consent: Democratic Liberalism in International Legal Theory," *Australian Yearbook of International Law*, 15 (1994): 103–128.

[11] Larbi Sadiki, "Al-La Nidam: An Arab View of the New World (dis)Order," *Arab Studies Quaterly* 17 (1995): 1–22.

[12] Michele E. Olivier, "Die Relatiwiteit van Menseregte met Spesifieke Verwysing na Zambië en Tanzanië" (MA thesis, Rand Afrikaans University, 1990) 34–35.

[13] Burchill, 62.

popular contention belies the diversity of Africa, consisting of 54[14] states very diverse in terms of size, population, culture, religion and wealth. Based on these differences, NA is usually distinguished from SSA in any analyses of political and socio-economic problems. The quest for African unity is, however, a highly symbolic notion and enjoys unanimous continental support. The contention of the research is that the distinction between, yet interconnectedness of, NA and SSA, informs the legal and political status of democracy in Africa. Bearing these differences in mind, modern African states share a historic context which should be considered when assessing the state of democracy on the continent.

Systems of governance were indeed present in pre-colonial African societies but differed significantly from western governance and bureaucracy as imposed by colonial rule. Before being demarcated and balkanised into states, traditional African societies were governed according to non-codified tradition, practices, beliefs and verbal communications handed from one generation to the next.[15] It is significant to note that these systems of governance, although varying between different tribes, contained inherent primordial democratic elements which contributed to the legitimacy thereof. Pre-colonial systems of governance did not conform to notions of constitutionalism followed by western states in that they accommodated the different laws and beliefs of Africa's heterogeneous peoples. In an analysis of the rule of law in pre-colonial African societies, Abioye points to a variety of tribal practices which are inherently democratic such as checks and balances on the power of rulers, institutional decision making (through heads of families and elders), the transferral of allegiance from one ruler to another where the former ceases to govern in the best interests of his/her subjects, political succession and 'removal' of a ruler guilty of dictatorial actions.[16] These examples challenge the perception that democracy is essentially a Eurocentric notion.[17]

The demarcation of Africa into states by its colonial rulers irrevocably changed the course of African governance. Arbitrarily constructed states created artificial units not taking account of geographical, historical and

---

[14] South Sudan became the most recent independent African state on July 2011.

[15] Funmilola T. Abioye, "Rule of Law in English Speaking African Countries: The case of Nigeria and South Africa" (LLD Thesis University of Pretoria, Sept 2011), p. 23.

[16] Abioye, 25–35.

[17] See Werner F. Menski, *Comparative Law in a Global Context: the Legal Systems of Asia and Africa* (Cambridge: Cambridge University Press, 2005), 385–390; Taslim O. Elias, *The Nature of African Customary Laws* (Manchester: Manchester University, 2005), 36.

tribal considerations.[18] In addition, features of colonial governance within these newly created territories must be born in mind in a discussion on the present state of democracy in Africa. Governance during the colonial period was aimed at serving colonial interests and disregarded or abolished traditional systems based on kinship or family units. Through the popular colonial practice of replacing traditional leaders with individuals responsive to colonial interests, legitimacy was sacrificed and an identity crisis was the result in most cases. Lacking the traditional authority to command popular obedience and respect, these leaders were often rejected and shunned by the people. In many cases the designated leaders (backed up by colonial rulers) became autocratic and corrupt. In addition, foreign law was introduced which, lacking local legitimacy and understanding, contributed to erode traditional systems of law. As a result traditional identities, beliefs and values mutated with those of the colonists within a newly demarcated space to create a new society where respect for the rule of law had to be established *de novo*.[19]

Colonially demarcated states nevertheless provided a blue print for politically independent African states in accordance with the principle of *uti possidetis*. This principle, originating from Latin America, was endorsed by the OAU in 1964[20] and was aimed at preventing the redrawing of boundaries to accommodate ethnic groupings.[21] The inherent conflict between the *uti possidetis* principle and the right to self-determination was acknowledged by the International Court of Justice in the *Frontier Dispute Case*.[22] The Court, however, noted that the maintenance of the territorial *status quo* in Africa was regarded as the wisest course under the circumstances and would avoid the disruption which would result from a redrawing of the boundaries that would deprive the continent of the sacrifices made in the name of national independence.[23] The principle of self-determination is closely associated with the notions of sovereignty and territorial integrity which appear amongst the 'Purposes" and

[18] Adekeye Adebajo, *The Curse of Berlin Africa after the Cold War* 2010 (New York: Columbia University Press, 2010). At the 1884–1885 Conference of Berlin, a collection of states, mostly European, established the rules for the partition of Africa. The consequences of their decision had immense historical and structural implications apparent in the domestic and international behaviour of the continent today.

[19] Abioye, 45–48.

[20] See AGH/Res 16(1).

[21] John Dugard, *International Law a South African Perspective*, 3rd ed. (Lansdowne: Juta, 2005), 131.

[22] 1986 ICJ Reports, 554.

[23] 1986 ICJ Reports, 567.

"Principles" of the Charter of the OAU. Non-intervention coupled with absolute sovereignty remained firmly engrained in African politics at the time when the West yielded to the forces of multilateral cooperation and global regulation.[24]

Rulers of newly independent African states were faced with high expectations and no past experience in governance. Moreover, the violent liberation struggles preceding independence from colonial rule did not facilitate sustainable democracies. In many cases colonial rule was replaced by autocratic leaders, one party states and military dictators often aimed at the enrichment of the political elite. During the 70s, 80s and 90s when other underdeveloped regions such as Asia experienced economic growth, living standards in Africa declined.[25] Not much remained of the democratic elements of pre-colonial models of governance. Non-democratic regimes made themselves guilty of a litany of human rights abuses which contributed to a perennial cycle of poverty and stalled development in SSA. A more prosperous NA with oil based economies displayed an equal disrespect for democracy and human rights.

Generally speaking, Africa became characterised by political intolerance, the unwillingness of their leaders to stand down and the rigging of election results leading to a wave of Afro-pessimism. The high level of human rights abuses, armed conflicts, regional instability, poverty and corruption associated with unrepresentative and illegitimate governance became the focus of civil society as well as the international community contributing to a positive turn taking root in the late 1990s.[26] Efforts to tackle Africa's problems with a new zeal coincides with the idea of an African renaissance, articulated and popularised by the former South African

---

[24] Tom Farer (ed.), *Beyond Sovereignty: Collectively Defending Democracy in the Americas* (Baltimore: John Hopkins Press, 1992), 1–25; Vasiliki Saranti, "A System of Collective Defense of Democracy: The Case of the Inter-American Democratic Charter," *Goettingen Journal of International Law* 3 (2011) 2: 688. Saranti refers at p. 688 to the Organization of American States (OAS) where "democracy emerges as a *conditio sine qua non* for the achievement of regional security and stability" after the end of the Cold War. In terms of resolution 1080 of the OAS General Assembly on "Representative Democracy" (AG/RES080 (XXI-O/91, 5 June 1991, member states of the OAS agreed to intervene collectively, with diplomatic means, in the domestic affairs of a member state to protect the diplomatic order.

[25] Edward Miguel, "Africa Unleashed Explaining the Secret of a Belated Boom," *Foreign Affairs Journal* Nov/Dec (2011): 1 (Http://www.foreignaffairs.com/articles/136547/edward-miguel/africa unleashed).

[26] Michèle Olivier "Civil society and democratisation in Africa with specific reference to the African Peer Review Mechanism," *Strategic Review for Southern Africa* XXXIII No. 2 (November 2011): 106–112.

president Thabo Mbeki in the 1990s.[27] This period is also characterised by positive economic growth rates and the introduction of multiparty elections in many African states.[28] Internationally, the growing importance of democratisation through the electoral process was reinforced by numerous UN and other international observer missions to elections in African states.[29] Political crisis following elections in Sierra Leone (1997)[30] and the Ivory Coast (2010)[31] resulted in action under Chapter VII of the UN Charter, or press statements in the case of the Central Africa Republic (2011).[32] Despite the fact that international election monitoring remains a very controversial issue in Africa, it has managed to reinforce the importance of democratisation on the African agenda.[33]

Miguel argues that establishing democratic footholds in the face of entrenched dictatorships has indeed introduced a nascent transformation of many African states since the late 1990s.[34] International interest, AU

---

[27] The phrase was first used in 1994 in South Africa following the first post-apartheid democratic election. In April 1997, former South African President Mbeki listed the elements seen to comprise the African Renaissance: social cohesion, democracy, economic rebuilding and growth, and the establishment of Africa as a significant player in geo-political affairs.

[28] See Steven Radelet, *Emerging Africa How 17 Countries are leading the way* (Baltimore: Brookings Institution Press, 2010), 47–90. Radelet singles out democratisation as the factor that has contributed most to Africa's nascent transformation.

[29] For further discussion see Douglas G. Anglin, "International Election Monitoring: The African Experience," *African Affairs* 97 389 (1998): 471–495.

[30] By its unanimous adoption of resolution 1132 (1997), the Security Council demanded that the military junta in Sierra Leone take immediate steps to relinquish power and make way for the restoration of the democratically elected Government and a return to constitutional order.

[31] Following the Ivory Coast's disputed presidential election of November 2010 and the refusal of former President Laurent Gbagbo to relinquish power, the Security Council adopted resolution 1962 (2010) backing Alassane Ouattara as the winner of the election urging all parties and stake holders respect the outcome of the election.

[32] The following was noted in Security Council Press Statement on the Central African Republic (SC/10313, AFR/2206): The members of the Council acknowledge the efforts made by the Independent Electoral Commission and the authorities of the Central African Republic to organize peaceful presidential and legislative elections. They note that the near absence of a political opposition in the democratic institutions of the Central African Republic since the elections may constitute a considerable challenge to the process of national reconciliation and nation-building. In this regard, the members of the Council encourage the Government to take the necessary measures to address irregularities experienced in the electoral process in order to ensure the improved conduct of the municipal and subsequent elections.

[33] The Carter Center is an example of an NGO that has observed 86 elections in 35 countries in Africa, Latin America, and Asia since 1989, including Liberia, Tunisia, Democratic Republic of the Congo, Egypt, and Cote d'Ivoire. http://www.cartercenter.org/peace/democracy/index.html accessed on 14/12/11.

[34] Miguel, 155.

efforts and pressure from a better informed civil society all contributed to democratisation and have boosted governmental accountability and transparency. Ironically, African autocrats, most notably perhaps former Libyan leader Muammar Gaddafi, soon learnt that portraying themselves as democrats implied legitimacy, access to donor money and favourable diplomatic relations. (Such claims are made possible by the vague and variable content of the notion of 'democracy'.) Numerous recent AU initiatives have contributed to balance the post-colonial absolutist approach to sovereignty with human rights and regional integration and to make democratisation a priority on the African agenda.

4. African Initiatives on Democracy and Human Rights

The international law status of principles of democratic governance needs to be determined against the background of the sources of international law namely treaties, custom and general principles[35] with due regard to evolving or 'soft law'. It is suggested that the evolvement of a right to democracy within Africa should be assessed by looking at the complimentary effect of all three formal sources.

Most African states became party to the United Nations human rights treaties soon after independence. Despite the wide endorsement of these agreements, little was done as far as domestic implementation and enforcement were concerned due to a variety of reasons ranging from a lack of resources and knowledge to the absence of political will and the rule of law. Consequently many African states lagged behind in submitting their compulsory reports to the relevant treaty monitoring bodies with the result that the treaties had no visible effect in the domestic legal systems of African countries. The regional protection of human rights started when the AU adopted the African Charter on Human and Peoples' Rights, also known as the Banjul Charter[36] in 1981, recognising not only civil and political and socio-economic rights but also peoples' rights and duties. The core elements of democracy appearing in the UDHR and the ICCPR are reflected in the following articles of the Banjul Charter:

[35] According to article 38 of the Statute of the International Court of Justice, the Court shall apply international conventions, international custom and general principles of law to international law disputes submitted to it. Judicial decisions of the most highly qualified publicists of the various nations shall be used as a subsidiary means to determine rules of law.

[36] Entered into force in October 1986.

- Equality before the law (art 3),
- freedom of conscience (art 8), association (art 10) and assembly (art 11),
- the right to self-determination (art 20),[37]
- the right of every citizen to participate freely in the government of his country, either directly or through freely chosen representatives in accordance with the provisions of the law as well as the right of equal access to the public service of the country (article 13), and
- the right of all peoples to their economic, social and cultural development with due regard to their freedom and identity and in the equal enjoyment of the common heritage of mankind (art 22).

With the exception of the indirect reference to representative governance through article 13, no mention is made of democratic governance.

By the time that the AU replaced the OAU in 2001, the continental priorities had shifted from decolonisation to promoting African unity through regional integration. Although the agenda is set by the AU for regional integration in Africa, integration at regional levels is facilitated through a number of Regional Economic Communities (RECs)[38] and sub-regional organisations such as the Arab League.

The Preamble of the Constitutive Act of the African Union refers to important contextual features justifying the establishment of the AU:

- the importance of African unity,
- the affirmation of a common identity,
- the challenge faced by Africa on an economic, social and political level,
- the need to accelerate the implementation of the Treaty establishing the African Economic Community,
- the promotion and protection of human and peoples' rights, to consolidate democratic institutions and culture and to ensure good governance and the rule of law.

---

[37] "All peoples shall have the right to existence. They shall have the unquestionable and inalienable right to self-determination. They shall freely determine their political status and shall pursue their economic and social development according to the policy they have freely chosen."

[38] Many of these RECs have overlapping membership. These RECs include: Community of Sahel-Saharan States (CEN-SAD), Common Market for Eastern and Southern Africa (COMESA), East African Community (EAC), Economic Community of central African States (ECCAS/CEEAC), Economic Community of West African States (ECOWAS), Inter-governmental Authority on Development (IGAD) and Southern African Development Community (SADC).

The latter commitments establish a firm link between African integration and democratisation. This is reinforced by the Objectives of the AU namely to achieve greater unity and solidarity between African countries and the peoples of Africa (art 3 (a)), promotion of the integration of African economies (3(j)), promotion of democratic principles and institutions, popular participation and good governance (3(g) and 4(m)) and the promotion of human rights (art 3(h)). In addition familiar reference is made to the defence of sovereignty, territorial integrity and independence of member states (art 3(b)).

The commitment to democratic principles portrayed by these provisions should thus be balanced by provisions defending the sovereignty, territorial integrity and independence of its Member States and non-interference by any Member State in the internal affairs of another.[39] The AU may only intervene under limited circumstances:

> The right of the Union to intervene in a Member State pursuant to a decision of the Assembly in respect of grave circumstances, namely war crimes, genocide and crimes against humanity.[40]

The AU is often compared to the European Union (EU) but differs in many important respects. Unlike the EU, the AU allows African states as members on an indiscriminate basis. All African states are currently AU members with the exception of Morocco. Africa is still regarded to be in the phase of "shallow integration" or intergovernmental co-operation.[41] Consequently supra-national decision-making is as yet entirely absent. Compliance with AU treaty obligations is not monitored and enforced by supranational institutions as in the case of the EU[42] nor does the AU require direct enforcement of legal obligations by the domestic systems of member states.

It is this context of intergovernmental co-operation set by AU instruments that the present status of democratic entitlement within Africa will be discussed below.

---

[39] 4(g).

[40] 4(h). The restricted conditions for intervention are referred to as the doctrine of non-indifference. See Paul D. Williams, "From non-intervention to non-indifference: the origins and development of the African Union's security culture," *African Affairs* vol. 106 Issue 423 (April 2007): 253–279.

[41] Gerrit C. Olivier, "Regional integration in Africa: Cooperation without integration," *Strategic Review for Southern Africa* Vol. XXXII No. 2 (Nov 2010): 17.

[42] Burchill, 60.

5. African Charter on Democracy, Elections and Governance, 30 Jan 2007

The African Charter on Democracy Elections and Governance (the Charter) read together with the Constitutive Act of the AU provides guidance as to the legal status of democracy under the AU.

According to the official website of the AU[43] 38 AU members, have signed the said Charter on 09/02/2011. Twelve states (Burkina Faso, Chad, Ethiopia, Ghana, Guinea-Bissau, Lesotho, Mauritania, Niger, South Africa, Rwanda, Sierra Leone and Zambia) have deposited instruments of ratification/accession, rapidly homing in on the required fifteen ratifications to come into effect. It is interesting to note that none of the NA states have either signed or ratified the Charter.

Inspired by the endorsement of universal values and principles of democracy, good governance and human rights as set out by articles 3 and 4 of the Constitutive Act, the Charter deals with different components of democratic governance and provides useful indicators of what Africa would consider to be building blocks of democracy. The Preamble to the Charter expresses a commitment to "universal values and principles of democracy, good governance, human rights and the right to development". Although the right to development is singled out, AU members align themselves with what is universally considered as encapsulating general principles of democracy. Despite the fact that the Charter is not yet in force, it is a decisive indication of the political commitment amongst African decision makers supporting the validity of the notion of democracy as the preferred system of governance for Africa.

The Charter focusses not only on the content of democracy but also on what is lacking from the African experience. Given the African context, the Preamble identifies the need to entrench a political culture of change of power, based on the holding of free, fair, transparent elections conducted by independent, impartial national electoral bodies. It alludes to an AU understanding of democracy by stating that the institutionalisation of transparency, accountability and participatory democracy are keys to promote and strengthen good governance. These sentiments are echoed in and elaborated on by the text of the Charter. The objectives[44] include the promotion and enhancement of the rule of law, regular free and fair

---

43 www.africa-union.org. Accessed on 1 Jan 2012.

44 Art 2.

elections, an independent judiciary, promoting a democratic culture and inculcating political pluralism and tolerance, promoting the fight against corruption, promoting the establishment of conditions to foster citizen participation, transparency, access to information, freedom of the press and accountability.

It is interesting to note that the Charter provisions are mostly phrased in soft language: "The objectives of the Charter are to *promote*...";[45] "State Parties shall commit themselves to *promote* democracy, the principle of the rule of law and human rights";[46] "State Parties *shall undertake to develop* the necessary legislative and policy frameworks to establish and strengthen a culture of democracy and peace"[47] and "State Parties *shall take all appropriate measures* to ensure constitutional rule" (own emphasis).

The Charter is, however, not devoid of examples of hard and enforceable obligations for example: "State Parties *shall eliminate* all forms of discrimination, especially based on political intolerance... as well as any other form of intolerance"[48] and "... *shall ensure* that citizens enjoy fundamental freedoms and human rights."[49] The reason can probably be found in the fact that the prohibition of discrimination and respect for human rights belong to general international law already independently applicable to all member states.

Notwithstanding the number of non-enforceable obligations and the fact that the Charter is not yet operative, it is suggested that the value of the Charter lies not in the enforceability of it provisions but in the fact that it is a firm suggestion for national policy and an authoritative indication of *opinio iuris*[50] of the participating states. The Charter does however provide for sanctions in one particular set of circumstances namely that of unconstitutional changes of government.[51] The provision does add an uniquely African flavour to our understanding of democracy. Unconstitutional changes are listed to include any putsch or *coup d'état* against a democratically elected government, intervention by mercenaries, armed

45 Art 2.

46 Art 4.

47 Art 11.

48 Art 8.

49 Art 6.

50 *Opinio iuris* which refers to a sense of obligation on the part of states that they are bound to a rule, together with state practice or *usus*, form the twin requirements for the development of a rule of customary international law as referred to by art 38(1)(b) of the ICJ Statute.

51 Chapter 8, art 23.

dissidents or rebels to replace a democratically elected government. This provision appears to hold a number of difficulties. How may a democratically elected but unconstitutional government, that fails to adhere to the rule of law and does not hold regular, free and fair elections, such as that of Mugabe[52] and former NA leaders Gaddafi and Mubarak, be replaced? These leaders claimed to be democratically elected and enjoy the continued support of their people to such a degree that it entitles them to lifelong rule. The AU is reluctant to act against undemocratic rulers accused of war crimes.[53] The AU's unwillingness to endorse the International Criminal Court's genocide charge against Sudanese President Omar Hassan al-Bashir and to disregard the International Criminal Court's arrest warrant for Gaddafi are open to interpretation. The decision passed by the 54-member AU states that the warrant against Gaddafi "seriously complicates" efforts by the organisation to find a political solution is a case in point.

6. NEPAD and the APRM

Another notable initiative in this regard is NEPAD or "The New Partnership for Africa's Development which is the Strategic Policy Framework and Socio-economic Development Programme of the African Union (AU)".[54] In an effort to address shortcomings in the quality of governance, the 6th Summit of the Heads of State and Government Implementation Committee adopted the Memorandum of Understanding on the African Peer Review Mechanism (MOU on the APRM) and the Declaration on Democracy, Political, Economic and Corporate Governance in March 2003. The MOU on the APRM contains prioritised and approved codes and standards in four focus areas: Democracy and Good Political Governance; Economic Governance and Management; Socio-Economic Development; and

52 Zimbabwe is not a signatory to the Charter.

53 Max du Plessis and Antoinette Louw, "Justice and the Libyan Crisis: the ICC's role under Security Council Resolution 1970," *Institute for Security Studies*, May 31, 2011, 4.

54 The vision of NEPAD is "to eradicate poverty and to place countries, individually and collectively, on a path of sustainable growth and development, and at the same time to participate actively in the world economy and body politic". The realisation of this vision calls for improved governance, action plans outlining realistic sustainable development targets, reinforcing successful best practices, identifying deficiencies and assessing the needs for capacity building in all African countries.

Corporate Governance. Participation is not compulsory[55] as the APRM may be voluntarily acceded to by AU Member States. Participating states include the NA states, namely Egypt and Algeria.

The purpose of the APRM is to establish a self-monitoring mechanism of the AU with the aim of fostering the adoption of policies, standards and practices that will lead to political stability, high economic growth, sustainable development and accelerated regional and economic integration. Despite the fact that the APRM reports do not contain enforceable findings, it underscores the commitment to implement the codes and standards contained in the Declaration on Democracy, Political, Economic and Corporate Governance.

Subscribed to by 33 AU members,[56] the APRM provides a strong indication that the foothold of democracy and a new accountable sovereignty are gaining on the continent.

7. State Practice as an Indication of a Developing Right to Democracy

The above discussion indicates that despite ambitious AU efforts to promote and give legal substance to democratic governance, existing AU treaty mechanisms are either not yet in force or of a non-binding nature. In lieu of any binding continentally supported treaty commitment to democracy, examination must inevitably turn to establishing whether a rule of customary international law encapsulating a right to democracy is developing. In order to justify the formation of a customary rule the requirements of supporting state practice and a coupled obligation to be bound must be met. In the state practice department, many African states fall short in their compliance with various human rights which form components of democratic governance as they appear in both African and universal human rights instruments. The wide political support of pro-democracy instruments and the increase in democratic elections may be indicative of a sense of obligation that is developing. It is, however, suggested that despite rapid development since the 1990s, the absence

---

[55] The African Peer Review Mechanism ("APRM") foundation base document [AHG/235 (XXXVIII) Annex 2] defines the APRM as: "an instrument voluntarily acceded to by Member States of the African Union as an African self monitoring mechanism."

[56] According to African Peer Review Mechanism (APRM) | NEPAD www.nepad.org/economicandcorporategovernance/african visited on 2/01.2012.

of consistent supporting state practice stands in the way of a customary international entitlement to democratic governance.

The African scholar Ibegbu makes a comparative analysis of state practice of the national constitutions of African states to justify the existence of democracy as a general principle of international law,[57] a third source of international law after treaties and custom. General principles of law as indicated by article 38(1)(c) of the ICJ Statute refer to those common principles of law found in national legal systems which can be turned to in the absence of applicable treaty or customary international law. References to democracy appear misleadingly often in African constitutions. The following NA constitutions predating 2011 may be referred to: Art 1 of the Constitution of Algeria states that Algeria is a democratic and people's Republic.[58] The Moroccan Constitution of 1996 predating the protests and present constitutional reform stated that "Morocco is a constitutional, democratic and social monarchy".[59] Prior to its current review the Egyptian Constitution[60] as amended proclaims Egypt as a "Democratic State", deriving its sovereignty from the people. It describes the system of government as a multi-party semi-presidential system within the framework of the basic principles and components of the Egyptian society. Ironically the constitution of Libya[61] in place prior to the civil unrest that started in 2011 also stated that "Libya is an Arab democratic free republic in which sovereignty is vested in the people."

Notwithstanding constitutional references to popular participation in governance, many African states remain dominated by a single strong party often ruled by a strong leader. In a single-party state, there may be theoretical or legal protection for opposition parties, but there is no legitimate chance of a candidate outside the ruling party winning an election; often there are constitutional provisions protecting one-party dominance. While no AU state is constitutionally defined as such, Egypt was effectively a one-party state under the National Democratic Party. Although other parties existed, they faced various restrictions.

---

[57] Jude I. Ibegbu, *Right to Democracy in International Law* (Lewiston, NY: Edwin Mellen Press, 2003), 4.

[58] The Constitution of the People's Democratic Republic of Algeria, approved by the Referendum of November 28, 1996.

[59] Art 1.

[60] The Egyptian Constitution was adopted on September 11, 1971 through a public referendum. It was later amended in 1980, 2005 and 2007. On the 13th of February, 2011, the Constitution was suspended following the resignation of President Hosni Mubarak as a result of the 2011 Egyptian Revolution.[1]

[61] Libya Constitution, 1969, art 1.

The following SSA states, many of whom have embraced the process towards democratic governance, are considered dominant-party systems: Angola (Popular Movement for the Liberation of Angola—Party of Labour); Botswana (Botswana Democratic Party); Burkina Faso (Congress for Democracy and Progress); Cameroon (Cameroon People's Democratic Movement); Chad (Patriotic Salvation Movement); Republic of the Congo (Congolese Labour Party); Djibouti (Progress People's Assembly); Equatorial Guinea (Democratic Party of Equatorial Guinea) ; Ethiopia (Ethiopian People's Revolutionary Democratic Front); Gabon (Gabonese Democratic Party); The Gambia (Alliance for Patriotic Reorientation and Construction); Guinea (Party of Unity and Progress); Mozambique (Mozambican Liberation Front); Namibia (South-West Africa People's Organisation); Nigeria (People's Democratic Party); Rwanda (Rwandese Patriotic Front); Seychelles (Seychelles People's Progressive Front); South Africa (African National Congress); Tanzania (Chama Cha Mapinduzi); Togo (Rally of the Togolese People); Zambia (Movement for Multiparty Democracy); Zimbabwe (Zimbabwe African National Union—Patriotic Front).[62]

Being dominant-party systems does not necessarily imply the absence of democracy. South Africa is a prime African example where the dominant African National Conference (ANC) has ruled the country with a two thirds majority as a constitutional democracy since the abolition of apartheid and experienced a succession of three different Presidents since 2004. Smaller parties exist but are not able to secure sufficient support to act as effective opposition. There is, however, a very real possibility that where one particular political party has such an overbearing influence, political tolerance will be low, it will be considered to be in the interest of individuals to openly ally with the ruling party and it is generally speaking difficult for democratic culture and a plurality of opinions to take root.

Prior to 2011, the process of democratisation in NA has not received the same encouragement as in its southern neighbours. Economic affluence has shielded NA from the amount of international scrutiny and involvement the southern part of the continent was exposed to. Economically NA could get by without yielding to the forces of human rights and international transparency. A process of democratisation started in NA when a Tunisian man burned himself to death in December 2010 in protest

---

[62] List of African Union member states by political system, Wikipedia accessed 4 July 2011.

against his treatment by police, soon spreading to pro-democracy rebellions across the Middle East.

8. North Africa

In the light of the civil uprising commonly referred to as the "Arab Spring" which erupted in early 2011 and has now continued to span over many seasons, focus will be turned to the effect this quest for democracy has had on reinforcing the international law status of an entitlement to democratic governance in Africa. The discussion will investigate why protests did not spread to SSA and highlight the role played by civil society and a middle class as catalysts for change. Finally the role of human rights in NA will be discussed.

African Arab states have a dual identity in many respects, including at an institutional level. The following African states belong to the League of Arab States,[63] a regional organisation comprised of Arab states, whilst they are also members of the AU namely Mauritania, Algeria, Tunisia, Libya, Egypt, Sudan, the Comoros and Somalia. Morocco is a member of the Arab League but not the AU. The region wide wave of popular protest was started by the NA states (NAS) of Egypt and Tunisia. Despite fears to the contrary it did not spread to SSA but proceeded to spread to other Arab regimes of NA.

A reason for the uprisings not spreading to SSA states may be explained against the racial, religious and ideological cleft between NA and SSA—a divide that Gaddafi, former Libyan leader, opportunistically attempted to straddle in order to widen his support base and thus secure power. Gaddafi was Chairperson of the AU in 2009. He advanced the ambitious target of a "United States of Africa",[64] and was a vigorous proponent of the idea that only a true pan-African state can provide stability and wealth to Africa. In addition the Libyan government contributed significantly to a

[63] It was formed in Cairo on 22 March 1945 with six members: Egypt, Iraq, Transjordan (renamed Jordan after 1946), Lebanon, Saudi Arabia, and Syria. Yemen joined as a member on 5 May 1945. The Arab League currently has 22 members and four observers. The main goal of the league is to "draw closer the relations between member States and co-ordinate collaboration between them, to safeguard their independence and sovereignty, and to consider in a general way the affairs and interests of the Arab countries."

[64] This was done at two regional African summits: in June 2007 in Conakry, Guinea, and again in February 2009 in Addis Ababa, Ethiopia.

cash strapped AU.[65] The divide is clear within some national states crossing the geographical divide such as Sudan where the south has succeeded to become a separate and independent state in 2011.

Another possible reason is that many SSA states have already started on the road to democratisation. South Africa and Ghana have introduced competitive elections and constitutional reforms. In addition, a number of SSA states have participated in the APRM process whilst only one NAS has been peer reviewed namely Algeria. Despite being wealthier than SSA, NAS have not made any strides towards constitutionalism prior to 2011. NAS are less dependent on foreign aid and less open to successful transition to democracy. In other words, NAS are more isolated and not open and receptive to international law.

9. The Role of Civil Society

Civil society organisations (CSOs), by virtue of their voluntary nature, are regarded as important in promoting democratic citizenship, and provide a voice to those marginalised by governments. They operate in the political space between families/households and government, providing an alternative vehicle for political change.[66] Colonial rule, as mentioned above, destroyed much of the social fabric of pre-colonial societies not leaving room for civil CSOs to operate. Post-colonial governments in turn continued to disempower civil society not accommodated in the ruling party by introducing autocratic measures to restrict independent civil society activities, thereby yet again depriving them of a role in the political process. Governmental control over civil society became even more important when they were seen as competitors for political influence. Given the influence of the Cold War and lack of tolerance for political pluralism that characterised post-independent African politics, local CSOs have not achieved a high level of sophistication.[67] This was especially true in NAS where ordinary citizens, but especially women, were traditionally isolated from outside contact. Modern modes of communication such as the internet and twitter, and the influence of globalisation,

[65] "Libya makes its full required contribution to AU Not all countries do and that buys it influence," according to a senior African Union official. pakdefenceunit.wordpress.com/.../gaddafi-placed-97-billion-on-table funds, accessed on 4 Jan 2012.

[66] Michèle Olivier, 107.

[67] Michael Bratton, "Civil Society and Political Transition in Africa," *Institute for Democratic* 11 no. 6 (1994): 5.

however penetrated NAS, exposing its citizens to new ideas prompting them to mobilise to challenge human rights abuses and the hold on power by "lifelong dictatorships".

10. Middle Class Formation

A growing middle class[68] challenges authoritarian regimes and demands popular participation in governance issues. According to a report released by the African Development Bank (AfDB) "The middle of the pyramid: Dynamics of the middle class in Africa",[69] Africa's middle class has tripled over the last three decades to 313 million, or approximately 34% of Africa's population.[70]

The AfDB report emphasises the rapid increase in middle class citizens which has occurred since 2000. In 1980, there were approximately 111 million middle class citizens: 26% of Africa's population. In 1990, the number had risen to 151.4 million (27%), and in 2000, to 196 million (27.2%). By 2010, the NAS of Tunisia (90%), Morocco (85%) and Egypt (80%) had the highest percentage of middle class citizens. The increase in the number of middle class citizens can be attributed to strong economic growth and a shift towards a stable, salaried job culture as well as entrepreneurial activity, as opposed to traditional agricultural activities.

It is therefore not surprising that both Tunisia and Egypt toppled their oppressive governments. SSA states with a high percentage of middle class citizens are Botswana, Cape Verde, Gabon, Ghana, Kenya, Namibia and South Africa.[71]

11. Interpretation of Universal Human Rights

NAS are notorious for their interpretation of universal human rights in line with the provisions of the Islamic Sharia. The reservations to the

68 Middle class refers to individuals with annual income exceeding $3,900 in purchasing power parity terms or with daily per capita expenditure between $2 to $4 and those with daily per capita expenditures between $6 and $10.

69 Maurice Mubila and Mohamed-Safouane Ben Aissa, www.afdb.org. 20 April 2011.

70 Masahudu A. Kunateh, "Africa: Continent's middle class triples to 313 million—Report," The Chronicle, 17 May 2011, http://ghanaian-chronicle.com.

71 Casper H. Claassen "Africa's burgeoning middle class: The rise of the plebeians," *Consultancy Africa Intelligence* (11 Jul 2011), http://www.consultancyafrica.com accessed on 13 July 2011.

Convention on the Elimination of All Forms of Discrimination against Women, for instance, includes reservations by Egypt indicating that Egypt would only be willing to comply with treaty provisions that does not run counter to the Islamic Sharia. Similar reservations were made by Libya and Morocco.

The Arab Charter on Human Rights[72] was adopted by the Council of the League of Arab States 22 May 2004 and entered into force on 16 March 2008, 60 days after ratification by the seventh member state of the Arab League. There are little academic analyses available on this very recent regional instrument. The product of several drafting attempts, the final text is criticised by human rights movements in Arab countries for containing inconsistencies with international human rights instruments. An example referred to is a reference to Zionism as 'an impediment to human dignity and a major barrier to the exercise of the fundamental rights of all peoples'. Being party to standard setting human rights instruments would bar Arab states from agreeing to a lesser degree of protection.[73]

Generally speaking, the Arab Charter affirms the principles contained in the UN Charter, the UDHR, the two Covenants and the Cairo Declaration on Human Rights in Islam. A number of traditional human rights are provided for, including the right to liberty and security of persons, equality of persons before the law, protection of persons from torture, the right to own private property, freedom to practice religious observance and freedom of peaceful assembly and association. States that have ratified the Charter are: Algeria, Bahrain, the United Arab Emirates, Jordan, Libya, Palestine and Syria, two of whom are African states and AU members.

In the absence of any direct reference to democracy, article 24, dealing with political rights, is of particular interest in this discussion, especially the wide nature of the limitation clause:

> Every citizen has the right to:
> 1. Freedom of political activity.
> 2. Take part in the conduct of public affairs, directly or through freely chosen representatives.

[72] An English translation is available at: http://www1.umn.edu/humanrts/instree/loas2005.html.

[73] Mervat Rishmawi, "The Arab Charter on Human Rights and the League of Arab States: An Update," *Human Rights Law Review* vol. 10 issue1 (2010): 169–178.

3. Stand for election and to choose his representative in free and fair elections under conditions guaranteeing equality between all citizens and ensuring the free expression of the will of the electorate.
4. The opportunity to gain access, on general terms of equality, to public service in his country under equal conditions of opportunity.
5. Form associations with others and to join associations.
6. Freedom of peaceful assembly and association.
7. No restrictions may be placed on the exercise of these rights other than those imposed in conformity with the law and which are necessary in a society that respects freedom and human rights, in the interests of national security or public safety, public order, the protection of public health or morals or the protection of the rights and freedoms of others.

Ironically, many of the rights proclaimed by the Charter were called for by protestors in the NA uprising such as a free press, freedom of association, a plurality of parties and open elections.[74] At a legal level, the Charter does not contribute to establish an entitlement to democratic governance, but does endorse the value of several of the democratic core components as restated in article 24.

12. Conclusion

Democratic elements of decision-making inherent in the way many pre-colonial African societies governed themselves were suppressed under colonial rule and did not re-emerge when newly independent African states entered the international community after the demise of colonialism. The struggle against colonialism did, however, contribute to securing a position for the right to self-determination amongst universally recognised human rights at a time when the international community did not concern itself with preferred systems of domestic governance. During the post-colonial period Africa, as a developing region, remained vulnerable to external influences, limiting the development of legitimate systems of government be it through the destructive forces of the Cold War or through what is perceived as self-serving new-colonialist involvement of powerful western states. The political dictatorships and human rights abuses which flourished in these murky waters were only challenged in the 1990s which saw economic growth coupled with a more enlightened and growing body of CSOs, an expanding middle class and tentative steps

[74] "Libya Keep Calm, Keep Going," *The Economist*, 2nd July 2011, p. 10.

towards democratic rule and constitutional governance. NAS, being more economically prosperous compared to SSA, did however not follow suit with democratisation during this period.

Democracy steadily established credibility as a system of choice able to foster economic growth and stability and has accordingly enjoyed a prominent position in the AU. A number of pro-democratic instruments emanated from the AU, underlining the universal characteristics of democracy but also giving substance to an African understanding of democracy. Democratic governance enjoys support at an institutional level through voluntary peer review assisting with the implementation of international standards guiding governance and the protection of human rights. Important African and Arab human rights instruments in place help to secure a pro-democratic environment. Practical results are evident in the increase in regular democratic elections, the adoption of constitutional rule and references to human rights and democracy in many SSA states. NAS are behind their southern neighbours in this respect, but received a pro-democratic injection through the events of the Arab Spring.

The above discussion focus on the question of whether AU efforts and state practice have progressed sufficiently to give legal authority to democratic entitlement, especially in the light of pro-democratic protests in NA. It is suggested that despite significant strides towards democratisation, the international law requirements towards the establishment of binding law are still very much in a process of development. Reasons include the fact that the African Charter on Democracy, Elections and Governance is in place but not yet operative and weak implementation of the various individual human rights components of democratic governance as embodied in AU and UN treaties. Wide spread *opinio iuris* is not sufficiently supported by state practice in SSA for the establishment of a customary rule.

Recent events in NA have indeed challenged our understanding of governance in Africa. It underscores the important contribution of non-state actors to state practice advancing the establishment of a right to democracy. Despite the fact that SSA states have progressed further in ridding themselves of dictatorships, events in NA set the tone for more pro-active action against the dictatorships and reluctant rulers to yield to democratic forces in SSA.

CHAPTER THREE

HUMAN RIGHTS, DEMOCRACY AND THE LEGITIMACY OF GOVERNMENTS IN INTERNATIONAL LAW: PRACTICE OF STATES AND UN ORGANS

Jure Vidmar*

1. Introduction

The statehood criteria under international law require that a state has a government which exercises effective control over a defined and permanently populated territory.[1] The existence of a government is thus presupposed by the very concept of the state. At the same time, the concept of the government presupposes that this is an authority which *represents* the state and speaks on its behalf.

Consequently, it is important that there exists no doubt as to who constitutes the government which is entitled to speak and act on behalf of a certain state. As Crawford argues, "governmental authority is the basis for normal inter-State relations; what is an act of a State is defined primarily by reference to its organs of government, legislative, executive or judicial."[2] In principle, the legitimate governmental authority is determined by effective control over a territory.[3] In contemporary international law, however,

* Faculty of Law, University of Oxford. The author's research is supported by the Early Career Fellowship of the Leverhulme Trust.

[1] The Montevideo Convention on Rights and Duties of States, in its Article 1, provides: "The State as a person of international law should possess the following qualifications: (a) a permanent population; (b) a defined territory, (c) government; and (d) capacity to enter into relations with other states." The Montevideo Convention on Rights and Duties of States 165 LNTS 19 (1933), Article 1. These provision is generally-accepted as being reflective of customary international law.

[2] James Crawford, *The Creation of States in International Law*, 2nd edn (Oxford OUP, 2006), 56.

[3] See Anthony Aust, *Handbook of International Law* (Cambridge: CUP, 2005), 136–37, arguing: "There must be a central government operation as a political body within the law of the land and in effective control over the territory . . . The government must be sovereign and independent, so that within its territory it is not subject to authority of another state." See also David Raič, *Statehood and the Law of Self-Determination* (The Hague: Kluwer, 2002), 75, defining independence of a state as possessing "the legal capacity to act as it wishes, within the limits given by international law."

practice has emerged which may well deny legitimacy to a government despite its effective exercise of control over the state's territory.[4]

One part of scholarship has argued that governmental legitimacy stems from democratic electoral procedures.[5] Although this view is not universally-accepted,[6] it cannot be denied that it does have some limited support in practice of states and UN organs.[7] Moreover, the question arises of what other considerations, apart from effectiveness and democracy, may be determinant of governmental legitimacy.

Further issues that arise from the concept of governmental legitimacy are how effective governments lose their legitimacy as well as what the consequences are of a lost legitimacy. Traditionally, international law also knew of the concept of recognition of governments.[8] This institute indicated which authority is internationally considered to be the legitimate government of a certain state. In contemporary international law the practice of explicit recognition of governments is an exception rather than rule and most states resort to the Estrada doctrine;[9] but some recent

---

[4] See notes 46–48 and 60–66.

[5] See especially Thomas M. Franck, "The Emerging Right to Democratic Governance," *AJIL* 86 (1992): 46; Thomas M. Franck, "Democracy as a Human Right," in *Human Rights: An Agenda for the Next Century*, ed. Louis Henkin & John Lawrence Hargrove (Washington: ASIL, 1994); Thomas M. Franck, "Legitimacy and the Democratic Entitlement," in *Democratic Governance and International Law*, ed. Gregory H. Fox & Brad R. Roth (Cambridge: CUP, 2001); Fernando Teson, "The Kantian Theory of International Law," *COL LR* 92 (1992): 53; Fernando Teson, *A Philosophy of International Law* (Boulder: Westview, 1998); Anne-Marie Slaughter, "International Law in a World of Liberal States," *EJIL* 6 (1995): 503; Anne-Marie Slaughter, "The Real New World Order," *FOREIGN AFFAIRS* 76 (1997): 183.

[6] See Susan Marks, *The Riddle of All Constitutions* (Oxford: OUP, 2000); Brad R. Roth, *Governmental Illegitimacy in International Law* (Oxford: OUP, 1999), Jose Alvarez, "Do Liberal States Behave Better? A Critique of Slaughter's Liberal Theory," *EJIL* 12 (2001): 183; Jean d'Aspremont, "The Rise and Fall of Democratic Governance in International Law: A Reply to Susan Marks," *EJIL* 22 (2011): 549.

[7] See SC Res 940 (31 July 1994) (Haiti) and SC Res 1132 (8 October 1997) (Sierra Leone).

[8] See generally Stefan Talmon, *Recognition of Governments in International Law: With Particular Reference to Governments in Exile* (Oxford: Clarendon Press, 1998); M. J. Peterson, *Recognition of Governments: Legal Doctrine and State Practice* (Basingstoke: Macmillan, 1997).

[9] This doctrine is named after the Mexican minister of foreign affairs Genaro Estrada who, in 1930, made a proclamation on behalf of Mexico that its government in the future shall issue "no declaration in the sense of grants of recognition, since [Mexico] considers that such a course is an insulting practice and one which, in addition to the facts that it offends sovereignty of other nations, implies that judgment of some sort may be passed upon the internal affairs of those nations by other governments, inasmuch as the latter assume, in effect, an attitude of criticism when they decide, favourably or unfavourably, as to the legal qualifications of foreign regimes." Estrada Doctrine (1930), reprinted in Roth, *Governmental Illegitimacy*, 137–38.

international developments have brought a partial revival of this practice.[10] Moreover, collective practice may have emerged of 'abusive', albeit effective, governments being stripped of their legitimacy and the right to represent the people they claim to represent.

With special references to post-Cold War developments and to recent international practice developed in the context of the 'Arab Spring', this chapter will (i) consider the contemporary limitations on the notion 'legitimacy through effectiveness'; (ii) demonstrate to what extent the concept of recognition of governments has returned to international legal practice; and (iii) argue that the concept of 'non-democratic government' in international law needs to be separated from the notion of 'abusive government'. Recent international practice may deny legitimacy to governments that are abusive of their people(s), but 'governmental abusiveness' in this context is not necessarily understood in terms of democratic electoral procedures.

2. Speaking on Behalf of a State: Effectiveness

It follows from the statehood criteria that government is (or should be)[11] a *sine qua non* of a state.[12] At the same time, the governmental authority needs to be attached to a certain state or it is not a government properly-so-called.[13] It is the government who acts on behalf of a state internationally and domestically. Consequently, the state's policies are perceived through the actions of its government. Thus, there should exist no doubt as to who is the authority entitled to speak on behalf of a certain state. The criteria relevant for the determination of who constitutes the actual government are associated with the questions of effective control and legitimacy.[14]

The consideration for effectiveness does not deal with the question of how the new government has come to power but merely acknowledges

---

[10] See *infra* notes 90–92.

[11] Contemporary practice demonstrates that the Montevideo criteria are not applied thoroughly when new states are created. Therefore, "the question remains whether [the Montevideo] criteria are sufficient for Statehood, as well as being necessary." Martin Dixon and Robert McCorquodale, *Cases and Materials in International Law* (Oxford: OUP, 2003), 137.

[12] See *supra* note 1.

[13] Roth, *Governmental Illegitimacy*, 130, argues: "just as there is no government without a state, there is no state without a government."

[14] Roth, *Governmental Illegitimacy*, 136–37.

that an effective government *is* in power. This understanding is well-expressed in the following statement: "The government brought into permanent power by a revolution or a *coup d'état* is, according to international law, the legitimate government of a State, whose identity is not affected by these events."[15] Two legal rules apply in this context. First, a new government is not the legitimate authority before effective control over the territory of a state in question is achieved; second, after an old government loses its effective control, it should be no longer treated as the government of that state.[16] In other words, an authority becomes the legitimate government of a state by meeting the criterion of effectiveness.[17] This doctrine was supported by practice of most states in the twentieth century.[18]

This section now considers how it is internationally decided which authority is entitled to speak on behalf of a state and what the limits are on the criterion of effectiveness in contemporary international law.

2.1. *Recognition of Governments*

The act of recognition in international law is a complicated relationship between law and politics; recognition is "a political act that has legal consequences."[19] In contemporary international law, one is predominantly dealing with the act of recognition of states the legal effects of which remain controversial.[20]

The act of recognition of governments is even more controversial, as, unlike the recognition of states, it is not a one-time act.[21] This opens the possibility of much more frequent politicisation of this type of recognition than this is the case with the recognition of states. Recognition of governments can thus become "a political tool for reaching foreign policy goals."[22]

---

15 Hans Kelsen, *Principles of International Law* (New York: Holt, Rinehart & Winston, 1966), 220.

16 Peterson, *Recognition of Governments*, 35.

17 Robert McCorquodale, "The Creation and Recognition of States," in S. Blay, R. Piotrowicz and B. M. Tsamenyi (eds.), *Public International Law: An Australian* Perspective, ed. Sam Blay, Ryszard Piotrowicz & B. Martin Tsamenyi. (Melbourne: OUP, 2005), 198.

18 McCorquodale, "The Creation and Recognition of States," 198.

19 McCorquodale, "The Creation and Recognition of States," 197.

20 See generally Jure Vidmar, "Explaining the Legal Effects of Recognition," *ICLQ* 61 (2012): 361.

21 McCorquodale, "The Creation and Recognition of States," 198.

22 Peterson, *Recognition of Governments*, 3.

Where the change of government occurs in accordance with constitutional provisions of the state in question, the new government would not become subject to recognition. This is different where a new government usurps power against the constitutional provisions.[23] For example, if a government changes after democratic elections, the new government will be automatically accepted without an international enquiry into its legitimacy.[24] This may be different where a democratic government is overthrown in a coup.[25]

The practice of explicit recognition of governments has declined and most governments now resort to the "Estrada Doctrine", which perceives an explicit declaration of recognition of governments as an insulting practice that interferes with the internal affairs of other states.[26] Instead of an explicit proclamation of recognition the approach of the "Estrada Doctrine" is less formal and "confines itself to the maintenance or withdrawal . . . of . . . diplomatic agents, and to the continued acceptance . . . of . . . accredited diplomatic agents."[27] This doctrine was quietly accepted even by the United States with the Department of State statement in 1977.[28]

2.2. *Beyond Explicit Recognition of Governments and the Shortcomings of the Effectiveness Doctrine*

Although practice of explicit recognitions of governments has declined, there is significant practice of factual non-recognition of governments. Such practice has been identified in three types of situations:

> [1] [There exist] [t]wo or more local *de facto* authorities each claiming to be the only legitimate government of a (recognized) State . . . [2] the government of a State claims to continue to be the government of a part of the State's territory that has *de facto* seceded . . . [3] an authority in exile claims to be the government of a State which is under the effective control of a

---

[23] David J. Harris, *Cases and Materials on International Law* (London: Sweet & Maxwell, 2004), 156.

[24] Harris, *Cases and Materials*, 156.

[25] See *infra* note 48.

[26] See *supra* note 9.

[27] Harris, *Cases and Materials*, 156.

[28] Harris, *Cases and Materials*, 159. The United States Department of State argued that "establishment of relations does not involve approval or disapproval but merely demonstrates a willingness on our part to conduct affairs with other governments directly." US Department of State statement (1977), reprinted in Harris, *Cases and Materials*, 159.

> colonial power, a belligerent occupant or its local puppet, or an authority which came to power by *coup d'état* or revolution.[29]

In the absence of explicit recognition in such situations, actions of states imply their views with regard to the problem of which government is considered the legitimate representative of a certain state.[30]

Important clarification on the acceptance of governmental authority stems from the practice of UN organs. From 1949, governments of the People's Republic of China and of the Republic of China have both claimed to be the legitimate government of China.[31] The Government of the Republic of China initially represented China in the UN.[32] In 1971, however, the General Assembly adopted Resolution 2758[33] which recognized:

> [T]he representatives of [the Government of the People's Republic of China] as the only legitimate representatives of China [and expelled] the representatives of [the Government of the Republic of China (Taiwan)] from the place which they unlawfully [occupied] at the United Nations and in all the organizations related to it.[34]

The General Assembly thus pronounced that the Government of the Republic of China was not the legitimate government of China as it was in effective control of only a fraction of the Chinese territory, i.e. of Taiwan. In so doing, the General Assembly also confirmed that the Government of the People's Republic of China is the legitimate government of the entire Chinese territory, including Taiwan, although this authority obviously did not (and still does not) exercise effective control over Taiwan. This suggests that the requirement for effectiveness is not absolute and may be limited by other principles in international law. Indeed, to accept that the government of mainland China is not the government of Taiwan could imply that Taiwan is a separate state. This would, however, invoke a number of other international legal questions.[35]

Although recognition of governments should not be conflated for recognition of states, there are also several other instances which indicate

---

29 Talmon, *Recognition of Governments*, 7–8.
30 Talmon, *Recognition of Governments*, 7–8.
31 Crawfod, *The Creation of States*, 200.
32 Crawford, *The Creation of States*, 200.
33 GA Res 2758 (25 October 1971).
34 GA Res 2758, para. 4.
35 The question is not only how would China react on that and whether any potential use of force would fall within the ambit of Article 2(4) of the UN Charter; but also whether Taiwan could be considered a state although it does not claim to be one.

that acceptance of a certain authority as being the legitimate government of an entity could be perceived as recognition of the entity as a state.

For example, Southern Rhodesia declared independence in 1965.[36] However, the racist government of Ian Smith was seen as an illegal authority, not authorized to declare independence of the entity as such declaration would be issued in violation of the right of self-determination and in pursuance of racist policies.[37] Although the government was illegitimate, the issue was broader and resulted in universal non-recognition of Southern Rhodesia as a state.[38] The situation with the South African homelands[39] was similar and so was collective non-acceptance of the Turkish puppet-government in Northern Cyprus which has resulted in the Turkish Republic of Northern Cyprus not being recognized as a state.[40]

Another relevant example may be the Iraqi occupation of Kuwait in 1990. Non-recognition of the Kuwaiti government as the only legitimate government of Kuwait after the Iraqi occupation could have implied acceptance of the Iraqi annexation. Although the Kuwaiti government was ineffective in the territory of this state, the Security Council acted under Chapter VII, condemned the occupation and proclaimed the Government of Kuwait to be the only legitimate government of that territory.[41]

However, in these circumstances territorial illegality was at issue while the regime type *sensu stricto* played no role. Indeed, Southern Rhodesia, the Homelands, Northern Cyprus and Kuwait were not about democracy. Rather, violations of certain fundamental norms of international law (*jus cogens*)[42] created territorial situations that were effective yet illegal. In other words, at issue here were breaches of *jus cogens* and territorial illegality.

---

36 John Dugard, *Recognition and the United Nations* (Cambridge: Grotius Publications 1987), 90.

37 See SC Res 216 (12 November 1965), para. 1; SC Res 217 (20 November 1965), para. 3; and SC Res 277 (18 March 1970), para. 2.

38 Ibid. See also Jericho Nkala, *The United Nations, International Law, and the Rhodesian Independence Crisis* (Oxford: Clarendon, 1985), 57.

39 See Status of Transkei Act 100 (26 October 1976); Status of Bophuthatswana Act 89 (6 December 1977); Status of Venda Act 107 (13 September 1979); Status of Ciskei Act 110 (4 December 1981); GA Res 2671 F (8 December 1970), see especially para. 3; GA Res 2775 (29 November 1971); GA Res 31/6 A (26 October 1976), para. 3; GA Res 402 (22 December 1976); GA Res 407 (25 May 1977); GA Res 37/43 (3 December 1982); GA Res 37/69A (9 December 1982).

40 SC Res 353 (20 July 1974); SC Res 541 (18 November 1983), para. 6.

41 See SC Res 661 (6 August 1990).

42 Dugard, *Recognition and the United Nations*, 102.

In sum, governmental legitimacy is traditionally rooted in effective control over the territory. But this doctrine is not unqualified. It is well-established in international law that an effective governmental authority will be denied its legitimacy in situations of territorial illegality. Now it needs to be considered what the limitations are on the effective-control principle beyond territorial illegality.

3. Legitimacy of Governments in the Post-Cold War Era

In the post-Cold War era, some writers have advanced the view that only democracy legitimizes a governmental authority.[43] Non-democratic governments lose their legitimacy both internally and internationally.[44] In the most extreme interpretations, the consequence of the lack of democratic governmental legitimacy could even be that the state in question loses the protection of Article 2(4) of the UN Charter.[45] This argument for pro-democratic intervention is very far-reaching and not supported by international law. However, in the post-Cold War era, democracy has nevertheless played some role in determining governmental legitimacy. This section will argue that such practice may be developing in respect of coup governments.

3.1. *The Limits on Democratic Legitimacy*

Some significant collective practice has developed which denies recognition to coup-governments overthrowing democratically-elected ones. Sierra Leone and Haiti are examples of such. In the case of Sierra Leone, the Security Council, acting under Chapter VII, demanded that "the military junta take immediate steps to relinquish power in Sierra Leone and make way for the restoration of the democratically-elected Government and a return to constitutional order."[46]

In relation to Haiti, the Security Council went even further and authorized an intervention for the return of an ousted democratically-elected government. Acting under Chapter VII of the UN Charter, the Security Council in 1994 adopted Resolution 940. Based on this Resolution, the United States led a multi-national effort to bring the overthrown elected

---

43 See, for example, Franck, "The Emerging Right to Democratic Governance," 41–47.
44 See Franck, "The Emerging Right to Democratic Governance," 41–47.
45 See, for example, Teson, "The Kantian Theory of International Law," 90–91.
46 SC Res 1132 (8 October 1997), para. 1

President Jean-Bertrande Aristide back to power.[47] The Resolution, *inter alia*, spelled out:

> Reaffirming that the goal of the international community remains the restoration of democracy in Haiti and the prompt return of the legitimately elected President, Jean-Bertrande Aristide, within the framework of the Governors Island Agreement
>
> ...
>
> 4. Acting under Chapter VII of the Charter of the United Nations, authorizes Member States to form a multinational force under unified command and control and, in this framework, to use all necessary means to facilitate the departure from Haiti of the military leadership, consistent with the Governors Island Agreement, the prompt return of the legitimately elected President and the restoration of the legitimate authorities of the Government of Haiti; and to establish and maintain a secure and stable environment that will permit implementation of the Governors Island Agreement, on the understanding that the cost of implementing this temporary operation will be borne by the participating Member States....[48]

Importantly, Resolution 940 thus authorized an intervention for the purpose of restoration of an elected government and not for imposition of democracy.

The entire role of the UN in the Haiti events, which ultimately led to intervention under Chapter VII, is particularly interesting from the point of view of pro-democratic advocacy within international law.[49] One can argue that the internationalization of the internal matters of Haiti was the very instrument which opened the door to an intervention.[50] Namely, the UN observed the Haitian election in 1990 and, after it had verified the electoral results, it was unwilling to accept nullification of these results by a coup (four years later).[51] As Resolution 940 also demonstrates, the Governors Island Agreement[52] further internationalized the internal conflict. In the process of the negotiation of this agreement between the *de facto* government of Haiti and the government-in-exile, the UN also became a

[47] See generally Richard Falk, "The Haiti Intervention: A Dangerous World Order Precedent for the United Nations," *HARV ILJ* 36 (1995): 341.
[48] SC Res 940 (31 July 1994).
[49] Compare *supra* note 5.
[50] Roth, *Governmental Illegitimacy*, 385.
[51] Roth, *Governmental Illegitimacy*, 385.
[52] The Governors Island Agreement, concluded on 3 July 1993, was a UN-sponsored agreement between the elected overthrown president Aristide and the *de facto* government of Haiti which foresaw a retreat of the non-elected de facto government from power in exchange for amnesty. For more see UN Doc S/26063 (12 July 1993).

party and thus also responsible for the implementation of solutions foreseen by the agreement.[53] According to Resolution 940, the failure of the *de facto* government of Haiti to comply with this agreement was also a reason for intervention.

Notably, the Security Council acted under Chapter VII of the UN Charter, although it is generally perceived that, strictly speaking, no breach of or threat to *international* peace existed.[54] However, the interpretation of Article 39 of the UN Charter nowadays is different than in the time when it was drafted. The Security Council thus acts even where the situation is clearly domestic. Moreover, gross and systematic human rights violations are also seen as breaches or threats to international peace. The reaction to Haiti may even suggest that, under some circumstances, the lack of democracy could also trigger such an interpretation.[55]

However, Resolution 940 should not be understood too broadly, as the previous engagement of the UN in the electoral process in Haiti makes the situation somewhat specific. Moreover, it is questionable to what degree other Chapter VII resolutions addressing the governance problem in a certain territory have been founded on express pro-democratic rather than general human rights arguments. There exists practice established with regard to the legitimacy of those governments which are in effective control but are "unwilling to carry out essential international law duties and obligations."[56] Grave breaches of international human rights and threats to international peace fall under this category, but absence of a democratic government does not.

3.2. *Beyond Democracy: Human Rights and Legitimacy*

This subsection turns to the international response to the Taliban government of Afghanistan. This may be an example where the government, which may well have been effective, lost its international legitimacy. However, the lost legitimacy and the call for a regime change were not based on democratic considerations.

Acting under Chapter VII of the UN Charter, the Security Council adopted Resolution 1363, in which it insisted:

53 Ibid.
54 See Falk, "The Haiti Intervention," 342.
55 Compare Franck, "The Emerging Right to Democratic Governance."
56 Roth, *Governmental Illegitimacy*, 149.

> [T]hat the Afghan faction known as the Taliban, which also calls itself the Islamic Emirate of Afghanistan, comply promptly with its previous resolutions and in particular cease the provision of sanctuary and training for international terrorists and their organizations, take appropriate effective measures to ensure that the territory under its control is not used for terrorist installations and camps, or for the preparation or organization of terrorist acts against other States or their citizens, and cooperate with efforts to bring indicted terrorists to justice.[57]

With the formulation "the Afghan faction known as the Taliban, which also calls itself the Islamic Emirate of Afghanistan",[58] the Security Council suggested that it did not recognize the Taliban government as the legitimate government of Afghanistan. With regard to the situation in Afghanistan, the Security Council in several instances invoked obligations of "the Taliban, as well as other Afghan factions".[59] This raises doubts as to whether, in the Security Council's perception, the Taliban government exercised effective control over the territory of Afghanistan. Consequently, the authority of the Taliban government of Afghanistan might have also been partly denied on the grounds of non-effectiveness. Indeed, the lack of effective control over the entire territory was clearly one of the considerations in the pronouncement that the government lacked legitimacy.

But effectiveness, or the lack of it, was certainly not the only consideration; and perhaps even not the most important one. The Security Council in its resolutions on Afghanistan under Taliban control stated that the Taliban were obliged to comply with duties imposed by international law—most notably threats to international peace[60] and human rights[61] were at issue here—while it strictly avoided using the term "the government of Afghanistan". Instead, terms such as "the Afghan faction known as the Taliban",[62] "the Taliban authorities",[63] "the territory of Afghanistan under Taliban control"[64] were used, or it was demanded that "the

[57] SC Res 1267 (15 October 1999), para. 1.

[58] SC Res 1267 (15 October 1999), para. 1.

[59] See SC Res 1214 (8 December 1998), para. 1.

[60] See SC Res 1267 (15 October 1999), SC Res 1333 (19 December 2000) and SC Res 1363 (30 July 2001), where the Security Council acted under Chapter VII of the UN Charter.

[61] See SC Res 1267 (15 October 1999), preamble: "[D]eep concern over the continuing violations of international humanitarian law and of human rights, particularly discrimination against women and girls."

[62] See SC Res 1267, para. 1.

[63] See SC Res 1333, preamble.

[64] See SC Res 1363, para. 3 (b).

Taliban [and not "the government of Afghanistan"] comply"[65] with previous resolutions.

Security Council Resolution 1378, *inter alia*, condemned "the Taliban for allowing Afghanistan to be used as a base for the export of terrorism by the Al-Qaida network and other terrorist groups"[66] and expressed deep concern about "serious violations by the Taliban of human rights and international humanitarian law"[67] and further spelled out:

> [I]ts strong support for the efforts of the Afghan people to establish a new and transitional administration leading to the formation of a government, both of which:
>
> – should be broad-based, multi-ethnic and fully representative of all the Afghan people and committed to peace with Afghanistan's neighbours,
> – should respect the human rights of all Afghan people, regardless of gender, ethnicity or religion,
> – should respect Afghanistan's international obligations.[68]

The Security Council thus denied legitimacy of the Taliban government in Afghanistan based on its grave human rights violations and threats to international peace and expressed its support for a change of government. However, despite some references to democratic principles, such as "broad-based" government, which is "multi-ethnic and fully representative of all the Afghan people",[69] one cannot argue that Security Council Resolution 1378 expressed support for a particular political system—that of Western style liberal-democracy.

The use of the term 'democracy' itself was avoided. The resolutions also failed to call for an enactment of a particular political system or electoral method. References to 'a broad based government' clearly cannot be seen as a call for democracy as a political system; it should rather be understood as a requirement for representativeness of various ethnic groups and peoples in the context of the right of self-determination.[70] The internal mode of the exercise of the right of self-determination is, however, not a synonym for democracy.[71]

---

[65] See SC Res 1333, paras 1 & 2.
[66] SC Res 1378 (14 November 2001), preamble.
[67] SC Res 1378 (14 November 2001), preamble.
[68] SC Res 1378, para. 1.
[69] SC Res 1378, para. 1.
[70] See, generally, Jure Vidmar, "The Right of Self-Determination and Multiparty Democracy: Two Sides of the Same Coin?" *HRLR* 10 (2) (2010): 248–250.
[71] Vidmar, "The Right of Self-Determination," 266–68.

With regard to the Taliban government of Afghanistan, the Security Council specifically invoked the rights of women and girls.[72] This is a powerful pronouncement that governments which exclude women from political participation and girls from education are illegitimate. Yet the Security Council did not make any pronouncements on representativeness on the basis of formation of political parties.

The Security Council's expressed support for the change of government in Afghanistan was therefore no pro-democratic activism. It was rather a collective response to serious breaches of internationally protected human rights and involvement in international terrorism. Moreover, some prominence was also given to the fact that the Taliban government was not in effective control over the entire territory of Afghanistan. Even in this example, therefore, the question of governmental legitimacy and representativeness was not entirely liberated from the test of effective control.

4. The 'Arab Spring' and the Implications for Democratic Legitimacy in Contemporary International Law

In 1990s, some writers discussed the possibility of the use of force against 'non-democratic states'.[73] After the terrorist attacks of 11 September 2001, the debate on expanding the zone of democracy, if necessary by military means, became less prominent. What some scholars were questioning was no longer whether the prohibition of the use of force protects non-democratic states; but whether it protects 'rogue states'.[74] There was no exact overlap between the two labels. However, the 'Arab spring' revived the debates on democracy, human rights, regime change and intervention. This section seeks to demonstrate that international responses to these developments have little to do with democracy. They may rather confirm that even an effective government may, under some circumstances, lose international legitimacy; but this conclusion should not be overstretched.

---

72 SC Res 1378 (14 November 2001), preamble.

73 Teson, "The Kantian Theory of International Law"; Teson, *A Philosophy of International Law*.

74 See, for example, Jonathan B. Schwartz, "Dealing with a "Rogue State": The Libya Precedent," *AJIL* 101 (2007): 553.

4.1. *International Legitimacy and Libya: How Far Beyond Effectiveness?*

The developments in Tunisia and Egypt attracted significant international interest but, unlike in some other instances, did not lead to a collective international response. Although the, then, opposition movements in these two states progressively gained notable international sympathy,[75] previous governments were not collective pronounced as being illegitimate. This was to a certain degree different in the situation of Libya.

Security Council resolutions 1970 and 1973 on Libya were adopted under Chapter VII of the UN Charter; the Security Council identified the existence of a threat to international peace and security and drew a number of legal consequences; for example, a travel ban,[76] asset freezing,[77] referral to the International Criminal Tribunal,[78] and an arms embargo.[79] In order to protect civilians, the Security Council, in all likelihood in a manner of deliberate ambiguity, authorized the use of all necessary means, which can be seen as a euphemism for the use of force.[80] But in so doing it excluded "a foreign occupation force of any form on any part of Libyan territory."[81]

The Resolutions are, however, not concerned with the choice of a political system. Resolution 1970, for example, urged the Libyan authorities to: "Act with the utmost restraint, respect human rights and international humanitarian law, and allow immediate access for international human rights monitors."[82] Resolution 1973 condemned "the gross and systematic violation of human rights, including arbitrary detentions, enforced disappearances, torture and summary executions."[83]

---

75 See Joint UK, France, Germany, Italy and Spain Statement on Egypt (3 February 2011), at http://www.number10.gov.uk/news/joint-uk-france-germany-italy-and-spain-statement-on-egypt. In the Joint Statement, the governments, *inter alia*, argued: "Only a quick and orderly transition to a broad-based Government will make it possible to overcome the challenges Egypt is now facing." This was only a political statement without any legal effects.

76 SC Res 1970 (26 February 2011), para. 15.

77 SC Res 1970, paras 17–21.

78 SC Res 1970, paras 4–8.

79 SC Res 1970, paras 9–14.

80 See Christian Henderson, "International Measures for the Protection of Civilians in Libya and Cote D'Ivoire," *ICLQ* 60 (3) (2011): 770–71.

81 SC Res 1973 (17 March 2011), para. 4.

82 SC Res 1970, para. 2 (a).

83 SC Res 1973, preamble, para. 4.

Unlike the relevant resolutions on Afghanistan,[84] the resolutions on Libya did not explicitly deny legitimacy of the sitting government or call for a regime change, not even when, at that time, the Benghazi-based government of the National Transitional Council was already in control of large parts of Libyan territory. Indeed, the language used in the resolutions on Afghanistan clearly disputed legitimacy of the Taliban government,[85] while the resolutions on Libya referred to the Gaddafi government as 'the Libyan authorities'.[86] Moreover, the resolutions on Libya did not call for a regime-change; the authorization of the use of force was limited to the protection of the civilian population.[87]

Nevertheless, the government-change in Libya clearly was not only a domestic but an internationalized issue.[88] It is debatable whether the international support for the National Transitional Council overstepped the Security Council's mandate and at what point the international involvement should have stopped.[89] As argued above, an internationalized government-change was not authorized by the applicable Security Council resolutions and neither was a requirement expressed for an enactment of a particular political system.

In the case of Libya a number of states (including the United Kingdom) departed from the Estrada doctrine and decided to grant explicit recognition to the National Transitional Council.[90] This is a notable exception to the general practice developed over the past decades. The recognizing states clearly expressed preference to one of the competing authorities and their decisions were rooted in human rights considerations and in the grave humanitarian situation. Indeed, for many states the Gaddafi government lost its legitimacy by the escalation of abusiveness against its people.

---

84 See *supra* notes 60–66.

85 Ibid.

86 SC Res 1970, para. 2 (a).

87 See Henderson, "*International Measures for the Protection of Civilians*,' 772.

88 See generally Mehrdad Payandeh, "The United Nations, Military Intervention, and Regime Change in Libya," *VJIL* 55 (2) (2012): 355.

89 Payandeh, "The United Nations, Military Intervention, and Regime Change in Libya."

90 See Dapo Akande, 'Recognition of Libyan National transitional Council as Government of Libya' EJIL Talk! (23 July 2011), http://www.ejiltalk.org/recognition-of-libyan-national-transitional-council-as-government-of-libya.

See also Stefan Talmon, 'Recognition of the Libyan National Transitional Council ASIL Insights (16 June 2011), http://www.asil.org/insights110616.cfm.

It is nevertheless notable that recognition of the competing authority did not come before the National Transitional Council managed to establish a degree of control over parts of the Libyan territory. In other words, governmental legitimacy was not denied to a firmly-established and entirely effective government. It was rather that the international community progressively shifted toward one of the competing authorities neither of which was in effective control over the entire territory of Libya. Still, the Gaddafi government was in control of the capital and several governmental institutions, so it seemed to have had a better claim on the basis of effectiveness. But it lost this claim due to gross and systematic human rights violations and the grave humanitarian situation.[91]

Attempts were also made to link Gaddafi's governmental illegitimacy with democracy. When the United Kingdom recognized the National Transitional Council as the only legitimate government of Libya, Foreign Secretary William Hague stated that this recognition would contribute toward "more open and democratic Libya . . . in stark contrast to Gaddafi whose brutality against the Libyan people has stripped him of all legitimacy."[92] But this reference to democracy should not be interpreted too broadly. It is merely political and without legal consequences. References to democracy in such situations seem to be mantra repeated by politicians but their legal value is, at least, questionable.

The National Transitional Council expressed its commitment to democratic institutions and procedures.[93] It is highly questionable what precisely this means. In political theory, there is no single definition of democracy. While the procedural definition focuses on democratic elections which need to be held in a multiparty setting,[94] the substantive definition cautions that elections do not (necessarily) bring democracy.[95] It is, however, difficult to define substantive democracy in legal terms, as it becomes unclear on whom fall the obligations arising under the ideal of consolidated democracy; clearly not only on states and their governments. Indeed, it is in the end also individuals who need to assure that they do

---

[91] Compare *supra* notes 81–83.

[92] See UK Expels Gaddafi Diplomats and Recognises Libya Rebels, BBC News (27 July 2011), http://www.bbc.co.uk/news/uk-politics-14306544.

[93] See 'A Vision of a Democratic Libya', The Libyan Interim National Council, http://www.ntclibya.org/english/libya.

[94] See, for example, Samuel P. Huntington, *The Third Wave* (Norman: University of Oklahoma Press, 1990). See also, generally, Franck, "The Emerging Right to Democratic Governance."

[95] See, for example, Roth, *Governmental Illegitimacy*, 32–38.

not vote extremist politicians into power. Domestic and regional courts have even developed notable practice of dissolving extremist political parties.[96] This is a good illustration that elections and electoral choice are not synonyms for democracy.

It is also of little value to perceive 'democracy' as a synonym for human rights. Indeed, the two concepts can work against each other. For example, majoritarian decision-making can lead to the tyranny of the majority. It is then on human rights to protect minorities, so that they do not become the victims of 'democratic decision-making'.[97]

Moreover, international (human rights) law, treaties and custom, does not bind states to a particular political system or electoral method. This was established by the ICJ in the *Nicaragua* case and, in the post-Cold War era, confirmed in a number of widely-supported General Assembly resolutions.[98] These resolutions are capable of reflecting a uniform *opinio juris*.[99] Even the Human Rights Committee avoided a pronouncement that the right to vote under the ICCPR requires elections in a multiparty setting.[100]

Libya is thus internationally not bound to any particular political system or electoral method and neither was the Gaddafi government in breach of any norms simply by not holding Western-style multiparty elections. It was rather gross and systematic violations of human rights and the grave humanitarian situation which triggered a collective response and denial of governmental legitimacy to Gaddafi. And even in this case the international support to the National Transitional Council did not come before this authority established effective control over a part of the territory of Libya.

---

96 See Jure Vidmar, "Multiparty Democracy: International and Human Rights Law Perspectives," *LJIL* 23 (2010): 228–237.

97 See Article 27, ICCPR.

98 See *Military and Paramilitary Activities in and Against Nicaragua* (*Nicaragua v. United States*), Merits, Judgment of 27 June 1986, [1986] ICJ Rep. 14, at 132, para. 261. GA Res 50/133 (20 December 1995), GA Res 51/31 (13 December 1996), GA Res 52/18 (21 November 1997), GA Res 53/31 (23 November 1998), GA Res 54/36 (29 November 1999), GA Res 55/43 (27 November 2000), GA Res 58/13 (17 November 2003), GA Res (9 February 2004), GA Res 60/253 (2 May 2006), GA Res 61/226 (22 December 2006), GA Res 55/2 (8 September 2000)—the Millennium Declaration. These resolutions invoke some democratic standards but do not prescribe an electoral method or specify that elections need to be held in a multiparty setting.

99 See The *Nicaragua case*, para. 188.

100 HRC, General Comment 25, UN Doc CCPR/C/21/Rev.1,Add.7 (1996), para. 1.

Libya was thus a situation in which two competing authorities claimed they were the legitimate government of the state. Neither of them was in effective control of the entire territory of Libya. A number of states decided to grant an explicit recognition to the National Transitional Council on the basis of the Gaddafi government's record of gross human rights violations. It is, however, very unlikely that the competing authority would have been recognized, if it did not control part of the territory and demonstrate the capability of taking full control over Libya.

With regard to democracy, Libya is yet another example proving that calls for respect of human rights should not be taken as an equivalent for democracy as a political system. The post-Gaddafi Libya is certainly at liberty to enact a democratic political system. However, an international imposition of a particular political system would mean a violation of the right of self-determination.[101] Moreover, 'a democratic Libya' is presently not a reality. The international community should rather pressure the new government of Libya to respect the internationally-guaranteed human rights standards. Such international pressure on the basis of specific human rights provisions would be much more effective than flowery-phrases on democracy; whatever this term precisely means.

4.2. *The Security Council and Syria in Light of the Debate on the Responsibility to Protect and Humanitarian Intervention*

The human rights violations and grave humanitarian situation in Syria initially triggered an international response and a draft Security Council resolution.[102] The draft went much further than the resolution on Libya and explicitly called for a regime-change. The draft thus calls for a transition "to a democratic, plural political system"[103] and for the formation of a national unity government.[104] The draft did not specify or operationalize the meaning of a democratic, plural political system and neither did it challenge the legitimacy of the government of Syria on the basis of democracy. For this purpose it rather invoked human rights and humanitarian grounds. But the draft nevertheless reflects the view that respect for

---

101 See Vidmar, "The Right of Self-Determination," 266.

102 See Draft of Security Council Resolution on Syria, New York Times (1 February 2012), at http://www.nytimes.com/2012/02/01/world/middleeast/draft-of-security-council-resolution-onsyria.html?_r=1&pagewanted=all.

103 Draft of Security Council Resolution on Syria, para. 7.

104 Draft of Security Council Resolution on Syria, para. 7.

human rights can only be achieved upon the change of the government and in a democratic setting.

If it were adopted, the resolution would have been rather far-reaching. Yet it was subject to a double veto (China and Russia).[105] The subsequently adopted Resolution 2042 uses a much milder language, does not call for a regime change and does not challenge the legitimacy of the government of Syria.[106] The Resolution called for the end of violence in Syria and made some provisions to achieve this goal (e.g. authorization of unarmed military observes).[107] However, this is not a Chapter VII resolution. Moreover, the preamble reaffirms the "commitment to the sovereignty, unity and territorial integrity of Syria,"[108] while the operative paragraphs make references to Syrian Government[109] and Syrian authorities.[110] The Resolution also uses the phrasing "all parties, including the opposition."[111] The language thus clearly suggests that the Resolution does not challenge the legitimacy of the authority of the government of Syria.

This indicates that the universal perception of governmental legitimacy has not entirely shifted away from the requirement of effective control over a territory. As Stefan Talmon argued in the context of the Gaddafi regime in Libya: "Even gross and systematic violations of human rights by a government . . . do not *automatically* lead to its loss of status as a government in international law or make it any less a government than it would otherwise be."[112] With regard to Syria this means that in the absence of the Security Council's action or collective de-recognition of Syrian government, the latter remains the government of Syria; despite gross and systematic human rights violations.

In recent years, international legal doctrine has prominently started to debate the concepts of humanitarian intervention and the responsibility to protect.[113] What remains problematic about these two concepts is, however, that it is generally not accepted that they constitute an exception

---

105 See 'Russia and China Veto Resolution on Syria at UN, BBC News (4 February 2012), http://www.bbc.co.uk/news/world-16890107.

106 SC Res 2042 (14 April 2012).

107 SC Res 2042, para. 7.

108 SC Res 2042, preamble, para. 3.

109 SC Res 2042, paras 2, 5, 6, and 7.

110 SC Res 2042, paras 8 and 10.

111 SC Res 2042, para. 4.

112 Stefan Talmon, "De-Recognition of Colonel Qaddafi as Head of State of Libya?" ICLQ 60 (3) (2011): 765.

113 For an overview see International Coalition for the Responsibility to Protect, http://www.responsibilitytoprotect.org/.

to the general prohibition of the use of force in international relations, contained in Article 2(4) of the UN Charter.[114] In other words, humanitarian intervention and responsibility to protect can only be given effect via Chapter VII Resolutions of the UN Security Council, otherwise the use of force is illegal.

This, of course, raises the question of whether international law is not ill-fit for solving humanitarian disasters if an action to avert such disasters can be prevented by a (political) veto in the Security Council.[115] However, social life is too complex that law could envisage any situation and always grant an appropriate exception. If the law attempted to do so, very little would be left of the original prohibitions. If states alone could authorize an exception to the prohibition of the use of force to themselves, little imagination is needed to see where this practice would end.

It is thus perhaps better to admit that sometimes intervention will simply be illegal, yet morally justified. It is indeed interesting to read the academic responses where the authors were at pains admitting that the intervention against Yugoslavia in 1999 was illegal, but it nevertheless ended a grave humanitarian situation in Kosovo.[116] It is not the intention of this chapter to revisit these debates. Here it is rather suggested that law and morality do not always go hand-in-hand and that we should perhaps stop trying to square with international law humanitarian intervention outside of Chapter VII. As far as the law is concerned, such intervention is illegal. But moral responsibilities may well go further than the law.

The example of Syria proves that states, especially permanent members of the Security Council, have not accepted the responsibility to protect and humanitarian intervention as a collective obligation where gross and systematic violations are taking place and where a grave humanitarian situation exists.

This leads to the question of what precisely is the added value of the concepts of humanitarian intervention and the responsibility to protect if (i) they need to be accommodated within Chapter VII; and (ii) permanent members of the Security Council do not automatically agree to

---

[114] Exceptions to the prohibition contained in Article 2(4) are only self-defence and authorization of the Security Council (Chapter VII, UN Charter).

[115] Compare *supra* note 105.

[116] See Christine Chinkin, "Kosovo: A 'Good' or 'Bad' War?" *AJIL* 93 (1999): 843, arguing: "How can I, as an advocate of human rights, resist the assertion of a moral imperative on states to intervene in the internal affairs of another state where there is evidence of ethnic cleansing, rape and other forms of systematic and widespread abuse, regardless of what the Charter mandates about the use of force and its allocation of competence?"

intervention on humanitarian grounds. The UN Charter, with its Chapter VII, has been there since 1945.

What can be said of this is that a breach of international peace and security, as referred to in Article 39 of the UN Charter, nowadays has a different meaning than back in 1945. At the end of the Second World War, a breach of international peace was understood as an illegal use or a threat of use of force in international relations.[117] It has been shown in this chapter that nowadays even purely domestic situations of governments being abusive of their people can fall within the scope of Article 39. But this is a matter of Chapter VII of the UN Charter, not a matter of customary international law. In international law *de lege lata* the responsibility to protect[118] and humanitarian intervention may thus be no more than a contemporary interpretation of Article 39. This practice is indeed well-grounded in the practice of this organ.

Some scholars and occasionally governments have even advanced the view that pro-democratic intervention could be legal under international law.[119] The idea often tags along with the concept of humanitarian intervention. Yet there is no support for pro-democratic intervention in international law *de lege lata*.[120] There exists no right or even duty to intervene on pro-democratic grounds under customary law.[121] As far as Chapter VII-authorization is concerned, it was argued above that the example of Haiti should not be overstretched and that it was limited to a coup situation. In other instances, the Security Council's involvement was exemplary limited to bringing to an end humanitarian disasters and/or gross and most systematic violations of fundamental human rights, often those of *jus cogens* character.

In sum, collective action on humanitarian grounds is exclusively a matter falling under Chapter VII of the UN Charter. It is not a matter of ad hoc coalitions or other international organizations or alliances. And when such action is authorized by the Security Council, this does not result from a lack of democratic (electoral) practices. It is rather a response to gross and systematic violations of fundamental human rights and to grave humanitarian situations.

117 See Payandeh, "The United Nations, Military Intervention, and Regime Change in Libya," 364.

118 See *supra* note 113.

119 See Teson, "The Kantian Theory of International Law,"; Teson, *A Philosophy of International Law*.

120 See Alvarez, "Do Liberal States behave better?," 189.

121 Compare *supra* note 114.

5. Conclusions

In the post-Cold War practice, recognition of governments in its "pre-Estrada Doctrine" meaning has not been re-established.[122] But there is some evidence of collective non-recognition of governments. Some effective governments were denied recognition because they were deemed illegitimate due to their unconstitutional establishments by overthrowing democratically-elected ones. Such were the examples of Haiti and Sierra Leone.

But there exists no example in collective practice that would deny legitimacy to a firmly-established non-democratic government, based solely or predominantly on its non-democratic nature. As the example of the Taliban government in Afghanistan shows, the legitimacy of a government may be questioned on the basis of threats to international peace and grave violations of human rights; but not on the basis of non-democratic practices.

In response to the developments in Libya, some states departed from the Estrada doctrine; but the denied legitimacy of the Gaddafi government did not originate in the lack of democratic practices; it may be said that it resulted from the combination of a loss of effective control over part of the territory and a record of gross and systematic human rights violations. However, as cautioned by Talmon, gross and systematic violations of human rights do not automatically de-recognize a government internationally or make it 'less of a government'.[123] This only happens through international action. The present chapter demonstrated that such action can be channeled either through the Security Council's binding powers or by the institute of recognition of governments.

With regard to the responsibility to protect, this is not a duty or right under customary international law. Where force is used in order to protect civilians, such action needs to be authorized by the Security Council or it is illegal. This chapter thus questioned the added value of the responsibility to protect as an international legal concept. The use of force to protect civilians can be legally-grounded in Article 39 of the UN Charter which is nowadays read much more widely than was the case when the Charter was drafted.

---

122 Compare *supra* note 9.

123 Talmon, "Derecognition of Colonel Qadhaffi."

Gross and systematic human rights violations may be considered a threat to international peace and thus trigger the Security Council's action under Chapter VII. However, absence of democratic political elections is not enough for such action to be triggered. Not even the somewhat special case of Haiti is a good example as it was a response to a coup and not exclusively based on democratic considerations.

Thus, effective control is still of central importance for determining the legitimacy of a government. It seems that where an 'abusive government', which is not the same as 'non-democratic government', loses control over part of the territory, the international community may be more willing to accept the legitimacy of the competing authority. But this only happens through an international response to the situation. By being abusive, an effective government does not lose its right to represent the state automatically.

CHAPTER FOUR

THE ARAB PEOPLE'S REVOLUTION—MODERNISING THE LEGAL ENVIRONMENT

Abdullah Nawafleh*

1. Introduction

The entire Arab world is witnessing mass demonstration and regime changes (popularly termed the Arab Spring) as a result of increased living costs, unemployment, corruption and poverty.[1] Unemployment rates in the Arab world are among the highest in the world.[2] By 2050 there will be 55 million unemployed Arabs.[3] This increased unemployment is due to the absence of investment in their economies and particularly in the agriculture and manufacturing sectors.[4]

The Arab Spring has raised challenges for their respective governments to create jobs for the large growing number of young people reaching working age. Every year 2.8 million young Arab people enter the labour markets.[5] This chapter illustrates that Arab countries could create a sustainable increase in employment, by setting up an efficient legal environment, based on a rule of law that is friendly and attractive to investors both local and foreign (labour intensive manufacturing).[6] The following

* LLB in Law, Amman University, Jordan, LLM in International Law and Diplomacy, University of Derby, UK, PhD in Law, University of Westminster, UK.

1 World Economic Forum and OECD, *Arab World Competitiveness Report 2011–2012* (World Economic Forum and OECD, 2012).

2 Imad A. Moosa, "Economic Growth and Unemployment In Arab Countries: Is Okun's Law Valid?," in *International Conference on "The Unemployment Crisis in the Arab Countries"* (Cairo-Egypt: Arab Planning Institute, 17–18 March 2008), p. 2. See also Boris Mirkin, *Population Levels, Trends and Policies in the Arab Region: Challenges and Opportunities* (RB f. A. States. New York: United Nations Development Program, 2010).

3 El Hassan bin Talal, *West Asia—North Africa and the Euro-Atlantic: Finding Common Solutions to Shared Challenges* (Armbrustergasse: Bruno Kreisky Forum for International Dialogue, 18 May 2009). Prince El Hassan bin Talal of Jordan is President of the Arab Thought Forum and President Emeritus of the World Conference of Religions for Peace.

4 El Hassan bin Talal, "Policy options for modernising the Middle East's industrial base," *Europe's World* (Summer 2009): 139.

5 World Economic Forum and OECD, *Arab World Competitiveness Report 2011–2012*, 6.

6 For the purpose of this chapter an efficient legal environment is a legal order which decreases the transaction costs of local and foreign investors, and consequently, their legal

sections will explore the importance of the legal environment on economic performance, private investment, and how the Arab world could make improvements.

2. The Inter-Relationship between Law and Economic Development

The shift to a market economic policy is a complex task. It involves making fundamental changes on the economic, legal, social and political fronts. Such a process represents an unprecedented challenge for policy makers in most developing countries.[7] Any successful transformation into a market economy requires the creation of a comprehensive legal infrastructure. This legal infrastructure should encourage entrepreneurial initiative, fair competition, the operation of market forces and investor confidence. The success of any economic transformation is dependent on the creation of such an infrastructure.

The inter-relationship between law and economic policy is apparent.[8] Laws in any given state do not function in isolation; they are interrelated with, and at the same time reflective of the state's economic and political ideology.[9] Reform of the law is a task for politicians, in government and parliament, and not for judges, who are not usually able to consider the wider legal implications of a particular decision.

The type of legal framework needed to allow private business, regardless of whether it is domestic or foreign, to grow and flourish, may be found in theoretical works on law and economic development which will be explored in the next two sections.

2.1. *The Law and Development Movement in the Early 1960s*

The notion that "law matters" is not entirely new. The statement itself figured prominently in the first law and development movement of the

---

uncertainties, and makes the investment climate in the host country more attractive for investors.

7 Third World nations choose to call themselves 'emerging markets', rather than 'developing countries', a term originally coined within the international financial community. See J. W. Salacuse, "From Developing Countries to Emerging Markets: A Changing Role for Law in the Third World," *The International Lawyer* 33 (4) (1999): 884.

8 Bahaa Ali El-Dean, *Privatisation and the Creation of a Market Based Legal System: The Case of Egypt* (Leiden: Brill Academic Publishers, 2002).

9 El-Dean, *Privatisation and the Creation of a Market Based System.*

early 1960s.[10] However, this movement focused on the reform of developing countries' legal systems, seen by the United States Agency for International Development (USAID), the Ford Foundation, and American lawyers and law academics as an important step towards developing countries' economic development. These groups assumed that the American legal system provided a good paradigm for development. Ultimately, it had a major role to play in the process of economic development of developing countries.[11] Some legal scholars saw the law and development movement as a result of the Cold War objectives of the United States to 'modernize' developing countries and bring them within the orbit of the West rather than that of the Soviet bloc.[12]

The movement started by adopting Max Weber's thesis about the relationship between the law and capitalism. It also took theoretical support from Moore's 1966 work on "routes to the modern world." The ideas of both Weber and Moore indicated that "in order to flourish, modern liberal capitalism required the kind of stability, predictability and calculability provided by a rational legal system."[13]

The main assumption of the 1960s movement was that law would provide the necessary elements for the functioning of a modern market system, including contract and private property rights, and universal and uniformly applied rules that allow for predictability and planning. In addition, modern law was viewed as essential to political development as it would help create a pluralist, liberal democratic state, and serve as the primary restraint on arbitrary state action.[14] This latter point illustrates the powerful instrumentalist conception underlying the view of the relationship between law and development maintained by participants of the movement.

---

[10] Trubek and Galanter refer to it as "liberal legalism." See Tamara Lothian and Katharina Pistor, "Local Institutions, Foreign Investment and Alternative Strategies of Development: Some Views from Practice," *Columbia Journal of Transnational Law* 42 (1) (2003): 101–22.

[11] David Trubek and Mark Galanter, "Scholars in Self-Estrangement: Some Reflections on the Crisis in Law and Development Studies in the United States," *Wisconsin Law Review* 4 (1974): 1070.

[12] James A. Gardner, *Legal imperialism American Lawyers and Foreign Aid in Latin America* (Madison: University of Wisconsin Press, 1980), 6–38.

[13] C. Jones, "Capitalism Globalization and rule of law," *Social and legal studies* 3 (1) (1994): 198.

[14] David Trubek, "Toward a Social Theory of Law: An Essay on the Study of Law and Development," *The Yale Law Journal* 82 (1) (1972): 44.

This conception "sees law as a force which can be moulded and manipulated to alter human behaviour and achieve development."[15] It "focuses above all on substantive rules of law, looking to the state for the promulgation of these rules and reserving for the legal profession a prominent role in formulating them."[16] Such a conception of law as an instrument of development (and not merely a response to it), and of the lawyer as a 'social engineer' was entirely in line with the "perceived need for rapid, directed change" underlying the modernisation school's notion of development.[17]

The 1960s movement also aimed to transform the legal culture and institutions, through educational reform and the selected transplantation of modern institutions.[18] It placed great emphasis on legal education and the provision of legal services as a major focus of aid. Adherents believed that legal education would train lawyers to use the law as a tool for social change and thus advance development.[19] It was also presumed that reform of legal education and the legal profession would stimulate other forms of modernisation, including the emergence of other institutions, integral to an effective legal system such as those responsible for administering and enforcing legal rules.

There was some recognition that there might be a gap between law in the books and law in action. The response of the law and development movement was still to rely on legal education reform and better 'penetration'. However, penetration defined as "the degree to which a rule, code, or law takes hold in a population."[20]

In both legal education and the development of modern law reform, the movement's emphasis was on economic law and the training of business lawyers. This was the case not just in the private sector, but also in the public sector, which was believed to play a major role in many third world economies.[21]

---

[15] Elliot M. Burg, "Law and Development: A Review of the Literature and a Critique of 'Scholars in Self-Estrangement," *American Journal of Comparative Law* 25 (1977): 505–506.

[16] Burg, "Law and Development," 505–506.

[17] Burg, "Law and Development," 505–506.

[18] David Trubek, "The Rule of Law in Development Assistance: Past, Present and Future," in *Haben wir wirklich Recht?*, ed. Michael Bäuerle, Alexander Hanebeck, and Carola Hausotter. (Berlin: Nomos, 2004).

[19] Trubek, "The Rule of Law in Development Assistance: Past, Present and Future."

[20] Lawrence Friedman, "Legal Culture and Social Development," *Law and Society Review* 4 (29) (1969): 43.

[21] Trubek, "The Rule of Law in Development Assistance: Past, Present and Future."

The movement was criticised for its ethnocentricity, its reliance on American models, and its assumptions that United States institutions represented appropriate goals for legal systems regardless of history, culture, and social system. The movement was roundly criticised by American academics and in an atmosphere of doubt, uncertainty, and lack of confidence, the movement withered away, and the funding it had received came to an end.

By 1975 the law and development movement had been declared a failure by some of its leading figures.[22] The conclusions were that reform of formal legal institutions had little or no effect on economic conditions in developing countries, that the American model of liberal legalism is ultimately based on the view that perhaps the culture and the history of the United States differ from those of developing countries, and therefore the United States legal system cannot be easily copied in developing countries.[23] In addition, the deterioration in this movement was affected because its participants did not set out well-developed theories to explain their choice of programmes and projects.[24]

By contrast, some commentators put forth the view that the work done on law and development neglected the fact that some countries clearly benefited from such legal reform. They cited, as an example, the experience of Brazilians who benefitted from the programmes funded as part of law and development. The Brazilians secured access to the United States legal technologies, qualifications, and contacts. They were able to use these toward creating impressive careers as brokers, serving businesses in their home countries and multinational business investors.[25]

2.2. *The New Law and Development Movement*

In the 1980s and 1990s, the majority of developing countries implemented economic reform programmes that included the liberalisation of trade

---

[22] See Trubek and Galanter, "Scholars in Self-Estrangement: Some Reflections on the Crisis in Law and Development Studies in the United States."; John Merryman, "Comparative Law and Social Change: On the Origins, Style, Decline & Revival of the Law and Development Movement," *Journal of Comparative Law* 25 (1977): 457; Gardner, *Legal imperialism American Lawyers and Foreign Aid in Latin America.*

[23] Merryman, "Comparative Law and Social Change: On the Origins Style, Decline & Revival of the Law and Development Movement."

[24] Trubek, "The Rule of Law in Development Assistance: Past, Present and Future," 5.

[25] Dezalay Yves and G. Garth Bryant, *The Internationalization of Palace Wars: Lawyers, Economists, and the Contest to Transform Latin American States* (Chicago: University of Chicago Press, 2002).

and capital movements. The enormous developments made in technology and in particular, in the field of communications, helped to speed up the transfer of data and statistics and consequently, accelerated investment-related decision-making in various countries. They also helped in facilitating and reducing the cost of foreign investors' funds transfer from the host country to the home country and vice versa, thereby assisting foreign investment flow. This change in the attitude of developing countries towards Foreign Direct Investment (FDI), has made law and development a hot topic.[26] The return of the movement was a result of civil strife and economic failures in Africa, the collapse of dictatorships in Latin America, the politico-economic changes in Eastern Europe, and the collapse of the former Soviet Union.[27]

The new movement differed in several significant ways from the earlier movement. It did, however, continue to assign a central role to the law and legal institutions in economic development.[28] In other words, the new movement perceived the law as restraining the state and empowering private actors. The International Financial Institutions (IFIs), such as the World Bank and the International Monetary Fund (IMF), as well as individual aid agencies such as the USAID, were the major participants in this new movement.[29] For one thing, the involvement of the international development institutions meant that the orientation of the programme was more practical than academic.[30] In addition, the interest of the IFIs

[26] See for example Anthony Carty, *Law and development* (Dartmouth: Dartmouth Pub. Co., 1992).

[27] Anthony Ogus, "The Importance of Legal Infrastructure for Regulation (and Deregulation) in Developing Countries," in *CRC Annual Conference* (Manila: CRC, 2003); Ibrahim F. I. Shihata, "The Role of Law in Business Development," *Fordham International Law Journal* 20 (5) (1997).

[28] Randal Perenboom, *China's Long March toward Rule of Law* (Cambridge: Cambridge University Press, 2002); Carol V. Rose, "The 'New' Law and Development Movement in the Post-Cold War Era: A Vietnam Case Study," *Law and Society Review* 32 (1998): 93.

[29] A new set of development policy prescriptions emerged from the Washington-based international financial institutions. This approach is popularly referred to as a "Washington Consensus." The term 'Washington Consensus' was coined by John Williamson, a former World Bank manager, to characterise consensus reached among economists in three important agencies with headquarters in Washington, DC—the IMF, the World Bank and the US Treasury Department—on the 'the lowest common denominator of policy advice being addressed . . . to Latin American countries as of 1989.'See John Williamson, "What Should the World Bank Think About the Washington Consensus?," *The World Bank Research Observer* 15(2) (2000): 251.

[30] Richard Bilder and Brian Z. Tamanaha, "The Lessons of Law-and-Development Studies," *American Journal of international law* 89 (1995): 470.

in law and economic development is further evidence in support of the argument that rule of law is important for economic development.

For these development organisations, the central function of the state is to create and enforce rules that support economic growth.[31] According to this new consensus, the law plays a crucial role in the process of market development. The function of the law has two elements: to define and enforce private rights, especially the rights of local and foreign investment, and to create the legal foundation for market reform, which alone guarantees the basis for economic development, stability and growth.[32]

3. Developing Countries and Law Reform

The reforms adopted by some developing countries required the abolition of controls on investment, prices, and production; the liberalisation of trade in goods and services; the privatisation of public enterprises; and labour and market reforms.[33] The adoption by many developing countries of a market-friendly approach to development since the 1990s, has coincided with the movement to promote 'good governance'[34] and thus to create attractive investment conditions and a sustainable allocation of investment capital.[35] In his foreword to the 1989 World Development Report, the Bank's President stated that "private sector initiative and market mechanisms are important, but they must go hand-in-hand with Good Governance."[36]

The 1989 report defined 'governance' as encompassing the following: the state's institutional arrangements; the processes for formulating policy, decision-making, and implementation; information flows within

[31] Lothian and Pistor, "Local Institutions, Foreign Investment and Alternative Strategies of Development: Some Views from Practice," 101–102.

[32] Ibrahim F. I. Shihata, *Legal treatment of foreign investment: "the World Bank guidelines"* (Dordrecht: M. Nijhoff, 1993).

[33] Claudio Ciborra and Diego Navarra, "Good Governance, Development Theory, and Aid Policy: Risks and Challenges of E-Government in Jordan," *Information Technology for Development* 11(2) (2004): 141.

[34] The contemporary origin of the term (good governance) is attributed to the World Bank. In its 1989 report on Sub-Saharan Africa, the Bank clearly identified the role of governance as "a central component of a development strategy," Ibrahim F. I. Shihata, *The World Bank in a Changing World, Vol. II* (Cairo: Martinus Nijhoff Publishers, 1995), 55.

[35] Saladjn Al-Jurf, "Good Governance and Transparency: Their Impact on Development," *Transnational Law and Contemporary Problems* 9 (1999): 193.

[36] World Bank, *Sub-Saharan Africa from crisis to sustainable growth. a long-term perspective study* (Washington, DC: World Bank, 1989), xii.

government; and the respect of citizens and the state for the institutions that govern economic and social interactions among them.[37] In addition, the Bank's 1992 World Report defines governance as "the manner in which power is exercised in the management of a country's economic and social resources for development."[38]

The terms 'governance' or 'good government' were commonly used in the 1990s by international organisations such as the United Nations, the World Bank, the World Trade Organization (WTO) and the IMF. As part of their programmes to help foster sound economic frameworks and encourage stable economic growth and foreign investment flow to developing countries, members of the development community have stressed the necessity for good governance. Their programmes aimed to help developing countries to establish well-functioning market economies, with stable property rights, enforceable contracts, high levels of transparency and low levels of corruption. With the recognition of the importance of 'good governance' for macroeconomic growth and stability, the IMF and the World Bank even extended the conditions they applied to borrowing members to cover domestic governance and the institutional framework of economic policy-making. Then in 1995, the establishment of the WTO created a new set of binding commitments on member states, which extend into many areas of domestic legislation.

For the development community, "weak institutions—tangled laws, corrupt courts, deeply biased credit systems, and elaborate business registration requirements"[39] may delay economic development. This belief in the importance of legal and judicial reform in encouraging economic development has been supported by research, showing that economic development is strongly affected by the quality of the legal institutions.[40]

The development community in their legal assistance often focus on establishing a more efficient and functional legislature. Their legal assistance projects have helped draft rules of procedure, designed induction programmes, provided information about establishing committees and

---

[37] World Bank, *Sub-Saharan Africa from crisis to sustainable growth*, p. xii.

[38] World Bank, *Governance and Development* (Washington, DC: World Bank., 1992), 3.

[39] See World Bank, *World Development Report 2002: Building Institutions for Markets* (New York: Published for the World Bank, Oxford University Press, 2002).

[40] World Bank, "Economic Development and the Quality of Legal Institutions", available from http://siteresources.worldbank.org/INTLAWJUSTINST/Resources/LegalInstitutionsTopicBrief.pdf (accessed 10/12/2011).

caucuses and funded the establishment of systems for transcription and publication of legislative proceedings.[41]

In 2004, however, the note concerning the Good Governance in Investment Promotion (GGIP) presented by the United Nations Conference on Trade and Development (UNCTAD) secretariat discussed what constitutes GGIP. It drew lessons from successful international cases and using knowledge gained through UNCTAD technical cooperation activities, including project activities in Ethiopia, Lesotho, Maldives, and the United Republic of Tanzania under the GGIP programme.[42] This note by the UNCTAD secretariat outlines the elements of the good governance that it considered important in creating a suitable legal environment for FDI. These elements are: (i) Accountability; (ii) Participation; (iii) Predictability and (iv) Transparency.

4. Law and Economic Development in Arab Countries

The 1990s wave of political changes that occurred in much of the world after the fall of socialist regimes in the Soviet Union and Eastern Europe, has not taken place in the Arab political systems.[43] In addition, war, violence, and social conflicts are and have been widespread throughout the Arab World since they gained their independence from colonial powers.[44]

This political instability has contributed to the continued deterioration of the business environment. However, political instability is not the only problem that deters potential investors in many Arab countries.[45] There are also other factors that impact upon the business environment in Arab countries such as instability and the complexity of business regulations, licensing, and other institutional distortions which are often unclear and usually inconsistent with the rules that apply in the rest of the world.[46]

---

[41] Bureau for Development Policy, *Legislative Assistance Retrospective* (United Nations Development Programme, 2001).

[42] United Nations Conference on Trade and Development, *Good Governance in Investment Promotion: Note by the UNCTAD secretariat* (United Nations Conference on Trade and Development, TD/B/COM.2/EM.15/2, 2004), p. 3.

[43] Marina Ottaway and Julia Choucair-Vizoso, *Beyond the facade: political reform in the Arab world* (Washington, DC: Carnegie Endowment for International Peace, 2008), 3.

[44] Xavier Sala-i-Martin and Elsa Vila-Artadi, *Economic Growth and Investment in the Arab World* (Universitat Pompeu Fabra, Economics and Business Working Paper No. 683, 2003), 17.

[45] Sala-i-Martin & Vila-Artadi, *Economic Growth and Investment in the Arab World*, 20.

[46] Sala-i-Martin & Vila-Artadi, *Economic Growth and Investment in the Arab World*, 20. See for example United Nations, *Foreign Direct Investment Report* (New York: United

Stability is one of the important pillars upon which legal systems are based. Legal changes that cause instability to the legal system will prevent investors from predicting with any accuracy the potential outcome of their investments. The reason is clear: if a legal system undergoes constant changes, investors naturally feel uncertain as to whether the assumptions made at the beginning of an investment project will hold true through the life of the project, and thus whether the expected results of their investment will be accomplished. Local and foreign investors could view an unstable legal environment as an obstacle for their business to grow. Stability in the legal environment is essential for business people to be able to make reasonable assessments of the risks involved in their decisions. Such a stable legal environment is integrally related to certainty and predictability in the law. Any rights and privileges giving rise to opportunities for business, will naturally flow from a regulatory framework, established according to legal principles and with the force of law.[47]

Stability in laws provides local and foreign investors with confidence in the legal environment which their businesses are going to operate in. This stability is brought about through laws that contain stable provisions, which guarantee that the contractual rights and fiscal regime applicable to foreign investors at the time of making the investment will not be altered. Instability in laws may increase costs to the investors and resultantly reduce project revenues, which in turn could destroy a prospective investment.

For foreign investors, instability in laws, the risk of unpredictable negative changes in the laws and regulations, or the risk of inconsistency between laws, can substantially deter foreign investment.[48] They could also create concerns, especially when changes may lead to expropriation

---

Nations-E/ESCWA/EDGD/2008/Technical Paper.1, 2008), 14–15. This report has suggested that numerous and lengthy Government procedures, inconsistent interpretation of Government regulations and favouritism in decisions of Government officials often constitute an additional burden for foreign investors. The report quoted the World Economic Forum which indicated that Bahrain, the Syrian Arab Republic and Kuwait were ranked 56th, 72nd and 78th respectively out of a total of 117 countries in terms of favouritism by Government officials, a clear indication that Government officials are not providing fair and equal treatment for all.

[47] For instance, Brunetti and Weder analysed data collected by 310 firms, in 28 developing countries, and concluded that instability in laws and policies reduce rates of economic growth. *See* Aymo Brunetti and Beatrice Weder, *Subjective Perceptions of Political Instability and Economic Growth* (Mimeo Basel: University of Basel, 1995).

[48] Abdullah Nawafleh, "The Legal Environment and Foreign Direct Investment: Jordan as a Case Study." (University of Westminster, 2008).

of their property rights.[49] Foreign investors usually look for guarantees against unreasonable law changes from the host country or international organisation, such as the Multilateral Investment Guarantees Agency (MIGA).[50]

Laws that are outdated or not easily understood by domestic and foreign parties, pose a major obstacle to sustainable economic activities.[51] They increase transaction costs and commercial risks and seriously impede the participation of commercial entities in the host country.[52] In such a legal environment, small and medium-sized enterprises with limited experience and access to legal advice, encounter difficulties in penetrating new markets.[53] When laws are passed quickly without debate, they frequently lack the support of stakeholders and legal professionals. These laws are subject to change by the legislature or by future ordinances, due to lobbying by businesses. Such laws are therefore unlikely to contribute to legislative stability, and to facilitate the entry of new businesses into the formal economy, by establishing supportive structures for awarding them legal recognition and legal personality. Reform to laws affecting companies, partnerships, antitrust, bankruptcy, securities markets, banking, property rights, currency and foreign exchange, labour, privatisation, taxation, competition, and association need to provide clear and liberal rules for the establishment of businesses.[54]

The creation of law can supplement and enhance the ability of parties to order their private investments.[55] A body of written law clearly defining

---

49 Nawafleh, "The Legal Environment and Foreign Direct Investment: Jordan as a Case Study."

50 The MIGA, an international organisation and member of the World Bank Group was founded in 1988, to protect foreign investments in its developing member countries by issuing guarantees against political risks to investors from other member countries. However, Bakker and Gill went further by suggesting that 'governance' refers to public and private partnership, rather than government. They also argued that governance is the path to economic success in today's globally integrated economy. United Nations Conference on Trade and Development, *Good Governance in Investment Promotion: Note by the UNCTAD secretariat.*

51 Jeswald W. Salacuse, "Direct Foreign Investment and the Law in Developing Countries," *ICSID REVIEW Foreign Investment Law Journal* 15 (2000): 382–400.

52 Salacuse, "Direct Foreign Investment and the Law in Developing Countries."

53 Hans Corell, "Law, Justice and Development: A Challenge for Africa in the 21st Century," in *All Africa Conference on Law, Justice, and Development* (United Nations, 2003).

54 Poonam Gupta, Rachel Kleinfeld, and Gonzalo Salinas, *Legal and Judicial Reform in Europe and Central Asia* (Washington, DC: World Bank Operations Evaluations Department, 2002).

55 Frank B. Cross, "Law and Economic Growth," *Texas Law Review Association* 80 (2002): 1737.

a person's rights and responsibilities and embodying market-friendly economic policies in Arab countries, is a necessary step towards the development of a well-functioning legal environment, for a market economy and local and foreign investment. Failure to take this step may have systemic costs that go beyond the direct consequences of flaws in individual laws. When laws are passed that incorporate major inconsistencies, uncertainties, or economic flaws, this can deepen public and private sector mistrust in the law in general. Transaction costs for local and foreign investment will rise where laws are difficult to access, ambiguous or conflicting. The possibility of immediately knowing applicable laws, constitutes one of the basic tenets of a state governed by the rule of law, and is also an essential element of legal security. This is also important for local and foreign investors who will know their commercial legal obligations and rights, and be able to reduce their transaction costs.[56]

For laws to be effective and for them to actually change behaviour, they must be fully understood and embraced not only by law enforcers, but also by those using the law. They must be understood and embraced by legal intermediaries including courts, judges, and lawyers.

4.1. *Arab Countries and Law Reform*

Reform becomes necessary in Arab countries to ensure that the principles underpinning the law, and the way it is applied, are just and consistent. Also reform should make law more certain, easier to locate and easier to understand for local and foreign business people, and by doing so, to enable the maintenance of the essential relationship between law and the needs of business society. Legal reform that aims to develop a business-friendly legal environment at a national level, should rely on two principles. The first principle determines that legal rules governing economic activities should take into account new economic realties. The second is the enforcement of legal rules, regardless of their content. Without the first process, law is not likely to be sound or useful; without the second, it is not law.[57]

Market-friendly laws need to be promoted to generate trust in the markets, alongside sound investments, minimal risk, and sound allocation of resources. The laws must be passed by the legislative body. The legislative body should take into consideration that the law should be market-

[56] Shihata, "The Role of Law in Business Development."
[57] Shihata, "The Role of Law in Business Development."

friendly, and should aim to encourage economic actors to carry out their economic activities with confidence. The law should also extend and open the market economy to participation from both, local and foreign private business.[58]

A country that makes the law accessible to the public, contributes to equality before the law and to the reduction of transaction costs for private sectors. In those countries where legislation is difficult to access and where case law is even harder to find, discrepancies between resources available to different parties are exacerbated. When one party has access to better information sources than other parties, whether such sources are commercial or personal, such a situation undermines equality under the law and creates an obstacle for local and foreign investors and their investment projects. However, to date there are no laws on access to information in Arab countries, apart from Jordan.[59] Although Arab countries might be tending to adopt access to information laws for economic development, however, evidence shows it is possible to foster legislative transparency in Arab countries, but with difficulties.[60]

Transparency in Arab countries will allow local and foreign investors to obtain relevant information quickly and efficiently. If laws let companies hide material information from the public, investors will be forced to make investment decisions based on inaccurate or incomplete data. Greater transparency, the "unfettered access to timely and reliable information on decisions and performance,"[61] is the key to generating confidence, and attracting and guiding productive investment. The law provides the framework to unite information and capital.[62] Availability of information does not mean allowing public officials to use *private* information (i.e., information that is available to only a few people, such as the

58 Shihata, "The Role of Law in Business Development."

59 J. E. Relly and D. Cuillier, "A comparison of political, cultural, and economic indicators of access to information in Arab and non-Arab states," *Government Information Quarterly* 27 (4) (2010). See Jordan's Freedom of Information Law No. 47 of 2007.

60 See the first study on this subject by Relly and Cuillier "A comparison of political, cultural, and economic indicators of access to information in Arab and non-Arab states," which compared key quantitative indicators associated with information access among Arab nations and non-Arab nations, with and without access-to-information laws.

61 United Nations Department for Economic and Social Affairs and United Nations Development Programme, *Public Sector Transparency and Accountability in Selected Arab Countries: Policies and Practices* (United Nations, New York, ST/ESA/PAD/SER.E/71, 2004), 2.

62 Robert Cooter, *Information, Innovation, and the Poverty of Nations* (Berkeley Program in Law and Economics, Working Paper Series, 2005).

recipe for Coca Cola, a commercial secret) to divert wealth to themselves, or to friends and cronies, for private purposes.[63] The misuse of private information leads to corruption, requiring officials to explain and justify their policies and actions with respect of using public information. It also creates a basis for accountability.[64]

Non-transparency of government policies increases the risk and uncertainty faced by economic actors, particularly foreign investors.[65] This increase in risk and uncertainty arises from bribery and corruption, unstable economic policies, poorly enforced property rights, and inefficient government institutions. Analysis of non-transparency and FDI shows that the degree of non-transparency is an important factor in a country's attractiveness to foreign investors.[66] A nation which takes steps to increase the degree of transparency in its policies and institutions can expect significant increases in the level of foreign investment.[67]

Hence, transparency in government decision-making and public policy implementation is important because it facilitates governmental accountability, participation, and predictability of outcomes. Transparency and the ready availability of information cannot be assured without legal frameworks that set clear and enforceable rules and procedures.

4.2. *Enhancing Government Accountability*

The majority of Arab countries have experienced a persistent corruption which has cost them nearly one trillion dollars.[68] The losses accounted for nearly a third of the total income earned by the Arab countries between 1950 and 2000.[69] Most countries affected by the Arab Spring score poorly, in International's Corruption Perceptions Index (2011).[70] In addition, they widely perceived as very corrupt, with an average score of less than 4 on

63 Cooter, *Information, Innovation, and the Poverty of Nations*.

64 Cooter, *Information, Innovation, and the Poverty of Nations*.

65 Zdenek Drabek and Warren Payne, "The Impact of Transparency on Foreign Direct Investment," *Journal of Economic Integration* 17 (4) (2002): 777–810.

66 Drabek & Payne, "The Impact of Transparency on Foreign Direct Investment."

67 Drabek & Payne, "The Impact of Transparency on Foreign Direct Investment."

68 Nadim Kawach, "Unemployment and Poverty Fuel Arab Revolt: Joblessness is High While Prices Rise and Per Capita Income Shrinks" *Emirates 24|7*, 06/02/2011.

69 Kawach, "Unemployment and Poverty Fuel Arab Revolt: Joblessness is High While Prices Rise and Per Capita Income Shrinks."

70 See Transparency International, *Corruption Perceptions Index 2011* (Transparency International, 2011).

a scale from 0 to 10, where 0 indicating the highest level of corruption and 10 "very clean".[71]

Corruption exists when the official diverges from the system to serve their personal interests.[72] Government officials should be accountable for their actions, for the quality and speed of their work, and for its reliability. Reducing the complexity of procedures and providing better services will contribute to the reduction in opportunities for corruption. It must be noted that corruption can only exist where there is a receiver and obviously a supplier. Suppliers generally exist outside the political system.

The continuation of corruption among officials and suppliers implies a certain level of tolerance for corruption in society. Regardless of whether corruption is culturally acceptable, the fact remains that investors have a choice of where to invest and they may not share the foreign country's tolerant attitude.[73]

In 2004, a study on "Transparency and Accountability in the Arab Region" commissioned and prepared by the UNDP's Programme on Governance in the Arab Region argued that accountability is needed not only for an effective, efficient, and equitable management in public institutions but also for private investment, whether foreign or domestic.[74]

Corruption in Arab countries can create a significant obstacle to foreign investment and raise the costs of doing business, thereby reducing returns to the investor.[75] For example, John Taylor, under Secretary for International Affairs, United States Treasury, announced at the 2005 conference on Good Governance for Development in the Arab Countries that "at [the] treasury, we are always hearing the complaints from all kinds

---

[71] Transparency International, *Corruption Perceptions Index 2011*, p. 3.

[72] Indem Foundation, *Russia Vs. Corruption: Who Wins?* (Moscow, 1998).

[73] Andrea Kennedy King, *The Link between Foreign Direct Investment and Corruption in Transitional Economies* (The Norman Paterson School of International Affairs, Carleton University, Ottawa, Ontario, 2003). In 2000, Wei investigated whether or not FDI flows from United States and other source countries were statistically different, by using data on bilateral flows between 14 source countries and 45 host countries for the years 1990 and 1991. He concluded that corruption has a significant negative impact on the levels of FDI. *See* Shang Jin Wei, "How Taxing is Corruption on International Investors," *Review of Economics and Statistics* 82 (1) (2000): 1–11.

[74] M. Henry Clement, *Transparency and Accountability in the Arab Region—A Political Economy Perspective* (United Nations Development Programme—Programme on Governance in the Arab Region, 2004), 1. This paper examined the changing composition of global capital flows over the past decade and the Arab Region's limited success in harnessing them to there developmental needs.

[75] See for example Salacuse, "Direct Foreign Investment and the Law in Developing Countries."

of investors about poor governance in countries all over the world. They are frustrated because they want to invest, but are driven away by what they perceive as rampant corruption or excessive bureaucracy. 'Why don't these governments understand that public governance influences investment decisions, and that investment brings jobs and growth?' they say."[76] In addition, research investigated whether or not FDI flows from United States and other source countries were statistically different, by using data on bilateral flows between 14 source countries and 45 host countries for the years 1990 and 1991. The research concluded that corruption has a significant negative impact on the levels of FDI.[77]

According to the UNCTAD, apart from legal accountability, other issues which need to be addressed are those related to the attitude of many civil servants in ministries and other government organisations toward foreign investors, as they still do not see investors as parties to whom they are accountable for prompt, competent, and impartial performance of their duties.[78]

Law reform in Arab countries should aim to improve accountability in the use of public resources and set up a mechanism for overseeing the performance of government official functionaries and their interaction with investors. It is important to identify to whom and for what these government officials are accountable. A government official is required to make decisions based on the established rules of the state (constitution, laws, and regulations). They should also be accountable for applying and enforcing specific sets of laws, regulations, and policies; they are legally bound to do so.

4.3. *Reform of Judicial Institutions*

Most of the Arab states judicial systems tend to suffer from poorly trained judges, overcrowded dockets, corruption and antiquated facilities.[79] The significance of judicial reform is derived from appreciation of the fact that

---

[76] J. B. Taylor, *The Governance/Investment Nexus: Measuring Results for Better Performance*, Stanford University (Remarks at Good Governance for Development in the Arab Countries: An Arab Regional Initiative in Partnership with OECD and UNDP; Stanford University, 2005), 1.

[77] Wei, "How Taxing is Corruption on International Investors."

[78] United Nations Conference on Trade and Development, *Good Governance in Investment Promotion: Note by the UNCTAD secretariat*, 5.

[79] See Sharif Ali Zu'bi and Zeid D. Hanania, *Legal and Judicial Reform in the Arab World a Primer* (DAVOS-SWITZERLAND: Arab Business Council, 2004), 3–4. See also Eric Wiebelhaus-Brahm, "False Starts: Transitional Justice in the Arab World," *SSRN eLibrary* (2010).

laws, however sophisticated, are mere pieces of paper that only come to life when implemented by the courts. Laws are seldom self-executing. They always need a judiciary to ensure their correct application and enforcement and to settle disputes that inevitably arise in the course of their application. Without a judiciary, laws may remain abstract concepts; they may not always reflect the law in force.[80]

The judicial system that provides access to justice and speedy outcomes, supports a market economy and contributes to development of a well-functioning legal environment, which facilitates economic activities in the private sector. An inefficient judiciary system in Arab countries hampers their economic performance in various ways: it narrows the range of economic activity, destimulating specialisation and making it difficult to exploit the economies of scale; it discourages investment and the utilisation of available capital; it distorts the price system by introducing additional sources of risk into business; and diminishes the quality of economic policy.[81]

The performance of the judiciary should be evaluated in terms of the services that it produces, particularly in terms of 'guarantee of access, predictability and promptness of results, in addition to the adequacy of the remedies.'[82]

Studies undertaken for the World Bank indicate that amongst global investors, the predictability of judicial enforcement is the most robust predictor of economic growth.[83] The majority of the developing countries reform their judicial system as part of a larger effort to establish a market friendly legal environment.[84] Much of the development community work on aid for judicial reform has also been spurred by the recognition that a well-performing judiciary is important for economic development.[85]

---

80 Ibrahim F. I. Shihata, "Judicial Reform in Developing Countries and the Role of the World Bank," in *Judicial reform in Latin America and the Caribbean: Conference: Papers*, ed. Waleed Haider Malik, Malcolm Rowat, and Mar Dakolias (Washington, DC: World Bank, 1995), 219.

81 A. C. Pinheiro, *Economics and Justice: Concepts and Empirical Evidence* (Working Paper BNDES, 2000), 4.

82 Robert Sherwood, Geoffrey Shepherd, and Celso De Souza, "Judicial Systems and Economic Performance," *The Quarterly Review of Economics and Finance* 34 (1994): 7.

83 See for example Frank, "Law and Economic Growth."

84 See for instance World Bank, *Doing Business in 2006: Creating Jobs* (Washington: World Bank, 2006).

85 See for example Richard E. Messick, *Judicial Reform: The Why, the What, and the How* (Prepared for Delivery at a conference on Strategies for Modernizing the Judicial Sector in the Arab World, Marrakech-Morocco, 15–17 March, 2002).

The core of their judicial reform programmes, typically consists of measures to improve the operation of the judicial system and related entities such as bar associations and law schools. This has been part of a larger effort to make the legal systems in developing countries and transitional economies more market friendly.[86]

According to the World Bank three characteristics should prevail in a good judicial system: independence, strength of instruments for the implementation of its decisions, and general efficiency. The Bank defines independence as a situation where the judicial system is protected from executive or legislative influence. It is also considered the most important character of the three.[87]

The effectiveness of the judicial system in Arab countries depends on its capacity to implement its decisions. In practice, this means the availability of sufficient power of coercion, not only in legal terms, but also in terms of human and financial resources. For example, an effective police force is an essential element in the adequate functioning of the judicial system. The characteristic needed for a judicial system to be effective is efficient organisation. There should not be any great delay experienced in deciding of cases.[88] The major elements for evaluating and identifying problems in Judicial Systems:[89]

a. the legal framework of the country and the role of judges within this framework
b. positions of judges in society and the perception of the system of administration of justice by the community
c. the integrity of the justice system
d. the administration of the judicial system
e. the economic cost of justice in the country
f. access to justice
g. the availability of legal information

---

[86] Ibrahim F. I. Shihata, "Legal Framework for Development: Role of the World Bank in Legal Technical Assistance," *International Business Lawyer* (1995): 360–8.

[87] World Bank, *World Development Report 1997: The State in a Changing World* (New York: Oxford University Press, 1997).

[88] In its report (ibid.), the Bank notes that a suit takes an average of 1500 days to be concluded in countries like Brazil and Ecuador, as against only 100 days in France. Long delays increase the costs of transactions in the resolution of disputes and can block access to the judiciary for potential users.

[89] Ibrahim F. I. Shihata, "The World Bank," in *Justice Delayed: Judicial Reform in Latin America*, ed. Edmundo Jarquín and Fernando Carrillo (Inter-American Development Bank, 1998), 120.

h. legal education and training
i. the actual functioning of legal procedures
j. physical facilities of courts
k. the impact of court decisions on society; and
l. alternative dispute resolution mechanisms

Evidence shows that a poorly functioning court system adds cost and risk to business transactions. Surveys of Latin American firms show how poorly-functioning courts affect business. In Peru, almost a third of World Bank survey respondents said they would not switch from a trusted supplier to a new one, even if a lower price was offered. They indicated that their reasoning was based on a fear that a new supplier could not be held to a bargain.[90] A similar survey in Ecuador found that businesses were hesitant to use the judicial system because of the lack of certainty and the probability of delay in enforcing contractual rights.[91]

Under most investment treaties, foreign investors are entitled to take legal action against the host state directly for violation of investment strictures, either in the national court system of the host state or before international trade tribunals, whose rulings are then lodged within the host state's legal system. The efficiency of the national judicial system tends be an important factor in implementing the decisions of international tribunals.

4.4. *The Rule of Law*

It appears from the foregoing that law and judicial reform in Arab countries should aim to promote the rule of law. Economic growth and the attraction of private investment are believed to hinge, at least in part, on the 'rule of law'. This mechanism ensures that the content of law is clear and understood by the private sector. It also helps to reduce risks, particularly the risk of arbitrary governmental action. For foreign investors, the rule of law in a host country is a risk reduction device and it saves on transaction costs.[92] Legal reform should, therefore, be in line with the rule of law.

90 Maria Dakolias, *The Judicial Sector in Latin America and the Caribbean: Elements of Reform* (World Bank, Washington, DC, 1996).
91 Dakolias, *The Judicial Sector in Latin America and the Caribbean: Elements of Reform.*
92 Salacuse, "Direct Foreign Investment and the Law in Developing Countries."

There are elements the rule of law must have, to create a suitable environment for private investment:[93]

1) It should provide a 'set of rules known in advance'.
2) The law must be enforced, not just written in 'the book'; this requires effective administration: 'law is not only a set of rules but also encompasses procedures and institutions for implementing those rules.'
3) The rule of law must ensure application of the rules to all, including state officials.
4) It must be able to rely on an independent and credible judicial system that provides an effective dispute settlement mechanism, away from government intervention.
5) There must be a publicly known procedure for amending the rules, because laws that are created or amended without known and established procedures will lead to a general lack of credibility for the whole legal system.

The above elements could be categorised as the classical concept of the rule of law and focus on the formal or procedural aspects that any "legal system allegedly must possess to function effectively as a system of laws, regardless of whether the legal system is part of democratic or nondemocratic society, capitalist, liberal or theocratic."[94]

The notion of the rule of law is supported by the international development community, which believes that if developing countries wish to succeed economically they should develop the rule of law.[95] One area of work

---

[93] Ibrahim F. I. Shihata, "The Word Bank and 'Governance' Issues in Its Borrowing Members," in *The World Bank in a changing world: selected essays*, ed. Ibrahim F. I. Shihata, Franziska. Tschofen and Antonia. R. Parra (Dordrecht & Boston: Martinus Nijhoff, 1991), 85.

[94] R. P. Peerenboom, "Varieties of Rule of Law: An Introduction and Provisional Conclusion," in *Asian Discourses of Rule of Law: Theories and Implementation of Rule of Law in Twelve Asian Countries, France, and the U.S.*, ed. R. P. Peerenboom, RoutledgeCurzon law in Asia (London: RoutledgeCurzon, 2004), 2.; The rule of law is seen in this paper as a concept, focusing on the formal or procedural aspects, which any legal system allegedly must possess to function effectively as a system of laws, regardless of whether the legal system is part of a democratic or non-democratic society, capitalist, liberal or theocratic. See also Sabine Schlemmer-Schulte, "The World Bank's Role in the Promotion of the Rule of Law in Developing Countries," in *Liber Amicorum Ibrahim F. I. Shihata*, ed. S. Schlemmer-Schulte and K. Tung (Leiden: Kluwer Law International, 2001).

[95] The rule of law elements have been adopted by the World Bank as a basis that countries should have in order to obtain loans from it. World Bank, *Governance and Development*, 38.

focuses on foreign investment, considering that countries without the rule of law will not be able to attract substantial amounts of foreign investment and therefore will not be able to finance development.[96] The rule of law is considered a necessary criterion for law reform. In its reports in the early 1990s, the World Bank argues that the rule of law has come to be seen as necessary for creating appropriate conditions for the market to function, by keeping transaction costs at a low level. Additionally, the Bank believes that the rule of law allows the state to regulate the economy and empowers private individuals to contribute to economic development, by confidently engaging in business, investments and other transactions.[97]

The rule of law facilitates economic activity and protects the rights of individuals who wish to execute contracts, thus providing the people with predictability of the actions of contractual parties as well as those of government. [98] Thus, the rule of law helps to provide predictability for investors in Arab countries and facilitates investment.

Under the rule of law, decisions taken by governments should comply with and be founded in law. This ensures that private firms and individuals are protected from arbitrary decisions. Arab governments that work under the rule of law should be free from distortionary incentives through corruption, nepotism, patronage, or capture by narrow private interest groups; this guarantees property and personal rights. This provides a degree of reliability and predictability essential for firms and individuals to be able to take good decisions.[99] Although the term 'rule of law' means many things to many people, the rule of law means 'governance' by general and settled rules, impartially applied.

Legal predictability flows from legal stability and is a fundamental part of "what people mean by the Rule of Law"[100] However, the legal element of predictability is whether the legislative changes follow a clear path, which investors may predict and value as progressive. Analysing this element may lead to the conclusion that in general, the legal reforms

---

[96] Thomas Carothers, *Promoting the Rule of Law Abroad: The Problem of Knowledge* (Carnegie Paper No. 34. Carnegie Endowment for International Peace, 2003).

[97] World Bank, *The World Bank and Legal Technical Assistance: Initial Lessons* (World Bank Legal Department, Policy Research Working Papers No. 1414, 1995)

[98] Salacuse, "Direct Foreign Investment and the Law in Developing Countries."

[99] Organisation for Economic Co-operation and Development, *Report of a Workshop on Public Management in Support of Social and Economic Objectives* (Organisation for Economic Co-operation and Development: Paris, 1998).

[100] Maimon Schwarzschild, "Keeping it Private," *San Diego Law Review*, 44 (Summer 2007): 686.

introduced by the host country have been progressive and ought to improve the business climate. Furthermore, in order for law and regulation reform to be predictable, the reformed laws and regulations should set out the criteria by which government officials take decisions. The greater the clarity of the standards applied, the greater the degree of predictability and the smaller the risk for foreign investors.[101]

Another important element in predictability is the fulfilment of promises to carry out legal reforms, especially when investors factor this into their business plans. For instance, implementation of a long-awaited legislative reform by the host country, enabling private sectors to carry on certain activities that had previously been banned, or legislative reform which will reduce foreign investors' transaction costs, such as allowing the ownership of land by foreign investors, which will lead to significant increases in foreign investment in real estate, or the tax law reforms aiming to reduce tax in general. If host country governments are committed to the implementation of the reforms they have passed, a predictable legal environment will emerge. A legal environment based on laws and an effective enforcement mechanism has been regarded as the basic condition for economic development on this basis. Such an environment protects the rights of individuals and ensures the enforcement of contracts, thus giving foreign investors predictability in the actions of contractual parties as well as those of government.[102]

The UNCTAD recognised that predictability is the most important concern of investors.[103] To evaluate new projects by investors, the risks involved, and a high degree of uncertainty can easily be a deterrent.[104] For investors clear policies and a comprehensive legislative framework are essential, along with the consistent application of laws and regulations.[105] In other words, for prospective investors, the entire economic environment hinges on an element of predictability. Also, studies undertaken by the World Bank indicate that amongst global investors, the predictability

---

[101] United Nations Conference on Trade and Development, *Good Governance in Investment Promotion: Note by the UNCTAD secretariat.*

[102] Hiroshi Matsuo, "The Rule of Law and Economic Development: A Cause or a Result?," in *The Role of Law in Development—Past, Present and Future* (Tokyo: Nagoya University, 2003).

[103] United Nations Conference on Trade and Development, *Good Governance in Investment Promotion: Note by the UNCTAD secretariat*, 4.

[104] United Nations Conference on Trade and Development, *Good Governance in Investment Promotion: Note by the UNCTAD secretariat*, 4.

[105] United Nations Conference on Trade and Development, *Good Governance in Investment Promotion: Note by the UNCTAD secretariat*, 4.

of judicial enforcement is the most robust predictor of economic growth.[106] Predictability of the legal environment is crucial for foreign investors' decision-making and any system that lacks predictability does not generate much confidence in the investor community.[107]

Laws should provide freedom of information (transparency) and should be capable of being followed and enforced. Such rules need to be legitimated if they are to be stable. In addition, lack of transparency, accountability and participation encourage corruption and hinder investment. The relationship between the rule of law and good governance is one of interdependence. The rule of law and good governance are likely to advance each other. The inter-relationship between good governance and the rule of law will help create an efficient legal environment for economic activities.

5. Conclusion

The international development community recognises the rule of law in the economic growth of developing countries. Their works provide an interesting outline of the interlocking relationship between law and economic growth. The emphasis and importance attached to the law is primarily because it provides a measure of calculability, and a means for guaranteeing the right of contract and protection of the property rights of individuals. It is also the security provided by general law that is critical for the economic activities of local and foreign investments, which Arab countries need to create jobs, and to increase the domestic production capability, leading to increased welfare for their citizens.

Setting the rule of law in the Arab world is the first prerequisite for an efficient legal environment, because without rule of law, the state would not have any limitations on its arbitrariness, and the private sector would face complete uncertainty regarding what it may or may not do. In addition, not only the existence of formal laws in the books, but also the quality of those laws, defines the level of legal certainty for local and foreign investors in Arab countries. These types of qualitative or procedural characteristics of laws, such as their stability, predictability, transparency,

106 Frank, "Law and Economic Growth," 1768–1769.

107 United Nations Conference on Trade and Development, *Good Governance in Investment Promotion: Note by the UNCTAD secretariat.*

clarity, consistency, enforceability and nonviolent character are the decisive criteria for an efficient system of laws and regulations.

Proposals for reform in any Arab countries may well not be satisfactory unless they are preceded by research, and by wide consultation with the political parties; public opinion stimulated by the mass media; pressure groups of differing sizes and influence; permanent officials in government departments; more forward-looking members of the practising and academic legal professions, official law reform bodies and with those who may be affected by such reforms.

There is no doubt that for the Arab world legal reform is necessary, or that it will also be effective in protecting property rights, and reducing uncertainty for both local and foreign investors. Legal reform will provide a framework for a legal environment, which will create long-term stability in the Arab states. However, the content and direction of a legal reform that aims to establish an efficient legal environment based on the rule of law must be friendly and attractive to investor both local and foreign (labour intensive manufacturing.) These laws should be the responsibility of the Arab countries themselves and should conform to the individual country's needs and social norms.

CHAPTER FIVE

THE UNITED NATIONS SECURITY COUNCIL, LIBYA AND RESOLUTION 1973: PROTECTION OF CIVILIANS OR TOOL FOR REGIME CHANGE?

Gary Wilson*

1. Introduction

The spring of 2011 witnessed uprisings in a number of Arab/North African states, broadly taking the form of protests against long standing authoritarian regimes and calls for their replacement and/or transition towards democracy. Regimes in Tunisia and Egypt were soon toppled in essentially peaceful 'revolutions', before the uprisings spread to other states in the region, most prominently Libya, Syria and Yemen. Unlike in Tunisia and Egypt, uprisings in these states were met with repressive responses from the regimes in power, resulting in a tense atmosphere marked by the perpetration of violence by the state against rebel movements and the civilian population. Events in Libya are particularly interesting as a result of the international reactions which they provoked. Unlike Syria, where repression of the civilian population by the Assad regime has met with limited international measures, widespread condemnation of Libyan authorities' repression of opposition movements soon resulted in action on the part of the UN Security Council, initially taking the form of the imposition of sanctions against Libya, to be quickly followed by the conferment upon willing actors of the authority to conduct military operations against Libya with the objective of affording protection to civilian populations under threat, as the country degenerated into civil war. By the end of August the rebels had effectively seized power in Libya as Tripoli fell to their forces and Colonel Gaddafi was forced to flee, before being killed on 20 October 2011.

The objective of this chapter is to examine the international response to Libya, with particular reference to resolution 1973 adopted by the UN Security Council, and to consider the extent to which it represents a continuation of recent trends in the practice of the Council and the

* Dr Gary Wilson, Phd, LLB (Hons.), Senior Lecturer in Law, Liverpool John Moores University, Liverpool, UK. E-mail: G.Wilson@ljmu.ac.uk

wider international community and the extent to which it may signal new departures—particularly in relation to the possible endorsement of regime change—and the implications of these. The chapter begins by providing brief background on Libya's relationship with the international community to date, before moving on to explain the nature of the international response to events in Libya during 2011. The main part of the chapter is then devoted to attempting to make sense of this response within the context of wider debates on the appropriate handling of conflict situations by the Security Council.

2. Libya and the International Community 1969–2010

Colonel Gaddafi came to power in Libya in 1969 following a military coup and ruled uninterruptedly until his fall from power in August 2011.[1] The first quarter century of Gaddafi's rule was marked by two dominant themes: the desire to forge Arab unity,[2] and his support for a variety of rebel, often terrorist, movements dispersed around the globe, including the IRA in Northern Ireland, Basque separatists in Spain and the Palestine Liberation Organisation. Libya's support for such causes had the effect of turning it into something of an international pariah, especially in the eyes of Western states.[3] With the exception of its protracted involvement in Chad's civil war,[4] the external impact of Gaddafi's regime was principally achieved indirectly through such assistance. While the Cold War deadlock within the UN Security Council meant that any response through that forum was unlikely, relations between Libya and the US deteriorated during the 1980s as a result of Libya's foreign policy objectives,[5] culminating in the 1986 US

---

[1] On background to the coup and an overview of Libya's earlier years post-independence, see Omar I. El Fathaly & Monty Palmer, *Political Development and Social Change in Libya* (Lexington & Tornto: Lexington Books, 1980), ch. 2; Jonathan Bearman, *Qadhafi's Libya* (London: Zed Books, 1986), chs. 1–4.

[2] On efforts to merge Libya with other states in the region, see El Fathaly & Palmer, *Political Development* ch. 3; Bearman, *Qadhafi's Libya*, ch. 5; Ronald Bruce St John, *Qaddafi's World Design: Libyan Foreign Policy, 1969–1987* (London: Saqi Books, 1987), chs. 2 & 4.

[3] On Libyan support for various terrorist and insurgent causes, see generally Geoff Simons, *Libya: The Struggle for Survival* (2nd ed.) (Basingstoke & London: Macmillan, 1996), 281–6. On support for the PLO, see Yehudit Ronen, "Libya's Qadhafi and the Israeli-Palestinian Conflict, 1969–2002," *Middle Eastern Studies* 40 (1) (2004): 85–98.

[4] On Libyan involvement in Chad, see St John, *Qadhafi's World Design*, 100–102; Bearman, *Qadhafi's Libya*, ch. 11; Simons, *Struggle for Survival*, 286–95.

[5] On Libyan-US relations, see Veronica Nmoma, "Power and Force: Libya's Relations with the United States," *Journal of Third World Studies* XXVI (2) (2009): 137–159; Edward Schumacher, "The United States and Libya," *Foreign Affairs* 65 (7) (1986): 329–348.

bombing of Libya in retaliation for a terrorist attack at a West Berlin discotheque which Libya was alleged to have been responsible for.[6]

The UN Security Council only really became concerned with Libya in the early post-Cold War period following the Lockerbie incident, in which a US air flight was brought down over Scotland as a result of sabotage by Libyan nationals.[7] Following pressure wrought by the US, UK and western states, the Council proclaimed international terrorism to constitute a threat to international peace and security, demanded that Libya hand over for trial those alleged to have perpetrated the attack,[8] and imposed sanctions in order to encourage its compliance with these demands.[9] After a number of years during which Libya remained an international outcast, a deal was eventually brokered whereby Libya handed over the alleged 'bomber' for trial under Scottish law in the Netherlands, leading to the eventual lifting of sanctions in 2003.[10] Following the successful resolution of the Lockerbie issue, western states quickly moved to re-establish relations with Libya and in many respects Libya became reintegrated within the international community.[11] British Prime Minister Tony Blair visited Tripoli in 2004 and spoke of a 'new relationship' with Libya,[12] and US Secretary of State Condoleeza Rice referred to Libya in similarly positive language on a trip to Libya four years later.[13] It is important to note that prior to the 2011 developments in Libya, the country had only attracted serious international attention as a result of the threats to international peace and security which its activities had projected externally. Its own internal structures and domestic policies had never been the focus of the Security Council's attention, making its sudden emergence as a conflict hot-spot during 2011 all the more remarkable.

---

6 For discussion of the 1986 US bombing, see Bearman, *Qadhafi's Libya*, ch. 16; Simons, *Struggle for Survival*, 334–45.

7 On the Lockerbie incident, see especially Simons, *Struggle for Survival*, ch. 1.

8 SC Res. 731 (1992).

9 SC Res 748 (1992).

10 SC Res. 1506 (2003).

11 On the shift in Western, especially US, attitudes towards Libya, see further Ronald B. St John, "Libya and the United States: A Faustian Pact?," *Middle East Policy* XV (1) 2008: 133–48; Yahia H. Zoubir, "The United States and Libya: From Confrontation to Normalization," *Middle East Policy* XIII (2) 2006: 48–70; Yahia H. Zoubir, "Libya in US foreign policy: from rogue state to good fellow?," *Third World Quarterly* 23 (1) 2002: 31–53.

12 See "Blair hails new Libyan relations," BBC News, 25 March 2004, http://news.bbc.co.uk/1/hi/uk_politics/3566545.stm.

13 See "Rice in talks with Libya's Gaddafi," BBC News, 5 September 2008, http://news.bbc.co.uk/1/hi/7599199.stm.

3. The 2011 'Revolutions', Libya and the UN

In early 2011 a spate of apparently spontaneous uprisings broke out in several North African and Middle Eastern states. While each state has its own dynamics, a common theme of the uprisings was dissatisfaction with long-standing authoritarian governments and pressure for political reform. Relatively quickly, the pressure brought about by mass protests in Tunisia and Egypt resulted in the presidents of those two states relinquishing power in January and February respectively.[14] However, while uprisings in Tunisia and Egypt effected peaceful change, similar calls for change in other states, principally Libya, Syria and Yemen, led to all out violent conflict between opposition movements and government forces.[15] As Fisher and Biggar noted in the Libyan context, while "the popular uprisings in Egypt and Tunisia had successfully led to regime change ... in Libya [they] seemed likely to be suppressed by the determination of one tyrant to use force to hold onto power."[16]

Anti-Gaddafi protests in Libya began on February 15th in the so-called "rebel stronghold" of Benghazi and soon opposition forces had taken control of parts of the country as it plunged into civil war.[17] A huge counter-offensive military campaign on the part of the Gaddafi regime soon followed,[18] prompting international concern at the use of force against civilian populations, human rights abuses and the ensuing humanitarian crisis which by late April was reported to have resulted in over 600,000 Libyans fleeing the country.[19] Following condemnation from the Arab League and African Union, the situation in Libya met with a response from the United Nations Security Council in the form of resolution 1970. Adopted under chapter VII of the UN Charter, the resolution condemned "the violence and use of force against civilians" and demanded "an immediate end to the violence and ... steps to fulfil the legitimate demands of

[14] See *Keesing's Record of World* Events, 57 (2011), 50254, 50308.

[15] Discussion of events in Syria and Yemen are outside of the scope of the present chapter. For discussion of the scale of hostilities, see media reports, for example, "Syria: hundreds flee scorched earth tactics of Assad regime," The Telegraph, 16 June 2011, http://www.telegraph.co.uk/news/worldnews/middleeast/syria/8573582/Syria-hundreds-flee-scorched-earth-tactics-of-Assad-regime.html.

[16] David Fisher & Nigel Biggar, "Was Iraq an unjust war? A debate on the Iraq war and reflections on Libya," *International Affairs* 87 (3) 2011: 701.

[17] Keesings, 57 (2011), p. 50309.

[18] Keesings, 57 (2011), p. 50365.

[19] *Time Magazine*, 9 May 2011, 11. 615,339 were reported to have fled as of April 21, most of whom went to Tunisia or Egypt.

the population."[20] A wave of sanctions were imposed upon Libya, consisting of an arms embargo,[21] travel ban[22] and assets freeze.[23] The situation in Libya was also referred to the Prosecutor of the International Criminal Court,[24] with a view to consideration whether charges ought to be brought against Libya's leadership for crimes against humanity.

Following a call from the Arab League for the imposition of a no-fly zone over Libya in order to afford protection to civilians, the Security Council decided to adopt more robust measures to respond to the situation in Libya. Resolution 1973, adopted with just ten positive votes in favour,[25] determined that the situation in Libya continued to constitute a threat to international peace and security and demanded an immediate ceasefire and the cessation of violence against civilians.[26] In its most pertinent parts, the resolution authorized "member states ... acting nationally or through regional organizations or arrangements ... to take all necessary measures ... to protect civilians and civilian populated areas under threat of attack ... while excluding a foreign occupation force of any form on any part of Libyan territory,"[27] and established a no-fly zone in Libyan airspace, which member states were authorized to enforce through the use of all necessary measures.[28] Acting on the basis of resolution 1973, beginning on 19th March, NATO member states resorted to a campaign of air-strikes against Libyan targets,[29] purportedly taken in pursuit of the resolution's objective of affording protection to the civilian population. These air-strikes were wide-ranging, going beyond the most obvious forms of humanitarian inspired action to include targeting the military and political infrastructure of the Gaddafi regime. Significant sections of Libya's military apparatus were destroyed and in one attack one of Gaddafi's sons was killed.[30] In one of its most controversial strikes, Libyan state television was targeted, prompting criticism from several quarters

[20] SC Res. 1970 (2011), para. 1.
[21] SC Res. 1970, paras. 9–10.
[22] SC Res. 1970, para. 15.
[23] SC Res. 1970, para. 17.
[24] SC Res. 1970, para. 4.
[25] Brazil, China, Germany, India and Russia abstained from voting on the resolution.
[26] SC Res. 1973, para. 1.
[27] SC Res. 1973, para. 4.
[28] SC Res. 1973, paras. 6, 8.
[29] See UN Doc. S/PV.6505. Notification that they had commenced operations against Libyan targets was communicated to the Secretary-General by the UK, France, the US, Denmark, Canada, Italy, Qatar, Belgium, Norway, Spain, the UAE and NATO.
[30] Keesings, 57 (2011), 50426.

including UNESCO's director-general, who commented that "Media outlets should not be targeted in military actions."[31] NATO's role in conducting operations against Libya's state military apparatus undoubtedly significantly weakened the regime's capability to combat the rebel opposition movement's gradual capture of more areas within Libya, which by the end of August had extended to its seizure of the reins of power in Tripoli. Although Gaddafi was not killed until October, the extent of the opposition TNC's control of the country was sufficient for the UN General Assembly on 16 September to decide that its representatives would occupy Libya's seat within the Assembly.[32]

4. The Scope of Resolution 1973: Continuity and Controversy

4.1. *The Security Council's Broad Conception of Collective Security under Chapter VII*

The UN Security Council is given broad powers to respond to situations which threaten international peace and security. The strength of these powers is reinforced by Articles 24 (1) and 25 of the UN Charter which respectively confer upon the Council primary responsibility for the maintenance of international peace and security and provide that member states agree to accept and carry out the Council's decisions. Article 39 has been described as the 'gateway' provision: it empowers the Security Council to determine that there exists a threat to the peace, breach of the peace or act of aggression. Following such a determination, it can move to authorise the application of non-military sanctions[33] or military enforcement measures[34] in response. While the Council made little use of these chapter VII powers during the Cold War period, in the post-Cold War era a considerable range of situations have been considered to constitute "threats to the peace",[35] by far the most commonly used of the phrases referred to in Article 39. The Council itself has formally acknowledged that a wide range of situations can threaten international peace and security

---

[31] 8th August 2011, http:www.un.org/apps/news/story.asp?NewsID=39255&CR=Libya&Cr1.

[32] UN Doc. GA/11137 (Press Release).

[33] Article 41.

[34] Article 42.

[35] See Robert Cryer, "The Security Council and Article 39: A Threat to Coherence?" *Journal of Armed Conflict Law* 1 (2) 1996: 161–95.

and its resolutions have reinforced this view.[36] Internal armed conflict, humanitarian crises, human rights abuses, and international terrorism have all been labelled as threats to the peace,[37] and non-military sanctions and military measures have been authorised in response to these on several occasions. The Council's increasingly humanitarian focus has been reinforced by the UN's endorsement at its millennium summit of the responsibility to protect doctrine,[38] as developed and advanced by the International Commission on State Sovereignty.[39]

Prima facie, the Security Council's response to events in Libya is compatible with its recent approach to the use of chapter VII measures. Determining the situation to constitute a threat to international peace and security, the Council moved to impose non-military sanctions before having resort to the authorisation of military measures in order to afford protection to the civilian population of the country. The Council had previously authorised the use of military measures under chapter VII to protect civilians, create a secure environment for humanitarian relief operations, or facilitate the provision of humanitarian assistance in relation to a number of situations deemed to threaten international peace and security including Somalia,[40] Rwanda,[41] Bosnia-Herzegovina,[42] Kosovo,[43] and Cote d'Ivoire.[44] In one respect, resolution 1973 was the latest in a line of measures which sanctioned military intervention for broadly humanitarian purposes. However, the Council's approach to Libya gives rise to a number of issues of potential controversy. These concern the nature of the mandate conferred on coalition forces by resolution 1973 and action taken under it, implementation of the *Responsibility to Protect* doctrine and the prosecution of Libya's leaders for crimes against humanity, and international support for regime change.

---

36 See UN Doc. S/PV.3046, at p. 124.

37 For discussion, see Karel Wellens, "The UN Security Council and new threats to the peace: back to the future," *Journal of Conflict and Security Law* 7 (1) 2002: 34–47.

38 World Summit Outcome Document, UN Doc. A/RES/60/1, paras. 138–9.

39 International Commission on State Sovereignty, *The Responsibility to Protect*, http://www.iciss.ca/pdf/Commission-Report.pdf.

40 SC Res. 794 (1992).

41 SC Res. 929 (1994).

42 SC Res. 1031 (1995).

43 SC Res. 1244 (1999).

44 SC Res. 1464 (2003).

4.2. *The Authorisation of Force: Clarity and Conformity with the Security Council's Objectives*

In resolution 1973 the Security Council clearly authorised the use of force for humanitarian purposes and to enforce a no fly zone over Libya, providing that member states were authorized "to take all necessary measures . . . to protect civilians and civilian populated areas under threat of attack" and "to enforce compliance with the ban on flights."[45] This much is undisputed. In the post-Cold War era, the term "all necessary measures" has been universally understood as the Security Council's chosen term of language when authorising the use of force. Authorisation of force to effect humanitarian objectives is also largely uncontroversial, the Council having adopted a broad conception of international peace and security—which incorporates respect for human security—for some time, and which has led to the authorisation of military measures for humanitarian purposes on a not insignificant number of occasions previously, as noted above. Again in line with its past approach, the resolution confers authority to use force on member states acting individually or through regional organizations or arrangements, the organization contemplated by the Council in particular being NATO, which had previous experience of taking military measures under UN authority (as well as sometimes in the absence of such authority).[46]

The authorisation contained in resolution 1973 is, arguably, more problematic as a result of its lack of clarity, reinforced by some controversies over the manner in which it has been acted upon by NATO member states. The fact that the Council doesn't have its own forces, as originally envisaged by the UN Charter,[47] makes it all the more important that it exercises sufficient control over those whom it authorises to take military action in order to ensure that they remain faithful to the objectives of the Council. Three particularly useful tools of control are clarity in resolutions authorising the use of force which leave no ambiguity as to the extent to which force may be applied and for what purposes, the imposition of time limits on such authorisations, and a requirement that those who act

[45] SC Res. 1973, paras. 4 & 8.

[46] NATO first took military enforcement action under UN authority in support of humanitarian objectives during conflict in the former Yugoslavia during the early 1990s and subsequently undertook a non-UN sanctioned military campaign against the FRY in 1999, as well as being deployed in Afghanistan from 2001 onwards. See further Tarcisio Gazzini, "NATO's Role in the Collective Security System," *Journal of Conflict and Security Law* 8 (2) (2003): 231–263.

[47] Article 43.

under UN authority report regularly on the action which they have taken. The merits of these requirements have been explained in greater detail elsewhere.[48] While there was some evidence that early post-Cold War resolutions had a patchy record of meeting these requirements, in more recent years the Council has generally proven better at endowing its resolutions under chapter VII with greater clarity.[49] However, resolution 1973 is arguably in certain respects a regressive step in this context.

To some extent it does appear to safeguard against states exceeding the humanitarian nature of the mandate conferred upon them by "excluding a foreign occupation force of any form on any part of Libyan territory."[50] This provision was emphasised by some of the states voting in favour of its adoption,[51] and is particularly important with reference to the legacy of Iraq where intervening states had sought to justify their invasion and subsequent occupation of the country on the basis of a poorly worded earlier resolution adopted for another purpose.[52] The resolution nevertheless falls short in other respects. Although member states are to inform the Council via the Secretary-General of measures taken under the resolution, there is no time limit upon the authorisation conferred upon them. This is of particular concern given the propensity of some states to seek to rely upon mandates conferred in the distant past for other purposes, as did the US and UK in claiming that their invasion of Iraq in 2003 could be based upon a resolution adopted over a decade earlier to deal with Iraq's invasion of Kuwait. Williams suggests that, "one would have thought that the Russians . . . would have learned to put a sunset clause in the resolution so that its effect would not be prolonged past its useful life."[53]

---

48 Gary Wilson, "The Legal, Military and Political Consequences of the 'Coalition of the Willing' Approach to UN Military Enforcement Action," *Journal of Conflict and Security Law* 12 (2) (2007): 295–330. See also Niels Blokker, "Is the Authorization Authorized? Powers and Practice of the UN Security Council to Authorize the Use of Force by "Coalitions of the Able and Willing,"' *European Journal of International Law* 11 (2001): 541–68.

49 Wilson, "Legal, Military and Political Consequences," 303–313; Blokker, "Is the Authorization Authorized?," 560–7.

50 SC Res. 1973, para. 4.

51 UN Doc. S/PV.6498. See, for example, the comments of the representatives of Lebanon (p. 3) and Colombia (p. 7).

52 On the dubious legal arguments employed by states intervening in Iraq, see for example Helen Duffy, *The 'War on Terror' and the framework of International Law* (Cambridge: Cambridge University Press, 2005), 197–209; Marc Weller, *Iraq and the Use of Force in International Law* (Oxford: Oxford University Press, 2010), 144–73; Philippe Sands, *Lawless World: America and the Making and Breaking of Global Rules* (London: Allen Lane, 2005), 174–203.

53 Ian Williams, "Resolution 1973: Responsibility to Protect, Not Humanitarian Intervention," *Washington Report on Middle East Affairs* 30 (4) (2011): 44.

In the event, the Council did terminate the authority conferred by resolution 1973 once the NATO military campaign came to an end.[54] Given the evident concerns of a number of Council members over the nature of the resolution, which only received ten positive votes, it is perhaps surprising that there were no real efforts to tighten its provisions. Russia raised a number of issues within the Security Council, arguing that "a whole range of questions ... remained unanswered [concerning] how the no-fly zone would be enforced, what the rules of engagement would be and what limits on the use of force there would be ... Provisions were introduced into the text that could potentially open the door to large-scale military intervention."[55] Certainly the authority to use force was couched in very general terms, leading to alternative possible interpretations of what it permitted. As Fisher & Biggar noted, "some international lawyers and countries read the resolution restrictively; others read it permissively."[56]

Debates over the scope of the mandate to use force contained in resolution 1973 are borne out by tensions over actions taken under it. The application of force by NATO forces was, in many ways, more extensive than that applied on the basis of UN resolutions in the past that had authorised the use of force for humanitarian purposes. Previous operations inspired by humanitarian objectives had applied force to remove obstacles to the delivery of humanitarian assistance or to respond to direct attacks on civilian targets. Military action taken by NATO in Libya went beyond simply responding directly to assaults on civilian populations within Libya to strikes directly aimed at weakening the infrastructure of the Gaddafi regime, indirectly strengthening the ability of rebel forces to wage their military campaign against the regime. Concern that military action taken exceeded what was permissible based upon a reasonable interpretation of resolution 1973 appears to be hinted at in comments made in the Security Council in early May by the Russian and Chinese representatives respectively. Noting "that actions by the NATO-led coalition forces are resulting in civilian casualties", the Russian representative went on to reinforce that "any use of force ... should be carried out in strict compliance with resolution 1973 ... Any act going beyond the mandate established by that resolution in any way or any disproportionate use of force is unacceptable."[57]

---

[54] SC Res 2016 (2011).

[55] S/PV.6498, 8.

[56] "Was Iraq an unjust war?," 707. See also 'Coalition bombing may be in breach of legal limits', *The Guardian*, 29 March 2011, 5.

[57] UN Doc. S/PV.6528, 8–9.

Evidently concerned that military action was being taken for wider purposes than the simple protection of civilians, China "[called] for the complete and strict implementation of the relevant resolutions of the Security Council. The international community must respect the sovereignty, independence, unity and territorial integrity of Libya. The internal affairs and fate of Libya must be left up to the Libyan people to decide. We are not in favour of any arbitrary interpretation of the Council's resolutions or of any actions going beyond those mandated by the Council."[58]

Arguably for the first time, action taken on the basis of Security Council authority was exercised with the intention of destabilising a regime in power and facilitating 'regime change', a theme to which we will return below. While military action in Afghanistan in 2001 and Iraq in 2003 was undoubtedly conducted with regime change in mind, neither operation proceeded on the basis of express UN authority. The clumsiness of the formulation contained in resolution 1973 makes it difficult to say whether NATO forces exceeded the mandate conferred upon them. As Williams writes, "certainly the resolution could have been better written."[59] Determining what measures are necessary to protect civilians under threat of attack leaves considerable scope for interpretation, but arguably any resolution authorising the use of force should be interpreted restrictively in order to prevent against its abuse. The indications are that this has not been the case.

Some international lawyers have raised potential legal difficulties with the scale of NATO's operations. Sands noted that, "The resolution is concerned with the protection of civilians, so a military attack on Gaddafi's retreating forces could only be justified if it could be shown to be related to that objective."[60] Grief suggested that the NATO military campaign potentially amounted to taking sides, noting that it "may have gone beyond the terms of the resolution ... It is almost as if we have entered the fray openly on behalf of the rebels. We have taken sides."[61]

While it does seem that NATO's actions evidence a very wide interpretation of resolution 1973, going beyond simply protecting civilians to aiding the overthrow of the incumbent regime, Shaw correctly notes that the resolution's authority extended not only to the protection of civilians from attack, but from the "threat of attack". He suggested that as long

58 S/PV.6528, 10.
59 "Resolution 1973: Responsibility to Protect."
60 "Coalition bombing may be in breach of legal limits," 5.
61 "Coalition bombing may be in breach of legal limits," 5.

as the Libyan regime had a fighting force employing a forcible stance, it could constitute a legitimate target.[62] While plausible, allowing such a broad interpretation of a Security Council mandate could arguably set a dangerous precedent. An analogy can arguably be made with the concept of pre-emptive self-defence, which pertains to permit states to take pre-emptive action to remove a threat which may materialise in the future. The concept is regarded with disdain by most states and international lawyers alike.[63] Shaw's argument is similarly problematic in that because of the actions of the Gaddafi regime, its implication is that as long as it had a military apparatus it was a legitimate target, conferring effective authority for its total destruction and the facilitation of a seizure of power by rebel forces. If this had been the intention of the sponsors of the resolution it should have been made explicit, and may well have resulted in its rejection by some of those states who abstained from voting upon it given their uneasiness over its actual implementation in practice.

Members of the Security Council themselves appear to have had different understandings of the scope of authority conferred by resolution 1973. Those who abstained from voting for it generally seem to have been concerned by the authorisation of force per se, although as noted above Russia clearly had problems over the lack of clarity contained in the resolution. Brazil felt the authority conferred went too far and may exacerbate tensions on the ground.[64] Even some supporters of the resolution at the time evidently disapproved of the manner in which it was acted upon by NATO, most prominently South Africa, whose representative within the Security Council commented that, "When South Africa voted in favour of resolution 1973 (2011), our intention was to ensure the protection of civilians ... Our intention was never regime change; nor was it the targeting of individuals. The future of Libya should be decided by the Libyans themselves, and not by outsiders."[65] Clearly there was far from universal support for the view that resolution 1973 permitted the scale of military operations which NATO ultimately came to undertake. Of course it must be remembered that resolutions of the Council are inherently political and are on occasion deliberately phrased in language which enables states to agree upon their adoption while holding different views on their

62 "Coalition bombing may be in breach of legal limits," 5.

63 See generally Christian Henderson, *The Persistent Advocator and the Use of Force* (Farnham: Ashgate, 2010).

64 S/PV.6498.

65 UN Doc. S/PV.6566, 4.

meaning. This is not, however, ideal from a legal perspective and disagreements over the scale of action taken on the basis of resolution 1973 may well have been a key consideration on the part of Russia and China when vetoing a draft resolution calling on Syria to cease its oppression of civilians during 2012.[66] While the resolutions sponsors maintained that it did not sanction any military measures,[67] memories of Libya might warrant an overly cautious approach on the part of those resolutely opposed to the prospect of military intervention in Syria.

4.3. *The Responsibility to Protect and Crimes against Humanity*

The *Responsibility to protect* doctrine has come to heavily influence contemporary thinking on responding to human rights abuses and humanitarian crises. First set out in the ICISS report of 2001,[68] the doctrine essentially holds that states have a responsibility to protect their people from harm, but where the population of a state suffers serious harm as a result of internal war, insurgency or state failure, which the state is unwilling or unable to halt, there then falls upon the international community a responsibility to protect the affected population.[69] Importantly, the doctrine does not give rise to any independent right of humanitarian intervention but is to be affected in accordance with existing legal norms. The *Responsibility to protect* received the support of the international community at the 2005 World summit where UN member states agreed that each individual state had a responsibility to protect its population from genocide, war crimes, ethnic cleansing and wars against humanity,[70] although its impact on Security Council decision-making is debatable. The stated purpose of the authorisation to use force in resolution 1973 was to protect civilian populations under threat and specific reference was made to the doctrine here and in the Council's earlier resolution on Libya.[71] However, the significance of this in the evolution of the importance of the doctrine can easily be overstated for two reasons. Firstly, Libya does not mark the first invocation of the *Responsibility to protect* in a resolution.

66 UN Doc. S/2012/77.
67 See UN Doc. S/PV.6711.
68 International Commission on State Sovereignty, *The Responsibility to Protect*, http://www.iciss.ca/pdf/Commission-Report.pdf.
69 Ibid., p. XI.
70 UN Doc. A/Res/60/1, paras. 138–40.
71 SC Res. 1970.

This occurred in resolution 1674.[72] It was also invoked shortly after resolution 1973 in a resolution pertaining to Cote d'Ivoire.[73] Secondly, references to the doctrine in Council resolutions have been very brief and entailed no real effort to make any meaningful connection between the requirements of the doctrine and the situation facing the Council or the specific measures which it adopts in response. Resolution 1674 simply reaffirmed the relevant parts of the World Summit document which referred to the *Responsibility to protect*. Tensions between some permanent members over the modern meaning of state sovereignty and the extent to which intervention in other states is appropriate have meant that the responsibility to protect has never explicitly played a significant role in the responses of the Council to humanitarian crises. For example, in early 2007 a resolution on the situation in Burma[74]—where human rights abuses were being perpetrated by the ruling military junta—was vetoed by Russia and China, as they considered events within Burma to be its internal affairs and incapable of constituting a threat to international peace and security.[75] Thus, while intervention in Libya may be heralded by some as a clear example of implementation of the *Responsibility to protect*, the limited references to the doctrine in the official statements of the Council and the tensions among its members which its discussion provokes, suggest some caution is warranted before making such assumptions. Nonetheless, importantly the Council does not need to recognise any such doctrine in determining situations to amount to threats to the peace and adopting enforcement measures in response.

Arguably, however, the *Responsibility to protect* doctrine has indirectly become more significant in light of the expansion in the reach of international criminal law in holding to account leaders for their treatment of their populations. This began with the creation of international criminal tribunals for Former Yugoslavia and Rwanda and culminated in the establishment of the International Criminal Court. Where prosecution takes place against members of a state's leadership for their responsibility for crimes against the population of their state, this can be seen as very much complementing the responsibility to protect: holding to account those individuals who have not only failed to protect their population, but

[72] SC Res. 1674 (2006), para. 4.

[73] SC Res. 1975 (2011).

[74] UN Doc. S/2007/14.

[75] UN Doc. S/PV.5619, 2–3 (China), 6 (Russia). Similar reasoning was employed by South Africa (4).

actively taken steps to cause harm to them. The Security Council first contemplated in resolution 1970 that "the widespread and systematic attacks currently taking place in [Libya] against the civilian population may amount to crimes against humanity" and referred it to the Prosecutor of the International Criminal Court.[76] Subsequently, the ICC prosecutor reported to the Council on its investigations into crimes against humanity alleged to have been committed in Libya,[77] and an arrest warrant for Colonel Gaddafi, his son Saif al-Islam and head of intelligence Abdullah al-Sanussi was issued by the ICC.[78]

The Libyan episode does not mark the first occasion on which a head of state has been subject to international criminal prosecution. As former heads of state, Slobodan Milosevic of Serbia[79] and Charles Taylor of Liberia[80] were indicted to face trial at the International Criminal Tribunal for Yugoslavia and Special Court for Sierra Leone respectively, and more recently President Bashir of Sudan became the first sitting head of state to be indicted by the ICC following a referral from the Security Council.[81] In this sense, the issue of an arrest warrant for Gaddafi arguably marks the continuation of a trend in which the reach of the ICC has been extended to anyone culpable for international crimes irrespective of status. However, there is still an argument to be made that the issuing of an arrest warrant for Gaddafi marks a departure from past practice in light of the fact that the Security Council's referral to the ICC and its issue of an arrest warrant related to very recent events which went back over a period of several weeks. By contrast, the events which led to the prosecution of Milosevic, Taylor and Bashir had endured for some time. Milosevic was charged with genocide, crimes against humanity and war crimes going back over several years to the civil war which accompanied the break-up of Yugoslavia. Taylor's alleged commission of crimes against humanity, war crimes and breaches of international humanitarian law took place during his six year tenure as Liberian President from 1997–2003. More recently, the charges faced by President Bashir of Sudan (war crimes and crimes against humanity) date back to 2003, some two years before the case was referred to the ICC. In this sense, the referral of Gaddafi and key

76 Para. 4.
77 S/PV.6528, 2–4.
78 Un Doc. SC/10297.
79 Indicted on 22 January 2001.
80 Indicted on 4 June 2003.
81 Indicted on 4 March 2009. Referred to the ICC Prosecutor by SC Res. 1593 (2005).

members of his regime to the ICC is in some respects surprising and suggests that either a more robust approach is now favoured for responding to international crimes, and/or that the decision to refer events in Libya to the ICC was a politicised one.

It is particularly interesting to compare the Security Council's approach to the decision to refer the leadership of Sudan and Libya respectively to the ICC. Four states abstained from supporting resolution 1593's referral of the Sudanese situation for reasons broadly related to their own general opposition to the ICC and the fact that Sudan was not a party to the Rome Statute creating the ICC. Interestingly, the US explicitly stated that it opposed the referral of those from non-state parties and alluded to its concerns over the risk of politicised prosecutions.[82] This makes it remarkable to think that resolution 1970 was adopted unanimously, receiving the positive votes of the US, China and three other states not party to the Rome Statute. Given the grounds for the opposition of the US and China to resolution 1593, it is difficult to see what had changed to lead to such a radically different approach to Libya. Like Sudan, Libya is not a party to the Rome Statute, and if anything the severity of events in Libya at the time of the referral to the ICC could not be realistically compared to the situation existing in Sudan when resolution 1593 was adopted, the country having been the focus of international concern for several years. It is too soon to say whether the Security Council's approach to prosecuting crimes against humanity in respect of Libya amounts to the emergence of a more robust approach to holding individuals to account for abdicating their responsibility to protect their own citizens, but suffice it to say the apparent shift in attitudes of some key states—particularly China, a long time adherent to a broad conception of state sovereignty—is arguably quite remarkable.

4.4. *Regime Change*

'Regime change' is a popular buzzword in the context of contemporary international relations and can be broadly understood as a term which describes either a process whereby a longstanding, usually authoritarian, government is replaced by a broadly democratic successor, or a policy aimed at achieving such a result. More usually, however, it is used to refer to "the forcible replacement by external actors of the elite and/or governance

[82] UN Doc. S/PV.5158, 2–4. See similarly the comments of China (5).

structure of a state so that the successor regime approximates some purported international standard of governance."[83] While international law places no restrictions upon the ability of a state's population to take action which results in the replacement of an existing government, this being a straightforward exercise in internal self-determination, it does so in respect of the actions of external actors intended to produce regime change. The prohibition on the use of force contained in Article 2 (4) of the UN Charter, taken together with the principle of non-intervention in states' internal affairs,[84] means that states may not apply force with the objective of replacing a government of another state unless authorised to do so by the UN Security Council.[85]

'Regime change' has never formally featured in the objectives of Security Council resolutions authorising the use of force previously. Although the Council has authorised military enforcement action for the purpose of restoring a democratically elected government that had been overthrown by a military coup in Haiti,[86] this is clearly something different: the objective was not the removal of a longstanding regime, but simply the restoration of a recently deposed government perceived to enjoy democratic legitimacy.[87] While military action in Afghanistan and Iraq played a significant role in effecting a change of government in those states, in neither case was action taken on the basis of any authorising resolution of the Security Council. Furthermore, the primary concern of the intervening states in those countries was the external threat posed by the incumbent regimes as opposed to their treatments of their civilian populations. Increased emphasis upon the importance of democratisation and human rights and the experience of Afghanistan and Iraq would, however, appear to suggest that 'regime change' is increasingly becoming the objective of a number of states when faced with threats to the peace which emanate

---

83 W. Michael Reisman, "The Manley O. Hudson Lecture: Why Regime Change is (Almost Always) a Bad Idea," *AJIL* 98 (3) (2004): 516–25, at 516.

84 For discussion of the non-intervention principle, see Maziar Jamnejad & Michael Wood, 'The Principle of Non-Intervention,' *Leiden Journal of International Law* 22 (2009): 345–381.

85 The Council has never authorised action to replace one government with another. Resolution 940 (1994) authorised the use of force to bring about the restoration of the democratically elected President Aristide to power in Haiti, but that is best seen as action to defend the democratic status quo and give effect to the clear expression of the population in electing him.

86 SC Res.940 (1994).

87 See Mehrdad Payandeh, "The United Nations, Military Intervention, and Regime Change in Libya," *Virginia Journal of International Law* 52 (2) (2012): 355–403, at 368–70.

from the actions of authoritarian regimes. The statements of some states would appear to reinforce the belief that action in respect of Libya, albeit not specifically mandated for such an objective by the Council, was taken with a view to effecting or supporting regime change. Many, arguably, shared the view of Fisher & Biggar, who "hoped that affording protection to the Libyan people will give them the opportunity to choose their own destinies, in the way the Egyptian and Tunisian peoples are doing, and that this will indeed lead to a just peace and democratic future for them."[88] In Security Council proceedings the African Union spoke of giving Libyans an opportunity to elect their leaders.[89] The US similarly believed that Libya "deserve leaders who share and support their aspirations to freedom, democracy and dignity"[90] Even Germany, which opposed the adoption of resolution 1973, felt that Gaddafi "must relinquish power immediately."[91]

However, there is a difference between supporting in principle a change of government in Libya and explicitly taking measures to bring that about, and states and international actors appear to have been careful not to go as far as actually endorsing international action to topple the Gaddafi regime. For example, President Obama stated that while "there is no question that Libya ... would be better off with Gaddafi out of power ... broadening our military mission to include regime change would be a mistake."[92] The UN Secretary-General's Special Envoy for Libya emphasised that "responsibility for finding a solution lies with the Libyan people themselves,"[93] and Under Secretary-General for Political Affairs Lynn Pascoe warned that "Taking sides in any internal conflict situation in an effort to institute regime change in Libya sets a dangerous precedent that will surely damage the credibility of the Council and its resolutions."[94] Not only is there evidence of states' unwillingness to invoke regime change as a formal objective of their actions, but the very notion is treated with disdain by many states. The views of many were arguably represented in the comments of President Museveni of Uganda, that "if there is a doubt about the legitimacy of a government and the people decide to launch an

88 "Was Iraq an unjust war?," 703.
89 UN Doc. S/PV.6555, 2–5.
90 UN Doc. S/PV.5428, 12.
91 UN Doc. S/PV.6498, 4.
92 Quoted in Michael Elliott, 'The Libyan Muddle', *Time*, 9 May 2011, 18.
93 UN Doc. S/PV.6509, 4.
94 UN Doc. S/PV.6595, 5.

insurrection, that should be the decision of the internal forces. It should not be for external forces to arrogate themselves that role."[95]

However, while it is one thing for states and international actors to formally deny any intention of effecting regime change, the reality is that the very actions which they have taken or supported have directly resulted in this. Although unwilling to make this an express objective of the military action—action against Libya being officially taken with the sole objective of affording protection to civilian populations under threat—given that Libya was effectively in a state of civil war and NATO's extensive actions seriously weakened the military infrastructure of the Gaddafi regime to the benefit of the opposition rebel forces which may not have been able to seize power in their absence, they undoubtedly contributed to regime change in Libya and it is somewhat dishonest to suggest otherwise. As Henderson succinctly comments in relation to the NATO contribution to the rebel cause, "it is hard to see how providing them with such assistance does anything other than assist them in winning the civil war and changing the political leadership of the country."[96]

While aiding rebel movements in civil wars is generally unlawful, the Security Council can confer states with express authority to aid a rebel movement to remove from power a discredited regime. However, such authority was clearly lacking in resolution 1973. Any such measure would meet with the veto of at least two permanent members within the Council. Regime change can logically be an unintended consequence of legitimate measures taken for another objective. This may have been what occurred in Libya, although that presumes that NATO interpreted the mandate contained within resolution 1973 appropriately, and as noted above there are good grounds for arguing that this was not the case.

The Libyan episode suggests that we may be witnessing the possible emergence of new tensions within the UN system whereby some states favour using its collective security machinery to remove threats to the peace by toppling rogue regimes whereas others adhere vehemently to traditional norms of non-intervention in the internal affairs of states and state sovereignty in resisting such moves. If regime change is not a formal objective of the Council, doubts are cast over the legitimacy of action taken under its authority when this is undoubtedly a desired outcome

95 'Museveni: It's not for foreigners to sponsor rebels in Libya', *New African*, May 2011, 25.

96 Christian Henderson, "International Measures for the Protection of Civilians in Libya and Cote D'Ivoire," *International and Comparative Law Quarterly* 60 (2011): 772.

of the states undertaking it. Such controversies could quite easily be resolved through the adoption of watertight resolutions which leave no doubt as to their objective or the permissible modes of effecting them.

5. Conclusions

In some respects the situation which events during 2011 in Libya produced for the Security Council to deal with was rather different from most of the threats to the peace with which the Council had been faced in the past. While most of the Council's post-Cold War activity has been concerned with situations that, broadly speaking, take the form of internal conflict or crises occurring within individual states, the events in Libya during 2011 were rather sporadic as opposed to the escalation of long-running tensions or disputes into graver crises. Previously, military enforcement measures had only been authorised in response to internal conflicts which had been ongoing for some time, usually following the failure of attempts at pacific settlement, peacekeeping or sanctions. In this sense, the Council's response was perhaps unusual.

Nonetheless, in some key respects the response of the Council followed a similar pattern to that of earlier authorisations to member states to use force in pursuit of humanitarian objectives. There is nothing particularly noteworthy about the fact that a humanitarian crisis within a state was deemed to pose a threat to international peace and security and that military measures were sanctioned to protect endangered civilian populations. That the mandate could have been defined with greater clarity is a matter meriting greater attention but, again, is something which the Council has not handled ideally on other occasions. Likewise, states have interpreted mandates conferred by the Council in broader terms than may have been intended by some states at the time of their adoption. In other respects there does not appear to be any prima facie departure from established approaches on the part of the Council: there is little real express emphasis upon the responsibility to protect despite this situation arguably being of the very kind the doctrine is designed for, the referral of the incident to the ICC which led to the issue of arrest warrants for key Libyan leaders is not the first instance of its kind, and despite the apparent implicit support for regime change on the part of several states they have been cautious not to formally make this part of the established objectives of the military operation authorised by resolution 1973.

However, several general observations can be made about the international response to events in Libya which suggest that it is more significant than may appear to be the case on the surface. Firstly, despite the apparent non-distinctiveness of resolution 1973 and action taken under it, it must be stressed that the situation posed by Libya is in many ways a new kind of problem for the Council. The sporadic nature of the Arab uprisings and the radical changes which they promise provide the Council with a unique situation which perhaps merits consideration of unique solutions. Secondly, the Security Council's response to events in Libya suggests a greater willingness on the part of some permanent members to make use of the ICC machinery to complement the UN collective security machinery in holding to account leaders who fall foul of the responsibility to protect their populations, even where their wrongdoing in this respect is only recent. Thirdly, the statements of some states and the scale of the actions taken on the basis of resolution 1973 also suggest that whereas the notion of 'regime change' does not feature formally in the justifications offered for international action over Libya, it is of paramount importance to them and may increasingly come to influence decision-making and action in respect of situations in which authoritarian regimes are responsible for serious human rights abuses.

Without doubt, action taken under resolution 1973 had the effect of assisting the opposition rebel movement in Libya to overthrow the regime of Colonel Gaddafi. The resolution never authorised action to be taken with this objective, although it did not of course preclude action which indirectly aided this outcome. The real difficulty lies in determining how extensive military action was actually permitted to be by the resolution, as it is apparent that a number of states and international lawyers believe NATO's interpretation of its authority under the resolution to have been unjustifiably broad. If these criticisms of NATO's actions are accepted, the NATO role takes on the form of a partially unlawful intervention in a civil war in support of one side. To avoid such controversies it is imperative that the Security Council begins to endow its resolutions with a much greater degree of clarity in specifying the objectives for which military action may be taken and the limits which apply to its exercise.

CHAPTER SIX

WOMEN OF THE REVOLUTION: THE FUTURE OF WOMEN'S RIGHTS IN POST-GADDAFI LIBYA

Olga Jurasz*

1. Introduction

17 February 2011 marked the beginning of the historical overthrow of the oppressive regime of Colonel Muammar Gaddafi in Libya. The Libyan Uprising, which was triggered by the protests of women in Benghazi on 15 February 2011 against the arrest of Fethi Tarbel, human rights lawyer for the victims of the 1996 Abu Salim massacre, soon spread around the whole country. Protesters demanded the removal of Gaddafi as head of state and called for an open and inclusive Libya. They demanded the end of an era of oppression and gross human rights violations in the country, such as those committed in the Abu Salim prison. The response of Gaddafi to this protest with armed violence against civilian protesters ignited a civil war between the government forces in support of Gaddafi and the opposition armed forces formed by the rebels. By the end of February 2011, it became clear that Libyans, with the support of the UN-led international community, were determined to transform their country into a democratic, pluralist and equal state.

If there is one thing, which symbolizes the Libyan Revolution, it is the unity of Libyans in taking responsibility for the shape of their country after 42 years of Gaddafi's rule. In demanding long-awaited changes, Libyans appeared to join in solidarity and abandoned the differences, which permeated the society thus far. One of the key boundaries, which was set aside during the civil war in the most visible way (even for an external observer) and enabled the unity of Libyans was gender.

Since its very inception, Libyan women were actively participating in the course of the Revolution. Their role during the uprising stretched much beyond the traditional gender roles expected of women and performed by them in Libyan society. Libyan women stood arm in arm with

* Lecturer in Law, Open University, UK (olga.jurasz@open.ac.uk).

Libyan men in fight against the Gaddafi regime. They played a central role in the Revolution by providing essential support to the fighters and often taking up arms themselves.

They sent a clear message: by showing their strength and willpower through their full participation in Libya's political transition, women wanted to be citizens of a free Libya in their own right and on a basis equal with men. This rather powerful image of what may be labelled as 'a step towards empowerment of Libyan women' raises the important question of the legal position of women in the aftermath of the Revolution.

The opportunities that lie ahead for Libyan women greatly depend on the shape of the new Libyan legal system. For that reason, it is crucial that in times of post-conflict transition women's rights are no longer marginalized and take a strong place on the agenda 'for the change'. In the context of the upcoming new Libyan Constitution, debate regarding the status of human rights in post-conflict Libya and women's rights in particular, is very timely. It is thus through the creation of adequate laws and their thorough implementation, that women's rights can be secured and the foundations of gender equality in post-conflict Libya can be set.

Would the post-Gaddafi government, strongly aspiring to build a democratic, pluralist state respecting human rights and the rule of law, adequately address the problem of gender inequalities and discrimination of women in the Libyan society? Would human rights of Libyan women be secured and enshrined in the new Constitution and the new legal system? Or would (s)heros of the Revolution have to fight yet another battle—a battle for equality and empowerment?

2. Women and Their Rights in Gaddafi's Libya

Approaching the challenge of securing women's rights in the liberated Libya in a complete and effective manner requires a thorough understanding of the current legal position of women in Libya, which was shaped over 42 years of Gaddafi's rule.

Prior to 17 February 2011, women were not actively present in the socio-political sphere in Libya. In traditional and conservative Libyan society, the vast majority of women were not involved in the political consultation or decision making processes. The existence of a patriarchal system which was supported by Gaddafi's dictatorship resulted in the majority of decisions, including laws relating to women and directly impacting on their lives, being made without women's participation. This situation has continued despite the fact that the numbers of educated women in Libya have continued to rise over the years, with over 50% of the current graduates in Libya being female.

While in power, Gaddafi created a system dominated by a false sense of gender equality. Whilst policies and laws aimed at making women equal citizens of Libya were created, such as widening access of women to education and employment, the regime in fact perpetuated further gender inequality. In particular, the unequal status of women under various family laws and in cases involving gender-based violence strengthened the transparency of this problem. Furthermore, the semblance of equality fades away in light of laws (discussed below), which not only contradict the legal clauses facilitating an apparent empowerment of women, but also diminish women's position in society by restricting the enjoyment of their social and economic rights. Such a situation further inhibits the real chance for active participation and advocacy for women's rights.

2.1. *The National Perspective*

From a legal perspective, the reasons behind the critical situation of women's rights appear to be twofold. On the one hand, laws enacted under Gaddafi's rule provided, at least in principle, for the equality of men and women in the society. Nevertheless, a range of commitments to gender equality appear to fade away when contrasted with the more specific provisions of the Libyan law. The contradiction between the principle of equality guaranteed by law and the discriminatory nature of many specific laws, in particular those governing the private sphere of women's lives, created a major factor behind the perpetuation of gender inequality. The critical areas, in which women attain significantly lower status than men are primarily provisions of family law,[1] which are deeply enshrined in Shari' a principles. However, the unequal treatment of women before the law is not limited to family law but also includes laws on nationality, ownership, political rights as well as freedom of expression and movement of the person.

On the other hand, women under Gaddafi's regime had a limited opportunity to advocate for a change of discriminatory laws. The possibility of even beginning the process of advocating for change in legal

[1] Amnesty International, *Annual Report 2011* [*Libya*], 2011, available at: http://www.amnesty.org/en/region/libya/report-2011#section-81-7 (accessed 12 April 2012).

status of women's rights was inhibited by the laws restricting freedom of expression and assembly in Jamahiriya. Under Article 3 of Law No. 71 of 1972 on the Criminalization of Parties, 'forming, joining, financing or supporting groups based on a political ideology opposed to the principles of the al-Fateh Revolution of 1 September 1969, and encouraging that by whatever means is punishable by death'.[2] The Libyan Penal Code also prohibits under the punishment of death penalty, any form of calls "for the establishment of any grouping, organization or association proscribed by law" (Article 206) as well as makes illegal any "theories or principles aiming to change the basic principles of the Constitution or the fundamental structures of the social system" (Article 207).[3] Furthermore, Gaddafi's government prohibited the establishment of any independent human rights groups or non-governmental organizations, with the exception of the Human Rights Society of the Gaddafi International Charity and Development Foundation, headed by Saif al-Islam al-Gaddafi.[4]

In effect, these restrictions created barriers to development of any form of women's advocacy group or any other form of forum, where women's rights could be publicly discussed and advocated for. As a result, for 42 years Libyan women were deprived of a real chance to have a say regarding their legal rights—a status quo, which was considerably changed with the outbreak of the Libyan Revolution.

2.1.1. *Equality Principle*

In the *Green Book*,[5] which outlines his political and social thought ideas as a basis for the establishment of the Libyan Jamahiriya, Gaddafi manifests the equality of genders and condemns any form of such discrimination. In chapter 5 of the *Green Book* (part 3), which is dedicated to the issues relating to women, he describes gender equality as a 'self evident fact' and condemns 'discrimination between man and woman [as] a flagrant act of oppression without any justification'.[6] Nevertheless, in the later part of the book, he elaborates about the biological differences between

---

[2] Libyan Arab Jamahiriya: Amnesty International submission to the UN Universal Periodic Review, Ninth Session of the UPR Working Group, November–December 2010, available at: http://lib.ohchr.org/HRBodies/UPR/Documents/Session9/LY/AI_Amnesty International.pdf (accessed 12 April 2012).

[3] Ibid., n. 3.

[4] Ibid., n. 3.

[5] Muammar al-Qadhafi, *The Green Book* (Tripoli: World Centre for the Study and Research of the Green Book, 1983).

[6] *The Green Book*, part 3, chapter 5.

the sexes, with particular focus on pregnancy, and concludes, paradoxically, that these differences result in functions, which set women apart from men and make equality of genders unachievable for that particular reason.[7]

One of the key provisions in the Libyan Constitution Proclamation from 1969[8] (the 1969 Proclamation) is equality of citizens before the law.[9] Commitment to gender equality was reinstated in 1988 in both the preamble and the text of The Great Green Charter of Human Rights of the Jamahiriyan Era[10] (The Green Charter), which condemned the inequality in rights between men and women as:

> (...) *a flagrant injustice that nothing whatsoever can justify.*[11]

The article also incorporates the principle of equality between spouses:

> (...) *marriage is an equitable association between two equal partners. No one may be coerced into a marriage contract, nor divorce except by mutual consent or after a fair judgment.*[12]

The principle of equality was once again repeated by Article 1 of Law No. 20 (1991):

> *Citizens in Great Jamahiriya, male and female, are free and equal in rights. These rights are not to be violated.*[13]

2.1.2. *Family Law*

In the context of family law, women's position remains heavily disadvantaged by traditional and cultural norms. For example, divorce is still regarded as matter of shame and subject to considerations within a broadly understood family domain. The Freedom House observed in its 2010 Report that:

---

[7] "All these innate characteristics form differences because of which man and woman cannot be equal."

[8] *Constitution Proclamation* [Libya], 11 December 1969, available at: http://www.unhcr.org/refworld/docid/3ae6b5a24.html (accessed 10 April 2012), hereinafter: the 1969 Proclamation.

[9] Article 5, The 1969 Proclamation.

[10] Article 21, *Great Green Charter of Human Rights of the Jamahiriyan Era* [Libya], 12 June 1988, available at: http://www.unhcr.org/refworld/docid/3dda540f4.html (accessed 10 April 2012).

[11] Article 21, The Green Charter.

[12] Article 21, The Green Charter.

[13] *Law No. 20, Endorsement of Freedom* [Libya], 9 November 1991, available at: http://www.unhcr.org/refworld/docid/3dda542d4.html (accessed 10 April 2012).

> although women are permitted to represent themselves before the court during divorce proceedings, in practice they are usually represented by a male family member. Divorce is still considered to be a family affair, meaning a woman's ability to secure a divorce is often dependent on the extent to which her family supports her decision. Moreover, it is generally easier for men to secure a divorce than women, and society is more accepting of divorced men than divorced women.[14]

In cases where a woman is pronounced to be the guilty party in divorce, she is required to forfeit her right to sadaq (deferred dowry payment) and custody of the couple's children.[15] Also, unlike men, in cases where a spouse is not consenting to the divorce, women must base their claim on one of the following grounds: husband's financial incapacity, absence without justification or unjustified abandonment.[16]

2.1.3. *Violence against Women*

Violence against women, including acts of domestic violence, is an urgent problem in Libya, which needs to be addressed. Although there exists a provision prohibiting a male spouse from causing physical or mental harm to his wife,[17] Libya has not yet adopted any fully comprehensive legal provisions specifically addressing all forms of violence against women.[18] Systems allowing for protection have also not been developed. Furthermore, socio-cultural conventions play an important role in shaping the attitudes towards the issue of violence against women and public attitude towards the victims as well as assistance available to them. In its 2009 Concluding Observations, the Committee on the Elimination of All Forms of Discrimination Against Women (CEDAW) expressed concerns about

---

[14] Freedom House, *Women's Rights in the Middle East and North Africa 2010—Libya*, 3 March 2010, available at: http://www.unhcr.org/refworld/docid/4b99012091.html (accessed 12 April 2012).

[15] Otherwise, the custody is presumptively granted to women (Law No. 10 (1984), chapter 3 (Consequences of the Dissolution of Marriage), section 6 (Custody), article 62. *Al-mara'fi al'tashiryat al-libaya* [Women in Libyan Legislation], (Tripoli: Publication of the Women's Affairs Secretariat of the General People's Congress, 1994), p. 113, cited in 2006 HRW Report, n. 21).

[16] International Federation for Human Rights (FIDH), 'Women and the Arab Spring: Libya', available at: http://arabwomenspring.fidh.net/index.php?title=Libya (accessed 12 April 2012).

[17] Article 17, Law No. 10 (1984).

[18] CEDAW, *Concluding Observations of the Committee on the Elimination of Discrimination Against Women: Libyan Arab Jamahiriya*, 6 February 2009, UN DOC. CEDAW/C/LBY/CO/5, para. 23 (CEDAW Report 2009).

> [...] the widespread practice whereby marriage between perpetrators of rape and women victims of rape is encouraged to protect victims from social stigma and marginalization and ensure clarity of linage if the victim is pregnant.[19]

Such practice not only allows impunity for the perpetrator, but also doubly victimizes the woman. The victim is effectively forced to live with the perpetrator throughout her life, which further traumatises her but also (in cases where the victim becomes pregnant as a result of rape) forces her to keep and bring up the child fathered by the rapist. As a result, the victim is not only failed by the national justice system in that she has no means of redress for violations of her rights. She also falls a victim to traditional stereotypes, cultural and social norms, which encourage and allow for such an unjust and demeaning arrangement to take place.

2.1.4. *Unlawful Detention*

Another area of concern is the unlawful detention of women and girls in social rehabilitation centres. The centres were created for women in order to provide protection for them in cases where families disowned them where they were suspected of transgression of social mores. Human Rights Watch further notes that these 'facilities are supposed to "protect" these women and girls from violence by relatives in the name of "family honour," and to rehabilitate women deemed to have transgressed socially-accepted norms of behaviour'.[20] Women and girls, who were detained in these facilities were not criminally convicted, but transferred there by the public prosecutor, too often against their will. They were also deprived of a possibility to challenge the decision about their detention before a court.[21] In fact, the majority of women were kept in facilities based on accusations of extramarital sexual relations (*zina*[22] crimes, punishable as

---

19 CEDAW Report 2009, para. 23.

20 Human Rights Watch, *A Threat to Society? The Arbitrary Detention of Women and Girls for "Social Rehabilitation"*, (New York: Human Rights Watch, 27 February 2006), available at: http://www.hrw.org/sites/default/files/reports/libya0206webwcover.pdf (accessed 12 April 2012).

21 CEDAW Report 2009, para. 23.

22 *Zina* is defined under Art. 1 Law No. 70 (1973) "Regarding the Establishment of the *Hadd* Penalty for *Zina* modifying some of the Provisions of the Penal Law" as intercourse between a man and woman who are not bound to each other by marriage. Articles 3 and 4 prescribe flogging as a method of punishment for those convicted of the *zina* offenses.

a criminal offence under the Libyan law), including victims of rape[23] as well as women, who suffered domestic violence. Women and girls were also detained for minor breaches of social norms, such as smoking or talking back.[24]

While in confinement, women suffered further abuses of their rights. Human Rights Watch reports that women in social rehabilitation centres were forced to undergo invasive virginity tests in order to determine whether they engaged in recent sexual intercourse. Girls, who were detained were refused access to further education—a right guaranteed under Convention on the Rights of the Child (CRC)[25] and the International Covenant on Economic, Social and Cultural Rights (ICESCR).[26] Furthermore, the conditions of detention were not compliant with standards set out in international human rights instruments, to which Libya is a party.[27]

2.1.5. *The State Response*

Multiple instances of violations of women's rights in Libya receive a very limited (if any) response from the state authorities. The problem is often underestimated, marginalized, and, as in the case of gender-based violence, authorities refuse to acknowledge its real extent.[28] There is a lack of facilities for victims of violence as well as limited access to the necessary health and counselling services. This situation takes place despite the fact that the State may be "responsible for private acts if they fail to act with

[23] Human Rights Watch, *World Report 2011: Libya*, (New York: Human Rights Watch, January 2011), available at: http://www.hrw.org/sites/default/files/related_material/libya_1.pdf (accessed 12 April 2012).

[24] 2006 HRW Report, p. 28.

[25] Article 28 of The Convention on the Rights of the Child, (entered into force 2 September 1990, acceded to by Libya on 15 May 1993), 1577 U.N.T.S. 3 (CRC).

[26] Article 13 of the International Covenant on Economic, Social and Cultural Rights 1966, (entered into force 3 January 1976, acceded to by Libya on 15 May 1970), 993 U.N.T.S. 3, (ICESCR).

[27] Article 9 of The International Covenant on Civil and Political Rights 1966, (entered into force 23 March, 1976 and acceded to by Libya on 15 May 1970), 999 U.N.T.S. 171 (ICCPR), prohibits arbitrary arrest and detention. Article 10 ICCPR provides that 'all persons deprived of their liberty shall be treated with humanity and with respect for the inherent dignity of the human person'. Art. 7 ICCPR guarantees that 'no one shall be subjected to torture or to cruel, inhuman or degrading treatment or punishment'.

[28] *"Violence and rape is very rare. You might find two cases [in Libya] from people belonging to non-Libyan cultures."*—Amal Safar, deputy of social affairs in the General People's Congress, Tripoli, April 25, 2005, cited in: 2006 HRW Report, p. 10.

due diligence to prevent violations of rights or to investigate and punish acts of violence".[29]

2.2. *The International Perspective*

In addition to the national regulations regarding women's rights and their legal status, Libya is bound by the relevant provisions of the international human rights framework. Libya is a party to a majority of the core international human rights instruments, including International Covenant on Civil and Political Rights 1966,[30] International Covenant on Economic, Social and Cultural Rights 1966,[31] Convention Against Torture and Other Cruel, Inhumane or Degrading Treatment or Punishment 1984[32] and Convention on the Rights of the Child 1989.[33]

In 1989, Libya acceded to the Convention on Elimination of All Forms of Discrimination Against Women 1979 (CEDAW).[34] Nevertheless, Libya entered reservations in relation to two important articles in the Convention: Article 2 concerning non-discrimination in relation to the right to inheritance and Article 16 (c) and (d) relating to marriage and divorce. Reservations were made on the ground that both articles need to be interpreted and implemented in accordance with provisions of the Shari'a. Given that Article 2 is considered the very core of the Convention, entering reservations to it undermines the object and purpose of this treaty: elimination of all forms of discrimination against women. These reservations were criticised by other governments,[35] but also by the Committee on the Elimination of All Forms of Discrimination against Women

[29] Committee on the Elimination of Discrimination against Women (CEDAW Committee), General Recommendation 19, Violence against women, U.N. Doc. A/47/38 (1992), para. 9.

[30] The International Covenant on Civil and Political Rights 1966, (entered into force 23 March, 1976 and acceded to by Libya on 15 May 1970), 999 U.N.T.S. 171 (ICCPR).

[31] International Covenant on Economic, Social and Cultural Rights 1966, (entered into force 3 January 1976, acceded to by Libya on 15 May 1970), 993 U.N.T.S. 3, (ICESCR).

[32] Convention Against Torture and Other Cruel, Inhumane or Degrading Treatment or Punishment 1984, (entered into force 26 June 1987, acceded to by Libya 16 May 1989), 1465 U.N.T.S. 85 (CAT).

[33] The Convention on the Rights of the Child, (entered into force 2 September 1990, acceded to by Libya on 15 May 1993), 1577 U.N.T.S. 3.

[34] Convention on Elimination of All Forms of Discrimination Against Women 1979, (entered into force 3 September 1981, acceded to by Libya on 16 May 1989), 1249 U.N.T.S. 13 (CEDAW).

[35] Denmark, Finland, Germany, Mexico, the Netherlands, Norway, and Sweden have entered objections to these reservations. These governments emphasized the problem of incompatibility of Libya's reservation with the object and purpose of the Convention.

(CEDAW Committee), which rightly noted that "reservations to article 16, whether lodged for national, traditional, religious or cultural reasons, are incompatible with the Convention and therefore impermissible and should be reviewed and modified or withdrawn".[36]

The CEDAW Committee also noted in its Concluding Observations in 2009, concern over these reservations and highlighted their contrary nature to the object and purpose of the Convention, calling for their prompt withdrawal.[37] The entry of reservations to Articles 2 and 16 of CEDAW appears particularly peculiar in the context of the ICCPR, to which Libya is a party. Although the content of the ICCPR requires equality between men and women in the same areas as outlined in Articles 2 and 16 of CEDAW, Libya did not enter any reservation to the 1966 Convention. Despite a reservation to CEDAW, in 2004 Libya as the only Arab state, acceded to the Optional Protocol to the Convention on the Elimination of All Forms of Discrimination Against Women,[38] which provides a Communications Procedure which allows both individuals and groups of individuals to submit individual complaints to the CEDAW Committee.

3. (S)heros of the Revolution

There is little doubt that women played an active and crucial role in the Libyan Revolution. Their presence in the streets became a defining feature of the Libyan Revolution, but also the Arab Spring more generally.

3.1. *The Role of Women in the Revolution*

In overcoming the boundaries to political participation set over 42 years of Gaddafi's rule, women formed groups and organizations and publicly demonstrated against the oppressive regime. Although not many women became combatants per se, they supported the Revolution to a degree equal to men. Their involvement included smuggling weapons, medical supplies, organizing and ensuring safe passage for the fighters, but also

[36] *Report of the Committee on the Elimination of Discrimination Against Women* (Eighteenth and Nineteenth session), (United Nations: New York, 1998), UN Doc. A/53/38/Rev.1, p. 49.

[37] CEDAW Report 2009, para. 13.

[38] Optional Protocol to the Convention on the Elimination of All Forms of Discrimination Against Women 1999, (entered into force 22 December 2000, acceded to by Libya 2004), 2131 U.N.T.S. 83 (CEDAW Optional Protocol).

providing humanitarian support to them.[39] Women effectively became the backbone of armed operations and their active involvement was a crucial element, which contributed to the overall success of the Revolution. What is important, these initiatives were taken on by women in addition to their traditional gender roles and therefore demonstrated their strong commitment to the socio-political change in Libya. Moreover, women showed their sense of citizenship and manifested taking responsibility for their country by fighting not only for their own rights, but for the main objective of the Revolution: democratic change.

Nevertheless, the involvement of women in the Revolution also resulted in cases where women suffered repression because of public manifestation of anti-Gaddafi views either by women themselves or by a person closely associated with them. In some instances, women were detained and tortured or otherwise punished by the Gaddafi loyalist forces for expression of their views and/or support given to the rebels. However, as the Report of the International Commission of Inquiry[40] suggests, the opposition armed forces committed similar abuses, including acts of sexual violence, violating principles of human rights and international humanitarian law.

3.2. *Sexual Violence in the Revolution*

Amongst various human rights abuses and violations of international humanitarian law norms, acts of sexual violence appear to have become a forgotten part of the Revolution. The attention of the international community was first drawn to that matter in March 2011, when the media worldwide featured the story of Eman al-Obeidi. On 26 March 2011, al-Obeidi burst into the lobby of Rixos Hotel in Tripoli filled with western journalists, where she publically admitted to being stopped at the checkpoint, tortured and gang raped by a group of government militias.[41] A few

39 BBC News, 'Tripoli underground: handbags, dinghies and secret emails', 3 December 2011, available at: http://www.bbc.co.uk/news/magazine-16001247 (accessed 12 April 2012).

40 *Report of the International Commission of Inquiry to investigate all alleged violations of international human rights law in the Libyan Arab Jamahiriya*, (UN Human Rights Council: 1 June 2011), UN Doc. A/HRC/17/44.

41 Ian Black, 'Libyan woman is brutally silenced after accusing Gaddafi's forces of rape', The Guardian, 26 March 2011, available at: http://www.guardian.co.uk/world/2011/mar/26/libya-woman-silenced-accusing-gaddafi-forces-rape (accessed 12 April 2012). Steven Sotloff, 'The Rape of Iman al-Obeidi: The Libyan Regime's Other Crisis', The Time, 29 March 2011, available at: http://www.time.com/time/world/article/0,8599,2062007,00.html (accessed 12 April 2012); Al-Obeidi also described her story in a number of interviews, e.g.: Nic Robertson, "Interview with Eman al-Obeidi", CNN (7 April 2011), available at: http://edition.cnn.com/video/#/video/world/2011/04/07/robertson.libya.obeidy.intv.cnn?iref=allsearch

weeks later, at the beginning of June 2011, media reported allegations of the use of rape as a weapon of war in the Libyan civil war, following the statement of Luis Moreno-Ocampo, the Chief Prosecutor of the International Criminal Court (ICC).[42]

However, the occurrence of rapes was later confirmed by the Human Rights Watch[43] and the International Commission of Inquiry[44] as well as local women's organizations working on the ground in Libya.

3.2.1. *Sexual Violence in War and International Law*

Sexual violence has been used for centuries as a weapon of war in armed conflicts beyond Libya and the Middle East. Historically, it has been considered an 'integral' part of armed conflict, a socially acceptable behaviour well within the rules of warfare and was conducted almost simultaneously with acquiring property of the defeated. The main objective behind resorting to sexual violence, and rape in particular, was not only to exercise and demonstrate power over a particular part of the society, but also to stigmatize women from that group. As a result, these wartime acts will affect the entire life of the victim, but also will have a destructive impact on her community, becoming effectively a weapon not only cheaper than bullets, but also causing a severe, irreversible and life-long harm. As Margot Wallström, the UN Special Representative on Sexual Violence in Conflict, notes: 'armed groups continue to use rape as a weapon of war because it is cheaper, more destructive and easier to get away with than other methods of warfare'.[45]

(accessed 12 April 2012), Jonathan Miller, "Eman al-Obeidi: in her own words", Channel 4 (20 May 2011), available at: http://www.channel4.com/news/eman-al-obeidi-in-her-own-words (accessed 12 April 2012).

[42] BBC News, 'Libya: Gaddafi investigated over use of rape as weapon', 8 June 2011, available at: http://www.bbc.co.uk/news/world-africa-13705854 (accessed 12 April 2012).

[43] 'Human Rights Watch documented 10 cases of apparent gang rape and sexual assault of men and women by Gaddafi forces during the conflict, including of detainees in custody. The extent of sexual violence during the conflict remains unknown, due in part to the stigma surrounding rape in Libya and the dangers that survivors may face when they publicize such crimes', in: Human Rights Watch, *World Report 2012: Libya*, (Human Rights Watch: New York, January 2012), available at: http://www.hrw.org/sites/default/files/related_material/libya_2012.pdf (accessed 12 April 2012).

[44] *Report of the International Commission of Inquiry to investigate all alleged violations of international human rights law in the Libyan Arab Jamahiriya*, (Human Rights Council: 1 June 2011), UN Doc. A/HRC/17/44, pp. 71–74.

[45] Margot Wallström, UN Secretary-General's Special Representative on Sexual Violence in Conflict, Statement made in speech on 10 June 2011. Available from: http://www.unmultimedia.org/radio/english/2011/06/political-leaders-challenged-to-pass-laws-to-end-violence-against-women/ (00:16–00:23) (accessed 10 April 2012).

However, the gravity of rape as a weapon of war has only relatively recently received the desired attention of international law, following the conflicts in Rwanda and in Yugoslavia, which were marked by an extremely high prevalence of sexual violence. These tragic events led to the first international prosecution of rape by the International Criminal Tribunal for Rwanda in 1998 in *Akayesu*[46] and gave foundations to further jurisprudence relating to gender-based crimes committed in armed conflict. Since then, there has been growing attention paid to gender violence on the international level (especially United Nations Security Council Resolutions 1325[47] and 1820),[48] crimes of sexual violence have been incorporated into statutes of International Criminal Tribunals and the International Criminal Court (ICC) and, finally, crimes of sexual violence committed in war were prosecuted on international level.

Currently rape in war has been internationally recognized as amounting to a war crime,[49] a crime against humanity,[50] genocide[51] and torture.[52]

In the context of a non-international armed conflict, in which Libya was involved from 17 February 2011, the use of rape and sexual violence is explicitly prohibited both under human rights law (which continues to apply during armed conflict) and international humanitarian law (*lex specialis*, which applies to armed conflicts of both international and non-international character).

Article 4(2)(e) of the Additional Protocol II to the Geneva Conventions[53] prohibits

[46] *Akayesu* Judgement; ICTR-96-4-T, 2 September 1998; *Akayesu* has been widely acknowledged for its landmark contributions to international law. It was not only the first judgement prosecuting rape as a crime against humanity, but also the first international conviction for genocide in which rape and sexual violence have been recognized as constitutive acts of genocide. The judgement also held rape as a crime amounting to torture and highlighted the failure to charge it as war crimes.

[47] UNSC Resolution 1325 (2000), 31 October 2000, S/RES/1325 (2000).

[48] UNSC Resolution 1820 (2008), 19 June 2008, S/RES/1820 (2008).

[49] Article 8 (2)(e)(6) Rome Statute of the International Criminal Court 1998, U.N. Doc. A/CONF.183/9* (ICC Statute).

[50] Article 7 (g) ICC statute 1998.

[51] *Akayesu* Judgement; ICTR-96-4-T, 2 September 1998, para. 731–732 Article 6 (b)–(d) ICC Statute 1998.

[52] *Akayesu* Judgement; ICTR-96-4-T, 2 September 1998, para. 687, 690; *Čelebići* Trial Judgement, IT-96-21-T; (16 November 1998), para. 941.

[53] Protocol Additional to the Geneva Conventions of 12 August 1949, and Relating to the Protection of Victims of Non-International Armed Conflicts (Additional Protocol II), 1125 UNTS 609 (Libyan Arab Jamahiriya has been a party to the four Geneva Conventions of 1949 since 22 May 1956 and to Additional Protocols I &II since 7 June 1978).

> *Outrages upon personal dignity, in particular humiliating and degrading treatment, rape, enforced prostitution and any form of indecent assault.*

In addition, common Article 3 to the four Geneva Conventions of 1949 prohibits in situation of non-international armed conflict:

a) *Violence to life and person, in particular murder of all kinds, mutilation, cruel treatment and torture, (...)*
c) *outrages upon personal dignity, in particular humiliating and degrading treatment.*

Furthermore, in African context, special protection of women during armed conflict is foreseen in the Article 11 of the Protocol Additional to the African Charter Human and Peoples' Rights, the main human rights instrument in Africa:

1. *States Parties undertake to respect and ensure respect for the rules of international humanitarian law applicable in armed conflict situations, which affect the population, particularly women.*
2. *States Parties shall, in accordance with the obligations incumbent upon them under international humanitarian law, protect civilians including women, irrespective of the population to which they belong, in the event of armed conflict.*[54]

3.2.2. *The Response to Sexual Violence in Libya*

The occurrence of rape prompts the duty of the State under international[55] and regional human rights instruments[56] to independently investigate the alleged crimes, but also to provide victims with an effective remedy and reparations for the harm suffered. The State is further obliged to take preventive steps to stop the ongoing human rights violations as well as to prevent their reoccurrence in the future. As the example of al-Obeidi shows, the reports of gang rape allegedly committed by the pro-Gaddafi militiamen did not meet the desired State response.

However, when discussing sexual violence in the context of the Libyan civil war, one may not ignore a socio-cultural dimension of alleged crimes.

[54] Protocol to the African Charter on Human and Peoples' Rights on the Rights of Women in Africa (adopted by the 2nd Ordinary Session of the Assembly of the Union, Maputo, 11 July 2003), (Maputo Protocol), Article 11.
[55] Article 2(3) ICCPR.
[56] Article 4 Maputo Protocol 2003.

In Libya's conservative culture, rape is regarded as a matter of profound shame, not only for a victim, but also her entire family. It remains a taboo, a subject that, although critical, is not to be mentioned in public and often not even in the private sphere. These conditions have a significant impact on the process of investigation into sexual violence as due to these constraints the victims are very reluctant to come forward with their testimony. Furthermore, the inadequate laws and services (discussed in 2.1.3. and 2.1.4. above) as well as the social stigma associated with rape, leave victims of sexual violence without an effective remedy and deter women from reporting the events of such violence.

The case of al-Obeidi also demonstrates the conservative attitude of the state authorities as well as the Libyan society at large to the problem of sexual violence against women. Al-Obeidi's account of rape was immediately undermined: she was called a drunk, a prostitute and even a traitor. Her statement was summarized by the Libyan authorities as an act of insanity and intoxication.[57] The determination of pro-Gaddafi forces to restrain al-Obeidi and, by violating her freedom of expression, to silence her voice is also telling.

Surprisingly, the socio-cultural dimension of rape within the Libyan context was also ignored by some of the international commentators. Although the ICC chief prosecutor, Luis Moreno-Ocampo, publicly stated that there is evidence that Gaddafi ordered the rape of hundreds of women as a weapon against rebel forces, many suggest that allegations of rapes by pro-Gaddafi forces are a 'myth' and point out the lack of sufficient amount of evidence of rape victims to support such claim. In June 2011, the UN human rights investigator into the situation in Libya, Cherif Bassiouni, referred to rape allegations as a part of a 'massive hysteria'.[58] This statement, in addition to rather insensitive choice of language, can be seen as downplaying the rape allegations and diminishing the credibility of the victims. Furthermore, it also suggests that the main problem was the use of such claims to spread the fear of atrocities, rather than the commission of the atrocities, which grossly violate women's human rights. Margot Wallström's statement on sexual violence in Libya aptly encapsulates the

[57] Kelly Askin, 'When rape is a tool of war', CNN 7 April 2011, available at: http://edition.cnn.com/2011/OPINION/04/06/askin.libya.rape.war/index.html (accessed 12 April 2012).

[58] Stephanie Nebehay, 'Libyan envoy accuses rebels and NATO of war crimes', Reuters, 9 June 2011, available at: http://www.reuters.com/article/2011/06/09/us-libya-un-rights-idUSTRE7582 9J20110609 (accessed 12 April 2012); "Libya rape claims 'hysteria'—UN Human Rights Investigator Says", The Tripoli Post, 10 June 2011, available at: http://www.tripolipost.com/articledetail.asp?c=1&i=6155 (accessed 12 April 2012).

very core of the problem: "If we allow the lack of hard data to justify inaction, it will always be too late".[59]

Although there has been a considerable silence regarding the use of sexual violence during the Libyan conflict after June 2011, both in the media and within international organizations and agencies, the problem has certainly not disappeared. Furthermore, the independent investigations into alleged crimes of sexual violence as well as the question of accountability for these human rights abuses and reparations for victims are one of the main challenges yet to be addressed in the post-conflict, liberated Libya.

4. Women's Rights in the Aftermath of the Revolution

The successful liberation of Libya from Gaddafi's rule presents a great opportunity, yet also a great challenge, for securing women's rights in post-conflict reconstruction. However, one may wonder, why should women's rights should be at the forefront of the important tasks of (re)building the country, especially when there are a range of other priorities lying ahead in the process of transition from the conflict.

4.1. *Importance of Women's Rights in Post-Conflict Reconstruction*

International law recognized the need for the inclusion of women and their active participation in the peace processes as well as in post-conflict reconstruction. Security Council Resolution 1325 (2000)[60] on women, peace and security emphasizes the important role of women in peace-building processes calling for their equal participation in decision-making processes on national, regional and international levels. Furthermore, the Resolution calls for a 'full implementation of international human rights law and international humanitarian law, which protect women's rights during and <u>after</u> (emphasis added) armed conflict'. It also calls upon States to 'adopt a gender perspective', including with reference to 'the special needs of women and girls during repatriation and resettlement and for

[59] Statement by UN Special Representative of the Secretary-General on Sexual Violence in Conflict Margot Wallström, "Concern Over Sexual Violence in Libya" (20 April 2011), available at: http://www.stoprapenow.org/uploads/files/Statement_by_Special_Representative_of_the_Secretary.pdf (accessed 12 April 2012).

[60] UNSC Resolution 1325 (2000), 31 October 2000, S/RES/1325 (2000); However, UNSCR 1325 was not adopted under UN Charter chapter VII and therefore is not formally binding.

rehabilitation, reintegration and post-conflict reconstruction.' However, if women are to be truly involved in the implementation of UNSCR 1325 and actively participate in the process of post-conflict reconstruction, including post-conflict justice mechanisms, more attention must be paid to the support available to women in the process of transition. One area, through which this assistance may be realized is through the securing of women's rights and gender equality post-conflict.

Delivery of women's economic, social and political rights strengthens the durability of the peace process as well as facilitates the real chance for women's participation in democratic post-conflict processes. Therefore, it is necessary that a gender perspective is adopted and applied throughout all stages of the transition from conflict and post-conflict reconstruction. Otherwise, as Chinkin notes, 'the failure to address economic and social rights undermines the sought-after stability and human security post-conflict (including food, health, gender and physical security), which in turn lessens the ability or willingness of victims and witnesses to participate in the formal processes of post-conflict justice'.[61]

4.2. *Women's Rights in Post-Conflict Libya*

The new Libyan government faces a key challenge of addressing and delivering women's rights in the process of transition into a democratic and inclusive state. The importance of women's participation in the process of liberating Libya from Gaddafi's rule is unquestionable. Nonetheless, the question remains as to the legal status of their rights as well as to the role they are going to play in the new post-conflict government.

4.2.1. *Participation in Political and Decision-Making Process*

Securing women's rights in any post-conflict setting is a challenging and complex process, which requires active engagement of its main beneficiaries—the women themselves. Therefore, it is absolutely necessary to engage women in active participation in democratic and socio-political processes during and beyond the transitional period, to ensure that all decisions made incorporate a gender perspective and are representative of the views of all citizens.

[61] Christine Chinkin, "The Protection of Economic, Social and Cultural Rights Post-Conflict", paper series commissioned by the Office of the High Commissioner for Human Rights (2009), p. 4, available at: http://www2.ohchr.org/english/issues/women/docs/Paper_Protection_ESCR.pdf (accessed 12 April 2012).

In the immediate aftermath of the Revolution, the National Transitional Council (NTC), whose legitimacy becomes increasingly recognized by the international community, made promising statements giving assurances that women's rights will not be marginalized in the new political and legal system in Libya. Nevertheless, since then, the NTC have made decisions, which counteract efforts towards achieving inclusive and gender equal Libya.

Firstly, the representation of women in the government structure remains limited. The 28 person cabinet appointed by the NTC in November 2011 included only two women: Dr. Fatima Hamroush (Minster of Health) and Mabrouka Sherif (Minister of Social Affairs). The chance for ensuring women's representation was further significantly reduced by the abandonment of fixed quota for women in the new Electoral Law, announced in January 2011. The initial 10 % quota was dropped in a very brief decision by the Electoral Commission, which, as argued by a number of women's rights groups, lacked transparency especially at final stages of decision making (swift modification of laws and ratification) and 'left women at even greater risk of exclusion'.[62]

Fixed election quotas are commonly used in post-conflict elections (e.g. in Iraq and in Afghanistan) in order to ensure the participation of women in the political process. They also play an essential role in promoting gender equality by supporting an electoral process, where (male) gender of the representative is not the major decisive factor. As such, quotas can act as temporary special measures aimed at accelerating the realization of de facto equality between men and women, as provided by Article 4(1) CEDAW 1979,[63] and practically enable women to enter into the political governance and decision-making process. As Alaa Murabit, the founder of Voice of Libyan Women (VLW) observes, women often lack financial resources for political campaign or do not have established social networks to become elected. In addition, they have more societal and familial responsibilities than men, not to mention cultural obstacles, which create an impediment to women's political participation and

---

[62] "The drafting team of eight should have included women representatives and the whole process been more transparent." Statement made by Sara Maziq, founder of Women4Libya in: 'Women 4 Libya Say Draft Election Law Risks Failing Libyan Women', The Tripoli Post, 20 January 2012, available at: http://www.tripolipost.com/articledetail.asp?c=1&i=7711 (accessed 12 April 2012).

[63] Adoption of temporary special measures under Article 4(1) CEDAW 1979 was also recommended in the 2009 CEDAW Committee Concluding Observations on Libyan Arab Jamahiriya, para. 20.

representation.[64] The decision on the rejection of the fixed quota is therefore even more alarming, especially in the context of the upcoming elections to the Constitutional Assembly—a body responsible for drafting the new Libyan Constitution. It is crucial for women to be strongly represented in this process in order to secure women's rights and protection from any future possibility of their abuse.

4.2.2. *Legal and Constitutional Reform*

The drafting of the new constitution is a crucial step in building the post-conflict legal system in Libya. So far, this process has been marked by major obstacles, which prevent inclusiveness of women and their political participation. These include the reduction of the fixed quota in the new Electoral Law, the lack of other measures capable of promoting equal participation of women and the Draft Constitutional Charter,[65] which in its current form does not include any provisions expressly prohibiting discrimination against women.

It is undoubtedly important that the shortcomings of the previous legal system as well as the discriminatory nature of many laws are repealed and replaced with provisions which do not violate women's rights. However, the process of legal reform in Libya is concerned not only with the reform of laws, which were formed under Gaddafi's rule (discussed in further detail above, 2.1.) but also provisions of international law and international human rights law in particular.

The new government bears the responsibility for the thorough implementation of Libya's obligations under international law. One may hope that the pursuit of women's rights and gender equality will include the cancellation of reservations entered by Gaddafi's government to international instruments, in particular Articles 2 and 16 CEDAW 1979. Nevertheless, the real challenge is not in the ratification of international instruments, but in their implementation. As the example of the past four decades in Libya show, the mere acknowledgement of the rules of international human rights law in itself does not guarantee equality, non-discrimination and protection from human rights abuses. Education about women's rights

---

64 Alaa Murabit, 'Why are we not involved?', interview for The Institute of Inclusive Security, 12 March 2012, available at: http://www.youtube.com/watch?v=fZJ1F1ZjLws (accessed 12 April 2012).

65 *Draft Constitutional Charter for the Transitional Stage* [Libya], September 2011, available at: http://www.unhcr.org/refworld/docid/4e80475b2.html (accessed 12 April 2012); Article 6 of the Draft Charter prohibits discrimination based on religion, belief, race, language, wealth, kinship, political opinions or social status.

and gender plays a crucial role in advancement of their rights. Particularly in the aftermath of conflict, building awareness of rights and their extent helps to create a process, through which women's participation can be encouraged and the sense of citizenship may be strengthened.

Nonetheless, the issue of legal reforms raises a basic, yet vital question, namely: what law is the new legal system going to be built on and what impact is it going to have on women's rights?

In the liberation speech on 23 October 2011, Moustafa Abdel Jalil indicated that the future Libyan legal system will be based on Shari'a, citing polygamy and divorce as examples of areas where the law will remain the same. This statement causes concern from the perspective of delivering women's rights in a post-conflict Libya. Both in the national and international context, Shari'a, or as argued by some commentators, its incorrect interpretation,[66] was a key reason behind laws and practices perpetuating discrimination of women and violation of their human rights. It was also perceived as contradictory to some of the key provisions of international human rights, particularly those prohibiting discrimination of women in all areas of the law.[67]

Although the aim of this chapter is not to discuss the issue of the (im)possibility of securing women's rights in the context of Shari'a, it is nevertheless important to recognize the existence of a legal system based on religious laws as a potential challenge to securing such rights.

4.2.3. *Accountability for Human Rights Violations and Post-Conflict Justice*

The process of post-conflict transition must be accompanied by the transparency and accountability for past human rights violations, especially those committed during armed conflict. It is important that a gender perspective is applied throughout this process and that violations of women's rights are not marginalized or silenced.[68]

In post-conflict Libya, the allegations of wartime acts of sexual violence against women require thorough and independent investigation and

[66] However, Darwish argues that liberty and equality of women in the Middle East, especially following the events of the Arab Spring, is dependent upon defeating Shari'a. Nonie Darwish, "Will the Arab Spring Usher In a Feminist Movement?," in *The Devil We Don't Know. The Dark Side of the Revolutions in the Middle East*, ed. Nonie Darwish (Wiley: New Jersey, 2012).

[67] E.g. Art. 2 CEDAW 1979, to which Libya entered reservations.

[68] Security Council Resolution 1820 (19 June 2008) called upon States to ensure that women and girls have 'equal protection under the law and equal access to justice'.

prosecution of all those responsible for these acts in either international or national criminal courts. For the reasons discussed in 3.2.2. (above), the difficulties faced by female victims in seeking post-conflict justice must be recognized and effectively addressed by the responsible authorities.[69] The systems of protection of victims and adequate assistance is of particular importance, especially in the light of conservative Libyan culture, which traditionally stigmatizes victims of gender-based violence and fails to protect them from their perpetrators.[70] Furthermore, States are required to exercise due diligence to prevent, investigate, prosecute and punish gender-based violence against women that occurs post-conflict.[71]

However, the quest for justice for wartime gender crimes needs to be accompanied by a system of reparations for human rights violations suffered. It is important that reparations are gender-just and that women's right to effective remedy is not impeded by any traditional or socio-cultural obstacles.[72]

5. Conclusions

Since the very beginning of the Libyan Revolution, women played a crucial role, soon becoming the defining feature of the liberation, but also of the Arab Spring. (S)heros in the Revolution, women soon found themselves facing, unsurprisingly, yet another battle: a battle for empowerment, security and full enjoyment of their rights in the aftermath. Although women gained their voice during the Revolution, the obstacles to their greater political participation and long-term, sustainable gender equality

[69] The NTC failed to respond to the petition handed in by women participating in the silent march in Tripoli on 26 November 2011 demanding justice and support for victims of wartime rape. Women, with their mouths covered with tape, marched to the office of the Prime Minister, Abdurrahim El-Kib. Organizers handed him a letter calling for tougher sentences for those who commit rape as well as logistical and financial support for NGOs who provide assistance to victims. No such measures have so far been taken. (International Federation for Human Rights (FIDH), 'Women and the Arab Spring: Libya', available at: http://arabwomenspring.fidh.net/index.php?title=Libya (accessed 12 April 2012)).

[70] Rape victims are often forced to marry their rapist.

[71] Christine Chinkin, "The Protection of Economic, Social and Cultural Rights Post-Conflict", paper series commissioned by the Office of the High Commissioner for Human Rights (2009), p. 24.

[72] For further discussion see: Valerie Couillard, The Nairobi Declaration: Redefining Reparation for Women Victims of Sexual Violence, *International Journal of Transitional Justice* 1 (3) (2007): 444–453.

set by the new government, may prevent their voice from being heard in post-conflict Libya. The challenge therefore remains for the new Libyan government, and Libyan women in particular, to act upon securing and executing their rights in the aftermath of the Revolution. Though without women's rights secured and delivered, this Revolution is not finished.

CHAPTER SEVEN

SECURITY COUNCIL RESOLUTION 1973: A NEW INTERPRETATION OF THE NOTION OF PROTECTION OF CIVILIANS?

Mohamed A. E. Youssef*

1. Introduction

From the time Libyans took their turn, in the Arab Spring, to take to the streets and demand their political freedom and human rights, the international community burnt with curiosity about the fate of a leader who has been in absolute power for over 40 years. Confrontations started between a newly born "National Transitional Council" and Libyan forces. Gaddafi made ferocious statements against the opposition, with no indication of mercy, while the National Transitional Council decided to resist this intimidation and remained on the battlefield. The Security Council decided to intervene and implement a No-Fly Zone under Resolution 1973.[1] It was important not to deny the possibility "that outside assistance can do more harm than good or can become entangled in a local political economy that is built on structures of interest that favor war."[2]

Resolution 1973 was the first in which reference to the "Responsibility to Protect" served as a legal foundation for military intervention. It set precedence in international law and practice that the safety of civilians from grave human rights violations is a superior objective to state sovereignty. This article focuses on the process that the Security Council undertook in order to use the notion "protection of civilians." It also underlines the effects of making use of such terms. The situation in Libya did not fall under the traditional heads of conflict such as historical claims, ethnic cleansing or secession. Therefore it was not an easy task to legitimize intervention. Resolution 1973 implicitly recognized the Libyans'

* Licence en Droit, Université Paris 1—Panthéon Sorbonne; LLM in International Law, University of Dundee.

[1] UN Security Council, *Security Council resolution 1973 (2011) [on the situation in the Libyan Arab Jamahiriya]*, 17 March 2011, S/RES/1973(2011).

[2] Thomas G. Weiss, *Military-civilian interactions: humanitarian crises and the responsibility to protect*, 2nd edn. (Oxford: Rowman & Littlefield Publishers, Inc., 2005), 200.

self-determination without using the term "self-determination." Instead, the wording of the Resolution did not touch upon the political affiliation of the National Transitional Council and treated them as innocent civilians who deserved to be treated peacefully regardless of their demands.

This chapter questions whether it was legitimate of the Security Council to treat the NTC as a civilian group rather than an armed opposition group. It also draws attention to the consequences of not qualifying the situation in Libya as an internal armed conflict, unlike previous military interventions in non-international armed conflicts. The core critique of Resolution 1973 lies in the fact that the Security Council took two self-contradictory positions; on one hand it protected civilians in accordance with its general purposes under the UN Charter and its "responsibility to protect" and on the other it offered protection to those groups who might, at other times or by other people, be classified as an armed opposition group.

The remainder of this chapter is organized as follows: Section 2 discusses the issue of the Security Council's Global Governance. It studies the question of legitimacy as a political concept, distinguished from the principle of legality. The political accountability of the Security Council will then be analyzed by mainly making reference to the principle of transparency and the way in which the Security Council handled the advice given by the African Union and the International Crisis Group.

Section 3 establishes the criteria for qualifying the need for protecting civilians. These criteria will be drawn from previous and current authoritative guidelines. The first question that will be raised is *what* the "civilians" need to be protected from. This will lead to the importance of the careful assessment of the situation in Libya before taking the step of military intervention.

Section 4 studies the requirements for qualifying the Libyan situation as an internal armed conflict. Although it is difficult to find legally binding criteria, the Security Council had a resourceful authority of previous cases and of international texts and customs. Special focus will be put on the report of the International Commission of Inquiry on the situation of Human Rights in Libya.

Section 5 targets the definition of "civilians." First, it will explore how subjective this definition could be depending on who is making it, i.e. Gaddafi as opposed to the Security Council. The principle of distinction between a civilian and a combatant will then be discussed.

Section 6 follows Section 5 in defining an "armed opposition group." Authority will be taken from several important texts as well as jurisprudence from the International Criminal Tribunal for the Former Yugoslavia and the International Criminal Tribunal for Rwanda.

Section 7 raises the importance of ensuring the accountability of the NTC. It underlines the fact that Resolution 1973 provided impunity for the NTC from being held responsible for violations of rules and customs of war applicable on internal conflicts.

Finally, Section 8 explores the option that the Security Council had of engaging in a pro-democratic intervention and explicitly taking the side of the NTC. Several previous examples will be briefly mentioned and compared to the situation in Libya.

2. The Security Council's Global Governance

In tackling the first question considered herein, i.e. the Security Council's global governance, first, a distinction will be made between legality and legitimacy, highlighting the importance of legitimacy even when legality is established. The principle of political accountability will then be underlined, with reference to the SC's transparency while handling the situation in Libya.

Resolution 1973 was the Security Council's (SC) first step towards implementing the "responsibility to protect." The reasoning that the drafters employed certainly resulted in questions around the Security Council's global governance and the decision making process that led to authorizing the No-Fly Zone on Libya.

As the core question of this chapter is the definition of "civilians" and what distinguishes them from an armed opposition group, references will often be made to this distinction in the context of global governance.

2.1. *Legality vs. Legitimacy*

It is undeniable that violations of human rights and severe aggression against innocent civilians is an unacceptable act and that the perpetrator should not benefit from any impunity. However, one must note that a certain balance is required in order to warrant that military intervention responds to such violations as appropriately as possible, and that the intention is indeed the protection of civilians. If this balance is not established closely, it opens a door for claims that that intervention breaches the sovereignty of the concerned state, or is a tool to serve individual interests, or is viewed as adding fuel to the fire.

The Middle East has known the experience of Egypt where, despite grave violations of human rights and the direct killing of peaceful protesters, the legal process is being used to punish the alleged perpetrators, including Hosni Mubarak, without any foreign intervention. And yet, in

Libya, Resolution 1973 was prompt to such an extent that it gave no time for the so-called civilians to express their exact demands. It also left no chance for the Libyan nation to prepare itself for the consequences of a political vacuum and choose the potential replacement.

The resolution cannot be questioned on the basis of legality, as adoption without a veto is enough to grant the resolution standing in international law. However a distinction must be made between legality and legitimacy; after all, "[a] body has political legitimacy when its decisions are justified by moral and other socially embedded beliefs about the end to which it exercises power, and about the processes through which its power is exercised."[3]

It is certain that the essence of the legitimacy of the SC's resolution is manifested in the long-term goal of the resolution. But the drafters often underestimate the wide difference between long and short-term peace. The side effects of authorizing military action may well indeed, as obvious with the Libyan experience, lead to a short-term success, i.e. leading to Gaddafi's elimination and the end of his tyranny. But one cannot automatically claim that Resolution 1973 aimed for the long term protection of civilians. It is important to see the large difference between dissolving a dictatorial regime *per se* and guaranteeing the protection of civilians *a posteriori*.

> The haunting question (...) is whether intervention that tries to combine both the short-term and long-term goals of rescuing victims from starvation and lawlessness, and restoring legitimate authority, is always doomed to end in a humiliating exit.[4]

For this reason, the decision making process that was employed by the Security Council deserves to be put under the radar. Has Resolution 1973 provided comfort for the Libyan "civilians" that their future will be protected? The SC's political accountability is the most appropriate route to answer this question.

2.2. *Political Accountability*

The most comprehensive definition of political accountability is the combination between transparency, independent reporting, evaluation

[3] Dominik Zaum, "The Authority of International Administrations in International Society," *Review of International Studies* 32 (3) (July 2006), 457.

[4] Sebastian von *Einsiedel and David M. Malone*, "Peace and Democracy for Haiti: A UN Mission Impossible?" *International Relations* 20 (2) (Spring 2006), 153–74.

mechanisms, financial review and broader rights of participation.[5] Due to restrictions of space and relevance, the main focus will be on transparency although some reference will be made to the other elements.

The main concern around the SC's transparency was its interpretation of the notion of "protection of civilians". The most important critique worth mentioning is how the situation in Libya was assessed by the SC. There are several legal steps that the SC avoided in the process of adopting Resolution 1973. Once again, this only creates loopholes in the SC's legitimacy not legality, since the following criteria are not directly binding upon the Security Council.

The Security Council did not entirely follow the instructions provided by Article 42 of the UN Charter. Article 42 was supposed to be implemented in a chronological order, after the failure of non-military action, i.e. Article 41 under Resolution 1970. As worded in the UN Charter: "[s]hould the Security Council consider that measures provided for in Article 41 would be inadequate or have proved to be inadequate..."[6] military action may then be taken. It is very clear, that military action is not an automatic step. And even if the inadequacy of article 41 was not particularly proven, it would have served the Security Council's transparency to at least state the reasons behind the failure of the measures adopted under Article 41.

It is true that the there is no explicit rule forcing the Security Council to make such a statement, but it would have certainly increased its legitimacy, as a response to the "somewhat cautious argument that the Resolution was not properly thought through."[7]

The reality of the situation in Libya was only shallowly discussed in the writing of the Resolution and this puts question marks around a resolution that claims to protect civilians without having much knowledge about their status and the situation in which they were involved. Moreover, the nature of the conflict between the "civilians" and the government was not mentioned at all. Similarly, the details of the negotiations with Gaddafi were not shared with any clarity. Gaddafi was portrayed as most uncooperative, but the offers that he refused were not made public and the mandate of the Special Envoy to Libya was vague and with no

---

5 Kristen E. Boon, "New Directions in Responsibility: Assessing the International Law Commission's Draft Articles on the Responsibility of International Organisations," *The Yale Journal of International Law Online* 37 (Spring 2011), at: http://www.yjil.org/docs/pub/o-37-boon-new-directions-in-responsibility.pdf (Last visited: 10 April 2012).

6 United Nations, *Charter of the United Nations*, 24 October 1945, 1 UNTS XVI, Article 42.

7 Jason Hadden, "Flying under the radar?" NLJ 161 (7459) (2011): 454–455.

precise aim. The Secretary-General merely stated that the role of Adbdul Ilah Khatib, who was appointed as envoy, was to "undertake broad consultations with Libyan authorities on the immediate humanitarian, political and security situation."[8]

These considerations raise doubts about the impartiality of the investigations that led to concluding that military intervention was the most suitable option in the Libyan situation. Besides, it is worth mentioning that the SC had taken sides against Gaddafi from the very first moments of the conflict without admitting it through the Resolution. One was then left with the impression that the SC anticipated almost automatically that there was no hope in seriously negotiating with Gaddafi, so logically the talks were a matter of courtesy, not aiming to genuinely solving the conflict. Hence, the Special Envoy's 'talks' with Gaddafi were doomed to be a failure before he even arrived in Libya.

3. Criteria for Establishing the Need for Protection

3.1. *What to Protect the Civilians From?*

The basis of deciding to "protect the civilians" in Libya was unclear especially when Resolution 1973 is compared with other Security Council's Resolutions when "all necessary measures" were authorized. Examples are *inter alia*, Haiti, East Timor and Kosovo.

In Haiti, besides the "systematic violations of civil liberties, the desperate plight of Haitian refugees,"[9] actions that were taken into consideration before the intervention were also "the recent expulsion of the staff of the International Civilian Mission (MICIVIH), which was condemned in its Presidential statement of 12 July 1994 (S/PRST/1994/32)."[10] Furthermore, the military action was justified by "... the continuing disregard of [Governors Island and the New York pact] agreements by the illegal de facto regime, and the regime's refusal to cooperate with efforts by the United

[8] UN News Service, UN envoy expected in Libya next week to discuss humanitarian, political issues http://www.un.org/apps/news/story.asp?Cr=libya&Cr1=&NewsID=37744 Last visited: 10 April 2012.

[9] Resolution 940 (1994) Adopted by the Security Council at its 3413th meeting, on 31 July 1994.

[10] Resolution 940 (1994).

Nations and the Organization of American States (OAS) to bring about their implementation."[11]

In East Timor, Indonesia had made grave violations of the May agreements with Portugal on 5 May 1999[12] by opening fire on 2000 East-Timorese and deporting 200,000 to refugee camps following the vote for East-Timor's independence. The UN Mission in East Timor was also in charge of the supervision of the voting.

In the former Yugoslavia, the NATO air strikes, which the Security Council did not oppose, were a reaction to grave violations of the General Framework Agreement for Peace in Bosnia and Herzegovina (Dayton Agreements). The Serb and Bosnian Serb forces had committed crimes of ethnic cleansing, used rape and torture as a war weapon.[13]

Resolutions in all these examples showed what the perpetrators concretely violated. Hence the scope of the protection of civilians was determined in context. The demands to the perpetrators were precise and therefore the violations were clear. This is not to say that systematic violations of human rights are not a breach of international law, but further efforts were needed in order to concretely establish legal foundations of a less vague nature, and hence make sure the SC knows exactly what it is protecting the civilians from. In Resolution 1973, it was very well phrased that the "systematic attacks currently taking place in the Libyan Arab Jamahiriya against the civilian population may amount to crimes against humanity". One is to understand, from this wording, that the Resolution authorized intervention against systematic attacks rather than well established crimes against humanity.

For crimes against humanity to be established, further detailed assessment of the situation in Libya is a must.

3.2. *A Need for Further Assessment of the Situation in Libya*

The Security Council was called upon by several authoritative entities to improve its knowledge of the Libyan situation and the nature of the conflict in order to ensure the efficiency of the protection of civilians.

---

11 Resolution 940 (1994). See also Vaughan Lowe et al., *The United Nations Security Council and war: the evolution of thought and practice since 1945* (Oxford: Oxford University Press, 2008), 554.

12 Agreement between the Republic of Indonesia and the Portuguese Republic on the question of East Timor, New York, 5 May 1999. At: http://www.un.int/portugal/acordos.htm (Last visited: 10 April 2012).

13 Weiss, *Military-civilian interactions*, 82.

3.2.1. *The African Union*

The African Union's Peace and Security Council decided to send an *ad hoc* High Level Committee, which arguably increased the chances of peacefully settling the dispute, or at least reaching a temporary ceasefire until an agreement could be reached between Gaddafi and the NTC as two warring camps. Despite the fact that Resolution 1973 "noted" the African Union's PSC's decision, the appointed Heads of States were rejected authority to fly to Libya.[14] This closed a vital chance to explore the demands of Gaddafi and the NTC but also measure their willingness to cooperate.

3.2.2. *International Crisis Group*

The International Crisis Group's call was similar to that of the African Union's Peace and Security Council:

> A complete ceasefire to be followed by negotiations to secure a transition to a post-Qaddafi, legitimate and representative government should be the immediate objectives of the international community's approach to the Libyan crisis.[15]

This recommendation suggested that, for an effective ceasefire to be implemented, all parties should have been negotiated with, and *compromise* should have been expected from both sides. It is certain that insisting on demanding that Gaddafi alone should stop the violence without putting the pressure on the NTC implied that the SC considered Gaddafi to be the only one involved in the fighting, which most certainly did not reflect the facts on the ground. This was crystal clear from the report of the International Commission of Inquiry which will be studied below.

The essence of the demands put forward by the African Union and the International Crisis Group was to recognize the NTC at the other end of the negotiating table and not consider them as civilians. This meant that the situation should have been qualified as an internal armed conflict.

---

[14] Report of the Chairperson of the commission on the Activities of the AU High Level *Ad Hoc* Committee on the situation in Libya, PSC/PR/2 (CCLXXV) para. 16.

[15] A Ceasefire and Negotiations the Right Way to Resolve the Libya Crisis 10 March 2011, http://www.crisisgroup.org/en/publication-type/media-releases/2011/%D9%90a-ceasefire-and-negotiations-the-right-way-to-resolve-the-libya-crisis-%20.aspx Last visited: 10 April 2012.

4. The Qualification of an Internal Armed Conflict

There are several applicable criteria before a situation is qualified as an internal armed conflict. First of all, a distinction should be made between a civilian and combatant. Then there are other criteria that distinguish a combatant from a member of a group of saboteurs and a combatant in an organized opposition group. Before analyzing these two steps, it is important to underline the importance of determining the presence of an internal armed conflict.

4.1. *The Importance of Determining the Presence of an Internal Armed Conflict*

The reason why it was important to recognize the status of the NTC as an armed opposition group is to ensure the respect for international law by all sides at war, and hence truly guarantee the protection of civilians that are not in battle, and the protection of combatants *hors de combat*, as well as to ensure the implementation of the rule of proportionality.

The Report of the High Commissioner on the situation of Human Rights in the Libyan Arab Jamahiriya has shown that it was not only a case of internal armed conflict but it also contained violations of human rights by all the sides involved in the conflict.

4.2. *The Report of the International Commission of Inquiry*

The UN Human rights Council, distancing itself from the political implications of the situation in Libya, announced the three high-level experts to the independent International Commission of Inquiry.[16]

It has not been specified what the authority of this Commission was *vis-à-vis* the Security Council's drafting of the resolutions; in fact, it has not been mentioned in either one of the two Resolutions.

It is however important to draw attention to the outcome of the Report of the High Commissioner on the situation of Human rights in the Libyan

[16] Report of the High Commissioner under Human Rights Council resolution S-15/1, A/HRC/17/45, 7 June 2011. At: http://www2.ohchr.org/english/bodies/hrcouncil/docs/17session/A.HRC.17.45_AUV.pdf (Last visited: 10 April 2012). They were the Egyptian jurist Cherif Bassiouni, the Jordanian/Palestinian lawyer Asma Khader, and the Canadian lawyer Philippe Kirsch.

Arab Jamahiriya.[17] It stated that "human rights violations were committed by the Government forces in Libya," but "also included allegations of violations committed by armed groups, connected with the opposition, as well as allegations of casualties caused by international forces' air strikes."[18] It is true that the report was released several months after Resolution 1973; nevertheless, the question remains valid as to why the Security Council had not taken this step before the implementation of the No-Fly Zone, and why it had not taken into consideration the possible outcomes of the International Commission's report. It is evident that the Security Council's reaction towards Libya would have been different if it had admitted that the conflict contained violations from all warring camps or, that the No-Fly zone would inevitably lead to significant human causalities. And even if the SC had found that the implementation of the No-Fly Zone was so urgent that it could not wait for the finding of the independent commission, it should have taken the Commission's findings into consideration and admitted that Resolution 1973 was not "protecting civilians" anymore.

5. The Definition of Civilians

5.1. *A Subjective Definition of Civilians*

One must admit that, *in primis*, the general rules regarding the "protection of civilians" are legitimately addressed by Resolution 1973: they "shall enjoy general protection against dangers arising from military operations."[19]

However, are the individuals who are protected by the Resolution civilians themselves? The Security Council disregarded this very important question and avoided making a distinction between a civilian and a

---

[17] Report of the High Commissioner under Human Rights Council resolution S-15/1, A/HRC/17/45, 7 June 2011.

[18] *Human Rights Council holds interactive dialogue with High Commissioner for Human Rights on Situation of Human Rights in Libya, Human Rights Council*, 10 June 2011. At: http://www.ohchr.org/en/NewsEvents/Pages/DisplayNews.aspx?NewsID=11142&LangID=E (Last visited: 10 April 2012).

See also, The Report of the High Commissioner on the situation of human rights in the Libyan Arab Jamahiriya A/HRC/19/68, 2 March 2012, para. 799.

[19] The Protocol Additional to the Geneva conventions of 12 August 1949, and Relating to the Protection of Victims of International Armed Conflicts, June 8, 1977, (1125 UNTS 3), Article 51.

combatant in the Libyan matter. This distinction is nevertheless central to the Protocol Additional to the Geneva Conventions:

> The armed forces of a Party to a conflict consist of all organized armed forces, groups and units which are under a command responsible to that Party for the conduct of its subordinates, even if that Party is represented by a government or an authority not recognized by an adverse Party.[20]

Further emphasis was placed in Article 50 of the same text, defining a civilian as "anyone who is not a member of the armed forces or of an organized group of a party to the conflict."[21] This was confirmed by, *inter alia*, the ICTY, ICTR and the Inter-American Commision.[22]

It is true that there is a thin line between a civilian and combatant; "one person's innocent civilian is another person's dangerous rebel."[23] It is however very important to spend a considerable amount of effort in making this distinction. Defining a civilian is a question that requires attention to perspective for several reasons. As worded in the Additional Protocol II to the Geneva Conventions, "civilians shall enjoy protection ... unless and for such time as they take a direct part in hostilities."[24]

For example, Gaddafi viewed all individuals that opposed the regime as rebels not 'civilians.' Gaddafi claimed that he was defending Libya's national security against an insurgent movement; he even claimed that his actions sought to protect civilians—i.e. his supporters—against the rebels. Even if he did not seem to be willing to treat them as a legitimate opposition yet, the fact that the SC considered them civilians killed all chances for Gaddafi to recognize them as an opponent.

On a controversial note, one can see air strikes by the Libyan forces as similar to the bombing of Yemeni separatist rebels by the government with the help of the Saudi regime.[25] Another example could be the air strikes on Gaza in April 2011, at which point the Arab League's call for a No-Fly Zone was met with an oblivious stance on the part of the Security

20 Article 49 (2).

21 Article 50.

22 Liesbeth Zegveld, *The Accountability of Armed Opposition Groups in International Law* (Cambridge: Cambridge University Press, 2002), 75.

23 Weiss, *Military-civilian interactions*, 200.

24 The Protocol Additional to the Geneva conventions of 12 August 1949, and Relating to the Protection of Victims of International Armed Conflicts, June 8, 1977, (1125 UNTS 3.), Article 51.

24 Article 13(3).

25 "*Yemen troops 'kill Houthi rebel leader*", BBC, 19 November 2009, at: http://news.bbc.co.uk/1/hi/world/middle_east/8368442.stm (Last visited: 10 April 2012).

Council.[26] Such provocative arguments are only a result of the vagueness and ambiguity of Resolution 1973 regarding the distinction between rebels and civilians. After all, one may argue that the so-called rebels in Yemen and the so-called Palestinian terrorists were themselves civilians that deserved protection similar to the Libyan civilians. Of course, the answer to such a note would be that such actions would not be supported because of their political affiliation. For these reasons the SC should have answered Gaddafi's claims in a direct manner. It should have drawn out, clearly and with all transparency, that the difference between for example the situation in Yemen and the Occupied Palestinian Territories and the situation in Libya is the political affiliation. The Security Council would in that case endorse the demands put forward by the armed opposition in Libya but not in Yemen or the Palestinian authorities. This would have, at least, reflected the real views that the Security Council was implementing.

In the light of the question of 'whom' to protect, the type of civilians that were considered vulnerable, as defined by the Security Council, especially in Resolutions 1264 and 1265, were women, children, refugees and internally displaced persons. This surely is confirmed by several social psychological research studies proving that the willingness to offer help increases when the victim's characteristics are defined, *inter alia*, by "gender, ethnic-group affiliation, and age."[27] Such analyses increase the questions around the reasoning of Resolution 1973 because in its drafting there was no mention of the gender, ethnicity, or age of the conflict's victims. The most evident justification is that the vulnerability of 'civilians' in Libya was directly related to their political stance and weak fighting capacity relative to the current government. What distinguished them was their political affiliation, and since this was the important difference, it should have been recognized in the Security Council's Resolutions on Libya.

There are several important principles present in the Protocol Additional to the Geneva conventions of 12 August 1949, and Relating to the Protection of Victims of International Armed Conflicts, June 8, 1977.[28] Although these additions are not binding upon the Security Council, the Protocols are an important prevention tool used to reduce the risk posed

---

[26] Ayman Samir, Sarah Mikhail et al. *"Arab League calls for no-fly zone over Gaza"*, Reuters, Cairo, Apr 10, 2011. at http://www.reuters.com/article/2011/04/10/us-palestinians-israel-arabs-idUSTRE73923020110410 (Last visited: 10 April 2012).

[27] Michael Keren & Donald Sylvan, *International intervention: sovereignty versus Responsibility* (London: Frank Cass & Co. Ltd, 2002), 47–48.

[28] The Protocol Additional to the Geneva conventions of 12 August 1949, and Relating to the Protection of Victims of International Armed Conflicts, June 8, 1977, (1125 UNTS 3).

to civilians by military intervention and also serves to narrow the focus of the action and determine, with all fairness, the innocent and vulnerable objects. Once again, these Protocols represent a part of international law and taking them into account would have had a positive effect on the Security Council's determination to truly protect civilians.

5.2. *The Principle of Distinction*

The basic rule of distinction[29] entails that

> [i]n order to ensure respect for and protection of the civilian population and civilian objects, the Parties to the conflict shall at all times distinguish between the civilian population and combatants and between civilian objects and military objectives and accordingly shall direct their operations only against military objectives.[30]

The Additional Protocol's focus was on cases of wars between two combatants. In the Libyan case, in the terms of Resolution 1973, the two combatants were NATO and their target, the Libyan army. So, technically speaking, the implementation of the Resolution was in conformity with the rule of distinction given the fact that the rebels were not military targets. However, the true implementation of the rule of distinction should have been occurred before the Resolution was drafted, with all neutrality, between an armed individual and a non-armed civilian regardless of them being part of the Libyan army or the NTC.

Legally speaking, Resolution 1973, through paragraphs 13 to 16, reconfirmed the "enforcement of the arms embargo." Of course the implementing States, i.e. NATO members, are allowed to assist each other with arms. Furthermore, paragraph 8 allows "Member States" to implement the No-Fly zone through regional or national arrangements after notifying the UN Secretary-General and the Secretary General of the Arab League. However, the Resolution did not include permission for non-state actors to implement the "all necessary measures" action in Libya.

One of the explanations of the Security Council's abstention from qualifying the situation in Libya as an internal armed conflict is the fact that it was the best way to guarantee an efficient and quick end to Gaddafi's days. If the civilians were defined as an armed opposition group, the arms embargo enforced under Resolution 1970 and 1973 would have

---

29 Article 43 (1).

30 Article 48.

been imposed on them as well, since the embargo was applicable on the entirety of Libya. This calls for speculation that the Security Council made a cunning detour in order to allow NATO to arm the NTC without worrying about the NTC breaching international humanitarian law since this law was not binding on the NTC.[31] In other words, the wording of Resolution 1973 opens the door for giving implicit authorization to use legally unrecognized armed rebels to enforce a military intervention. The danger of using such a "detour," for future reference, lies in the fact that such unrecognized armed opposition groups in a SC Resolution are not necessarily trained in a manner consistent with general rules and customs of wars, and they do not necessarily have full knowledge of international humanitarian law.

6. The Definition of an Armed Opposition Group

The Security Council had a rich precedence of situations similar to that of Libya with the difference being that confrontations with the government were qualified as internal armed conflicts rather than mere protests organized by civilians demanding civil and political freedom and rights.

The process of qualifying a certain situation as an internal armed conflict certainly is complicated and controversial but it is very important to pass through it for several reasons. As mentioned above, the distinction between a civilian in a protest and a combatant in an organized opposition group is the only reference that determines which area of international law is applicable. This distinction determines the scope of responsibility entailing on the parties that are involved in a conflict.

The dangers of avoiding this crucial step are enormous, one of which is creating a legal gap in the laws and customs of war. In other words, the individuals that were in the battlefield on behalf of the NTC against Gaddafi, if defined as civilians, would simply run free from any international legal obligation related to the rules and customs of war. The resourceful applicable law on internal armed conflicts that was compiled from previous cases of insurgencies had no effect on the situation in Libya since it was not qualified as an internal armed conflict. The most important example was the fact that Gaddafi's murder was not considered as a war

[31] See, Laura Trevelyan, "*Libya: Coalition divided on arming rebels*", BBC, 29 March 2011, at: http://www.bbc.co.uk/news/world-africa-12900706 (Last visited: 10 April 2012).

crime against a wounded, *hors de combat*, individual, but rather a "simple" homicide under national jurisdiction.

Now that the distinction between a civilian and a combatant was established, the second criterion in order to qualify the situation in Libya as an internal armed conflict was to establish that the combatants acting on behalf of the NTC were in fact an armed opposition group.

6.1. *Recognition of the NTC as an Armed Opposition Group*

One must emphasize that not all violent actions against an incumbent government are translated into an internal armed conflict. This chapter does not suggest that, since the Libyan civilians were engaged in armed activities, they became automatically part of an armed opposition group. In this regard, there are several criteria set by general principles of international law, international and regional conventions as well as international criminal tribunals.

The International Committee of the Red Cross has underlined the importance of "distinguishing genuine armed conflicts from a mere act of banditry or an unorganized and short-lived insurrection,"[32] which would not in that case fall under international humanitarian law.

In terms of competence, it is in the hands of the SC to determine, under Chapter VII, the existence of an armed conflict and hence the applicability of international humanitarian law. Common Article 3 of the Geneva Conventions has also provided that it is legally possible to recognize the insurgents by their organization and territorial control.[33]

This was also in the powers of the International Court of Justice, when it qualified the conflict between the *Contras* and the Government of Nicaragua as an internal armed conflict. Nicaragua had taken a position similar to that of Gaddafi's in the sense that it did not recognize the *Contras* as an organized opposition group. The ICJ set things straight and decided that Common Article 3 was applicable, and it could have done the same with Libya, if requested by the Security Council to do so.[34]

---

[32] *Commentary Convention (I) for the Amelioration of the Condition of the Wounded and Sick in Armed Forces in the Field.* (International Committee of the Red Cross, Geneva) (1949), 50.

[33] *Commentary 4th Geneva Convention Relative to the Protection of Civilian Persons in Time of War* (International Committee of the Red Cross, Geneva) (1958), 35–36.

[34] Military and Paramilitary Activities In and Against Nicaragua (Judgment of 27 June 1986) (Merits) 1986 ICJ Rep. 14, para. 218.

The ICTY gave a similar ruling in the *Tadić* appeal case establishing that:

> [a]n armed conflict exists whenever there is a resort to armed force between States or protracted armed violence between governmental authorities and organized armed groups or between such groups within a State International humanitarian law applies from the initiation of such armed conflicts and extends beyond the cessation of hostilities until a general conclusion of peace is reached; or, in the case of internal conflicts, a peaceful settlement is achieved. Until that moment, international humanitarian law continues to apply in the whole territory of the warring States or, in the case of internal conflicts, the whole territory under the control of a party, whether or not actual combat takes place there.[35]

On the African level, in the 1960s, the Organization of African Unity set standards for recognizing national liberation movements as the sole legitimate representative of a people.[36] The criteria with regard to national liberation movements are twofold; either it must be a United Action Front that is acting against the incumbent regime, or "it must be broadly based, have effective following and popular support throughout Libya, and must have reasonable fighting strength."[37]

Therefore, it is well established that the two main criteria for recognizing an armed opposition group are, to "control and govern a substantial part of the state territory" and "engage in a widespread armed conflict."[38]

To put these rules into perspective, the Security Council must have kept track of the legal status of the NTC as a political entity with a military arm. It must have modified its position according to the way the NTC was being viewed by the international community, especially the countries involved in the intervention, mainly France and the UK. The NTC was becoming more politically reputable as Resolution 1973 was being implemented. Assuming that the SC's excuse for treating the NTC supporters as civilians in the start was the fact that they did not meet the criteria of an armed opposition group, this position was becoming less and less excusable

---

[35] Decision on the Defence Motion for Interlocutory Appeal on Jurisdiction, Case No. IT-94-1-AR72 (2 October 1995), para. 70; Tadić case, para. 70

[36] *General Report of the Goodwill Mission of the Coordinating Committee for the Liberation of Africa to the Angolan Nationalists, Léopoldville, July 13–18, 1964, reprinted in* John A. Marcum, The Angolan Revolution vol. 2: exile, politics and guerrilla warfare (1962–1976), Appendix 2, at 304–307 (1978).

[37] Stefan Talmon, "Recognition of the Libyan National Transitional Council," *American Society of International Law insights* 15 (16) (2011), 3.

[38] Zegveld, *The Accountability of Armed Opposition Groups in International Law*, 2.

in the chronology of events. With time, the NTC's military control grew larger and they became more organized. Practically speaking, their "civilian" status became a myth and should have been corrected by the Security Council in due course.

Ironically, the first States that recognized the NTC as the successor to Gaddafi's regime were the same states that still treated them as civilians on paper.

Some recognized the NTC in matters that concerned areas that the NTC controlled, and others recognized the NTC as the sole representative of the Libyan people. The Security Council, regardless, avoided applying the legal consequences of such recognitions. Of course the NTC did not get the full support of the entire international community, but their mere structure and the minimum support they received qualified the situation in Libya as a state where two parties were fighting over power, from the political but also the military point of view. Instead, the SC, despite remaining seized of the matter, held the same position from the first to the last day of the No-Fly zone.

7. The Accountability of the National Transitional Council

7.1. *The Accountability of the NTC as an Armed Opposition Group to Gaddafi*

As mentioned above, it is crucial to define "civilians" with strict care in order to determine as accurately as possible the applicable law to all parties that are involved in an armed conflict. As soon as the NTC gained control over parts of Libya and had an organized armed structure, it should have been recognized as such for the main reason of accountability.

Several legal texts and rules and customs of war were legally applicable to the NTC rebels but were not officially applied to them, and the Resolution did not provide for any framework to ensure such implementation. On the contrary, Resolution 1973 stripped NTC of their obligations under international humanitarian law, international criminal law and possible obligations under human rights law. The internal armed conflict in Libya became an unfair war, where Gaddafi was paradoxically responsible for protecting an armed group that he himself was fighting against. The NTC had, on the contrary, no responsibility whatsoever under Resolution 1973 since they were seen as civilians.

There were several legal consequences that should have applied to the NTC's armed opposition group. For instance, Common Article 3 of the

Geneva conventions and the Additional Protocols I & II to the Geneva Conventions, all to which Libya acceded, contained the obligations on armed opposition groups to respect international humanitarian and international criminal law. Despite the lack of clarity in international law over the applicability of human rights law to non-state actors, the NTC could have been held to such obligations through special agreements.[39]

7.2. *The Civilians' Impunity from International Accountability*

The Security Council avoided several opportunities to explicitly hold the NTC responsible for the manner in which they conducted their armed struggle against Gaddafi. It is true that, politically, crimes committed by the NTC rebels could have received frowning opposition from the international community or at least from the states that recognized it, but from a legal point of view, the NTC leaders escaped international accountability under international criminal law and international humanitarian law. For this reason, the murder of Gaddafi, for example, was treated as a crime under the national criminal jurisdiction of Libya instead of the war crime of murdering an individual injured and *hors de combat*. This is not to mention the other possible war crimes and crimes against humanity committed against the supporters of Gaddafi, whether they were civilians or for example war prisoners or *hors de combat*. The UN Declaration, on the Protection of All Persons from Being Subjected to Torture and Other Cruel, Inhuman or Degrading Treatment or Punishment, applied to all individuals regardless of their political affiliation. This declaration was "a guideline for all States and other entities exercising effective powers."[40]

Individual criminal responsibility was also established in the Statutes of the ICTY and the ICTR, in which, respectively in Article 7(1) and 6(1), "a person who ordered the execution of a crime referred to in the Statutes shall be individually responsible for the crime."[41] In addition to this, the ICTY has jurisdiction to try both military and civilian leadership.[42] This adds to the evidence that international criminalization of individuals in internal conflicts has become a common practice of international criminal courts. As done in these courts, the Security Council should have made a formal effort in assessing the situation in Libya further in order to understand the

39 At 10–11.

40 Adopted by the UNGA Res 3452 (XXX) 9 December 1975.

41 Zegveld, *The Accountability of Armed Opposition Groups in International Law*, 112.

42 At 117.

structure of the NTC as an armed opposition and ultimately ensure that the leaders use their power to prevent executions that are not in accordance with international humanitarian law, and that the leaders would be held accountable under the principle of command responsibility.

The terms of Resolution 1973 emphasized that the demands were solely directed at Gaddafi and not jointly to the NTC, unlike, for example, SC Resolution 794 (1992) on Somalia, in which it condemned "all violations of international humanitarian law occurring in Somalia, including in particular the deliberate impeding of the delivery of food and medical supplies essential for the survival of the civilian populations, and affirms that those who commit or order the commission of such acts will be held individually responsible in respect such acts."[43]

7.3. *Special Agreements*

Even in the absence of an express provision entailing responsibility upon the NTC in the Resolution itself, the Security Council had the power to compel the NTC to enter into special agreements with Gaddafi or into a unilateral declaration through which it would be bound to respect rules and customs of war in their armed activities against the Libyan army. This power to put pressure on the NTC to undertake legal responsibilities stemmed from the fact that without NATO's and the SC's backing, the NTC would have taken longer to achieve their goal or even lose the internal armed conflict.

Such Special Agreements were not foreign to internal conflicts in the past. Examples include the FMLN and the Salvadorian government.[44] The agreement contained "several human rights norms derived from the ICCPR and the American Convention on Human Right, Common Article 3 and Protocol II."[45]

There is no doubt that the NTC had the legal capacity to enter into such an agreement, given, once again, that the SC would cease from calling them civilians. This was the case with the San José Agreement in which the FMLN had "the capacity and the will and assumes the commitment to respect the inherent attributes of the human person."[46]

---

43 UN Security Council, *Resolution 794 (1992) Adopted by the Security Council at its 3145th meeting, on 3 December 1992*, 3 December 1992, S/RES/794 (1992), para. 5.

44 Agreement of 26 July 1990, A/44/971, S/21541. At *The United Nations and El Salvador 1990–1995* (UN Blue Book Series, United Nations, New York, 1995), 179.

45 Zegveld, *The Accountability of Armed Opposition Groups in International Law*, 50–51.

46 Preamble of the San José Agreement. 41.

One must clarify that imposing international law on the NTC does not necessarily mean that the Security Council cannot still help the NTC in their political and military struggle. Legal neutrality does not have to lead to political and military neutrality as well.

Even if the situation in Libya was qualified an internal armed conflict, the Security Council was not forced to be neutral. It could have still taken the side of the NTC since they had legitimate demands and they were attempting to overthrow a dictator, not a democratically elected president. The option of a pro-democratic intervention was available to the Security Council.

8. Taking Sides: Pro-Democratic Intervention

As found in the spirit of several previous Security Council resolutions, the true protection of civilians lies in ensuring the swift transition to a democracy that guarantees their rights and freedoms, and not merely an action that aims to get rid of a dictator.

In the Libyan situation, if the major concern was about the protection of civilians from being deprived of their political freedom and human rights, then logically Resolution 1973 should have been drafted in a manner that ensured that they would obtain these rights and freedoms.

The Resolution paradoxically put the entire burden of ensuring democracy on a regime that the SC itself knew was falling apart. It was out of courtesy that the resolution demanded Gaddafi guarantee the implementation of democracy, because his chances expired as soon as sympathy for the NTC became obvious. How could the SC expect a positive reaction from Gaddafi when what he views as an armed opposition group is treated as a group of civilians by the Resolution? Demanding that Gaddafi respect a responsibility to protect armed civilians is rhetorical and self-defeating, and it is unthinkable that Resolution 1973, in the way it was drafted, would have led Gaddafi to grant more freedoms to the Libyan people.

A realistic scenario would put forward the support of the NTC and encouraging them to take over and ensure democracy in the post-Gaddafi era.

Despite the fact that there are no "pro-democratic intervention" provisions present under Chapter VIII of the UN Charter, there are several cases in the past in which the Security Council took sides by authorizing a pro-democratic action, through replacing a regime by another or ensuring the independence of a state. Examples are, *inter alia*, the Operation Restore Democracy in Haiti in 1990, and Operation Stabilize in East-

Timor in 1997. There were several other practices by individual states or regional organizations to which the SC acquiesced, such as ECOWAS's military intervention in Sierra Leone in 1997 and in Guinea-Bissau helped by Senegal and Guinea; the intervention in the Central African Republic by the Inter-African Force to Monitor the Implementation of the Bangui Agreements; the intervention in Lesotho by Botswana and South Africa in accordance with several agreements by the Southern African Development community.[47]

There were several obstacles to the blunt recognition of the NTC as the democratic replacement for Gaddafi at the early stage of the conflict. The NTC was not a democratically elected government that for example suffered from a military coup. Gaddafi could not be trusted with an orderly transition to democracy but neither could the NTC; it was their first appearance on the political scene and were barely introduced to the international community. This is not to say that they were not competent or democratic *per se* but at that point in time they had not proven their good or bad faith to the international community.

The remedy to such uncertainty was available, as mentioned earlier, through the option of taking such guarantees from the NTC if it was compelled to sign agreements, under the auspices of the Security Council, ensuring their knowledge and commitment to the general principles of international law.

In that case the SC would explicitly take the side of the NTC and provide the authorization to use all necessary measures to overthrow the Gaddafi regime instead of using an intention as vague as "protecting civilians." Such action would have reflected the true views of the Security Council, or at least of the states that took the responsibility to implement the No-Fly Zone. Disagreements and questions of intervention in sovereign affairs would have surely been raised but at least the transparency of the Security Council would have been less questionable, especially as Gaddafi was already committing crimes against humanity as was established by the International Commission of Inquiry, and the NTC was gaining wider recognition and larger control over major parts of Libya.

47 Weiss, *Military-civilian interventions*, 198. See also Jeremy I. Levitt, 'African Interventionist States and International Law," in *African Interventionist States*, ed Oliver Furley and Roy May (Aldershot: Ashgate, 2001): 35.

9. Conclusion

It has been a difficult task to go through the Security Council's analysis of the situation in Libya and compare it with the reality of the conflict between Gaddafi and the National Transitional Council. The main critique lies in the way the SC defined the term civilians, and the way the SC abstained from treating the situation as an internal armed conflict.

Assuming that the way Gaddafi handled the demands of his people was shockingly brutal and undoubtedly in violation of human rights, the fact that he did not scare the National Transitional Council was a sign of the start of a fierce armed struggle over power.

The Security Council's reaction was indeed neutral; it distanced itself, on paper, from getting involved in the conflict itself, deciding to enforce a No-Fly Zone that ensured the protection of innocent civilians. However, this neutrality was destined to be self-defeating, for the reason that it did not pass through analyzing the reality of the conflict with all transparency. The drafters of the Security Council avoided considering the NTC as an armed opposition group, hence it did not establish that the situation in Libya was an internal armed conflict.

The way the SC reacted to Gaddafi's alleged violations of human rights created a loophole around the global governance of the SC, and raised questions around the true intentions of the SC in comparison with what was written in the text of Resolution 1973. Had the SC expressed its intentions more transparently, the doubts around the legitimacy of the Resolution would have decreased dramatically.

The Security Council, in assessing and analyzing the situation in Libya, has not only avoided recognizing the reality of the conflict but it also deliberately became oblivious to the calls and findings of important entities like the African Union, the International Crisis Group and the International Commission of Inquiry on the situation of Human Rights in Libya. The SC distanced itself the same way from previous cases and lessons learnt from the past.

The consequences of not qualifying the NTC as an armed opposition group and the situation in Libya as an internal armed conflict created confusion as to which international law is applicable. In other words, the NTC could not be held accountable for violations of international humanitarian law, such as the mistreatment of prisoners and individuals *hors de combat*. Common Article 3 of the Geneva Conventions was not applicable because they were not, in the eyes of international law, an armed opposition group.

Ensuring the implementation of the right applicable law on all sides in conflict would not have restrained the Security Council's arm to remain neutral. On the contrary, the Security Council, as it did in Haiti and East Timor, has the option to engage in a pro-democratic action while still taking guarantees from the NTC that they would respect the rules and customs of war.

The main concern emanating from the consequences of Resolution 1973 are for the legacy it could create. Ending the effects of the No-Fly Zone immediately after the assassination of Gaddafi gave an obvious impression that the intention of the No-Fly Zone was to end the regime rather than only protect civilians. One cannot resist creating the link with the current situation in Syria where, after the killing of nearly 10,000 individuals, the Security Council remains paralyzed with a Chinese and a Russian veto preventing it from authorizing a military intervention.

CHAPTER EIGHT

PRO-DEMOCRATIC INTERVENTION, INVITATION, OR "RESPONSIBILITY TO PROTECT"? CHALLENGES TO INTERNATIONAL LAW FROM THE "ARAB SPRING"

Vasiliki Saranti*

1. Introductory Remarks

According to chaos theory, "when a butterfly flaps its wings in the Amazon, a storm ravages China". Likewise, the self-immolation of an unemployed young man in Tunisia, on 17 December 2010, sparked a series of uprisings and violent demonstrations in North Africa and the Middle East, the consequences of which are still ongoing. However, as the butterfly effect cannot be cut off of the initial prevailing conditions, this chain of events cannot be seen independently of the political and social conditions prevailing for decades in Arab and North African countries: corrupted totalitarian regimes and dictatorships, unemployment and poverty of the lower and middle classes, flagrant violations of human rights and fundamental freedoms, permanent and institutionalized states of emergency, martial laws.

In this context, one of the challenges of the "Arab Spring" uprisings is that they marked a new phase in the decolonization process. The claims of the heterogeneous groups of demonstrators and insurgents, even though diversified, could be summed up as follows: freedom, democracy, human rights protection, establishment of functioning institutions and the rule of law, free and fair election and regime change; namely, especially regarding the latter, the people vindicated the right to self-determination, in its internal dimension. A right that has been left incomplete since the colonies attained their independence, insofar as in those countries totalitarian regimes have been imposed one way or another.

---

* LL.B. (Law School, Democritus University of Thrace); LL.M (International and European Studies, Panteion University); Ph.D (International Law, Panteion University); Researcher of the European Centre of Research and Training on Human Rights and Humanitarian Action, Panteion University, Athens, Greece; Lecturer, National Police Academy; Member of the Hellenic Society of International Law and International Relations. Comments are welcome at vasiliki_sarandi@hotmail.com.

Faced with these pro-democratic revolutions, the reaction of the international community ranged from a total inaction in certain cases (Yemen, Bahrain), limited response in others (e.g. EU sanctions against Syria), to the military intervention in Libya. In the latter case the serious indications of crimes against humanity triggered the UN Security Council activation, which authorized the use of all necessary means to protect civilians and civilian populated areas. In other cases, for instance in Tunisia and Egypt, the developments have been so rapid that the international community remained essentially a spectator in a play where the leading roles were held by the vast oppressed masses of those countries.

It goes without saying that the use of force, in pursuance of the "responsibility to protect" doctrine, is always the last resort. Having said that, the following questions arise:

- How is the right to democracy defined and who is the holder of the right?
- How is democracy consolidated, how could the international community contribute to its consolidation and what are the limits of such an action?
- Before resorting to violent means, what is the scope of protection and assistance that international and regional organizations and states can offer in the establishment and consolidation of democratic institutions? A question that is rendered even more interesting if we consider that the UN Summit Outcome (2005) refers to democracy and the rule of law in general, but refrains from proposing the establishment of special mechanisms for the consolidation of democratic institutions in a State in the same vein as the responsibility to protect doctrine.
- Is the pro-democratic intervention, whether it is exercised by invitation or UN Security Council authorization, reconciled with the principle of non-intervention and what is the relationship between the right to democracy, pro-democratic interventions and the principle of self-determination?
- If we assume that we are in a new phase of the decolonization process, could a foreign state intervene legitimately in a civil conflict by supporting the party claiming its internal self-determination—in the same manner that the assistance to a national liberation movement was allowed during the decolonization era—and what will this entail for international stability?
- On the other hand, could a regime that is imposed (e.g. Iraq) ever be democratic? Does it represent the people's will? Or is it a violation of the right to self-determination?

The abovementioned questions, though closely related with international law, are at the same time inextricably intertwined with the national—constitutional—law insofar as they relate to the form of the political organization of a state, thus creating an extremely interesting dialogue between the two fields: international and national law.

2. The Right to Democracy in International Law

2.1. *In Quest of a Definition*

There is no universally accepted definition for democracy. Indeed, it is a relative notion and if we ask 100 people about its meaning and scope we will receive 200 different answers. The principle of democracy is mentioned in the constitutive charters of various international organizations,[1] but as a right it has been delimited very recently. The Inter-American Democratic Charter, although it does not provide us with a clear-cut definition of democracy, nevertheless contains various provisions on the relationship between democracy and human rights and fundamental freedoms, separation of powers, economic and social development, regular, free and fair elections and election observation missions, respect for the rule of law and civilian authority, all of which actually define the term democracy. It also gives us guidance as to the holder and beneficiary of the right: "The peoples of the Americas have a right to democracy and their governments have an obligation to promote and defend it" (article 1). Thus, democracy is a collective right, it is a people's right. One may also maintain that it is an aspect of internal self-determination, since the latter actually consists in the right of the whole people of sovereign states to have a representative and democratic government.[2]

On the other hand, the African Charter on Democracy, Elections and Governance points out that: "popular participation through universal suffrage is an inalienable right of the people" (article 4 §2). Yet democracy is not confined to the principle of regular elections—it is not only the will of the majority. To the contrary, the protection of human rights is a cornerstone of democracy. A democratic state should protect the rights of

[1] See Treaty on European Union, art. 2, OJ C 83, 30.3.3010; Statute of the Council of Europe, preamble, CETS No. 001, 5.5.1949; OAS Charter, preamble, art. 3d, OAS Treaty Series, nos. 1-C and 61, 1609 U.N.T.S. 119, 30.4.1948. For the African Union and other regional organizations, see infra notes no. 35, 36.

[2] See *infra* IIIb). See also Antonio Cassese, *Self-determination of peoples: a legal reappraisal*, (Cambridge: Cambridge University Press, 1995, 101 et seq.

the minority/minorities; it should be a "moderate state". This delimitation is crucial in view of the likely imposition of the Sharia Law in the states that emerge from the "Arab Spring"—and the possible conflicts that may arise with universally accepted human rights standards[3]—and in view of the human rights violations perpetrated against the supporters of the incumbent regimes, for instance in the case of Libya.[4]

In international jurisprudence, the right to democracy is rarely mentioned. One should note though the case of *Jawara v. Gambia*,[5] before the African Commission on Human and Peoples' Rights, concerning the coup d'etat in the country on 11 November 1994 that resulted in the imposition of a military government. The African Commission held that the coup deprived the Gambian people of their right to freely determine their political status and violated article 20 §1 of the African Charter on Human and Peoples' Rights.[6]

A further consequence of the absence of a definition of democracy is that we also lack a universally accepted definition on unconstitutional alterations of the democratic order. Such delimitation is indispensable given that a disruption of democracy may bring about the imposition of sanctions against the state in question, in implementation of the relevant provisions of the charters of international organizations. The African Charter on Democracy, Elections and Governance is the only instrument that offers certain guidance, but it is of regional character. According to article 23 of that instrument, an unconstitutional change of government consists in: a) any coup d'etat against a democratically elected government; b) any intervention by mercenaries to replace a democratically elected government; c) any replacement of a democratically elected government by armed dissidents or rebels; d) any refusal by an incumbent government to relinquish power to the winning party or candidate after free, fair and regular elections; and e) any amendment or revision of the

[3] This is a complex and multi-dimensional issue that cannot be dealt with here adequately. See before the European Court of Human Rights, *Refah Partisi (The Welfare Party) and others/Turkey*, appl. no. 41340/98, 41342/98, 41343/98 and 41344/98, 13.2.2003, §123 and the statement of the UN High Commissioner on Human Rights (30.1.2008), upon entry into force of the revised Arab Charter on Human Rights, available at http://www.unhchr.ch/huricane/huricane.nsf/view01/6C211162E43235FAC12573E00056E19D?opendocument (last visited 6 February 2012).

[4] See *Human Rights Watch*, World Report 2012, Chapter: Libya 2012.

[5] Communications 147/95 and 149/96, 13th Annual Activity Report, §73.

[6] See also the references of the Inter-American Court of Human Rights to the Inter-American Democratic Charter in cases *Herrera-Ulloa v. Costa Rica*, Serie C-107, 2 July 2004, para. 115 and *Yatama v. Nicaragua*, Serie C-127, paras. 193, 207, 215 and concurring opinion of judge Garcia-Sayán, paras. 15–17.

constitution or legal instruments, which is an infringement on the principles of democratic change of government.[7] The last case is perhaps the most controversial and caused much discussion when it was put into practice in the Honduras case (2009).

2.2. *The "Cold War" Era*

The effective protection of democracy in the domestic legal order was not a matter of concern for the international community when the UN was established. Hence, the UN Charter does not make any reference to the notion of the democratic state, for instance as a condition for UN membership.[8] On the other hand, the principle of non-intervention in the domestic affairs of states (Art. 2 para. 7 UN Charter) would hinder any qualitative evaluation of the regime or the form of government of a state.

Similarly, the legality or legitimacy of a regime at the international level was not an object of study for international law. A governmental structure that was exercising effective control of a state, whether it was recognized or not and irrespective of the means it used to seize power, would enjoy legal standing in the international fora. Unlike the observance of human rights, which exited early enough from the ambit of the *domaine reserve*,[9]

---

[7] Another issue is that unconstitutional alterations of government presuppose the existence of a constitution that would be violated. This is not always the case. See e.g. Libya, Zimbabwe. It is interesting that the AU considered the armed uprising against Colonel Qaddafi as illegitimate, thus delaying the recognition of the NTC, because it violated the regional organization's norms on democratic transfer of government. See "Libye: l'Union africaine refuse de reconnaître le CNT", Le Monde 26.8.2011, http://www.lemonde.fr/libye/article/2011/08/26/les-rebelles-prennent-leurs-quartiers-a-tripoli_1563710_1496980.html.

[8] Art. 4 para. 1: "Membership in the United Nations is open to all other peace-loving states which accept the obligations contained in the present Charter and, in the judgment of the Organization, are able and willing to carry out these obligations". See also, the report of the former UN Secretary-General B. Boutros-Ghali, *Supplement to reports on democratization*, UN Doc A/51/761, 20 December 1996, paras. 26 et seq. The Pact of the League of Arab States (LAS), adopted in 1945, is even more explicit, stating in article 8 that: "Every member State of the League shall respect the form of government obtaining in the other States of the League, and shall recognize the form of government obtaining as one of the rights of those States, and shall pledge itself not to take any action tending to change that form".

[9] Document of the Conference on the Human Dimension of the CSCE (Moscow, 3 October 1991); Institute of International Law, resolution on "The Protection of Human Rights and the Principle of Non-intervention in the Internal Affairs of States", session of Santiago de Compostela, 1989. See also Marc Bossuyt, "Human rights and non-intervention in domestic matters" *Review of the International Commission of Jurists* 35 (1985): 45–52; Danilo Türk, "Reflections on human rights: sovereignty of states and the principle of non-intervention", in *Human rights and criminal justice for the downtrodden: essays in honour*

the legitimacy of a government was a matter essentially within the domestic jurisdiction of states.[10] An emblematic exception is the "Greek case"[11] before the then European Commission on Human Rights, when Greece was expelled from the Council of Europe after its democratic government had been overthrown by a military junta. However, the reaction of the organization was precipitated by the overall miserable human rights situation in the country, as ascertained by the European Commission on Human Rights in its reports,[12] and not especially because of the disruption of the democratic order.[13]

This approach has been upheld by the International Court of Justice. In its advisory opinion on Western Sahara, the International Court of Justice has noted that: "No rule of international law, in the view of the Court, requires the structure of a State to follow any particular pattern, as is evident from the diversity of the forms of State found in the world today."[14] Furthermore, in the *Nicaragua* case, exploring the extent of the

---

of Asbjorn Eide, ed. Morten Bergsmo. (Leiden: Martinus Nijhoff Publ., 2003): 753–766; K. Zemanek, "Human rights protection vs non-intervention: a perennial conflict?", in *Man's inhumanity to man: essays in honour of Antonio Cassese*, ed. Lal Chand Vohrah (The Hague: Kluwer Law International, The Hague, 2003): 953–975.

[10] For the relationship between the principle of non-intervention and the legality of national governments at the international level see Brad Roth, *Government Illegitimacy in International Law* (Oxford: Clarendon Press, 2000). For an in-depth analysis of the legitimacy of governments in international law see, Jean d'Aspremont, *L'Etat non Démocratique en Droit International. Etude Critique du Droit International Positif et de la Pratique Contemporaine* (Paris: Pedone, 2008); Jean d'Aspremont, "Legitimacy of Governments in the Age of Democracy," *New York University Journal of International Law and Politics* 38 (4) (2006): 877–917; Ahmed Mahiou, "Droit International et Droit Constitutionnel: de la Non-Intervention à la Bonne Gouvernance," in *Droit Constitutionnel et Mutations de la Société Internationale*, ed. Abdelfattah Amor (Académie Internationale de droit constitutionnel, XVIIe session, 6–21 July 2001): 157–228; Sean Murphy, "Democratic Legitimacy and the Recognition of States and Governments," *International and Comparative Law Quarterly* 48 (3) (1999): 545–581; Niels Petersen, *Demokratie als teleologisches Prinzip: zur Legitimität von Staatsgewalt im Völkerrecht* (Berlin: Springer, 2009); Allan Rosas, "International Legitimacy of Governments," in *The Living Law of Nations: Essays on Refugees, Minorities, Indigenous Peoples and the Human Rights of other Vulnerable Groups: in Memory of Atle Grahl-Madsen*, ed. Gudmundur Alfredsson & Peter McAlister-Smith (Kehl: N.P. Engel, 1996), 201–217.

[11] For a comprehensive analysis see *(in greek)* Stelios Perrakis, *The "Greek Case" before the International Organizations (1967–1974)* (Athens: Ant. N. Sakkoulas, 1997).

[12] *Denmark, Norway, Sweden, The Netherlands/Greece*, application no. 3321, 3322, 3323 and 3344/67, report 5.11.1969, vol. I and II.

[13] See also the special operation of the "derogation clause" (art. 4 ICCPR, 15 ECHR, 27 ACHR) of the major human rights treaties. According to the jurisprudence, one of the substantive conditions of the legality of derogation measures is that they are adopted by the legitimate government.

[14] *Western Sahara*, Advisory Opinion, ICJ Reports 1975, 12, para. 94.

fundamental principle of non-intervention in domestic affairs, it stressed the following:

> A prohibited intervention must accordingly be one bearing on matters in which each State is permitted, by the principle of State sovereignty, to decide freely. One of these is the choice of a political, economic, social and cultural system, and the formulation of foreign policy[15] [...] A State's domestic policy falls within its exclusive jurisdiction, provided of course that it does not violate any obligation of international law[16] [...] adherence by a State to any particular doctrine does not constitute a violation of customary international law; to hold otherwise would make nonsense of the fundamental principle of State sovereignty on which the whole of international law rests, and the freedom of choice of the political, social, economic and cultural system of a State.[17]

2.3. *The Post-Cold War Developments*

After the end of the Cold War and the democratization processes initiated in many states (Central, Eastern and Southern Europe, Latin America etc.) we witnessed the gradual emergence of the right to democracy as a rule of international law.[18] Democracy is propounded as the means to prevent international and internal armed conflicts, to establish the rule of law and to guarantee the effective protection of human rights and to achieve in general regional and international stability.[19] The recognition of a regime

15 *Military and paramilitary activities in and against Nicaragua*, para. 205.

16 Id., para. 258.

17 Id., para. 263.

18 On these developments, see in particular Rafaa Ben-Achour, 'Le Droit International de la Démocratie,' *Cours Euro-Méditerranéens Bancaja de Droit International* IV (2000): 359; Boutros Boutros-Ghali, "Pour un Droit International de la Démocratie," in *Theory of International Law at the Threshold of the 21st Century. Essays in Honour of Krzysztof Skubiszewski*, ed. Jerzy Makarczyk (The Hague: Kluwer Law International, 1996): 99–108; Gregory Fox & Brad Roth (ed.), *Democratic Governance and International Law* (Cambridge Cambridge University Press, 2000); Thomas M. Franck, "The Emerging Right to Democratic Governance," *American Journal of International Law* 86 (1) (1992): 46–91; Rein Müllerson, "Democracy promotion: institutions, international law and politics," *RCADI* 333, (2008); L.-A., Sicilianos, *L'ONU et la Democratisation de l'Etat: Systemes Regionaux et Ordre Juridique Universel* (2000); Société Française pour le Droit International, L'Etat de Droit en Droit International (2009). Fox maintains that it remains uncertain whether the practice of international organizations has coalesced into a "right" to democratic governance. See Gregory Fox, "The International Protection of the Right to Democracy," Max Planck Encyclopedia of Public International Law, March 2008, available at http://www.mpepil.com/ (last visited 2 April 2012).

19 See the relevant references in the report of the former UN Secretary-General, Boutros Boutros-Ghali, *An Agenda for Peace. Preventive diplomacy, peacemaking and peace-keeping*, UN Doc. A/47/277-S/24111, 17 June 1992; Vienna Declaration and Programme of Action:

does not only depend on the effective control it exercises over its territory, but also on its democratic/electoral legitimacy.[20]

The growing importance of democratization is further demonstrated by the electoral observation or electoral assistance missions[21] organized by the UN (Department of Political Affairs),[22] the EU (European Commission),[23] the OSCE (ODIHR),[24] the OAS (Department for the Promotion of Democracy),[25] the Council of Europe[26] etc. The change in the regional democratization process refers both to the engagement of international actors, particularly international organizations, therein, and the influence they can exercise in the outcomes of this process.

At the international level, the culmination of this process, regarding the importance of democratic governance, which developed rapidly but in an uneven way after the Cold War, was the report of the High-level Panel on Threats, Challenges and Change that proposed a mechanism: "to protect democratically elected governments from unconstitutional overthrows."[27] However, such a reference has not been included in the 2005 World Summit Outcome. This document contains only the well-known references on the interrelationship between human rights, democracy and the rule of law but avoids establishing particular mechanisms to cope with interruptions

---

Report of the World Conference on Human rights, UN Doc. A/CONF.157/23, 12 July 1993; Document of the Moscow Meeting of the Conference on the human dimension of the CSCE, 4 October 1991. See also, Rafaa Ben-Achour, 'La Contribution de B. Boutros-Ghali à l'Emergence d'un Droit International Positif de la Démocratie', in *Boutros Boutros-Ghali Amicorum Discipulorumque Liber. Paix, Développement, Démocratie* (1998): 909–923.

[20] See for a recent example, Jean D'Aspremont, "Duality of government in Côte d'Ivoire," EJIL: *Talk!* 4.1.2011.

[21] The election process is one of the issues that pertain to national sovereignty. Thus, in order to safeguard national sovereignty and the principle of non-intervention during election observation the UNGA has adopted a series of resolutions: Respect for the principles of national sovereignty and non-interference in the internal affairs of states in electoral processes, UN doc. A/RES/44/147 (1989), A/RES/45/151 (1990), A/RES/46/130 (1991), A/RES/47/130 (1992), A/RES/48/124 (1993), A/RES/50/172 (1995), A/RES/52/119 (1997), A/RES/54/168 (1999); Respect for the principles of national sovereignty and non-interference in the internal affairs of states in electoral processes as an important element for the promotion and protection of human rights, UN doc. A/RES/56/154 (2001).

[22] http://www.un.org/wcm/content/site/undpa/main/issues/elections.

[23] http://ec.europa.eu/europeaid/what/human-rights/election_observation_missions/index_en.htm.

[24] http://www.osce.org/odihr/elections.

[25] http://www.oas.org/en/topics/elections.asp.

[26] http://www.coe.int/web/coe-portal/what-we-do/democracy/elections-and-democracy.

[27] Report of the Secretary-General's High-level Panel on Threats, Challenges and Change, A more secure world: our shared responsibility, 2004, para. 94.

of the democratic order in the UN member states, in the model of the "responsibility to protect" doctrine.[28]

On the other hand, the developments at the regional level have been much more impressive and dynamic. In the framework of the Organization of American States, after the end of the Cold War, the member states decided to alter their strict stance regarding the principle of non-intervention. The gradual collapse of the military regimes in Latin America made the concept of democracy emerge as a *conditio sine qua non* for the achievement of regional security and stability. Thus, the American states decided to render the protection, respect and guarantee of the democratic order in a state a prerequisite for membership in the organization. They achieved this goal gradually; the first major step was the adoption of Resolution 1080 of the OAS General Assembly on "Representative Democracy" (1991),[29] the second was the adoption of the Protocol of Washington (1992) which amended the OAS Charter[30] and the third and most important was the approval of the Inter-American Democratic Charter (2001).[31] The common feature of all these instruments is that the organization has the right to suspend the membership of a state, if the democratic order or the constitutional regime in that state is unconstitutionally interrupted or altered. This mechanism, consolidated with the Inter-American Democratic Charter, has been implemented in its entirety in the Honduras' coup d'etat (2009).[32]

In Africa,[33] similar efforts begin to take place only in the last decade, both as to the main regional organization (Organization of African

---

28 UN Doc. A/60/L.1, 15 September 2005, see in particular paras. 119, 135–137.

29 AG/RES.1080 (XXI-O91), 5 June 1991, in Proceedings of the 21st Regular Session, OEA/Ser.P/XXI.O.2, Volume I, 20 August 1991.

30 Protocol of Amendments to the Charter of the Organization of American States "Protocol of Washington", approved on December 14, 1992, at the Sixteenth Special Session of the General Assembly (A-56), 1-E Rev. OEA Documentos Oficiales OEA/Ser.A/2 Add. 3 (SEPF).

31 AG/RES.1 (XXVIII-E/01), 11 September 2001.

32 See for an analysis of the system established in the OAS framework as well as an overview of the democratization processes at the international level, Vasiliki Saranti, "A system of collective defence of democracy: The case of the Inter-American Democratic Charter," *Göttingen Journal of International Law* 3 (2011): 675–714.

33 See for a general approach, Frederick Cowell, "Preventing coups in Africa: attempts at the protection of human rights and constitutions," *International Journal of Human Rights* 15 (2011): 749–764.

Unity[34]/African Union),[35] as well as to various sub-regional organizations (ECOWAS,[36] SADC,[37] East African Community[38] etc.). Indeed, democratic governance and the condemnation of unconstitutional changes of governments is one of the bases for cooperation under the new institutional framework of the African Union.[39] According to the Protocol on Amendments to the AU Constitutive Act, the Assembly can decide on intervention, inter alia, following a serious threat to legitimate order or to restore peace and security to the Member States of the Union upon the recommendation of the Peace and Security Council. The insertion of this provision was meant to cover situations where the provision relating to intervention due to genocide, war crimes and crimes against humanity would not be applicable.[40] Definition of these situations is not provided and in theory they could also include the chaos resulting from a government's refusal to hand over power after losing an election. However, up until now, threats to or disturbances of the democratic order were not

---

34 The Organisation of African Unity (OAU) was established on 25 May 1963. On 9 July 2002 it was replaced by the African Union (AU).

35 See the Declaration on the framework for an OAU response to unconstitutional changes of government (2000), the Constitutive Act of the African Union (2000, Arts 3 and 4), the Protocol on Amendments to the Constitutive Act (2003) and the Protocol relating to the establishment of the Peace and Security Council of the African Union (2002, Arts 3f and 7 para 1m). In 2007, the African Charter on democracy, elections and governance was adopted and has entered into force on 15 February 2012.

36 Protocol A/SP1/12/01 on Democracy and Good Governance Supplementary to the Protocol relating to the mechanism for conflict prevention, management, resolution, peacekeeping and security, adopted by the Economic Community of West African States (ECOWAS) in Dakar, in December 2001. During the recent turmoil in Côte d'Ivoire, where the outgoing president, Laurent Gbagbo, refused to recognize Alassane Ouattara as the winner of the elections, the country had been suspended on 7 December 2010 from participation in the decision-making bodies of ECOWAS, by virtue of Art. 45 of the aforementioned instrument, until the democratically elected president effectively assumed power. The same sanction, along with an array of financial, economic and political measures, has been imposed against Mali on 30 March 2012, due to the violent overthrow of the government only a month before the national elections, see "Emergency mini-summit of ECOWAS Heads of State and Government on the situation in Mali", press release no. 092/2012, 30.3.2012. On 10.1.2009, ECOWAS had also suspended Guinea, see press release no. 003/2009 "ECOWAS leaders reject military transition in Guinea".

37 See the suspension of Madagascar, discussed in Cowell, "Preventing coups in Africa."

38 It was actually the countries of the eastern african region and not the organization proper that imposed trade and economic sanctions against Burundi in 1996, following a coup d'etat against the democratically elected government and the assassination of the president of the country.

39 See Ben Kioko, "The right of intervention under the AU's Constitutive Act: from non-interference to non-intervention," *IRRC* 85 (2003): 807–825.

40 Article 4h of the AU Constitutive Act.

treated through military action. To the contrary, the strongest sanction that was adopted by the AU Peace and Security Council in relevant situations was suspension of membership.[41]

In the EU framework one should mention the diplomatic sanctions—albeit with little practical impact—imposed on Austria, when Joerg Haider's extreme right-wing "Freiheitliche Partei Österreichs" entered into the government (February 2000). It is also interesting that the League of Arab States, although it does not include provisions on human rights protection or democracy in its Pact, decided to suspend Syria from membership[42] in the aftermath of the violent repression of the "Arab Spring" uprising in the country. The Charter of the Organization of Islamic Cooperation (2008) as well as the Charter of the Association of Southeast Asian Nations (ASEAN, 2007) also include references to democracy[43] but we do not have instances of suspension of membership.

2.4. *Pro-Democratic Intervention and the Use of Force*

2.4.1. *Unilaterally*

The continuing importance of the right to democracy and democratization in international law has another aspect. More precisely, the illegitimacy of a regime was propounded as a valid argument to unilaterally intervene and overthrow it by employing violent means. Those early approaches were supported mainly by the USA due to the overall inaction of the UNSC during the Cold War.[44] However, the final legal argument that was put forward in all the cases of armed interventions against regimes that were characterized as illegitimate by the intervening power was not the protection or restoration of democracy and democratic institutions but other arguments such as self-defence for the protection of nationals abroad (Dominican Republic, 1965, Grenada, 1983,[45]

---

41 Côte d'Ivoire [PSC/PR/COMM.1(CCLII), 9.12.2010. The suspension was lifted on 21 April 2011, see PSC/PR/COMM.1(CCLXXIII)]; Mali [PSC/PR/COMM(CCCXV), 23.3.2012]; Madagascar (PSC/PR/COMM.(CLXXXI), 20.3.2009); Guinea (29.12.2008).

42 Follow-up on the developments of the situation in Syria, Resolution: No. 7438 of the LAS Council, R.Extraordinary Session, 2/11/2011, available at http://www.arableagueonline.org.

43 See preamble and article 2 and preamble, articles 1 §7 and 2 §2h respectively.

44 See in that respect Oscar Schachter, "Is there a right to overthrow an illegitimate regime?," in *Liber Amicorum: Le droit international au service de la paix et du développement*, ed. Michel Virally (Paris: Pedone, 1991): 423–430.

45 The protection of nationals was the principle legal justification of US action, see Christopher Joyner, "Reflections on the lawfulness of invasion," *AJIL* 78 (1984): 131–144,

Panama, 1989),[46] invitation (Afghanistan, 1979),[47] or humanitarian intervention (Vietnam in Cambodia, 1978).[48]

Therefore, one cannot validly contend that there is a legal right to use force in order to implement democracy. To support otherwise would be a violation of the Declaration on Friendly Relations, according to which: "No state shall organize, assist, foment, finance, incite or tolerate subversive, terrorist or armed activities directed towards the violent overthrow of the regime of another state."[49] On another level, the USA, once the proponent of this approach—through the "Reagan doctrine"—seems to have abandoned such aspirations. According to the statement of President B. Obama in the wake of the "Arab Spring": "broadening our military mission to include regime change would be a mistake."[50]

---

at 134. The second justification was the invitation by five members of the Organization of Eastern Caribbean States and the collective security provision of its Pact (art. 8). See Joyner, "Reflections on the lawfullness of invasion," 135. The third referred to an alleged invitation by the island's Governor-General. See Joyner, "Reflections on the lawfullness of invasion," 137. The purported political or regime change aims of the Reagan Administration were strongly condemned by the majority of the theory, see Francis Boyle et al., "International Lawlessness in Grenada," *AJIL* 78 (1984): 172–175; Louise Doswald-Beck, "The legality of the US intervention in Grenada," *Netherlands International Law Review* 31 (1984): 355–377. For the US official legal position, see Deputy Secretary of State Kenneth W. Dam's statement in Leigh M. Nash, "Contemporary practice of the United States relating to international law," *AJIL* 78 (1984): 200–204. The armed intervention was also condemned by the UNGA res. 38/7, 2.11.1983.

46 The invocation of article 51 UN Charter was explicit, see Ved Nanda, "The validity of UN intervention in Panama under international law," *AJIL* 84 (1990): 494. However, the restoration of democracy was still propounded as one of the objectives of the invasion, ibid. The armed intervention was once again criticized in theory and condemned by the UNGA res. 44/240, 29.12.1989. See also John Quigley, "The legality of the US invasion of Panama," *Yale Journal of International Law* 15 (1990): 276–315. In subsequent meetings the US administration stated that they did not claim a right to intervene in favour of democracy, see SC 2902nd meeting (1989).

47 The UNGA condemned the Soviet intervention in Afghanistan, see res. ES-6/2, 14.1.1980 and 37/37, 29.11.1982.

48 During the discussions at the UNSC, the French representative pointed out that: "The notion that because a regime is detestable foreign intervention is justifiable and forcible overthrow is legitimate is extremely dangerous. That could ultimately jeopardize the very maintenance of international law and order and make the continued existence of various regimes dependent on the judgment of their neighbours." (S/PV.2109, para. 36.).

49 See above. Principle III, para. 2. The intervention of one state by force in order to protect democracy in another country would also constitute a violation of the right to self-determination, which shall emanate from the people, see W. Michael Reisman, "Coercion and self-determination: construing Charter article 2 (4)," *AJIL* 78 (1984): 642–645.

50 See "The Obama doctrine on foreign intervention and war", 28 March 2011, available at http://usliberals.about.com/od/homelandsecurit1/a/The-Obama-Doctrine-On-War-Foreign-Intervention.htm.

2.4.2. *At the Initiative of Regional Organizations*

2.4.2.1. Introductory note

Is there a regional right to use force for the restoration of a democratic government? This question has arisen out of ECOWAS'[51] practice to intervene, in certain cases without a prior UN authorization, in order to restore a democratically elected government after elections usually monitored by international observers. In the following paragraphs we will examine three cases emanating from ECOWAS practice: Sierra Leone, Liberia and Côte d'Ivoire.

2.4.2.2. Practice

In 1997, the government that was elected under UN supervision in Sierra Leone following a longstanding civil conflict was overthrown by a coup d'etat. ECOWAS, through its military observer group ECOMOG, resorted to force to restore the democratic government, using as its legal basis the explicit consent of the democratically elected president. The Security Council did not condemn the use of force nor did it give explicit authorization for it, until the ECOMOG presence had been validated by the Lomé Peace Accord on 7 July 1999.[52] It is perhaps the most characteristic, pure and unique example of restoring democracy at the regional level through the use of force.

In 2003 the situation in Liberia presented considerable similarities with the case of Libya in 2011. Sanctions were been imposed for the support of the opposition in Sierra Leone and the elected president Charles Taylor, who controlled only one third of the country, was prosecuted by the Special Tribunal for Sierra Leone. Likewise, in 2011, sanctions were imposed against the former Libyan regime,[53] the International Criminal Court issued an arrest warrant on 27 June 2011 against Qaddafi and other Libyan

[51] The founders of ECOWAS envisaged an economic community similar to the European Community (Treaty of the Economic Community of West African States, 28.5.1975, 1010 U.N.T.S. 17, 14 I.L.M. 1200). Nevertheless, in the post-Cold War era ECOWAS has been particular active in military action in West Africa, see in that respect Christine Gray, *International law and the use of force*, 3rd ed. (Oxford: Oxford University Press, 2008), 383 et seq.

[52] See Funmi Olonisakin, "Nigeria, ECOMOG, and the Sierra Leone crisis," in *Between democracy and terror: the Sierra Leone civil war*, ed. Ibrahim Abdullah (Dakar: CODESRIA, 2004): 220–237; K. Nowrot & E. Schbacker, "The use of force to restore democracy: international legal implications of the ECOWAS intervention in Sierra Leone," *American University International Law Review* 14 (1998): 321–412.

[53] UNSC res. 1970 (2011).

officials,[54] while the opposition forces marched toward Tripoli. Although ECOWAS offered to send peacekeeping forces to Liberia, it was not until Taylor stepped down that the Security Council decided to authorize member-states to establish a multinational force under Chapter VII for the implementation of the ceasefire agreement.[55] The mission did not have as its goal the preservation or restoration of a democratically elected government, since the intervention was delayed until Taylor agreed to leave. Similarly, the intervention in Libya did not have as its objective the change of the 42-year old regime, but the protection of civilians under threat of attack.

In Côte d'Ivoire we can distinguish two phases: the armed uprising of 2003 after the coup d'etat of 2002 and the crisis that followed the presidential elections of 2010, when Gbagbo refused to recognize the result of the elections. In 2003 ECOWAS swiftly condemned the mutiny and offered its support to the lawful president Gbagbo, strengthening the presence of ECOMICI in the country. Yet the regional peace-keeping force was not mandated to protect or preserve the democratic institutions, and lacked Security Council authorization.[56] The Security Council, by virtue of resolution 1464 (2003), welcomed the deployment of ECOMICI and French troops, and referred to Chapters VII and VIII of the UN Charter but did not authorize the use of enforcement action for the restoration of the democratic government. On the other hand, in the 2010 crisis, the main actor was the UN forces (UNOCI) and not ECOWAS.[57]

2.4.2.3. Critical evaluation

It follows from the above that the restoration of democracy may be one of ECOWAS' aims, but not the explicit legal basis for its actions. As Professor Gray rightly points out: "Given that the SC has not recognized an autonomous right of the regional organizations to use force in order to restore

---

[54] ICC-01/11–01/11, *The Prosecutor v. Saif Al-Islam Gaddafi and Abdullah Al-Senussi.* The case against Muammar Qaddafi was terminated on 22 November 2011 following his death.

[55] Res. 1497 (2003). Limited references to democratic principles are included in paras. 12 and 13, whereby the opposition forces are urged to refrain from attempts to seize power by force. ECOWAS sent 3.500 soldiers, forming ECOMIL, on 4.8.2003.

[56] See John M. Kabia, *Humanitarian intervention and conflict resolution in West Africa: From ECOMOG to ECOMIL* (Dartmouth: Ashgate, 2009); Collett Moya, "Foreign intervention in Côte d'Ivoire: the question of legitimacy," in *Righeous violence: the ethics and politics of military intervention*, ed. Tony Coady & Michael O'Keefe (Melbourne: Melbourne University Press, 2005), 160–182.

[57] See infra 2.4.3.

democracy, it is extremely difficult to accept the emergence of such a new right and a fundamental change to the role bestowed on regional organizations by the UN Charter."[58] ECOWAS's practice is not enough to establish a right of regional organizations to use force for the restoration of democracy. Besides, even though the AU provides for intervention in its Constitutive Act, its relevant organs have never put it into practice, so far at least.

Although a right to democracy is emerging, this cannot be exercised through the use of force. Collective measures short of armed force are much more effective than armed interventions that bring death and devastation and cannot contribute in any way to the establishment and consolidation of democracy.[59] Regional organizations can help foster democracy in a country through election observation, human rights promotion, negotiation, mediation and other peaceful means of dispute settlement etc. and as an ultimate sanction suspension of membership.[60] In the case of Honduras this was the sole sanction that was adopted. The suspension was followed by political mediation, good offices etc. Similar solutions can be adopted in such cases (e.g. Libya), provided that the legal tools are at the states' disposal and provided that the violations are not so grave as to constitute crimes against humanity. Indeed, in such a case, mediation may be ineffective (see for instance the case of Syria).

2.4.3. *Following a UNSC Authorization*

This is true and generally accepted today as far as unilateral and regional intervention is concerned. What about intervention for the protection of democratic institutions following an authorization of the UN Security Council? Since the end of the Cold War, there has been a significant enlargement in the cases that constitute a threat to international peace and security. The Security Council has broadened the scope of application of

---

[58] Gray, *International Law and the use of force*, 418.

[59] The recent example of Operation Iraqi Freedom (2003–2011) corroborates that democracy can never be established by force. See, in that respect, Simone van den Driest, "'Pro-democratic" intervention and the right to political self-determination: the case of Operation Iraqi Freedom," *NILR* 57 (2010): 29–72.

[60] In the Grenada crisis (1983) one of the critical approaches concerned the Organization of Eastern Caribbean States stance towards the US invasion. According to such a point of view, "if the OECS truly believed the new regime in Grenada created a serious threat to the future peace and stability of the region, the appropriate remedy would have been to bring the matter to the attention of the OAS" (see Francis Boyle et al., "International Lawlessness in Grenada," AJIL 78 (1984): 173). Thus, whenever the democratic institutions are threatened or destabilised in a state, the competent regional organization can contribute decisively to resolve the crisis, through a mediation that will not involve the use of force.

articles 39 and 41 UN Charter, so as to include cases of flagrant violations of human rights and international humanitarian law. Yet, unless there is strong evidence that a dictatorial regime perpetrates crimes against humanity or war crimes to such a degree that regional or international security could be endangered, the violation of democratic institutions per se is not perceived as a threat to international peace and security.[61] In this context, the Security Council has rarely proceeded to the adoption of coercive measures in order to ensure respect for the democratic order. Up until now, there are only two cases: Haiti and Sierra Leone.

The coups d'etat in Haiti (1991) and Sierra Leone (1997), following elections that were monitored by international observers, led to the immediate reaction of the UN Security Council and the invocation of Chapter VII of the UN Charter. After the overthrow of the first democratically elected government in Haiti in 1991, the SC stated that the situation constituted a threat to international peace and security.[62] However, the SC showed caution, stating that it is a unique and exceptional situation. A later resolution that imposed sanctions and authorized the creation of a multinational force for the "restoration of the legitimately elected President and authorities of the Government of Haiti" also recognized the "unique character of the situation in Haiti and its complex nature that requires an exceptional reaction."[63] In the case of Sierra Leone the SC demanded: "that the military junta take immediate steps to relinquish power in Sierra Leone and make way for the restoration of the democratically elected Government and a return to constitutional order" but it did not explicitly authorize the use of force in order to achieve that aim.[64]

The political crisis of November 2010 in Côte d'Ivoire, when the incumbent president refused to accept the result of the elections, is a controversial case. The UN Security Council adopted res. 1962 (2010) under Chapter VII urging: "all the Ivorian parties and stakeholders to respect the will of the people and the outcome of the election in view of ECOWAS and African Union's recognition of Alassane Dramane Ouattara as President-elect of Côte d'Ivoire and representative of the freely expressed voice of the Ivorian people as proclaimed by the Independent Electoral Commission" and renewing the mandate of UNOCI as it was set out in res. 1933 (2010).

---

[61] See the arguments against a draft resolution on Myanmar and Zimbabwe in S/PV.5526 and S/PV.5933.

[62] Res. 841, 16 June 1993.

[63] Res. 940 (1994).

[64] Res. 1132, 8 October 1997.

According to the latter, UNOCI has been mandated, amongst others, to "support the organization of open, free, fair and transparent elections". In subsequent resolutions it has been even more explicit as to the need of state institutions to yield to the authority vested by the people in President A. Ouattara (UNSC res. 1975/2011). However, it did not authorize the use of force to pursue that aim. To the contrary, the UNOCI and French forces have been authorized by the Security Council to use force only in order to protect civilians. Though it was not a pro-democratic intervention, one could contend that the siege of Gbagbo's compound and his forced removal from the country demonstrates that the actual intention of the use of force was to remove Gbagbo from power for the sake of stability.[65]

It is manifest from the above that the collective reaction of the Security Council is fragmentary, since other serious disturbances of the democratic order have not attracted its attention (see e.g. Burma/Myanmar in 1990, Pakistan in 1999, Thailand in 2006, Bangladesh in 2007 etc.).[66] The exceptional cases that are portrayed as representing pro-democratic intervention are usually related to the restoration of democratically elected presidents whose illegal overthrow may jeopardize or threaten international or regional peace and security and not situations of longstanding dictatorial regimes that are not viewed as threat per se.[67] States are reluctant to adopt a legal doctrine of pro-democratic intervention, albeit this may be one of the political goals of their will to intervene by force in a third country. In absence of explicit or implied authorization of the UNSC under Ch. VII for the restoration of democracy and in absence of any such discussion during UNSC meetings, one cannot contend that there is such a right.

The "Arab Spring" has not so far offered any arguments to the proponents of the theory of pro-democratic intervention. Indeed, the armed uprisings and demonstrations in Tunisia, Egypt, Bahrain, Yemen, and

---

65 It all depends on the interpretation of the mandate, see Antonios Tzanakopoulos, "The UN/French Use of Force in Abidjan: Uncertainties Regarding the Scope of UN Authorizations," EJIL: *Talk!*, 9.4.2011. One could make a similar assumption in the case of Libya, see *infra* notes 127–128. But this would be a political and not legal interpretation.

66 For an analysis see Theodore Christakis, 'La Violation du Droit Interne en tant que Menace contre la Paix?' in Société Française pour le Droit International, *L'Etat de Droit en Droit International*: 107–122.

67 D'Aspremont maintains that the disruption of the democratic order as such does not constitute violation of an international rule, see Jean d'Aspremont, 'La Licéité des Coups d'Etat en Droit International', in Société Française pour le Droit International, *L'Etat de Droit en Droit International*: 123–142.

most notably Syria did not trigger the intervention of the international community, for the establishment of democratic institutions, while the authorization for the use of force in Libya does not include in its objectives the establishment of democracy. Indeed, the overthrow of Qaddafi is not an aim of the mission, as this is spelled out in UNSC res. 1973 (2011), although with the arrest warrant in force it was difficult to imagine, even before his death, how he could ever remain in power or at least active in the internal political scene, given that the issuance of an arrest warrant entails that the international community has a legal obligation to implement it (article 89 ICC Statute).

3. Invitation to Provide Assistance/Support

3.1. *The Principle of Non-Intervention and Invitations in Contemporary International Law*

The principle of non-intervention in the affairs of other states is a fundamental principle governing international relations, closely linked to those of sovereign equality, territorial integrity and political independence of states and enshrined in various international instruments and soft law documents.[68] It is true that today, in the age of globalization and international cooperation at its peak, the principle of non-intervention does not have the legal connotations it used to.[69] Nevertheless, it is still frequently used with emphasis especially by politicians as political rhetoric.[70]

[68] Art. 2 (7) UN Charter, Art. 8 Arab League Pact, Art. 19 OAS Charter, Art. 3 OAU Charter, Art. 4g AU Constitutive Act; Declaration on the Inadmissibility of Intervention in the Domestic Affairs of states and the protection of their independence and sovereignty, UNGA Res. 2131/1965; Declaration on principles of international law concerning friendly relations and cooperation among states in accordance with the Charter of the United Nations, UNGA res. 2625/1970; Declaration on the inadmissibility of intervention and interference in the internal affairs of states, UNGA res. 36/103, 1981. See in general Kawser Ahmed, "The domestic jurisdiction clause in the UN Charter: a historical view," Singapore Yearbook of International Law 10 (2006): 175–197. The said principle forms part of customary law. See the judgement of the ICJ in the case concerning *Military and paramilitary activities in and against Nicaragua (Nicaragua v. United States)*, Judgment, ICJ Reports 1986, 14, paras. 184, 203.

[69] For the principle in general and its present-day significance, see Antonio Cassese, *International law*, 2nd ed (Oxford: Oxford University Press, 2005), 53–55.

[70] See for instance the statement of Ecuadoran president R. Correa criticizing M. Qaddafi's killing: "We are not defending the regime of Gaddafi, we defend the sovereignty of countries, non-intervention", available at http://en.mercopress.com/2011/10/24/ecuador-president-condemns-killing-of-gaddafi-and-family-members-as-homicide.

Although there is no official definition, an unlawful intervention consists of "coercive action taken by one state to secure a change in the policies of another."[71] Thus, it consists of three elements: it must be forcible or dictatorial; it must bear on matters on which each state is permitted by the principle of state sovereignty to decide freely; and finally it must in effect deprive the state intervened against of control over the matter in question. A simple interference does not equate with intervention.[72] Those elements are confirmed by the jurisprudence of the International Court of Justice,[73] the Declaration on Friendly Relations, the Declaration on the inadmissibility of intervention, as well as UNSC resolutions.[74]

A further consequence of the principle of non-intervention is that "no State shall organize, assist, foment, finance, incite or tolerate subversive, terrorist or armed activities directed towards the violent overthrow of the régime of another State, or interfere in civil strife in another State."[75] Thus, forcible intervention in a civil war on the side of the insurgents is prohibited. On the other hand, "intervention is allowable at the request of the government of a state,"[76] notwithstanding the theoretical discrepancies[77] and the problems arising in the practical implementation of the

---

71 Maziar Jamnejad & Michael Wood, "The principle of non-intervention," *Leiden JIL* 22 (2009): 347–348.

72 See Robert Y. Jennings & Arthur D. Watts, *Oppenheim's international law*, 9th edn (Oxford: Oxford University Press, 1993), 428.

73 *Corfu Channel case, United Kingdom/Albania*, judgment of 9.4.1949, ICJ reports 1949, 35; *Nicaragua*, 202–209; *Case concerning armed activities on the territory of the Congo, DRC/ Uganda*, judgment of 19.12.2005, 164–165.

74 UNSC res. 1234 (1999) on the situation in DRC; UNSC res. 1343 (2001) on the situation in Liberia.

75 Declaration on Friendly Relations, Principle III, (2).; *Nicaragua*, 206 et seq.

76 In the *Nicaragua* case the ICJ examined the "invitation" argument, although it was not invoked by the US, saying that a government may invite outside help, but a third state may not forcibly help the opposition overthrow the government, at 246. Article 3e of the "Definition of aggression" (UNGA res. 3314/1974) acknowledges implicitly the right of a state to invite a foreign army, since it stipulates that failure of the foreign army to leave or actions that exceed the framework of the invitation would constitute aggression.

77 In traditional international law the legal right of the government to seek help is in full force. Each state was free to allow another state to use force on its own territory, in pursuance of the principle *volenti non fit injuria*, i.e. an illegal act is no longer such if the party whose rights have been infringed previously consented thereto, provided of course that the prohibition of the use of force—arguably a *jus cogens* norm—can be derogated from. See Cassese, *International Law*, 368–371. See for a thorough discussion Theodore Christakis & Karine Mollard-Bannelier, "Volenti non fit injuria? Les effets du consentement à l'intervention militaire," *AFDI* 50 (2004): 102–137; Georg Nolte, *Eingreifen auf Einladung. Zur völkerrechtlichen Zulässigkeit des Einsatzes fremder Truppen im internen Konflikt auf Einladung der Regierun* (Berlin: Springer, 1999); Antonio Tanca, *Foreign armed intervention in internal conflict* (Leiden: Martinus Nijhoff Publ., 1993).

"intervention by invitation" theory.[78] In such a case the question that arises is who is the legitimate government that may extend such an invitation?[79] This question has tormented the theory and practice of international law both in the case of Libya and—to a lesser extent—Syria.[80]

One of the features of the principle of non-intervention is the prohibition of interfering in the internal organization of a foreign state. A corollary is the approach of states not to recognize governments but only states.[81] Indeed, according to the "objective" standard, a regime was not recognized by virtue of its democratic legitimacy, but on the basis of the effective control it exercised over its territory and the obedience or allegiance of its population.[82] Given that forcible unilateral intervention in favour of an opposition group in civil conflict is prohibited, when armed interventions were launched against non-recognized regimes, the legal justifications put forward by those intervening referred—inter alia—to a request for such intervention by the group allegedly possessing lawful authority or supported by the majority of the people.[83]

This question arose upon the outbreak of the uprising in Libya (February 2011) and the series of recognitions of the National Transitional Council—the main and most supported opposition group—that followed (from March 2011 henceforth). Indeed, in the case of Libya there was a blurring regarding the entity that constituted the legitimate representative

---

[78] It is a notion that is open to abuse, since all instances of intervention by invitation are of dubious legality and may even constitute armed attack, e.g. USSR in Hungary (1956), France/Belgium in Zaire (1978), USSR in Afghanistan (1979), US in Grenada (1983) etc. For a thorough list see Tanca, *Foreign armed intervention in internal conflict*, 149 et seq.

[79] Although the ICJ examined the "invitation" argument in Nicaragua, it did not go so far as to elucidate which entity is to be considered the legitimate government of the country, the one that is entitled to invite outside help during a civil conflict.

[80] In the past, a similar confusion was created during the 1983 US intervention in Grenada. One of the justifications put forward by the invading party was an alleged invitation by the country's Governor-General. However, the latter did not have any real authority since according to the "Peoples' Laws", proclaimed by the Bishop government, all executive and legislative power were vested in the People's Revolutionary Government, the Governor-General being merely the Queen's representative—a relic of the British rule.

[81] See the famous "Estrada Doctrine" developed by the Mexican government in 1930, Philip Jessup, "The Estrada Doctrine", *AJIL* 25 (1931): 719–723. Also, http://www.diplomaticosescritores.org/obras/DOCTRINAESTRADA.pdf.

[82] See Joe Verhoeven, *La reconnaissance internationale dans la pratique contemporaine* (Paris: Pedone, 1975), 90–92. A salient exception to that was the United States, which refused for decades to recognize China, although the latter had an effective control over the whole of the territory. See L. Thomas Galloway, *Recognizing foreign governments: the practice of the United States* (Washington, DC: American Enterprise Institute, 1978); M. J. Peterson, "Recognition of governments should not be abolished," *AJIL* 77 (1983): 31–50.

[83] See, Oscar *Schachter*, "Is there a right to overthrow an illegitimate regime?": 425.

of the state.[84] Many states recognized the NTC whether as the legitimate representative of the Libyan people or as the legitimate government of Libya.[85] Recognition was not limited only to statements, which would have only political and not legal effects, but many states concluded diplomatic relations with the NTC and the EU opened a diplomatic representation in Benghazi.[86] Given that the NTC at that time controlled only the eastern part of the country and the Qaddafi forces still controlled the capital, its

---

84 See in that respect, Stefan Talmon, "Recognition of the Libyan Transitional Council," *ASIL Insights* 15 (16) (2011).

85 The first country to recognize the Libyan insurgents was France, stating that the NTC was "the sole legitimate representative of the Libyan people"; see Alan Cowell & Steven Erlanger, "France Becomes First Country to Recognize Libyan Rebels," NY Times, 10.3.2011. Soon Italy followed on 4.4.2011, declaring that it recognizes the NTC as the "sole legitimate interlocutor"; see statement of Franco Frattini in *Le Figaro*, 4.4.2011. Germany, though not participating in the UN authorized military mission, recognized the NTC as "the legitimate representation of the Libyan people."; see the statement of Foreign Minister Guido Westerwelle, reproduced in Judy Dempsey, "Germany officially recognizes Libyan rebel government," NY Times 13.7.2011. On 11.7.2011, Switzerland stated that: "En attendant l'élection d'un gouvernement légitime, le CNT est l'unique interlocuteur de la Suisse en Libye"; see http://www.eda.admin.ch/eda/fr/home/recent/media/single.html?id=40181. On 15 July 2011, the USA recognized the NTC as the legitimate government of the country, allowing the access to 30 billion dollars of Libyan assets in the US; see the statement of the Secretary of State, Hilary Clinton: "US will join more than 30 countries in extending diplomatic recognition to the main opposition group, known as the NTC", NY Times 15.7.2011.

A salient exception is Cuba that refused to extend any recognition, condemning this act as an illegitimate interference. In a statement the Cuban Ministry of Foreign Affairs stresses that "Cuba does not recognize the NTC or any provisional authority in Libya; it will only recognize a government set up in that country in a legitimate way and by the free, sovereign and unique will of the Libyan people... urgent need to allow the Libyan people to find peaceful and negotiated solution, without any foreign interference and in tune with their inalienable right to independence and self-determination, and their sovereignty over their natural resources and territorial integrity of their nation', NY Times 3.9.2011. See for a list of recognitions http://fr.wikipedia.org/wiki/Reconnaissance_internationale_du_Conseil_national_de_transition#cite_note-66.

As far as international organizations are concerned, on 16.9.2011, the UN General Assembly accepted the credentials of the delegation of Libya at its 66th session, giving thereby the seat of Libya to the NTC (res. 66/1 A). Until then 86 countries had recognized the NTC as the "legitimate authority". However, the AU declined until the very last moment to recognize the NTC and it was only after the UN recognition that it decided to call it to occupy the seat of Libya [PSC/PR/COMM/2.(CCXCVII), 20.10.2011].

86 In May 2011, the EU opened a delegation in Benghazi and offered more than 140 million euros for humanitarian needs, see Ana Gomes, "Was EUfor Libya an April fool's joke?," EU Observer, 13.7.2011. One should also pay attention to art. 41 par. 1 of the Vienna Convention on Diplomatic Relations, according to which "all persons enjoying privileges and immunities have a duty not to interfere in the internal affairs of the receiving state" and the extent to which it is related with the establishment of diplomatic missions in Benghazi.

recognition as the de jure government seemed premature or precipitated and could even be considered illegal intervention in the internal affairs of the state.[87]

Furthermore, one of the consequences of the recognition of the NTC as the legitimate government of Libya concerns the legality of providing support, such as military advisors and equipment, to the opposition forces. It is true that overall third states' intervention in Libya (through the NATO forces) is covered by the UNSC authorization for the use of force. However, there is a dispute over whether the boundaries of UNSC res. 1973 have been transcended or not.[88] Indeed, the aim of the mission was to "protect civilians and civilian populated areas, including Benghazi" (Benghazi had been directly the object of threats by the Qaddafi forces). In this context the provision of arms and the dispatch of military advisors to the NTC,[89] insofar as they were intended to achieve the aim of the "responsibility to protect" mission, are considered legitimate. However, the provision of general support for the long-term stabilization of the new regime and the assistance in the establishment of administrative infrastructure go one step further from the responsibility to protect. Actually these acts could substantiate a forcible intervention in favour of the opposition forces in the civil war,[90] an accusation the respective countries tried to avoid by recognizing the NTC as the legitimate government of the

---

[87] See also the statements of French officials, pointing towards the need of regime change: "Qaddafi can stay in Libya if he relinquishes power", NY Times 20.7.2011. To the contrary an Obama administration spokesperson was more careful. He said that "Qaddafi needs to remove himself from power... then it's up to the Libyan people to decide", NY Times 20.7.2011.

[88] See the posts of Dapo Akande in EJIL: *Talk!*; "Does SC Resolution 1973 Permit Coalition Military Support for the Libyan Rebels?"; "Which entity is the government of Libya and why does it matter?," 16.6.2011, "France admits to arming Libyan rebels—Was this lawful?," 1.7.2011. See also Gleider Hernández & Thomas Liefländer, "Can Gaddafi invoke self-defence against NATO? Have NATO leaders committed the crime of aggression?," EJIL: *Talk*! 6.7.2011.

[89] The United Kingdom, USA and France have admitted doing so; see NY Times 29.6.2011.

[90] See also the wording of the *Nicaragua* judgment: "The US aid to the contras in Nicaragua in recruiting, training, arming, equipping, financing, supplying and otherwise encouraging, supporting, aiding, and directing military and paramilitary actions in and against Nicaragua is a breach of the prohibition of the use of force... they participated in acts of civil strife in another state in contravention to the Declaration of Friendly Relations. Arming and training of the contras involves the threat or use of force. The mere supply of funds, while undoubtedly an act of intervention in the internal affairs of the state, it did not amount to the use of force", at para. 228. It is interesting that according to the same judgment there does not have to be intention. If one state supports and assists armed bands whose purpose is to overthrow the government that amounts to an inter-

country.[91] It is interesting to note that, when the Syrian uprising broke out the Syrian National Council[92] stated in a meeting in Turkey that "the Syrian people would welcome an intervention on the part of Turkey for the protection of civilians."[93] Until now no such initiative has taken place in the Syrian case,[94] while the recognitions of the Syrian National Council are by far fewer than those of the NTC.[95]

3.2. *Internal Self-Determination and the Right to Democracy: Towards a New Subject of International Law?*

The principle of self-determination is one of the cornerstones of the UN Charter, embodied in articles 1 (2) and 55.[96] Nevertheless, at that time the right to self-determination meant neither the right of a colonial people to achieve political independence nor the right of the people of a sovereign state to choose freely its government through democratic and regular elections. It was rather a means of furthering the development of friendly relations between states and averting as much as possible the possibility of conflicts between them.[97]

Self-determination as a right was for the first time enshrined in a binding instrument in the International Covenant on Civil and Political Rights (ICCPR) and in the International Covenant of Economic, Social and

vention whether or not the political objective of the state giving such support is equally far-reaching, at para. 241.

91 It is interesting that this runs contrary to the official position of the United Kingdom as it is reflected in the British Foreign Policy Document (1984, available in *BYIL* 57 (1986), 614): "the principle of non-intervention and the inalienable right of every state to choose its political, economic, social and cultural systems entails also the duty not to intervene to help a government in a civil war, *especially if control of the territory is divided between two factions*", which reflects exactly the situation in Libya (emphasis added).

92 It is the opposition coalition, based in Istanbul (see its official website http://www.syriancouncil.org/). Its military wing is the Free Syrian Army, composed mainly by defected Syrian armed forces personnel. Actually, the statement came by the leader of the Muslim Brotherhood, Mohamed Riad Chakfa, which is considered the backbone of the Syrian opposition.

93 Ignacio Cembrero, "La oposicion siria acepta que Turquia intervenga para proteger a los civiles," El Pais, 17.11.2011. This situation reminds us of the "humanitarian corridors" applied in Iraq after the First Gulf War (1991).

94 See, though, Steven Lee Myers, "U.S. Joins Effort to Equip and Pay Rebels in Syria," NY Times, 1.4.2012, according to which a group of countries are moving closer to direct intervention.

95 See for a list http://en.wikipedia.org/wiki/Syrian_National_Council.

96 See for the right to self-determination, Antonio Cassese, *Self-determination of peoples: a legal reappraisal* (Cambridge: CUP, 1995); Spyros Calogeropoulos-Stratis, *Le droit des peuples à disposer d'eux-mêmes* (Bruxelles: Bruylant, 1973).

97 Cassese, *Self-determination of peoples*, 42–43.

Cultural Rights (ICESCR), both adopted in 1966.[98] Article 1 of both instruments reads as follows: "1. All peoples have the right of self-determination. By virtue of that right they freely determine their political status and freely pursue their economic, social and cultural development. 2. All peoples may, for their own ends, freely dispose of their natural wealth and resources without prejudice to any obligations arising out of international economic co-operation, based upon the principle of mutual benefit, and international law. In no case may a people be deprived of its own means of subsistence. 3. The States Parties to the present Covenant, including those having responsibility for the administration of Non-Self-Governing and Trust Territories, shall promote the realization of the right of self-determination, and shall respect that right, in conformity with the provisions of the Charter of the United Nations". By virtue of those instruments, self-determination is a human right of collective character, namely the holders of the right are the peoples.[99]

Gradually, self-determination acquired an external and an internal dimension.[100] The external dimension refers to the right of a people to choose its international status and the territory where it lives; this concerns primarily people under colonial or other forms of alien domination or foreign occupation and entitles them to fight against such domination or occupation.[101] On the other hand the internal dimension concerns the

---

[98] The right to self-determination is not mentioned in the Universal Declaration of Human Rights. Before the adoption of the two Covenants, it had been enshrined in the Declaration on the granting of independence to colonial countries and peoples [UNGA res. 1514 (XV), 14.12.1960]. In 1981, the African Charter on Human and Peoples' Rights became the first (and only) regional instrument to refer to the right to self-determination. See also the Declaration on Friendly Relations, principle V.

[99] For a distinction between holders and beneficiaries, see Cassese, *Self-determination of peoples*, 141 et seq. See also Robert McCorquodale, "Self-determination: a human rights approach," *ICLQ* 43 (1994): 857. Despite the clear wording of the two Covenants, the jurisprudence of the competent organs demonstrates that the right is not justiciable in the context of individual communications, while a constant issue is the absence of a universally accepted definition for the term "people(s)". This refers particularly to applications submitted by (indigenous) peoples in America, Africa and Europe, that were rejected as inadmissible, see African Commission on Human and Peoples' Rights, Communication 75/92, *Katangese Peoples' Congress/Zaire*, 8th Annual Activity Report, 1995; Human Rights Committee, *Chief Bernard Ominayak and the Lubicon Lake Band/Canada*, Communication no. 167/84, views UN doc. supp. no. 40 (A/45/40), 26.3.1990, *Ivan Kitok/Sweden*, Communication no. 197/1985, views CCPR/C/33/D/197/1985, 27.7.1988, *Diergaardt/Namibia*, Communication no. 760/1997, views CCPR/C/69/D/760/1997, 25.7.2000.

[100] Cassese, Self-determination of peoples, 67 et seq.; General Comment No. 12: The right to self-determination of peoples, 13.3.1984.

[101] See Declaration on the granting of independence to colonial countries and peoples; Declaration on Friendly Relations, principle V; *Western Sahara*, Advisory Opinion, I.C.J.

right of the people to have a government that is representative of the whole people, without distinction regarding race, beliefs or colour.[102] In the former case the people have the right to seek independence, whereas in the latter one cannot question the territorial integrity of the state whatsoever.[103]

It has already been said above that when a civil war is raging in a foreign state, the other states shall refrain from assisting in any manner whatsoever the insurgents. This duty retreats whenever the insurgents qualify as national liberation movements.[104] In particular, in such a case, third states can assist them and even recognize them "without this being considered

---

Reports 1975, 55. During the decolonization phase, several groups of insurgents qualified as national liberation movements. Gradually, they acquired their independence from foreign domination and turned into proper states. The remaining two groups that bear the rights and duties of national liberation movements are the Frente Polisario in Western Sahara, fighting against the occupation by Morocco, and the Palestine Liberation Organization representing the Palestinian people fighting against Israeli occupation. For the status of national liberation movements as subjects of international law, see art. 1 (4) Additional Protocol I (1977) to the Geneva Conventions of 1949 relating to the Protection of Victims of International Armed Conflicts, whereby situations in which peoples are fighting against colonial domination and alien occupation and against racist regimes in the exercise of their right of self-determination are recognized as armed conflicts of international character.

102 Declaration on Friendly Relations, principle V (7); *Western Sahara*, Advisory Opinion, I.C.J. Reports 1975, 55.

103 See however, the analysis by Cassese, *Self-determination of peoples*, 118, regarding racial groups and whether they are entitled only to internal self-determination or they can go so far as to claim external self-determination, i.e. the right to secede from the oppressive state. This is a question strikingly opportune, given that during the Libyan crisis there have also been unofficial discussions regarding the possible secession of Eastern Libya and the formation of two states. Fortunately, there was no such *fait accompli* that would perplex even more international law and international relations that have yet to overcome the problems posed by Kosovo's declaration of independence (see the highly ambivalent advisory opinion of the International Court of Justice, *Accordance with international law of the unilateral declaration of independence in respect of Kosovo*, General List no. 141, 22.7.2010, where it actually refrained from examining the legal consequences of the declaration of independence, confining itself only to the legality of the declaration as such). The Committee on the Elimination of Racial Discrimination has overruled the existence of such a right for racial groups, see General Recommendation no. 21: The right to self-determination, 23.8.1996.

104 See Declaration on Friendly Relations, op. cit. Principle V, §5 "such peoples are entitled to seek and to receive support in accordance with the purposes and principles of the Charter". There is extensive discussion as to the kind of assistance peoples struggling for self-determination are entitled to, see in that respect George Abi-Saab, "Wars of national liberation in the Geneva Conventions and Protocols," *RCADI* 165 (1979), 371–372; Tanca, *Foreign armed intervention in internal conflict*, 100–110. On the other hand the ICJ in the *Nicaragua* judgment left on one side the question whether assistance to national liberation movements can be considered as an exception to the principle of non-intervention, para. 206. Be that as it may a foreign direct armed intervention is hardly considered legitimate.

a premature recognition or constituting an intervention in the domestic affairs of the colonial or alien government."[105]

In view of the widespread recognition of the NTC by the international community, could one maintain that there is a leaning of attributing particular status to peoples fighting for democracy (i.e. internal self-determination) similar to that which national liberation movements fighting for external self-determination enjoyed? Is there a tendency of recognizing the people fighting for democracy as a distinct subject of international law? Has the Arab Spring changed the way invitations are perceived in international law since the famous statement from the *Nicaragua* case: "no such general right of intervention, in support of the opposition within another state, exists in contemporary international law"? Or does the law remain—to a large extent—the same?

International practice recorded by the response of third states to the "Arab Spring" does not support such a theory. It is true that both the National Transitional Council and the Syrian National Council strive to acquire a distinct status in international law. In the aftermath of its formation, the NTC issued a document "A vision for a democratic Libya,"[106] where it exposed its aspirations for a "modern, free and united Libya". The aims comprised, inter alia, the drafting of a National Constitution endorsed by a referendum, the formation of political parties and the holding of free and fair elections, the upholding of political pluralism, overall the consolidation of democracy through the protection and guarantee of human rights (including social rights) and fundamental freedoms. Though it did not refer particularly to the right to self-determination, "the establishment of a political authority that will represent the free will of the people, without exclusion or suppression of any voice" actually describes the very essence of the term. The Syrian National Council moves on the same track.[107] Both groups seem to fulfill by and large the standards set by the OAU Coordinating Committee for the Liberation of Africa for the recognition of national liberation movements as the sole legitimate representatives of the people. According to these standards, in order to be recognized, the respective groups must be the united action fronts against the rulers (Qaddafi or Assad), they must be broad-based, they must have

---

105 Abi-Saab, "Wars of national liberation."

106 http://www.ntclibya.org/english/libya/

107 See http://www.syriancouncil.org/en/mission-statement.html.

popular support throughout the country and they must have a reasonable armed forces backing.[108]

The international community responded positively to these efforts by recognizing gradually the two entities. Nevertheless, one can not speak of a consolidated practice of recognizing "people fighting for democracy" as a distinct subject of international law, along with states, international organizations, national liberation movements and individuals. Consequently, there is no separate right of third states to offer direct or indirect assistance to peoples vindicating the right to democracy or the right to internal self-determination.[109] The only way to offer assistance legitimately is through the recognition of the said group as the legitimate representative of the people or as the legitimate authority of the state in question.

4. The "Responsibility to protect" Doctrine and the "Arab Spring"

Emanating from the controversial doctrine of "humanitarian intervention,"[110] the "responsibility to protect" (R2P) doctrine was spelled out in the 2005 World Summit Outcome.[111] The primary responsibility to protect the population from genocide, war crimes, ethnic cleansing and crimes against humanity, including by adopting preventive measures, lies with the territorial state.[112] Along with the state in question, the international

[108] One could question the fulfilment of these criteria, especially regarding the broad support, since it has not been upheld through national elections or through another objective mechanism.

[109] Such a right would actually be a restatement of the "Reagan Doctrine", which justified United States' military support to insurgents fighting against regimes considered to be totalitarian and illegitimate, see Robert Turner, "International law, the Reagan Doctrine and World Peace," *The Washington Quarterly* 11 (1988): 119–136. See also the wording of the ICJ in *Nicaragua*: "...a general right for States to intervene, in support of an internal opposition in another State, whose cause appeared particularly worthy by reason of the political and moral values with which it was identified. For such a general right to come into existence would involve a fundamental modification of the customary law principle of non-intervention", 206–207.

[110] *Humanitarian intervention: ethical, legal, and political dilemmas*, ed. J. L. Holzgrefe & Robert O. Keohane (Cambridge: Cambridge University Press, 2003). For the most recent controversial application see Christine Gray, "The legality of Nato's military action in Kosovo: is there a right of humanitarian intervention?," in *International law in the post-Cold War world: essays in memory of Li Haopei*, ed. Sienho Yee & Wang Tieya (London: Routledge, 2001), 240–253.

[111] Paras. 138–140.

[112] This is in line with the stipulations of the major human rights treaties, namely that the contracting parties shall secure to everyone within their jurisdiction the rights and

community, through the UN, has also the responsibility to use all appropriate peaceful means, in accordance with Chapters VI and VIII of the UN Charter, so as to assist in the protection of the population. Should such peaceful means prove inadequate and national authorities unwilling or incapable of affording protection to the population, the UN can proceed to collective action, through the Security Council, in accordance with the Charter, including Chapter VII (i.e. even authorize the use of force), on a case-by-case basis and in cooperation with relevant regional organizations as appropriate.

The uprising in Libya and the subsequent open armed conflict between the two factions in Tripoli and Benghazi posed a series of challenges for the international community. The alleged perpetration of crimes against humanity against peaceful demonstrators and the preannounced "no mercy" advance of the Qaddafi troops toward Benghazi, alarmed the international community that urged the intervention of the UN Security Council to halt the bloodshed.

The latter intervened first by adopting resolution 1970 (2011) which, while requesting an immediate end to violence, provided for a series of measures: a) referral of the situation to the International Criminal Court, in pursuance of article 13b of the ICC Statute, due to serious indications that the widespread and systematic attacks against the civilian population could amount to crimes against humanity, b) arms embargo, namely the prevention of direct or indirect supply, sale or transfer to Libya of arms and related materiel of all types, c) travel ban against Qaddafi, members of his family and high-level officials of the regime, d) assets freeze against Qaddafi and members of his family. Meanwhile, Libya had been suspended from participation in the UN Human Rights Council.[113]

The inability to find a solution to the crisis and the imminent threat to civilians created by the ongoing violence led to the adoption of UNSC Res. 1973,[114] which imposed a no-fly zone and continued the arms embargo and the targeted sanctions (including inter alia against the Libyan Ambassador to Chad, who was suspected of direct involvement in recruiting and coordinating mercenaries for the regime). This resolution has also been admittedly the first implementation of the R2P doctrine. The mission

freedoms defined in the respective instruments, see art. 2 (1) ICCPR, 1 ECHR, 1 (1) ACHR, 1 ACHPR.

113 UNGA res. A/RES/65/265, 3 March 2011.

114 Adopted on 17 March 2011 by 10 votes in favour and 5 abstentions (Brazil, China, Germany, India, Russian Federation). See S/PV.6498.

"Odyssey Dawn", carried out by French, British, US, Danish and Canadian armed forces (Germany abstained from any military action), lasted from 19–31 March 2011. It was followed by NATO mission "Operation Unified Protector" and had as its objective to "protect civilians and civilian populated areas under threat of attack in the Libyan Arab Jamahiriya, including Benghazi, while excluding a foreign occupation force of any form on any part of Libyan territory". The mission ended officially on 31 October 2011, after the NTC had effectively assumed power and declared Libya "liberated."[115]

There are certain issues in the application of the R2P doctrine in the Libya case-study that created a crack to the initial euphoria of international actors and public opinion. While it was felt that the UN was actually acting to prevent a mass killing rather than watching the events unfolding, the absence of clear objectives for the NATO mission, the violation of international humanitarian law by the parties to the conflict and the growing number of victims notwithstanding the UNSC resolution,[116] placed international public opinion in a somewhat awkward situation. Among the issues that emerged, one can distinguish the following:

- First and foremost, although the international reaction was timely enough, an important link seemed to be missing: the preventive dimension. Indeed, one should not forget that the R2P is a larger concept—requires prevention rather than repression—and cannot be limited simply to military action. The human rights organs have long ago reported the flagrant human rights violations in all the countries of the

115 See UNSC res. 2016 (2011), para. 5. Colonel Qaddafi was beaten and killed on 20 October 2011 by NTC forces, after having been captured alive during the battle of Sirte.

116 Articles and reports in the newspapers arguably demonstrate that the NATO mission was not impartial, while it also overstepped the mandate of the UNSC (emphasis added): "Information on Libyan forces filters up from CIA officers and allied special operations troops *working with the rebels on the ground*... These are used to build a round-the-clock campaign that allied officers say is *preventing Colonel Qaddafi from making sustainable attacks on rebel fighters... We're grinding down the regime*... The targeting process started in Brussels in March when *NATO ambassadors approved the broad objectives of the campaign*... the allied mission has largely achieved its goal of *protecting civilians, especially in eastern Libya*, and has seriously damaged the Libyan military"; Eric Schmitt, "Daunting Task for NATO in Libya as Strikes Intensify," NY Times, 24.5.2011; "*Les insurgés, soutenus par l'aviation de l'OTAN* (the NTC enjoyed overall support, not only for the protection of civilians), Confusion autour de négociations entre les rebelles et le régime libyen," Le Monde, 16.8.2011. Moreover, following the official fall of the Qaddafi regime, NATO forces offers military assistance to the NTC manifestly (see for instance the attack on Sirte on 26 September 2011—military assistance to the NTC and lack of protection of the civilians of "the other side").

"Arab Spring", including Libya,[117] but the long-lasting problems were not treated with adequacy by the international community.[118]

- A second issue is the selectivity in the application of the R2P doctrine.[119] The case of Syria is an emblematic one. While the EU[120] and the Arab League[121] have imposed sanctions against Syria, the UNSC could finally agree only on a presidential statement,[122] due to two consecutive vetos on a draft resolution by Russia and China.[123] After months of violent clashes, thousands of people killed, ongoing discussions about the urgency of allowing the passage of humanitarian aid for those in need[124] and un unsuccessful Arab League action plan to exit the crisis,[125] the UN in cooperation with the Arab League decided to dispatch a Joint Special Envoy, former UN Secretary General Kofi Annan, to break the deadlock.[126] The Joint Special Envoy put forward a six-point proposal to end the crisis that seeks to stop the violence and the killing, give access to humanitarian agencies, release detainees, and kick-start an inclusive political dialogue. In this context, the Syrian government had informed the Joint Special Envoy that it will complete the withdrawal of troops

117 See indicatively the concluding observations of the Human Rights Committee on Libya (CCPR/C/LBY/CO/4, 15.11.2007), Syria (CCPR/CO/84/SYR, 9.8.2005), Yemen (CCPR/CO/84/YEM, 9.8.2005), Egypt (CCPR, A/58/40, 2003) and the Committee against Torture on Bahrain (CAT/C/CR/34/BHR, 21.6.2005).

118 The martial laws in Egypt (1981) and Syria (1963) are salient examples.

119 World summit outcome: "on a case-by-case basis".

120 The EU has gradually introduced comprehensive restrictive measures (asset freeze, travel ban, ban on import/export of oil, arms etc.) starting in May 2011 against high-level institutions, officials and members of the al-Assad family (including the First Lady, Asma al-Assad), see Council Regulation EU 442/2011, 9.5.2011 concerning restrictive measures in view of the situation in Syria, OJ L 121/10.5.2011, p. 1 and Council Decision 2011/273/CFSP, 9.5.2011 concerning restrictive measures against Syria, OJ L 121, 10.5.2011, p. 11. In total 13 sets of restrictive measures have been introduced, see for an overview http://www.consilium.europa.eu/uedocs/cms_data/docs/pressdata/EN/foraff/128379.pdf.

121 The LAS Council decided to suspend Syria from membership on 16.11.2011 (Res. 7438—R.Extraordinary Session, 2/11/2011) and imposed economic embargo by virtue of Res. 7442-Ex.S. 27.11.2011.

122 S/PRST/2012/6 (21.3.2012). A first presidential statement has been issued on 3.8.2011. See S/PRST/2011/16.

123 Draft resolutions S/2011/612 (4.10.2011) and S/2012/77 (4.2.2012).

124 It is characteristic that after the fall of Homs (March 2012) the Syrian authorities had denied access to an ICRC convoy with medical supplies and food, see Neil McFarquhar & Alan Cowell, "Syria Blocks Red Cross Aid to Rebel Enclave in Homs," NY Times, 2.3.2012.

125 The Observer Mission was formed pursuant to the Protocol signed on 19.12.2011 by the Syrian Government and the LAS General Secretariat but did not manage to halt the violence. It was terminated on 12 February 2012 (see res. 7446/12.2.2012).

126 See Council of the LAS res. 7444/22.1.2012 plan to peacefully resolve the Syrian crisis.

and heavy weapons from population centres by 10 April 2012. Unless the plan succeeds every option is on the table, especially after the Arab League call on the SC to form a joint Arab-United Nations peacekeeping force to oversee implementation of the eventual ceasefire.[127]

- The third issue is the abstract mandate. Resolution 1973 (2011) urges the protection of civilians and civilian populated areas "under threat of attack". Indeed, the wording could be interpreted very broadly. Does Qaddafi resistance to relinquishing power pose a threat for civilians? Does it mean that Qaddafi should not prevail in this civil war, because this would mean that civilians would be under imminent threat of attack? Could NATO forces bomb the Qaddafi compound in pursuance of the SC resolution?[128] The vagueness in the mission is an additional argument for those that maintain that it was actually a "regime change" mission.[129]
- Finally, the UN should reflect on certain thorny issues regarding the overall character of R2P missions. Can a UN R2P mission take sides in a civil conflict? Are civilians of the opposite side less worth protecting? Shouldn't such missions be by definition impartial and neutral so that they can protect effectively all civilians under threat of attack? In case use of force becomes unavoidable, R2P missions should be governed by impartiality, neutrality and clear mandates.

---

127 Res. 7446/12.2.2012. Reservations were expressed by Algeria and Lebanon.

128 For a brief account on what the authorization permits see Dapo Akande, "What does UNSC resolution 1973 permit?," EJIL: *Talk!* 23.3.2011. On 30 April 2011 NATO shelled the Qaddafi compound killing one of his sons and three of his grandchildren "in the sharpest intensification yet of the NATO air campaign intended to *pressure the Libyan leader from power*" (emphasis added) as was reported in the NY Times. See also further references: "the campaign against Libya's most densely populated areas raised new questions about *how broadly NATO is interpreting its UN mandate to protect civilians*" (emphasis added). The Qaddafi administration complained that the attack was illegitimate because: "this was a direct operation to assassinate the leader of this country ... this is not permitted by international law. It is not permitted by any moral code or principle". On the other hand, NATO stated that its target was not Qaddafi. According to its operational commander: "all NATO's targets are military in nature and have been clearly linked to the Qaddafi regime's systematic attacks on the Libyan population and populated areas. We do not target individuals". Nevertheless, the resilience of the regime led NATO to intensify its strikes on the broader instruments of Qaddafi's power, including state television facilities and command centres in the capital.

129 See also the wording of UNSC 2009 (2011): "Looks forward to the establishment of an inclusive, representative transitional Government of Libya, and emphasises the need for the transitional period to be underpinned by a commitment to democracy, good governance, rule of law and respect for human rights", at 2.

5. Concluding Observations

In an interview, Noam Chomsky has criticized the Libya intervention, saying that: "... there was no effort to institute a no-fly zone. The triumvirate at once interpreted the resolution as authorizing direct participation on the side of the rebels. A ceasefire was imposed by force on Qaddafi's forces, but not on the rebels. On the contrary, they were given military support as they advanced to the West, soon securing the major sources of Libya's oil production, and poised to move on". He has also questioned the motives of overthrowing Qaddafi, saying that: "the vast territory of Libya is mostly unexplored, and oil specialists believe it may have rich untapped resources, which a more dependable government might open to Western exploitation."[130] Whatever interpretation one may give to the actions of third states vis-à-vis the Libya crisis, it is beyond doubt that the intervention was effectuated in full accordance with the UN Charter. Additionally, the legal justification of intervening in the country is clearly strengthened by the "responsibility to protect" doctrine, irrespective of its implementation defaults.

Indeed, it has already been mentioned that the "Arab Spring" uncovered two important deficits in the "responsibility to protect" doctrine. The first one is selectivity; and the second, prevention. Both can be overcome or at least handled by the initiatives of regional organizations. The reference to Chapter VIII in the World Summit Outcome regarding the responsibility of the international community to use all appropriate peaceful means, so as to assist in the protection of the population, means that regional organizations have an important role to play, including in the consolidation of democratic institutions as an indispensable condition for effective human rights protection and the establishment of the rule of law.[131] The institutional preparedness of various actors in areas such as the protection and promotion of democracy, as well as the economic and social development, is essential for the prevention of crises that could eventually escalate, especially in fragile states, in open conflicts.

---

130 "On Libya and the Unfolding Crises", Noam Chomsky interviewed by Stephen Shalom and Michael Albert, ZNet, 30.3.2011, available at http://www.chomsky.info/interviews/20110330.htm.

131 The unprecedented mobilization of the Arab League in the case of Syria, despite the serious shortcomings regarding its effectiveness, is nevertheless remarkable; see http://www.arableagueonline.org, especially the decisions of the LAS Council.

The African Union seems ready to start moving toward this direction, having to encounter the next major challenge in the region: in April 2012, as an indirect consequence of the turmoil in Libya, a mutiny had taken place in Mali and the MNLA (Mouvement National pour la Libération de l'Azaoud) secessionist group declared independence of the northern region of Azawad. In its struggle to achieve security, stability and the rule of law in the region, the AU and other sub-regional organizations (such as ECOWAS) should draw on OAS best practices. Despite the differences in the level of regional integration and the incomparable challenges and problems between the Americas and Africa, the OAS response in similar cases can function as a model both for the AU and other regional organizations.

CHAPTER NINE

THE POSSIBLE ROLE OF NATIONAL COURTS IN THE AFTERMATH OF THE ARAB SPRING

Tamas Vince Adany*

1. Introduction

The role of international law in the management of a political transition of a society is ever more increasing, yet that role is still severely limited. While strong arguments support international law describing several essential features of a democracy, as a system that is based on sovereignty and the consequent respect for domestic affairs, international law is capable of describing the *means* to (re)build democracy only in exceptional cases.

Furthermore, due to the differences among various post-conflict or transitional societies, there cannot be a readily available international legal solution to these problems. Instead, there are a number of tools described by international law that may aid that transition, yet the choice in most cases must be made by the effected society itself.[1] A set of these tools are aimed at facing the past, rather than building the future.

Apparently, only facing the past will not solve all the problems of a transition, and will not magically create a fully-fledged democracy. However, it is an assumption of this chapter, that in the course of transition, a

* Department of Public International Law of the Pázmány Péter Catholic University, Budapest, Hungary.

[1] The dilemma of retribution v. clemency is already present in the works of Hugo Grotius. "Pardon, say they, is the Remission of a Punishment that is due, but a wise Man will always do what he ought to do. Here the Fallacy lies in the Word due. For if by due be meant, that he, who has offended, deserves to be punished, that is, may be punished without Injustice, it will not follow from hence, that he, who forbears to punish him, does what he ought not to do. But if it be meant, that Punishment is in such a Manner due from a wise Man, that he is indispensibly obliged to exact it, we say, that that doth not always happen, and therefore in this Sense Punishment is not always due, but permitted only. And that may be true, as well before the penal Law as afterwards." "But as he [the Lawmaker] can take away the Whole Law, so he may suspend the Obligation of any Part of it"; See Chapter XX, sections XXI and XXIV of Book 2 of De Iure Belli ac Pacis, in Hugo Grotius, *The Rights of War and Peace*, ed. Richard Tuck (Indianapolis: Liberty Fund Inc, 2005).

decision on facing the past must be made in every society.[2] Even if in the end there is no institutionalised solution thereof, a public decision must be made to that end.

It is therefore not necessary in every transitional society to resort to criminal justice, nevertheless it can be one of the many factors a society needs to face its past.[3] Since the early 1990's, the time of the Eastern and Central European transitions, international law has undergone a considerable development in that field, inasmuch as it is somewhat easier today to select the wrongs or wrongdoers of the past subjected to criminal justice.[4] The aim of the present chapter is to identify such international standards that can be used in that selection, and to mark those other international legal requirements, that must be respected by the local authorities, if and when they resort to retribution. At the time of writing, Tunisia and Egypt have already advanced procedures against their former leaders.

The first part of this chapter summarises some of the most important arguments for accountability, offering some arguments to the dilemma of penalisation or clemency. The conclusion reached here is that a certain level of personal responsibility is required for a lasting social peace. As for the realisation thereof, based on the level of involvement of the international community, an imaginary scale may be drawn from international criminal procedures to the complete lack of individual responsibility. The present chapter assumes that it would be fortunate and in some cases necessary to rely on national courts in the realisation of such accountability. By application of a technique widely used in the business world, the second part therefore considers the strengths, weaknesses, options and threats of national criminal procedures conducted by various national courts of the Arab world. Even though preference is given to national procedures, such courts should remain aware of the international legal context of their work. A "good" judiciary shall be able to comply with the actually existing international requirements of a fair, expeditious and genuine procedure, both in terms of human rights and in terms of efficiency.

---

[2] Jamal Benomar, "Justice After Transitions," in *Transitional Justice: how emerging democracies reckon with former regimes, Volume I—General Considerations*, ed. Neil J. Kritz (Washington D.C.: United States Institute of Peace, 1995): 34.

[3] Luc Huyse, "Justice After Transition: On the Choices Successor Elites Make in Dealing With the Past," in *Transitional* Justice: 337–339.

[4] The set of international crimes have become much clearer after the completion of the Rome and Kampala conferences. The work of the *ad hoc* tribunals and the drafters of the Rome Statute provided for numerous evidence of the customary nature of genocide, crimes against humanity and to some considerable extent war crimes as well.

2. The Need for Accountability

Participation in mass human rights violations may entail either some form of responsibility or some form of clemency during or after a political transition. As a main rule, the dilemma between "retribution or reconciliation" must be solved by the effected society itself, and strong arguments support and also contradict both possible ways.

In a post-conflict or transitional society a demand for vengeance over persons formerly serving the previous system would most likely emerge.[5] Besides, peaceful integration of the former officials and the victims into a democratic society is needed as well.[6] There can be no general recipe for finding an equilibrium between these needs; the choice is a difficult one and should be reached by the effected society itself, for many factors, such as national culture, the history of the former regime and the actual political realities[7] may have an impact on the final decisions. Presumably all oppressive political systems rely on some sort of coercive machinery, which would typically be the police or armed forces of the state, whereas the extent of military penetration to society varies across authoritarian systems.[8] The role of these forces as instruments of repression and their respective position after the transition is also such an important factor, as is evidenced by the Argentinian,[9] the recent Egyptian[10] and countless other examples.

Examining the issue of retribution, some argue that criminal procedures are required to separate the old system from the new one,[11] while others

---

[5] Antonio Cassese, "Clemency versus Retribution in Post-Conflict Situations," *Columbia Journal of Transnational Law* 46 (2009): pp. 5–6. See also: "Egypt court to deliver Mubarak trial verdict on 2 June" BBC, 22 February 2012, http://www.bbc.co.uk/news/world-middle-east-17120915.

[6] Richard H. Solomon, "Preface," in *Transitional Justice: how emerging democracies reckon with former regimes, Volume I—General Considerations* ed. Neil J. Kritz (Washington D.C: United States Institute of Peace, 1995).

[7] Solomon, "Preface".

[8] Guillermo O'Donnell and Phillippe C. Schmitter, "Transitions from Authoritarian Rule: Tentative Conclusions about Uncertain Democracies," in: *Transitional Justice*: 61.

[9] Alejandro M. Garro, "Nine Years of Transition to Democracy in Argentina: Partial Failure or Qualified Success", *Columbia Journal of Transnational Law* 31 (1994): 9–10; Kathryn Lee Crawford, "Due Obedience and the Rights of Victims: Argentina's Transition to Democracy," *Human Rights Quarterly* 12 (1990): 50–51.

[10] Jeff Martini & July Taylor, "Commanding Democracy in Egypt: The Military's Attempt to Manage the Future," *Foreign Affairs* 90 (2011): 129.

[11] See mutatis mutandis: Eric A. Posner & Adrian Vermeule, "Transitional Justice as Ordinary Justice," *Harvard Law Review* 117 (2003): 764.

maintain that such show trials or other solutions with a dubious human rights background are alien from the essence of a democratic society.[12] The contradiction between these two observations is not inevitable, as the first statement refers to the content, the second one to the form of actions. It is a truism that show trials do not befit democratic societies, and young democracies are particularly vulnerable to such threats.[13] However, opting for criminal justice in the course of a political transition ought not to be equal to opting for mere vengeance.

As for the contents, there are convincing arguments approving the isolation of those who have planned, ordered, or executed atrocities and their removal from society are necessary elements of an efficient political transition.[14] Without some kind of retribution, wounds of the society cannot heal,[15] and may be infected by ideas of collective responsibility, which in turn brings lasting hatred. However, human rights considerations must be closely scrutinised in any attempted retribution in order to avoid sowing the seeds of future nostalgic sentiments towards the former officials. Criminal procedures seem to be an obvious solution to serve as an appropriate framework to achieve such goals, as modern criminal justice bears *inter alia* both retributive and preventive functions,[16] while the well-established case law on the requirements of fair trials is also available through several international courts.[17]

Nevertheless, criminal justice is not a "Swiss Army knife" of facing the past: by its nature it is suitable to answer the question of guilt in individual cases. In the course of a judicial process, the court would establish the facts of the case, attach a legal qualification thereto, and finally draw the legal consequences (apply the adequate sanctions), as derivable from the qualification itself. Finding the facts does not make the court a place

---

[12] Neil J. Kritz "The Dilemmas of Transitional Justice," *in: Transitional Justice*: xxi; Benomar, "Justice After Transitions," 32–33.

[13] See Decision of the Hungarian Constitutional Court No. 53/1993. (X.13.) AB. Para. 4 a) An unofficial English Translation is available at www.icrc.org, National implementation of international humanitarian law—National case law.

[14] Cassese, "Clemency versus Retribution," 4.

[15] See Cassandra Fox-Charles, "Truth vs. Justice: Promoting the Rule of Law in Post-Apartheid South Africa," *Scholar* (2010): 103.

[16] Eszter Kirs, *Demokratikus átmenet a háborús bűntettek árnyékában [Democratic Transition in the Shadows of War Crimes]* (Miskolc, Bíbor, 2012), 15–19.

[17] As the precise contents of the right to fair trial could be the subjects of independent volumes, only a few examples are mentioned here to illustrate the relevant ECHR case law: Case of Neumeister v. Austria, Application No. 1936/63, Judgement of 27 June 1968, Case of Golder v. the UK, Application no. 4451/70, Judgement of 21 February 1975 etc.

of historical justice, because it would be unwise from a non-common law court to attempt to rule anything but the given case. The right to generally qualify a rather large set of cases is reserved to the legislator, and that role is rarely played by judges.[18] The judge is not a historian[19] and in civil law legal systems neither is he making the law. Facing the past thus may very possibly require different methods as well, because when a society needs to face the troubles of its past, there are many perspectives possible.

First, the victims of an oppressive regime do not necessarily form a single group. Just as it is recognised in international humanitarian law, different categories of victims require different treatment, not just in the conflict, but after the conflict as well; a similar differentiation would be essential even if there was no preceding "conflict". Surviving family members of the murdered or disappeared persons, victims formerly imprisoned, tortured, raped, harassed or deprived of property may have different demands, and consequently require different treatment.

Second, different categories may describe the acts of former officials taking part in the atrocities, from the high-ranking masterminds to the mere auxiliary staff of the police or armed forces. Furthermore, an individual does not always fall into the separate category of victim or victimiser: the more totalitarian a system becomes, the more people it involves in upholding the oppression, and the more people become "links in the chain." In a country where the army is the primary instrument of the atrocities, some soldiers may try to turn from the policy of their superiors, and this way they become victims themselves. According to a BBC report from the 10th of April 2012, there are hundreds of army defectors among the 24,000 Syrian refugees in Turkey.[20]

Past-oriented elements of a political transition therefore include, but are not limited to, criminal justice. In order to build a lasting social peace, the society must choose a solution to the dilemma of retribution or reconciliation which gives due consideration to all groups within society. The relationship between retribution and clemency is often discussed alongside the contradicting ideas of two leading humanistic advocates of the 20th century, Simon Wiesenthal and Desmond Tutu. While Desmond Tutu argues even his chosen book title, that there is "No future without

---

18 Such as the lustration laws in former Czechoslovakia or recently in Egypt.

19 Cassese, "Clemency versus Retribution," 8.

20 Syria clashes continue as ceasefire deadline arrives, BBC, 10 April 2012 http://www.bbc.co.uk/news/world-middle-east-17661878.

forgiveness,"[21] Simon Wiesenthal concludes in one place that forgiveness is not possible on behalf of others.[22] Applying these two ideas at a social level, it is arguable that a society has the power to forgive offences committed against itself, yet there are crimes committed against mankind which should not be left unpunished.[23]

Regardless of the delicate structures of transitional societies, the most heinous acts of an oppressive political system, those reaching the level of an international crime, do demand prosecution. Some find a connection to common moral values behind the obligation to prosecute crimes of international concern;[24] others argue that this is like an entry ticket to the international community for transitional societies.[25] Avoiding impunity, prevention of future occurrences of similar acts, or the revival of the perpetrators as a relevant political power in the actual society all justify this demand, which is also reflected by international customary law, although this reflection is not crystal clear.[26]

To conclude this section, it can thus be stated that some form of criminal justice should be considered mandatory in some instances, where offences against peremptory or otherwise universally accepted norms of international have been allegedly committed.[27] On the other hand, as a judicial instrument, a criminal court is not suitable to achieve certain goals, *e.g.* to go beyond individual cases[28] or to declare finally each and

---

21 Desmond Tutu, *No Future Without Forgiveness: A Personal Overview of South Africa's Truth and Reconciliation Commission* (London: Rider, 1999).

22 Simon Wiesenthal, *The Sunflower: on the possibilities and limits of forgiveness* (New York: Shocken Books, 1997).

23 "But the Right of punishing Offences against human Society is not so exclusively theirs, but that other publick Bodies, or their Governours have a Right to procure the Punishment of them in the same Manner as the Laws of a particular State allowı every one an Action for certain Crimes. And much more have they this Right in regard to Offences, by which they are injured in particular, and which they may punish on that Account, in order to maintain their Honour and Safety, as we have said above. The State therefore, or Governour of the State, where the Delinquent is, ought to bring no Obstacle to the Right which belongs to the other Power"; Grotius, op. cit. Book II, Chapter XXI, section III,

24 Christian Tomuschat, "La Cristallisation Coutumière," in *Droit International Pénal* (Paris: Pedone, 2000), 28.

25 See the assessment of Decision of the Hungarian Constitutional Court No. 53/1993. (X.13.) AB in Tamas Vince Adany, "Individual Criminal Liability for the Crimes Committed in 1956," *Miskolc Journal of International Law* 3 (2003): 50–51.

26 Eszter Kirs, *Demokratikus átmenet a háborús bűntettek árnyékában*, 147–148.

27 In spite of the relatively large number of failures to comply with the obligation.

28 Apparently, even one successful judgement may prove that atrocities had occurred, an effect not to be neglected.

every aspect of the historical truth.[29] If social reconstruction and development demands simple historical research and publicity or management of collectives rather than individuals, judicial means are better avoided. In cases not falling within any of the categories mentioned in this paragraph, the choice to resort to judicial process or to rely on some alternative form of transitional justice is usually freely made by the effected society, or in other words by the domestic authorities.

3. A Case for and Against National Prosecution of International Crimes

Since developments taking place since the Second World War, international crimes can be prosecuted by an international, a domestic or by a mixed tribunal. In this section the strengths, weaknesses, opportunities and threats of procedures conducted by national courts are examined. SWOT analysis is a tool generally used in business life, consequently its notions should be understood *mutatis mutandis* in relation to criminal procedures. In the course of a SWOT analysis the helpful and harmful, external and internal factors are examined, usually in relation to an organisation, a new product, etc. Criminal prosecutions are rather unusual subjects for a SWOT table, therefore a few preliminary remarks are unavoidable.

When the SWOT technique is applied to identify the role of national criminal jurisdictions in a post-conflict or transitional society, certain features turn out to be able to have different functions, depending on a number of conditions. For example, a judge must keep a certain distance from the case in order to avoid becoming biased: an ultimate proximity to the case would result in a violation of the ancient maxim of *nemo iudex sua causa*. On the other hand, a judge who is completely ignorant to the cultural, linguistic, social and historical background of the case, needs to undergo a long learning (and evidential) process to adequately rule the case.

The legal and judicial structure of a transitional society to a considerable extent is rooted in that of the previous régime. Consequently, it would be a tremendous mistake to rely on an essentially rule of law logic, when assessing the legal system of an authoritarian political system, one

[29] Elizabeth B. Ludwin King, "Amnesties in a Time of Transition," *George Washington International Law Review* 41 (2010): 612.

without a functioning democracy. Substantive rules may be partly or completely ignored in such societies; as an historical example it is sufficient to mention the ratification status of the International Covenant on Civil and Political Rights.[30] By the end of the 1970s all Central and Eastern European communist satellite states, the Soviet Union itself (including Belarus and Ukraine as well) Chile and Spain had consented to be bound by the Covenant in some form or another. Nevertheless, for decades these rights remained "law in books" for all of these societies, without even the vaguest chance to transform them to "law in action."

Examining the acceptance of some relevant conventions by Arab countries reveals a similarly controversial picture. For example, most states had been parties to the Convention Against Torture well before the recent revolutions,[31] with some formulating reservations that are similar to the jurisdictional excuses of some of the former communist countries with regards to human rights conventions. A 2011 UN report has examined *inter alia* in Syria and in Yemen the situation regarding torture, and basically came to the conclusion that despite an impressive list of international conventions to prohibit torture, international rules are profoundly disregarded in both.[32] Other reports on routinely used torture and inhumane treatment have also regularly surfaced, from other Arab countries as well.[33]

The Statute of the ICC is applicable with regards to two states. Tunisian accession grants jurisdiction for events taking place after the 24th of June 2011, and by virtue of UNSC Resolution 1973, the ICC has also jurisdiction regarding the situation in Libya. Other Arab states where major demonstrations have taken place in 2011 have not yet accepted the binding force of the Rome Statute, and for the time being there is no feasible prospect that the Security Council could rely on this tool in the case of future or ongoing events, for example Syria. Nevertheless, the Rome Statute and its

---

[30] See the website of the United Nations Treaty Collection, Section IV. 4. at http://treaties.un.org as of 15.04.2012.

[31] Algeria, 1989; Bahrain, 1998; Egypt, 1986; Lybia, 1989; Morocco, 1993; Syria, 2004; Tunisia, 1988; Yemen, 1991.

[32] Report of the Committee against Torture Forty-third session (2–20 November 2009) Forty-fourth session (26 April–14 May 2010) General Assembly Official Records Sixty-fifth session Supplement No. 44 (A/65/44)A/65/44 pp. Syria: 127–139 Yemen: 139–154.

[33] A 2008 UN report on torture condemned several other Arab states (Algeria, Tunisia), for disregarding long-standing requests for invitation to country visits by UN personnel. See: Interim Report of the Special Rapporteur Manfred Nowak of the Human Rights Council on torture and other cruel, inhuman or degrading treatment or punishment, A/63/175 para. 10 A more recent report by BBC in March 2012 cited a former officer on atrocities involving the Egyptian police and security forces.

adjacent documents can be used as an academic standard for the definition of crimes and certain qualitative requirements in relation to criminal procedures beyond those discussed as "fair trial standards."

As a final preliminary remark it is noted here that due to the structure of this analysis a "strength" of a national court should not necessarily be understood as a "weakness" of an international or a mixed tribunal, unless otherwise stated.

"Strengths" are internal, helpful factors of national criminal judiciaries in the course of the political transition of a country. For the present chapter, any inherent features of national courts that would support choosing a national court over an international or a mixed tribunal are considered as strengths.

In this respect, the most convincing "strength" would be an international obligation prescribing prosecution of certain crimes by national courts. Actually, if such a general obligation exists, it would render any further elements of the SWOT table irrelevant. Meanwhile it is not really a "strength," it is much rather a "highly convincing motive" to prosecute.

According to international customary law there are certain offences subject to personal (criminal) responsibility alongside the duty to extradite or prosecute.[34] The principle *aut dedere aut iudicare* has existed in international law since early modern times, Hugo Grotius having already contemplated a version of this principle.[35] Still, both the precise scope and content of this principle deserve some explanation

The principle clearly establishes an alternative obligation on States.[36] The duty is to either extradite or prosecute the offender: performance of either of these alternatives achieves full compliance with the norm. At the time of Grotius the principle was applicable exclusively to offences committed in relation to other states.[37] By the end of the 20th century, certain crimes derived from international law became clearly explicable

---

34 Linos-Alexandre Sicilianos, "La responsabilité de l'état pour absence de prévention et de répression des crimes internationaux," in *Droit international pénal*, 120.

35 M. Cherif Bassiouni & Edward M. Wise, *Aut dedere, aut iudicare: The Duty to Extradite Or Prosecute in International Law* (Dordrecht: Martinus Nijhoff, 1995), 4–5. Other early examples for the idea of personal responsibility for atrocities date back at least to the late 19th century. See Jean-Marie Henckaerts & Louis Doswald-Beck, *Customary International Humanitarian Law Volume I: Rules* (Cambridge: ICRC/Cambridge University Press, 2005), 551.

36 As a norm of customary international law, the addressees of this duty are the states. See Bruno Simma & Andreas Paulus, "Le rôle relatif des différentes sources du droit international pénal (dont les principles généraux de droit)," in: *Droit international pénal*, 57.

37 M. Cherif Bassiouni & Edward M. Wise, "Aut dedere, aut iudicare," 4–5.

in an entirely non-international context as well.[38] In such cases other states may claim extradition only on grounds of universal jurisdiction or as custodial states. In theory an international court may present itself as a contester of national jurisdictions. Practically, however, there is hardly any chance that the International Criminal Court would be able to obtain jurisdiction over the situation in each and every affected Arab country.

The obligations deriving from the principle are usually to proscribe, prosecute and punish.[39] An arch model for later regulations was formed by the Genocide convention, which requires punishment of the offenders and the enactment of rules of law "[giving] effect to the provisions of the [...] Convention, and, in particular, to provide effective penalties for persons guilty of genocide".[40] Establishing an appropriate legal framework at the level of national law is a logical consequence of the obligation to extradite, since double criminality stands as a prerequisite. This connection was made even clearer by the scholarly interpretation of the later regulatory model first used in the 1970 Hague Convention.[41] Similar obligations are to be found in the 1949 Geneva Conventions, in the Convention Against Torture, and in a number of counter-terrorism conventions.[42]

Nevertheless, when the state is duly prepared (from a substantive legal point of view) to extradite offenders, who committed certain acts, that supposes—due to the double criminality rule—an adequate substantive legal framework also to prosecute them. Thus in the case of crimes committed in a non-international context, lacking another state or international court, compliance with the *aut dedere aut iudicare* principle is only possible by means of prosecuting the offender.

An international obligation to prosecute perpetrators of certain crimes so exists, but it does not require the exclusive involvement of national (territorial) forums and its practical scope does not seem overwhelming. The list of strengths of national courts should be examined from a different perspective, that is the nearness of these forums to the transitional or post-conflict society, because as courts established and functioning locally, they rely on a knowledge base which is virtually unavailable to an international or a foreign court.

---

[38] Genocide and crimes against humanity, torture. For a list of other crimes see *e.g.* Tomuschat, "La Cristallisation Coutumière," 28–29.

[39] M. Cherif Bassiouni & Edward M. Wise, "Aut dedere, aut iudicare," 8.

[40] Convention on the Prevention and Punishment of the Crime of Genocide, Article 5.

[41] M. Cherif Bassiouni & Edward M. Wise, "Aut dedere, aut iudicare," 16.

[42] Linos-Alexandre Sicilianos, "La responsabilité de l'état pour absence de prévention et de répression des crimes internationaux," 120–121.

First, national courts are better attuned to the cultural background of the atrocities. They have an inherent understanding of the relevant cultural surroundings, and this way they are closer to the parties, offenders, victims and witnesses alike. One particularly relevant cultural aspect with regards to Arab societies to be considered is the attitude of the given society to certain non-judicial forms of justice.[43] The impact of these traditional ADR methods is not necessarily beneficial from a criminal or an international human rights point of view, as was already briefly mentioned in the previous section—yet the fact that the judge is nested in the same legal culture as these alternative methods helps to come to a correct judicial evaluation thereof.

Co-operation of the local law-enforcement agencies with the judiciary is presumably better if the judiciary is local, since their co-operation is a cornerstone of national law. Moreover, since international criminal law has never really decided the dilemma of accusatory or inquisitorial procedure models, a foreign or international evidential procedure may have alien demands[44] that will put to the test even the most willing local authorities—not to mention distrusting local authorities.[45]

Another considerable strength of national courts is the linguistic factor. International tribunals face the problem of translating vast amount of documentary evidence into languages understood by the judges and the translation of judgements, decisions and other court materials is also a resource demanding task.[46] The lack of a need for translations have other beneficial consequences: if all other conditions are presumed equal to international prosecutions, judicial response to the events will be much faster in the common native language of all persons involved in the procedures.[47]

---

[43] Recent references in Western literature are concerned with the conformity of these solutions with the local state judiciary and the rule of law. See Donald Brown, "A Destruction of Muslim Identity: Ontario's Decision to Stop Shari'a-based Arbitration," *North Carolina Journal of International Law and Commercial Regulation* 32 (2007): 495–546; Mona Rafeeq, "Rethinking Islamic Law Arbitration Tribunals: Are They Compatible with Traditional American Notions of Justice," *Wisconsin International Law Journal* 28 (2010): 108–139.

[44] This is to be understood to the technicalities of the evidence procedure, such as e.g. the existence or lack of cross-referencing. Well established international human rights requirements are not to be disregarded based upon some insistence to national traditions.

[45] "ICTY Manual on Developed Practices" [ICTY-UNICRI, 2009], 19, para. 36 [hereinafter: ICTY Manual]

[46] ICTY Manual, 60–61, para. 36.

[47] That holds true to trial and appeal stages as well. See ICTY Manual, 123, para. 61; 136, para. 22.

The existing infrastructure of the national judiciary may also be understood as a strength thereof. This infrastructure extends to archiving and documenting capacities, rather than simply to buildings and such: detention facilities and courtrooms may require modifications to meet security and human rights standards. As a local forum, there is no inescapable need to transfer huge amounts of evidence to new locations, if securing it is possible in other ways as well.[48] Existing infrastructure and the lack of multilingual procedures both result in another significant strength of national courts: generally speaking the financial costs of their procedure are considerably lower than those of an international prosecution.

"Weaknesses" are internal factors of national judicial forums that are harmful to the desired outcome, namely to fair and genuine prosecutions of the offenders. The first set of such weaknesses also derive from the nearness of the authorities to the transitional society. According to the standard outlined by the complementarity clauses of the Rome Statute, if any single one of these weaknesses reaches a level where it renders the local authorities unable or unwilling to carry on a genuine procedure, every other field and record of the SWOT table becomes futile, or at least questionable. Consequently, these weaknesses must be treated before commencement of the procedures in order to fulfil the aforesaid goal of fair and genuine prosecutions.

The most obvious weakness of a national court immediately after a political transition is its connection to the previous system. A noteworthy feature of any authoritarian system is the abuse of law, including a non-independent or politically biased judiciary and law-enforcement agencies ignorant to human rights. It is highly unlikely, that by a flick of a switch, all persons on the payroll of judicial and law-enforcement authorities would become genuine and independent champions of retribution over former human rights atrocities of the previous régime. It should not be forgotten that a number of the personnel have actively participated in the atrocities.

Similar criticisms have been made with regard to the examination of a recent Egyptian case, where the complainant had been subject to forced virginity tests carried out by medical personnel of the army. The accused doctor was acquitted by a military court, resulting in loud disappointment extending beyond Egyptian borders.[49]

---

48 ICTY Manual, 7, para. 3; 8, para. 7.

49 See e.g. Human Rights Watch website, "Egypt: Military 'Virginity Test' Investigation a Sham," 9 November 2011 http://www.hrw.org/fr/node/102892 and "Egypt: Military Impunity

Even if those members of the legal community who were party to the offences of the previous political system are removed from the process, the sentiments of the society towards officials who have already served the state before the transition cannot be disregarded. A society-wide distrust of service members of the earlier justice system is understandable. This "weakness" must be addressed even if there is a publicly made decision that no retribution will take place, and instead a general amnesty or some other form of clemency is granted. Without treatment, this originally understandable distrust of the remaining law enforcement agencies can easily develop into a disregard of law as such, creating a very fertile ground for extremist political forces and possibly a well-paved road to recourse to a different tyranny. Distrust of the law-enforcement agencies is also harmful to the morals of the agencies and police forces themselves; such signs are already apparent in certain societies. A report by the BBC in March 2012 stated: "The police are less feared than before the revolution and at the same time less respected than ever. As a result, morale in the force is low. [...] Egyptians are dealing with a security vacuum."[50] Police morals are also disruptive in Bahrain, as evidenced by reactions to demonstrations resulting from tension over the Formula 1 Grand Prix. Human Rights Watch Director Tom Malinowski was also briefly detained by the police, and in a subsequent e-mail from Bahrain he stated: "The unresolved political tensions are being manifested on the streets, with increasing anger on both sides."[51]

At a much more technical level, distrust of the authorities has a direct effect on the collection of witness testimonies. The fear of witnesses of being exposed to officers of the very same former régime they are testifying against can effectively block judicial procedures. Such exposure to some extent is inevitable due to the fair trial requirement usually referred to as "equality of arms."[52] In case of protected witnesses such fears have hampered even the work of international tribunals as well.[53] Sometimes relocation of witnesses and their families to third countries

for Violence Against Women," 7 April 2012 http://www.hrw.org/news/2012/04/07/egypt-military-impunity-violence-against-women.

[50] Yolande Knell, "Egypt's police still in crisis after revolution," BBC, 5 March 2012 http://www.bbc.co.uk/news/world-middle-east-17128116.

[51] The Cable, American human rights activists arrested in Bahrain Posted By Josh Rogin, Sunday, April 15, 2012, http://thecable.foreignpolicy.com/

[52] *Mutatis mutandis*. See: Roger Gamble-Noel Dias, "International Fair Trial Protections in Criminal Trials," *Sri Lanka Journal of International Law* 20 (2008): 51.

[53] ICTY Manual, 7 paras. 4–5.

has been required,[54] hardly an option in the case of exclusively national procedures.

Lacunae of the substantive criminal law can be tantamount to another severely disrupting factor. Even though most Arab states have acceded to a number of international human rights instruments, domestic implementation may be less than desirable, as has already been mentioned above. Subsequent legislation seems a very charming and straightforward solution to cut this Gordian knot, yet a transitional society cannot morally allow itself to set aside basic human rights considerations in connection with either legislation or the judiciary. Retrospective criminal jurisdiction is to be avoided, since it is extremely dangerous to rely on tools of such dubious legal character in the course of building the rule of law: the long term effects are unpredictable.[55] Instead of retrospective national legislation the problem caused by crimes missing from the applicable national law can be solved by the direct application of the relevant international customary rules or treaty-based obligations of the given state.[56]

From the perspective of certain Arab constitutions the relationship between national and international law is not always apparent. The 1991 Constitution of Yemen declares in its Article 3: "Islamic jurisprudence is the main source of legislation," while in Article 5 this document accepts a special role for certain international norms as well. This submission is however limited, as it only refers to "the United Nations Charter, the Universal Declaration of Human Rights, the Charter of the League of Arab States and the generally accepted norms of international law."[57] The 1996 Constitution of Morocco sets out a list of international norms in a similar context. A section of the preamble reads: "Aware of the need of incorporating its work within the frame of the international organisations of which it has become an active and dynamic member, the Kingdom of Morocco fully adheres to the principles, rights and obligations arising from the charters of such organisations, as it reaffirms its determination to abide by the universally recognised human rights." From the perspective of international law, some of these norms are peremptory,[58]

---

[54] ICTY Manual, 8 para. 6.

[55] E.g. Act VII of 1945 in Hungary, designed to be an anti-Nazi legislation, became the foundation of Communist show trials.

[56] Adany, "Individual Criminal Liability for the Crimes Committed in 1956," 49–51.

[57] Translations are cited from the website Richmond University Constitution Finder, confinder.richmond.edu.

[58] Barcelona Traction Light and Power Company Ltd, Judgement in ICJ Reports 1970, 33, para. 33: "[...] an essential distinction should be drawn between the obligations of a

bearing an *erga omnes* character, consequently binding all states and all state authorities.

"Opportunities" are beneficial to the realisation of a fair and expeditious procedure, yet they are features of national forums dependant on a number of external factors, or possibly their impact registers outside the range of judicial work. Apparently punishment and prevention are the most obvious *goals* of a criminal procedure, yet these are not discussed here as "opportunities."

Any legal condemnation of former officials may help to prevent their return to power, as was already realised at the time of Nuremberg International Military Tribunal.[59] An additional benefit of achieving that at national level by Arab courts would be to mitigate the charges of alleged "colonialism" of the international community. A considerable non-judicial asset of genuine national prosecutions can be the avoidance of adding more fuel to an already heated debate, by giving due consideration to the sensitive national and religious surroundings of social reconstruction within the Arab world.

Prosecuting former officials within their own society can also increase the level of trust enjoyed by the local authorities. It symbolically helps to separate the state from the acts of its former representatives, while if done nationally, it can also enhance the integrity of the state, by decreasing the social shock of transition. Increasing trust in the authorities and in the procedures themselves even in the short term may be beneficial to social attitudes to the rule of law itself. Authorities bear a great responsibility, because these prosecutions may have tremendous impact on the role of human rights in the future of that society.

Genuine prosecutions can be carried out by persons of high moral character: such persons are best chosen from the effected society: firstly, because their examples as role models are closer to the people and secondly, because unlike international judges, they would probably stay after the completion of the procedure and may have a lasting impact within either the judiciary or through legal education, or maybe even in politics. In cultures where personal relations matter much more than

State towards the international community as a whole, and those arising vis-à-vis another State [...] By their very nature the former are the concern of all States. In view of the importance of the rights involved, all States can be held to have a legal interest in their protection; they are obligations erga omnes.".

59 Kristina Rutledge, "Giving the Devil His Due: The Pursuit & Capture of Nazi War Criminals—A Call for Retributive Justice in International Criminal Law," *Regent Journal of International Law* 3 (2007): 68.

in individualist Western societies the role of such models can accordingly be more significant.

Procedures by national courts also pose several major threats. "Threats" in this sense are external factors harmful to the desired outcome or harmful side effects of national procedures that may or may not occur.

The most important and obvious threat is the procedures being biased. That is possible in two extreme cases. The first one is the result of the judges being too closely related to the offences from the victims' side, which results in a vengeful procedure. More passionate authors like to call such procedures "witch-hunts".[60] This can be a very effective form of revenge, yet the medium and long term outcomes are less than favourable. Protecting the dignity of law[61] must therefore be set out as a short term goal during a political transition, as it is the foundation of a lasting and sustainable social transition to democracy. Although judges and prosecutors are not historians, they do bear a historical responsibility, as was observed in the opening address of Justice Robert Jackson in Nuremberg: "The former high station of these defendants, the notoriety of their acts, and the adaptability of their conduct to provoke retaliation make it hard to distinguish between the demand for a just and measured retribution, and the unthinking cry for vengeance which arises from the anguish of war. It is our task, so far as humanly possible, to draw the line between the two. We must never forget that the record on which we judge these defendants today is the record on which history will judge us tomorrow. To pass these defendants a poisoned chalice is to put it to our own lips as well. We must summon such detachment and intellectual integrity to our task that this Trial will commend itself to posterity as fulfilling humanity's aspirations to do justice."[62]

The fact that perpetrators of heinous and inhumane criminal acts still deserve fair treatment are sometimes hard to accept for victimised societies. The most recent fears of an unfair trial come from the news related to the fate of Saif Al-Islam Gaddafi in Libya. As reported by Reuters, Libya intends to try the son of its former leader on Libyan soil.[63] As the patience

---

[60] For several other phrases see: Maria Los, "Lustration and Truth Claims: Unfinished Revolutions in Central Europe," *Law and Social Inquiry* 20 (1995): 120.

[61] Georg Schwarzenberger, "The Judgement of Nuremberg," Tulane Law Review 21 (1946–7): 337.

[62] IMT Records, Session Two, Wednesday, 21st November, 1945 p. 51 (published at the website of The Nizkor Proejct, see: www.nizkor.org.

[63] Ali Shuaib, "Libya will not hand Saif al-Islam to ICC," 8 April 2012.

of the ICC is running short,[64] the unfolding question is whether the UN Security Council will back the Hague court or not.

Although the situation was referred to the ICC by the UNSC, complementarity still demands that national prosecutions shall enjoy a certain primacy: however, that primacy is anything but automatic or unconditional. The conditions are clear from the word and spirit of the Rome Statute: the state concerned must be able and willing to genuinely and fairly prosecute the persons charged with crimes within the jurisdiction of the Court. The content of these qualifiers—genuine and fair—are described by international law, more particularly by international human rights law.

Whenever the ICC has commenced an investigation, which is clearly the case upon Security Council referral, a state concerned may challenge the jurisdiction of the Court over a *situation* or the admissibility of an individual *case*. As for the trial of Saif Al-Islam Gaddafi, due to the fact and the wording of UNSC referral, jurisdiction of the ICC is unquestionable and admissibility seems also justified, yet challenges to admissibility of the case do not seem entirely futile due to the time that has passed since the referral. Nevertheless, such challenges should have been made "at the earliest opportunity."[65] Although it is not the most precise description of a deadline, it is clear that in the present case that earliest opportunity is long gone.

In the case of a challenge the ICC examines whether the state concerned is ready and willing to genuinely prosecute the individual. The examination of the fairness of the national trial is possible *inter alia* under Article 55 of the Rome Statute. Its list of the rights of persons in the procedure is narrower than the rights derived from Articles 9–15 of the International Covenant on Civil and Political Rights, and therefore may seem somewhat autologous. However, the Article 55 rights of the perpetrator represent additional protection in cases where the hearings are performed by national authorities, when different and to some extent unforeseeable national practices must be brought to a common and appropriate level.[66] These additional rights are apparently similar to the rights embodied in the Miranda warnings, aimed at the prevention of self-incrimination.[67]

---

64 Chris Stephen, "Libya's failure to hand over Gaddafi son must be referred to UN, says ICC counsel," The Guardian 12 April 2012, www.guardian.co.uk.

65 Rome Statute, Article 18 (6).

66 Rome Statute, Article 55 (2).

67 Aaron Fichtelberg, "Democratic Legitimacy and the International Criminal Court," *Journal of International Criminal Justice* 4 (2006): 779; Supreme Court Of The United

The Rome Statute also gives considerable powers to the ICC to scrutinise and in some cases even control national procedures.[68] Unilateral *denial* of surrendering a person wanted by the ICC is in violation of the rules on co-operation of the Rome Statute, applicable to Libya by means of the referring UNSC resolution. Articles 94 and 95 both offer opportunities to *postpone* execution of an ICC request, though none of those provisions seem applicable to the present case. For the application of Article 95 a challenge to admissibility is missing at the time of writing, while postponement under Article 94 is subject to the agreement of the ICC.

In some other societies, courts can be also biased in the opposite way: instead of a genuine prosecution being possible, they try to whitewash former officials and shield them from genuine responsibility. This problem is far from being a speciality of the aftermath of the Arab Spring. Going back in time numerous Western examples can be cited from the 20th century: from Eastern Europe[69] to Latin America,[70] through the treatment of the My Lai incident[71] or the Leipzig Trials,[72] the military proved highly efficient in "protecting" its officers, whenever it retained sufficient power to do so. This problem of shielding is highly relevant for the International Criminal Court and is therefore mentioned, if not detailed, in the Rome Statute.

While the Statute itself is only applicable in the case of Libya, and to some extent also in Tunisia, there is a model for identifying the features of genuine procedure that is independent from the Rome Statute, and is much more based on the practice of human rights courts. Due to the far ranging line of examples mentioned above, both the European and the Inter-American Courts of Human Rights have faced this problem before, and a few features can be derived from their case law which may serve as

---

States 384 U.S. 436 Miranda v. Arizona Decided: June 13, 1966, particularly sections 1. (b), (d) and (e).

68 Rome Statute, Article 56.

69 European Court of Human Rights, Kaya v. Turkey [GC], judgement of 19 February 1998, Reports of Judgements and Decisions 1998-I [hereinafter: Kaya].

70 Inter-American Court of Human Rights, Case of the Pueblo Bello Massacre v. Colombia, Judgement of January 31, 2006 (Merits, Reparations and Costs).

71 William George Eckhardt, "My Lai: An American Tragedy," *UMKC Law Review* 68 (2000): 671–704; Jeffrey F. Addicott, "The Lesson of My Lai," *Military Law and Law of War Review* 31(1992): 73–116.

72 Although the trials remain controversial, the reliance on the theory of military necessity suggests a tendency to protect the national military. Claus Kress, "Versailles—Nuremberg—The Hague: Germany and International Criminal Law," *International Lawyer* 40 (2006): 18.

models for the international evaluation of ongoing and future trials, including in the Arab countries. Several disappointed voices of the general public have already criticised the first trial against former Tunisian president Ben Ali,[73] and very bitter opinions have been published after the case on forced virginity tests by the Egyptian Army closed. International human rights standards may help the general public to understand not just the importance, but also the technicalities of a fair and expeditious trial. It is nonetheless important to demonstrate that in the course of the proceedings courts strive to avoid witch-hunts and whitewash alike. The requirements of a fair trial are widely discussed in international case law and literature,[74] and may help to establish that there are no unfair, vengeful trials carried on. On the other hand, a criminal procedure must also be "effective."[75] The question of "effectiveness" is a sensitive issue: at the time of writing this chapter, family members of murdered victims called for the death penalty for Hosni Mubarak, the former Egyptian president.[76] They could never accept a legal system that would help clear the name of the former leaders. For them "effectiveness" has a very special meaning. International law instead helps to identify features of a "genuine" procedure. According to the case law of the aforementioned human rights courts on the issue of shielding former or currently serving officials of law-enforcement agencies from responsibility, a genuine examination or prosecution shall meet the following criteria.[77]

73 "Ben Ali and wife 'guilty of theft'" Al Jazheera, 20 June 2011 http://www.aljazeera.com/news/africa/2011/06/2011620191756405734.html.

74 The existence or the lack of a jury is sometimes mentioned to deny an international definition of fair trial. It is understood here, that international law contains the basic requirements of a fair trial, and the right to be heard by a jury is not amongst those. This means, fair trials are possible without a jury, yet domestic constitutional regulation may demand such protection.

75 The quotation marks emphasise that any notions of effectiveness of criminal procedures must be treated with extreme caution. The final version of the Rome Statute (genuine procedures) have been reached through a number of proposals, like "diligently", "good faith", "sufficient grounds" etc. Any reference to effectiveness was deliberately avoided in order not to cause a controversy with issues of primacy or complementarity. See *Yearbook of the International Law Commission 1994*, Vol. II Part 2, 58, para. 7 and John T. Holmes, "The Principle of Complementarity," in *The Making of the Rome Statute*, ed. Roy S. Lee (The Hague: Kluwer Law International, 1999).

76 "Egypt court to deliver Mubarak trial verdict on 2 June" BBC, 22 February 2012 http://www.bbc.co.uk/news/world-middle-east-17120915.

77 For detailed reasoning see: Tamas Vince Adany, "Genuine Test of Genuine Prosecutions? A Human Rights Model for Complementarity," in: *State Responsibility and the Law of Treaties* ed. Marcel Szabo (The Hague: Eleven International Publishing, 2010), 141–161

The forum dealing with the case must be impartial: as a minimum the investigating authority must be independent from the accused *de iure et de facto*.[78] The procedure must incarnate a certain level of rigorousness, i.e. authorities must "take all measures necessary to attempt to find an answer."[79] Expeditiousness is a requirement of a fair trial as well,[80] yet from the perspective of genuine prosecutions it is also important that measures must be taken within a reasonable period. This reasonable period is rather short, arguably requiring immediate action and an unconditional commencement is required "as soon as practicable"[81] after the investigating authorities acquire knowledge of the facts and gain the ability to prosecute—or when the former political structure exists no more, which gives way to prosecutions.[82] Effectiveness of a procedure thus gains a completely different meaning as an element of a genuine procedure: "Such investigation must be conducted using all legal means available and should be aimed at establishing the truth and conducting the investigation, search, arrest, trial, and punishment of all masterminds and actual perpetrators of the crimes, especially when State officials are or may be involved."[83] Furthermore, although it can be a disappointment to certain groups of victims, the obligation to genuinely prosecute is about the means, not about the results.[84] The duty to investigate and prosecute remains a "best efforts obligation."

Amongst the threats to criminal justice in the course of a political transition there is the threat that the accused will attempt to use the courtroom as a political arena. Herman Göring attempted that on the second

---

[78] Kaya, 87, 91; Inter-American Court of Human Rights: Case of Baldeón-García v. Perú Judgment of April 6, 2006 (Merits, Reparations, and Costs), 95; Case of Durand and Ugarte. Judgment of August 16, 2000, 125 and 126; and ECHR Nachova & others v. Bulgaria, (Applications nos. 43577/98 and 43579/98) Grand Chamber Judgement Strasbourg, 6 July 2005, 112.

[79] Jesus Mohamad Capote, Andres Trujillo et al. v. Venezuela, Case 4348–02, Report No. 96/06, Inter-Am. C.H.R., OEA/Ser.L/V/II.127 Doc. 4 rev. 1 (2007), 68.

[80] Jesus Mohamad Capote, Andres Trujillo et al. v. Venezuela, Case 4348–02, Report No. 96/06, Inter-Am. C.H.R., OEA/Ser.L/V/II.127 Doc. 4 rev. 1 (2007), 72.

[81] Inter-American Court of Human Rights: Case of Baldeón-García v. Perú Judgement of April 6, 2006 (Merits, Reparations, and Costs), 92.

[82] See e.g.: Nachova, 75 & 112, ECHR Case of Güleç v. Turkey, Judgement of 27 July 1998, 81–82.

[83] Or in other terms 'a thorough and effective investigation capable of leading to the identification and punishment of those responsible and including effective access for the relatives to the investigatory procedure,' in Kaya, 107, also in Oğur v. Turkey, Grand Chamber Judgement, (no. 21594/93), 88.

[84] ECHR Bazorkina v. Russia, (Application no. 69481/01) ECHR Judgement, 27 July 2006, 118.

day of the Nuremberg trials, but probably the most successful politicizing was achieved by Slobodan Milošević. Sometimes, in complex cases it is not just a tool to abuse human rights protection, but is not necessarily beneficial to the accused from pursuing tactical perspectives. According to a summary of the respective worries of the ICTY, "the accused may not have a clear objective view of the case to be met [...] and therefore may not conduct the case in his best forensic or legal interests; the accused may not be able to cope with the volume of material; [and] any sanctions imposed for breaches of orders may have adverse side effects on the conduct of the trial."[85]

Some of the additional difficulties also suggest that self-representation of an accused official of the former régime in the same country would risk not only the ongoing criminal procedure, but possibly the security situation of the transitional society as well. The security situation of the state concerned may become threatened even without self-representation if the supporters of the former elite are still strong in the society. As the case of former Liberian President Charles Taylor shows, in such a situation it may become necessary to remove the trial physically from the territory of the country.

Lacunae of substantive national criminal laws, or in simpler terms the problem of missing crimes have already been mentioned, along with a potential solution, namely the direct application of universally recognised international customary law. The inherent threats in this solution are first, the task for a national judge to apply international norms that she or he may be unfamiliar with, and second, if the judge rejects assistance offered with the application of international law. A case concerning a volley fire upon civilians from the 1956 Hungarian revolution had to be examined by the European Court of Human Rights. The central question of international law examined in the case was if in 1956 a non-international armed conflict existed in Hungary or not. In deciding this question the Supreme Court of Hungary relied on the expert opinions of two historians and rejected hearing the expert opinion offered by two renowned, volunteering professors of international law from different Hungarian universities, citing a unanimous court practice based on the *iura novit curia* principle.[86] The subsequent misunderstandings of international law were among the

---

85 ICTY Manual, 90 para. 53.

86 Supreme Court Decision no. Bf. V. 1344/1998/3, 7. See Gellért Ádám: "A Legfelsőbb Bíróság újabb ítélete a Korbély-ügyben [A Recent Decision of the Supreme Court in the Korbély case]" JEMA, 2010/4, 37. o., footnote 14.

reasons that the case was closed amidst severe criticisms by international lawyers only in 2010.

4. Conclusions and Open Issues

A tyrannical political system holding to power for decades creates irreparable damage to numerous members of society, who would rightly demand some kind of retribution after political transition. International law may assist the building of the rule of law by setting out and enforcing certain standards. These human rights standards are not instruments of colonialism, but are derived from positive and negative experiences of successes as well as failures of previous transitions all over the World, from the Far East to Latin America. National prosecutions hold a number of strengths and opportunities; however, consideration of weaknesses and due consideration of the threats are essential prerequisites.

There are also several crucial issues, not answerable by the SWOT technique as it was applied here. Parallel performance of judicial work and political elections would obliterate the borders between these two processes, weakening and damaging both of them. Assessment of the choice between legislative or judicial regulation of the role of the past elite in the forming future societies would demand a political decision where the legal framework is not yet the obvious one for fair and genuine prosecutions. The timing of national procedures is both a political and a human rights issue: the judiciary and law-enforcement agencies should be the first to submit to the new democratic requirements, but this leads to the problem of "*Quis custodiet ipsos custodes?*" Procedures started by the international community and then transferred back to national jurisdiction seem pleasing, yet this is only a theoretical solution with regards to all but one Arab State. The only country where it should work is Libya, where the new leadership of the state is being tested along with the international community's own commitment to these standards.

CHAPTER TEN

PROTECTING CULTURAL HERITAGE: WAR CRIMES AND CRIMES AGAINST HUMANITY DURING CONFLICTS AND REVOLUTIONS IN NORTH AFRICA AND THE MIDDLE EAST

Edward Phillips*

1. Perspectives

From Troy to Carthage, the destruction of cultural property has been used to devastating effect in times of conflict and revolution. At the same time, cultural property has also served as an iconic focus of peoples' aspirations and as a crucible of identity. Throughout North Africa and the Middle East, cultural property has become an essential emblem, serving both constructive as well as destructive ends. Two instructive examples, although from outside the region of discussion, may be mentioned at this point. The first was the destruction of the Ottoman-era bridge at Mostar.[1] Its destruction encapsulated the extent to which ethnic cleansing had become the policy of the dominant warring states of the former Yugoslavia. The second example was the destruction of the statutes of the Buddha in Bamiyan.[2] There could be no better illustration of the fundamentalist iconoclastic policies of the Taleban in Afghanistan. The destruction of both these emblems of cultural property serve to indicate the powerful hold that such cultural icons have on the global imagination; they also demonstrate the extent to which cultural property may become instruments of aggression, used as pawns by the very people who might be expected to protect them.

---

* Law School, University of Greenwich, UK.

[1] The Mostar Bridge, in what is now Bosnia-Herzegovina, was destroyed by Bosnian Croats in November 1993. For images of the Old Bridge and its reconstruction in July 2004, see www.whc.unesco.org/en/list/946.

[2] For centuries the two colossal statutes of the Buddhas of Bamiyan, carved into sandstone cliffs, stood in central Afghanistan. Despite international protests and appeals, their destruction was ordered by the Taleban leader, Mullah Mohammed Omar, as part of the campaign to rid Afghanistan of all images considered to be un-Islamic. For images of the Buddhas of Bamiyan and further details of their destruction, see www.bbc.co.uk/world-south-asia-1267451. For further analysis, reference may be made to Francesco Francioni and Federico Lenzerini, "The Destruction of the Buddhas of Bamiyan and International Law," *EJIL* 14 (4) (2003): 619.

One further example of the outrage that is generated by threats against globally-recognised cultural artefacts of cultural property may be noted. In June 2011, it was reported that Colonel Gaddafi's forces had taken over the ruins of Leptis Magna and were determined, by using the ancient ruins as an ammunition store, to hold the ancient city to hostage.[3] The rebel leaders in Misrata, reporting on the movement of ammunition and rocket-launchers stated, "They are inside the old buildings because they know that NATO will never destroy the area."[4]

This acknowledges the legal consequences of the inscription of a site on the UNESCO World Heritage List and is dealt with in the World Heritage Convention 1972, Article 6.1:

> Whilst fully respecting the sovereignty of the States on whose territory the cultural and natural heritage mentioned in Articles 1 and 2 is situated, and without prejudice to property rights provided by national legislation, the States Parties to this Convention recognize that such heritage constitutes a world heritage for whose protection it is the duty of the international community as a whole to co-operate.[5]

Commenting on Article 6, Carducci points out:

> For the first time in the Convention's sequence of Chapters and Articles, what was merely 'heritage' under Articles 1 and 2, becomes '*world* heritage' under Article 6 para. 1.[6]

As virtually all of the NATO allies engaged in the military intervention in Libya had ratified the 1972 Convention, and therefore undertaken the obligation imposed upon them, this was a factor of considerable import.

The conflicts and revolutions in North Africa and the Middle East represent one facet of this cultural destruction. However, it is vital that attention should be paid also to those instances where cultural property has been a unifying force, protected and valued by the peoples involved in political uprising. There is no greater example of this than the manner in which Egyptians of all religious and political backgrounds reacted to the

---

[3] Leptis Magna, one of the best preserved and most spectacular Roman ruins in the Mediterranean and one of the greatest abandoned cities of the Ancient World, is on the UNESCO World Heritage list.

[4] *The Times*, June 14, 2011.

[5] For a more detailed treatment of the 1972 World Heritage Convention, reference may be made to: Fransesco Francioni and Federico Lenzerini (eds.), *The 1972 World Heritage Convention: A Commentary* (Oxford: Oxford University Press, 2008).

[6] Guido Carducci, "National and International Protection of the Cultural and Natural Heritage", in *The 1972 World Heritage Convention*, at 120 (emphasis added).

looting of the Egyptian National Museum, situated just off Tahrir Square, the epicentre of the Egyptian protests in Cairo. In a gesture demonstrating the emotional hold that the world-renowned Museum and its priceless store of antiquities has in modern Egypt, demonstrators from across a broad spectrum of Egyptian society gathered to link hands around the Museum and to safeguard it from any further attack. The emblematic nature of this action received global comment:

> ... in a city where the police have all but disappeared, and inmates have escaped from four prisons, how can the objects in a museum hold any sort of priority? Shouldn't all of Egypt's attention and resources focus on maintaining peace and order? This is, I hope, a false choice: achieving peace (and democracy) in Egypt, and protection of its cultural and archaeological heritage, should not be mutually exclusive.[7]

It is not too fanciful to see, in the actions of the demonstrators, an emphatic acknowledgement of the role that Egypt's cultural heritage plays in constructs of national identity, as well as a guttural foresight of the manner in which artefacts of cultural identity may serve as a focus for unity and reconciliation.

Finally, sufficient regard should also be paid to the ultimate thesis that cultural property of the kinds under discussion should be regarded as the common heritage of all mankind, transcending national boundaries or nationalistic claims of ownership, as an essential constituent of global civilisation.

2. The Centrality of Cultural Property to Identity

As the efforts of ordinary Egyptians to preserve their cultural heritage demonstrate, the legal and judicial construction of cultural (and historical / artistic) property is often central to the integrity of peoples and nations. Perhaps the paradigm example of this is the Athenian Acropolis:

> The Acropolis became the political symbol of the new Greece. As one archaeologist put it, speaking at a meeting of the newly formed Archaeological Society of Athens in 1838, "it is to these stones [the sculpture and architecture of classical Greece] that we owe our political renaissance." Or, as another archaeologist wrote more than a century later, in 1983, the

[7] Margaret Maitland, January 30, 2011; www.museumca.org/theoaklandstandard/museum-looting-cairo (the website also contains an image of the protesters linking hands around the Museum).

> Parthenon is "the most sacred monument of this country... which expresses the essence of the Greek spirit."[8]

It is not too far-fetched to see a virtually identical standpoint being adopted in North Africa and the Middle East. An example from Saddam Hussein's attempt to 'restore' Babylon for the 1987 Babylon International Festival is instructive. At a time when the Iraq-Iran War was still in progress, Saddam Hussein convened the festival which:

> ... unashamedly linked Saddam with the great historical figures of Hammurapi and Nebuchadnezzar, 'whose legacies transcended time and history to fuse with the great strides and magnificent splendour of H.E. President Saddam Hussein'. For this event a special medal was issued showing the portrait of Saddam alongside that of Nebuchadnezzar.[9]

The appropriation of cultural property to serve the interests of tyrants and regimes is common enough. However, the events in Egypt during the uprising at Tahrir Square offers another, much more inspiring, perspective.

3. The Global Impulse to Protect

The legal protection of cultural property reflects the universal nature of the impulse to protect those artefacts that, quite apart from national appropriation, serve as both archetypes of progress as well as symbols of our global civilisation. The issues relating to the international legal regime of protection, and the provision of sanctions, are best illustrated by the world-wide attention paid to the events of the war in Iraq.

> There can be no denying that what happened to Babylon in the Saddam era was bad, but what happened in the aftermath of the second Gulf War was inexcusable. In April 2003 a small military camp was established at Babylon by American forces. By June 2003 (when the writer visited Babylon with a group from the British Museum) the camp was still relatively small. Thereafter, however, it rapidly escalated in size so that by the summer of 2004 there was widespread concern about the potential damage that was being caused, with publication in newspapers and on the web of photographs showing the immense scale of the military activity at Babylon. The camp, 150 hectares in size, had been established right in the middle of the ancient city of Babylon, straddling the inner wall of the city, and at its height it was home to two

[8] James Cuno, *Who Owns Antiquity? Museums and the Battle Over Our Ancient Heritage* (Princeton: Princeton University Press, 2008), xi.

[9] John Curtis, "The Site of Babylon Today," in *Babylon: Myth and Reality*, ed. Irving L. Finkel and Michael J. Seymour (London: British Museum Press, 2008), 215.

> thousand soldiers.... It is impossible to overstress the insensitivity involved in establishing a military camp in the middle of one of the most famous sites of the ancient world—a site that is part of the cultural heritage of the whole world—irrespective of what might have happened there before.[10]

This is not an isolated comment but has been echoed by others all over the world:

> For thousands of years the ancient city of Babylon endured waves of war and upheaval with the waxing and waning of empires. Yet, few could have predicted its current destruction at the hands of American-led coalition forces.... Construction of a helipad in the heart of the ancient city required the removal of layers of archaeological earth from the site. The daily flights of the helicopters rattle the ancient walls and the winds created by their rotors blast sand against the fragile bricks.... Between May and August 2004, the wall of the Temple of Nabu and the roof of the Temple of Ninmah, both of the sixth century B.C., collapsed as a result of the movement of helicopters. Nearby, heavy machines and vehicles stand parked on the remains of a Greek theatre from the era of Alexander of Macedon.[11]

This global reaction to the infractions in Babylon illustrates the rationale for the international regime of protection. Cultural property of this nature transcends narrow nationalistic claims and boundaries. As James Cuno puts it, it is necessary to transcend

> ... the premise of nationalist retentionist cultural property laws: that it is the right of sovereign nations to legislate the protection of and access to whatever they consider to be *their* cultural property, that which they claim to be important to their national identities and self-esteem.... Antiquities are the cultural property of all humankind—of *people*, not *peoples*—evidence of the world's ancient past and not that of a particular nation.[12]

4. The Legal Protection of Cultural Property[13]

International Law has recognised the destruction of cultural property as both a crime against humanity as well as a war crime (accepting the overlap between these two categories). Further recognition of this has been

---

[10] Curtis, "The Site of Babylon Today," 216.

[11] Zainab Bahrani, "The Fall of Babylon" in *The Looting of the Iraq Museum, Baghdad: The Lost Legacy of Ancient Mesopotamia*, ed. Milbry Polk and Angela Schuster (New York: Abrams, 2005), 214.

[12] James Cuno, *Who Owns Antiquity? Museums and the Battle Over Our Ancient Heritage*, 146.

[13] It is not possible, here, to do more than to summarise the major points in the evolution of the principles of International Law towards a full protection of cultural property.

provided in a number of decisions of the International Criminal Tribunal for the former Yugoslavia.[14] One of the earliest proponents of the principle that the protection of cultural property was to be regarded as a norm of International Law was de Vattel (1714—1769):

> For whatever cause a country is ravaged, we ought to spare those edifices which do honour to human society, and do not contribute to the enemy's strength—such as temples, tombs, public buildings, and all works of remarkable beauty. What advantage is obtained by destroying them? It is declaring one's self an enemy of mankind...[15]

Further, it should be noted that the protection of culturally significant property was not exclusively a 'western' preoccupation. In traditional and precolonial Africa, as well as in India, there were innumerable sacred places (venerable trees, ancestral dwellings, shrines, places where initiation ceremonies were held) that received protection through common consent and acknowledgement, often though the imposition of strong taboos and enforced through customary law.

The customary nature of the legal principles relating to protection have been the source of much dissenting opinion. There are, however, weighty opinions which support these principles as tenets of customary International Law. In 1962, the ICJ in the *Temple of Preah Vihear Case*[16] dismissed considerations of cultural heritage. However, the Temple was damaged during repeated conflicts in the early 2000s, and in July 2011 the ICJ issued an order for provisional measures requiring, *inter alia*, that troops from both Cambodia and Thailand be removed from the Temple precincts. In a notable judgement, Judge Trindade remarked on the Temple's importance and outstanding universal value, going as far as to indicate that "The prohibition of destruction of cultural heritage of an outstanding value and great relevance for humankind is arguably an obligation of *erga omnes*."[17]

Reference may also be made to the principles and conventions dealing with the laws of war. An early attempt at legal protection was the so-called Leiber Instructions: Instructions for the Government of the Armies of the United States in the Field (General Order 100, 1863). Articles 34–36 address the status of cultural property while Article 35 specifically provides that

---

14 *Prosecutor* v *Strugar*, Case No. IT-01-42-T, Trial Judgment (31 January 2005), paras 298–312.

15 De Vatel, *The Law of Nations III*, Chapter 9, Section 168 (Joseph Chitty, editor, 1844).

16 ICJ Rep. 1962, 34.

17 Reliance was placed on the views expressed in Francioni and Lenzerini, "The Destruction of the Buddhas of Bamiyan and International Law."

"classical works of art, libraries, scientific collections . . . must be secured against all avoidable injury, even when contained in fortified places whilst besieged or bombarded."[18]

While it is not possible, or indeed necessary in the current context, to chronicle all the various developments leading up to the modern conventions and declarations, it is worth noting the Roerich Pact (Treaty on the Protection of Artistic and Scientific Institutions and Historic Monuments) of 1935, which deserves recognition as the first international treaty dedicated exclusively to the protection of cultural property. The Pact, signed in Washington on April 15, 1935 (sometimes referred to as the Washington Treaty), and which is still in force, states in its Preamble that the States parties to it "have resolved to conclude a treaty . . . to the effect that the treasures of culture be respected and protected in time of war and peace . . ." Article 1 then goes on to declare:

> The historic monuments, museums, scientific, artistic, educational and cultural institutions shall be considered as neutral and as such respected and protected by belligerents. The same respect and protection shall be due to the personnel of the institutions mentioned above The same respect and protection shall be accorded to the historic monuments, museums, scientific, artistic, educational and cultural institutions in time of peace as well as in war.[19]

This was followed by a series of other (often unsuccessful) attempts to codify the rules relating to protection. Among these was the Draft International Convention for the Protection of Historic Buildings and Works of Art in times of War, 1939. Although ultimately defeated by the outbreak of the Second World War, it is noteworthy that the Draft Convention adopts a universalist/internationalist perspective as set out in its Preamble:

> Whereas the preservation of artistic treasures is a concern of the community of States and it is important that such treasures should receive international protection; Being convinced that the destruction of a master piece, whatever nation may have produced it, is a spiritual impoverishment for the entire international community.[20]

---

[18] See D. Schindler and J. Torman, *The Laws of Armed Conflicts* (Leiden: Martinus Nihjoff, 1988), 3–23.

[19] The full text of the Roerich Pact can be accessed at the website of the International Committee of the Red Cross: www.icrc.org/ihl.nst/INTRO/325?OpenDocument.

[20] Orna Ben Naftali, *International Humanitarian Law and International Human Rights Law* (Oxford: Oxford University Press, 2011).

The explicit principle expressed here is that the countries possessing culturally significant treasure of this nature are merely custodians of the civilisation-enhancing sparks which they embody. Moreover, states remain accountable for them to the international community. The spirit of the Draft Convention finds an echo in the almost universal outrage that greeted the Taleban's destruction of the Bamiyan Buddhas and the repulsion of the international community at the acts of Colonel Gaddafi which threatened the very existence of the city of Leptis Magna.

It must be re-iterated, however, that charges of this nature could equally be levelled against the occupying forces of the Iraq invasion, as noted above. These charges, in addition to the depredations imposed by the American forces in the ruins of Babylon, included the shelling of the Iraqi National Museum and the failure to take effective measures to combat looting in 2003. By way of contrast, reference may be made to the following statement issued by General Eisenhower on May 26, 1944 as the Allies prepared for the D-Day landings at Normandy:

> Shortly we will be fighting our way across the Continent of Europe in battles designed to preserve our civilisation. Inevitably, in the path of our advance will be found historical monuments and cultural centers which symbolize to the world all that we are fighting to preserve. It is the responsibility of every commander to protect and respect these symbols whenever possible.... where military necessity dictates, commanders may order the required action even though it involves destruction to some honored site. But there are many circumstances in which damage and destruction are not necessary and cannot be justified. In such cases, through the exercise of restraint and discipline, commanders will preserve centers and objects of historical and cultural significance.[21]

The Nuremberg Tribunal further pursued this ethos: various Nazis on the German High Command were held accountable for crimes relating to cultural property, whether of looting or of wilful destruction. Commenting on this, Hensel points out that:

> The Nuremberg verdicts established what were basic normative standards, universally applicable to all people and states, against which the actions of all would be judged and against which they would be held accountable.[22]

---

21 Cited in Howard Hensel, "The Protection of Cultural Objects During Armed Conflicts," in *The Law of Armed Conflict: Constraints on the Contemporary Use of Military Force*, ed. Howard Hensel (Ashgate: Aldershot, 2007), 58.

22 Hensel, "The Protection of Cultural Objects During Armed Conflicts," 59.

Tragically, from Babylon to Bamiyan, this is a warning which continues to be ignored by all sides of the armed conflicts that are the subjects of the present discussion. Two particular questions remain unresolved. The first relates to the response to global terrorism and the legitimacy or otherwise of offensive preventive action which imperils cultural property. A case in point would be in relation to the use of remote-controlled armed drones, the legality of which is a continued issue of debate. The second focuses on the response of the peoples within whose territory this cultural property is situated; will this property be valued or will it be regarded as expendable?

5. Post-World War II Developments

The measures to protect cultural property put in place in the post-War period must be seen in the context of, and as an integral part of, the other measures dealing with minimal standards of conduct in times of war and of guaranteeing human rights. These include the 1948 Universal Declaration of Human Rights, the 1948 Genocide Convention and the 1949 Geneva Conventions on Humanitarian Law. In particular, the 1954 Hague Convention for the Protection of Cultural Property in the Event of Armed Conflict and the 1972 World Heritage Convention stand as ultimate symbols of the determination of the international community to protect those artefacts that are part of the common heritage of all mankind. Referring to the 1954 Hague Convention, John Merryman notes that in its cosmopolitan, internationalist terms, it became "a charter for cultural internationalism."[23]

The detailed exposition of these two instruments is outside the scope of the present study.[24] It is always worth, however, reiterating the inspirational statements of principles in the Preamble of the 1954 Convention, which in its turn refers to the aspirations of the Roerich Pact of 1935:

> Recognizing that cultural property has suffered grave damage during recent armed conflicts and that, by reason of the developments in the technique of warfare, it is in increasing danger of destruction; being convinced that damage to cultural property belonging to any people whatsoever means

[23] John Merryman, "Two Ways of Thinking About Cultural Property", *American Journal of International Law* 80 (4) (1986): 831, at p. 837.

[24] Reference may usefully be made to Wayne Sandholtz, "The Iraqi National Museum and International Law: A Duty to Protect," *Columbia Journal of Transnational Law* 44 (2005): 185; Hensel, *The Law of Armed Conflict: Constraints on the Contemporary Use of Military Force*; Francioni and Lenzerini, *The 1972 World Heritage Convention: A Commentary*.

> damage to the cultural heritage of all mankind, since each people makes its contribution to the culture of the world; Considering that the preservation of the cultural heritage is of great importance for all peoples of the world and that it is important that this heritage should receive international protection;...

The Convention is also especially useful in the definition it offers, for the avoidance of doubt, of what is to be considered 'cultural property':

> Article 1: For the provisions of the present Convention, the term 'cultural property' shall cover, irrespective of origin or ownership:
>
> (a) moveable or immoveable property of great importance to the cultural heritage of every people, such as monuments of architecture, art or history, whether religious or secular, archaeological sites; groups of building which, as a whole, are of historical or artistic interest; works of art; manuscripts, books and other objects of artistic, historical or archaeological interest; as well as scientific collections and important collections of books or archives or of reproductions of the property defined above;
> (b) buildings whose main and effective purpose is to preserve or exhibit the moveable cultural property defined in sub-paragraph (a) such as museums, large libraries and depositories of archives, and refuges intended to shelter, in the event of armed conflict, the moveable cultural property defined in sub-paragraph (a);
> (c) centres containing a large amount of cultural property as defined in sub-paragraphs (a) and (b), to be known as 'centres containing monuments.'

Despite the all-embracing nature of both the 1954 as well as the 1972 Conventions, the reality remains the willingness of the international community and international institutions to effectively police and enforce their provisions, especially in terms of the characterisation of breaches both as war crimes as well as crimes against humanity. The cases dealt with by the Tribunal for the Former Yugoslavia may indicate some measure of success. But is there any doubt that no prosecutions will follow on from the cultural atrocities attendant upon the Iraq invasion?

It is, of course, true that the United States has not ratified the 1954 Convention. However, neither has it criticized or objected to any of its specific provisions. Moreover, leaving aside the critical discussion of whether crimes against cultural property may truly be regarded as *erga omnes*, the fact remains that the Roerich Pact (i.e. the Washington Treaty), specifically mentioned in the Preamble to the 1954 Convention, remains in force and the United States continues to be a party to it.

Further, Egypt, Syria, Libya and Tunisia are all signatories to both the 1954 as well as the 1972 Conventions and it remains to be seen whether the regimes that eventually come to control the countries of the Arab Spring maintain their adherence to the principles and ethos of the Conventions.

6. Islam, Cultural Property and Identity

> Notwithstanding all the customary and conventional provisions embodied in international law designed to protect various cultural properties during periods of armed conflict, however, in the final analysis, the fate of cultural properties largely depends upon how these objects are perceived and the value placed upon these objects by the respective belligerents.[25]

The issues surrounding the protection of cultural property in the countries of the Arab Spring (but also including Afghanistan and the previous events of the second Gulf War in Iraq) inevitably centre on the intersection of political aspiration and national identity. This is par for the course as can be seen in the events leading up to and after the fall of the Berlin Wall in the states of Central and Eastern Europe. There is here, however, a further factor which is not discernible in those other situations. This added factor is the perspective, and imperatives, imposed by Islam. How is the regime of international protection of cultural property to be implemented in those nations where, as in Afghanistan and the countries of the Arab Spring, the principles of Islam constitute the ruling paradigm of political and national identity? Attempts must be made to explore the answer(s) to this question; witness the destruction of the Bamiyan Buddhas in the Taleban's version of the requirements of Islamic orthodoxy regarding 'graven images.'

It is no exaggeration to claim that the countries of the Arab Spring are located in the part of the world that was home to the civilisations that developed our prototype for civilisation. Is it too unlikely to wonder at the chilling possibility of fundamentalist Islamic governments coming to power and wreaking destruction, either by malign intent or benign neglect, on the symbols of this civilisation? Paradoxically, it is the theocracy of Iran that offers an illuminating example: the culture of Iran's pre-Islamic past is as much revered as is its Islamic culture. The ayatollah-dominated ruling regime recognises the visceral hold that cultural property has over an essential Iranian claim to identity. It is to be hoped that such an attitude prevails over the countries of the Arab Spring.

25 Hensel, "The Protection of Cultural Objects During Armed Conflicts," 59.

> *Considering* that cultural property constitutes one of the basic elements of civilisation and national culture, and that its true value can be appreciated only in relation to the fullest possible information regarding its origin, history and traditional setting,
>
> *Considering* that it is incumbent upon every State to protect the cultural property existing within its territory against the dangers of theft, clandestine excavation and illicit export,
>
> *Considering* that, to avert these dangers, it is essential for every State to become increasingly active to the moral obligations to respect its own cultural heritage and that of all nations...[26]

[26] The Preamble, UN Convention on the Means of Prohibiting and Preventing the Illicit Import, Export and Transfer of Ownership of Cultural Property, 1970.

CHAPTER ELEVEN

PALESTINIAN SELF-DETERMINATION AND A STATE OF ASPIRATION

James Summers*

1. Introduction

On 23 September 2011 Mahmoud Abbas the Chairman of the Palestine Liberation Organisation (PLO) and President of the Palestinian National Authority announced in the UN General Assembly the widely-anticipated bid for Palestine to join the United Nations as a member state.[1] He did not declare the independence of Palestine, instead relying on an earlier Declaration of Independence made on 15 November 1988. A letter for Palestine's admission to the UN was delivered the same day for the consideration of the Security Council.[2] This was the first step in an admission procedure which requires a positive vote in the Security Council and then the General Assembly. Abbas' speech sought membership of a Palestinian state based on territory occupied by Israel in 1967: the West Bank, Gaza Strip and East Jerusalem together with a just and agreed upon solution to the Palestine refugees issue.[3] However, at the same time as seeking UN membership for the declared state, he accused Israel of "undermining the realistic potential for the existence of the State of Palestine".[4] This highlighted that what he sought acceptance of was far from a functioning independent state.

The application in the United Nations was the culmination of a state-building programme initiated by Palestinian Prime Minister Salam Fayyad,

---

* Law School, Lancaster University, UK.

[1] http://gadebate.un.org/sites/default/files/gastatements/66/PS_en.pdf. Accessed 14 October 2011.

[2] Letter dated 23 September 2011 from President of Palestine to Secretary-General, S/2011/592, Annex II.

[3] Speech by Mahmoud Abbas to the United Nations General Assembly, 4. Available at www.gadebate.un.org/sites/default/files/gastatements/66/ps_en.pdf. Accessed 14 October 2011.

[4] Ibid. 2.

launched in August 2009.[5] It sought to build a capacity for *de facto* Palestinian statehood in a two year period. This programme, in turn, lay within a broader context of unsuccessful peace negotiations between Israel and the Palestinians. The principal body charged with promoting a negotiated settlement was the Quartet, composed of the United States, Russia, the UN and EU. It had sought to establish a two-state solution in its Roadmap Plan of 2003 of "an independent, democratic, and viable Palestinian state living side by side in peace and security with Israel and its other neighbours."[6] This plan envisaged a negotiating process in which an independent Palestinian state would initially be established within provisional borders, followed by an agreement with Israel on the final status of those borders, including Jerusalem and the settlements by 2005. That plan, however, was unsuccessful, as were subsequent attempts at a negotiated settlement. The Palestinian bid can be seen as both frustration with negotiation attempts, but also an effort to strengthen their position in future talks. The Quartet itself on 23 September responded to the Palestinian unilateral approach with new proposals for direct negotiations.[7]

The Palestinian application was taken up by the Security Council on 27 September, where it is still pending. The United States has publicly declared that it will veto the application, and has also lobbied Council members to prevent the 9 out of 15 majority for admission which would necessitate its negative vote.[8] In the 27 September meeting of the Council the contradictions of Palestinian statehood were expressed by Lebanon:

> Palestine ... meets all the criteria required to become a State under international law: a people, a land, a Government and the ability to establish relations with other States. But it is an occupied State, and we must therefore support the efforts of the State of Palestine and its people to end the occupation, achieve independence and return to their homeland.[9]

---

[5] Palestine: Ending the Occupation, Establishing the State. Available at http://unispal.un.org/UNISPAL.NSF/0/A013B65A5984E671852576B800581931. Accessed 27 April 2012.

[6] A Performance-Based Roadmap to a Permanent Two-State Solution to the Israeli-Palestinian Conflict. Available at http://www.mfa.gov.il/MFA/Peace+Process/Guide+to+the+Peace+Process/A+Performance-Based+Roadmap+to+a+Permanent+Two-Sta.htm. Accessed 27 April 2012.

[7] Statement of the Middle East Quarter, New York 23 September 2011. Available at http://www.unsco.org/Documents/Statements/Quartet/2008/Middle%20East%20Quartet%20statement%2023%20September%202011%20New%20York.pdf. Accessed 27 April 2012.

[8] "Palestinians to Make Statehood Bid," *BBC News*, 23 September 2011.

[9] Lebanon, UN Doc. S/PV.6623, 2.

An alternative, more scathing assessment of Palestinian statehood was made by Israel following the vote in the United Nations Educational, Scientific and Cultural Organisation, UNESCO on 31 October to admit Palestine as a member state:

> UNESCO deals in science not science fiction. However, a large number of states, though most emphatically less than two-thirds of the member states of this organisation, have adopted a science fiction version of reality by admitting a non-existent state to the science organisation.[10]

Is Palestine a state? The answer to that question is as much political as legal. It is not claimed that Palestine is seeking UN membership as a normal fully-functional state but as an incomplete one. There are clear limits on the authority and territorial scope of Palestinian self-government which renders independent statehood largely aspirational. However, there are a number of states which joined the UN lacking in the criteria for statehood or which were subsequently seen to fail as states. Palestine in this regard is by no means unique. Moreover, while there are criteria which can be used for identifying states they are not precise and represent boxes that Palestine can to a degree tick. Whether that degree is sufficient depends on perspective. Palestinian statehood is supported by the perception of a right to statehood, which is essentially forward-looking pointing to a desired future state of affairs. However, an alternative perspective is to look at states as entities which have already been constituted, even if they subsequently lose this capacity. Ultimately Palestine consists of a number of elements: self-governing institutions and various rights. However, the combination of these depends on how they are interpreted.

2. Palestine as a State

The standard criteria for testing claims to statehood are contained in Article 1, Montevideo Convention 1933, which lists four elements: a permanent population; a defined territory; a government; and a capacity to enter into legal relations with other states. The Montevideo Convention was never intended as a systematic international attempt to define statehood, rather it was a Latin American regional instrument intended to protect the sovereignty of South American states. However, its rather basic

---

10 Israel, http://www.unesco.org/new/fileadmin/MULTIMEDIA/HQ/GBS/36GC/audio/36-VR-11-68-Israel-E.mp3. Accessed 20 April 2012.

nature, which gives wide scope for political interpretation of what a state is, underpins its enduring appeal and it has provided a key reference point in subsequent attempts to identify states.[11] Palestine provides a suitably ambiguous foil to Montevideo's broad and simplistic criteria.

In terms of territory, the Application identified a specific territory occupied by Israel in 1967 and defined by the 1949 Armistice Line, or "Green Line". The territory is not contiguous. The West Bank and East Jerusalem are physically separate from the Gaza Strip. Lack of contiguity does not in itself undermine statehood, though politically it can make governance more difficult which has proved the case in Palestine. In June 2007 Palestinian self-government fragmented between the secular government of Fatah, which dominates the West Bank, and the Islamist party Hamas, which took control of Gaza in a violent conflict. The two sides have unsuccessfully attempted to forge a political unity. A reconciliation agreement was reached on 4 May 2011 but not implemented. A later accord was concluded in Doha in Qatar on 6 February 2012, again without success.[12]

In terms of population, the territory of the West Bank and Gaza corresponds to an identifiable permanent population. However, there are complications. The PLO is representative of all Palestinians, which includes Palestinian refugees in neighbouring countries, such as Lebanon and Jordan, and a wider diaspora. The status of these populations outside the 1967 borders remains ambiguous in the Application as an issue to be resolved in final status negotiations. In addition, there is the position of Jewish settlers within the 1967 borders. If the Palestinian state is defined by those borders do they constitute part of the population associated with the territory? A population for the purposes of statehood does not necessarily have to equate to a people for self-determination.[13] The construction of settlements in occupied Palestinian territory has repeatedly been found to be a violation of international law.[14] Nonetheless, settlements are also identified in the Application as a final status issue.

---

[11] See Conference on Yugoslavia Arbitration Committee (Badinter Commission), Opinion No. 1: "the State is commonly defined as a community which consists of a territory and a population subject to an organized political authority; that such a State is characterized by sovereignty." *ILM* 31 (1992): 1495.

[12] "Fatah, Hamas Unity Meet Ends without Deal," *AFP*, 3 May 2012.

[13] On the potential scope of the Palestinian people see John Quigley, "Self-determination in the Palestine Context," in *International Law and the Israeli-Palestinian Conflict*, eds. Susan M. Akram, Michael Dumper, Michael Lynk and Iain Scobbie (London: Routledge, 2011), 224.

[14] *Legal Consequences of the Construction of a Wall in the Occupied Palestinian Territory* [hereafter '*Wall* Opinion'], ICJ Rep. (2010), paras. 119–121.

In terms of the capacity to enter into relations with other states, Palestine superficially appears to have a number of assets. It has recognition by 128 countries[15] and is a member of UNESCO. The PLO has permanent representation in the United Nations and other international bodies and has concluded bilateral agreements with states, most notably the Oslo Accords with Israel.[16] Indeed, there is potentially greater scope for these external aspects of statehood as they depend less on Israeli cooperation and more on other countries for their exercise. The ability of Palestine to join UNESCO in the face of opposition from Israel and the United States is a case in point. However, there is a political division in Palestinian institutions which potentially undermines this capacity. The 1988 Declaration of Independence was made by the PLO, a national liberation movement, and it is this organisation that holds responsibility for Palestinian external relations. The Palestinian Authority, which exercises governmental control in the West Bank, does not have powers for foreign affairs. The two are united by the personal authority of Mahmoud Abbas, who has a dual role as Chairman of the PLO and President of the Authority. In the UN Application, Abbas signed both as President of the State of Palestine (based on the Authority) and PLO Chairman, reflecting the formal separation of the offices. Moreover, the Basic Law 2003, the Palestinian Authority's constitutional document, does not codify the relationship between the Authority and the PLO. Thus, in terms of its own constitutional law, there is a no Palestinian legal structure which combines the internal exercise of government authority and relations with foreign states. Nonetheless, in practice the Chairman of the PLO is also the President of the Palestinian Authority. Likewise members of the Palestine Legislative Council, the legislative body of the Palestinian Authority, have been also members of the Palestinian National Council, the PLO's legislative body. Therefore, whether Palestine fulfils this criterion depends whether one focuses on the formal legal powers of the Palestinian Authority or its political practice.

The problematic element in the Montevideo criteria is a Palestinian government and the ability of this government to exercise control over its territory. These represent the internal elements of its statehood. A distinction can be made between the 1988 Declaration and the 2011 request

[15] Negotiations Affairs Department, Palestine Liberation Organization. Available at http://www.nad-plo.org/etemplate.php?id=303. Accessed 09 May 2012.

[16] See Geoffrey R. Watson, *The Oslo Accords: International Law and the Israeli-Palestinian Peace Agreements* (Oxford: Oxford University Press, 2000), 91–99.

for admission. In 1988 the PLO, which the General Assembly recognised as the representative of the Palestinian people, did not control any of the occupied Palestinian territories. It was a liberation movement based in Tunisia.[17] In the UN debate that followed the Declaration in 1988, it is notable that Israel and the US specifically challenged Palestine on meeting the criteria for statehood,[18] while supporters generally avoided such criteria[19] and focused on statehood as a right.[20]

However, under the Oslo Accords of 1993 and 1995, Palestinians in the Occupied Territories achieved a degree of self-government. A Palestinian Authority was established under Article VII(2) of the 1993 Agreement which exercised governance in education, culture, health, social welfare, direct taxation and tourism. Nonetheless, the Authority notably did not have responsibility for foreign relations which remained under the authority of the PLO as an organisation. Policing and security under Article XIII of the 1995 Agreement was divided into three zones: A, in which the Palestinian Authority had powers for policing and security; B, in which the PA had authority for public order, but Israel retained power over security and C which remained under Israel security control. Zone C accounted for 60% of the territory of the West Bank. Zones A and B consisted of fragments of territory typically separated from each other by areas of Zone C. Israel also retained control of the external borders.[21]

There is also the political division between the West Bank and Gaza. This has not yet translated into a Gazan secession, though in some ways Hamas-controlled Gaza, despite its small size, closer resembles a functioning state than the West Bank. Israel withdrew from Gaza, except for its borders, in 2005 leaving it a far more consolidated political unit than the West Bank.

The extent of government as an element in statehood is a matter of considerable debate, especially in relation to Palestine, and differing practice. Two elements of government can also be distinguished. On one hand there is the institutional capacity of an entity to govern. On the other, there is the exercise of governmental control over a territory. The two are often related: weak government can translate into weak control of

---

17 See James Crawford, "The Creation of the State of Palestine: Too Much Too Soon?" *EJIL* 1 (1990): 307–313.

18 Israel, UN Doc. A/43/PV.79, 32; US, UN Doc. A/43/PV.82, 47.

19 A notable exception is Pakistan, UN Doc. A/43/PV.81, 104–105.

20 See, e.g. Saudi Arabia, UN Doc. A/43/PV.78, 67 and 73; Bahrain, ibid. 98; Kuwait, ibid. 114.

21 Watson, *The Oslo Accords*, 107–111.

a territory. But, an effective functioning government might be unable to exercise control over its territory if another state intervenes to prevent it from doing so.

This provides the context for the Palestinian Authority's two-year programme of state-building in 2009, which has improved the efficiency and capabilities of Palestinian institutions without expanding their reach, which remains dependant on a settlement with Israel. External observers have commented on the success of this programme and that the Palestinian Authority has attained an institutional capacity for statehood. The World Bank reported that: "In area where government effectiveness matters most—security and justice; revenue and expenditure management; economic development; and service delivery—Palestinian public institutions compare favourably to other countries in the region and beyond."[22] The Office of the United Nations Special Coordinator for the Middle East Peace Process (UNSCO) listed six areas where the functions of the authority were sufficient for a functioning state: governance; rule of law and human rights; livelihoods and productive sectors; education and culture; health; social protection; and infrastructure and water.[23] The IMF considered that: "the PA is able to conduct the sound economic policies expected of a future Palestinian state."[24] Lynn Pascoe, UN Under-Secretary-General for Political Affairs, asserted that: "The Palestinian Authority is capable of running a State."[25]

However, those same reports also stress the fragility and vulnerability of this state-building and its dependency on the wider context of self-government.[26] The reports record the inability of the Palestinian Authority to fund itself and its dependency on external aid,[27] as well as Israel.

---

[22] The World Bank, Sustaining Achievements in Palestinian Institution-Building and Economic Growth, 18 September 2011, 5, 13, 16, 24. http://siteresources.worldbank.org/INTWESTBANKGAZA/Resources/WorldBankAHLCReportSep2011.pdf. Accessed 18 April 2012.

[23] Office of the UN Special Coordinator for the Middle East Peace Process, Palestinian State-Building: An Achievement at Risk (Ad Hoc Liaison Committee Meeting, New York, 18 September 2011), 1, para. 1. Available at http://www.unsco.org/Documents/Special/UNSCOs%20Report%20to%20the%20AHLC%2018%20September%202011.pdf. Accessed 18 April 2012.

[24] International Monetary Fund, Recent Experience and Prospects of the Economy of the West Bank and Gaza: Staff Report Prepared for the Meeting of the Ad Hoc Liaison Committee, March 21, 2012, 4. Available at http://www.imf.org/external/country/WBG/RR/2012/032112.pdf. Accessed 18 April 2012.

[25] Lynn Pascoe, Under-Secretary-General for Political Affairs, UN Doc. S/PV.6623, 3.

[26] UNSCO, 2, 11.

[27] World Bank, 9–10.

70% of its budget revenue comes from clearance revenue, including customs and VAT, collected by Israel.[28] Strict Israeli restrictions on Palestinian development in Area C have hampered economic growth,[29] as have travel restrictions within the territory and also with Israel.[30] The territorial fragmentation of the West Bank has been seen as the key weakness in its potential for further development.[31]

The Palestinian authority thus exercises functions of statehood but it does so in an incomplete and severely fragmented way. Moreover, despite its institutionally-disconnected capacity for international relations, Israel's control over the majority of the West Bank, its borders and a large part of its finance, undermines the idea of a Palestinian state being an independent one. It is possible to separate a state from independence. John Quigley notably argued that Palestine is already a state based on its succession from Britain's Palestinian mandate.[32] The mandate was not an independent state but it could be seen as a dependent state under British rule. States today are generally conceived to have the element of independence, rather than being an emanation of another state. Nonetheless, practice is not entirely consistent, and as will seen below, freely associated territories, such as the Cook Islands and Niue, whose external relations are normally managed by another state have been treated as states for the purposes of the UN.

The inability to exercise independence or sovereignty over a territory is not considered fatal to statehood. The Iraqi invasion of Kuwait did not extinguish the Kuwaiti state. The continued internal failure of Somalia has not led to international rejection of its statehood. Established, recognised states continue to be treated as states even with a loss of sovereignty or independence. However, new states may also be recognised without control of significant parts of their territory or with an inability to perform government functions, if they are seen to have a right to independence. Congo was admitted to the UN on 20 September 1960 despite fighting in the capital and the secession of its wealthy Katanga region.[33] The General Assembly on 2 November 1973 recognised Guinea-Bissau as independent

---

[28] IMF, 23.

[29] World Bank, 8; IMF, 5–6; UNSCO, 5.

[30] IMF, 22.

[31] UNSCO, 6.

[32] John Quigley, *The Statehood of Palestine: International Law in the Middle East Conflict* (Cambridge: Cambridge University Press, 2010), esp. 248.

[33] GA Res. 1480 (XV) (1960). See also resolution based on report of the Credentials Committee, GA Res. 1498 (XV) (1960).

from Portugal, even though its government did not control the majority of the population or any major town.[34] Western Sahara, or the Saharan Arab Democratic Republic, is a member of the African Union, despite Morocco's continued occupation of most of the territory. These states were established in the context of decolonisation and a right of self-determination. Lack of control or effectiveness of these new states was compensated for by external support for their right to independence. Bosnia-Herzegovina joined the UN on 22 May 1992,[35] with its capital under siege and most of its territory outside government control. Self-determination is not established as a positive right outside the colonial context. However, Bosnia became a state in the context of the dissolution of Yugoslavia in which its federal units, the republics, became independent with their borders protected under the principle of *uti possidetis*.[36] Moreover, Bosnia was required to demonstrate popular support for independence,[37] and did so through a referendum,[38] which may be seen as an expression of self-determination. States which are perceived to lack effectiveness may still receive recognition and admission into international organisations if they have an established right to independence or if that right is consistent with international law.

3. The Palestinian Right to Independence

The right of Palestine to self-determination and independent statehood has considerable support from a variety of sources. The General Assembly has been the principal international forum for promoting a right of Palestinian self-determination. Since 1970[39] it has issued a string of resolutions proclaiming this right. While those resolutions were initially controversial, they have since become routine events and have been supported by the overwhelming majority of states, with consistent opposition only from Israel and the United States.[40] However, some Western states, like

[34] GA Res. 3061 (XXVIII) (1973).
[35] GA Res. 46/237 (1992).
[36] Conference on Yugoslavia Arbitration Commission (Badinter Commission), Opinion Nos. 2 and 3, *ILM* 31 (1992): 1497–1500.
[37] Conference on Yugoslavia Arbitration Commission (Badinter Commission), Opinion No. 4, *ILM* 31 (1992): 1501–1503.
[38] Keesing's March 1992, 38832.
[39] GA Res. 2649(XXV), (1970). (Passed by 71 to 12, with 28 abstentions).
[40] The latest was GA Res. 66/17, 30 November 2011 (Passed by 167 to 7, with 4 abstentions).

Germany and Britain, have sometimes abstained and there is a serious question as to whether these resolutions reflect legal intent or simply political concern.[41] Nonetheless, the ICJ in the *Wall* Opinion recognised a right of Palestinian self-determination and emphasised the role of General Assembly resolutions and the body's recognition of the right, "on a number of occasions",[42] in establishing it.

The impact of Security Council resolutions is less direct. A series of Security Council resolutions recognise a future Palestinian state alongside Israel.[43] SC Res. 1860 (2009) refers to: "the vision of a region where two democratic States, Israel and Palestine, live side by side in peace with secure and recognized borders".[44] These resolutions do not specifically refer to Palestinian self-determination or a right to statehood, nor are they framed in legally-binding mandatory terms. Nonetheless, they support the general context of Palestinian self-determination by outlining the goals which the right could be used to achieve.

Another source of Palestinian self-determination may be Article 1 of the Twin Human Rights Covenants 1966. Reports to the Human Rights Committee on implementation of the International Covenant on Civil and Political Rights show broad recognition of a Palestinian right of self-determination.[45] Palestine may also be encompassed by Article 1(4) of Additional Protocol I 1977 to the Geneva Conventions 1949,[46] which referred to: "armed conflicts in which peoples are fighting against colonial domination and alien occupation and racist régimes in the exercise of their right of self-determination, as enshrined in the Charter of the United Nations and the Declaration on ... [Friendly Relations]".[47]

---

41 See Tal Becker, "Self-Determination in Perspective: Palestinian Claims to Statehood and the Relativity of the Right to Self-Determination" *Isr. LR* 32 (1998): 342; Kurt René Radley, "The Palestinian Refugees: The Right to Return in International Law" *AJIL* 72 (1978): 606–608.

42 *Wall* Opinion, para. 118.

43 SC Res. 1397 (2002); SC Res. 1515 (2003); SC Res. 1850 (2008); SC Res. 1860 (2009).

44 SC Res. 1860 (2009).

45 See e.g. Jordan, (CCPR/C/1/Add.55) *YHRC* 11–16 (1981–82) II, 198; Italy, *YHRC* 11–16 (1981–82) I, SR.261, para. 38; Japan, *YHRC* 11–16 (1981–82) I, SR.324, para. 15; France, *YHRC* 17–22 (1983–84) I, SR.445, para. 16; Australia, *HRCOR* 31–33 (1987–88) I, SR.807, para. 18; Columbia, *HRCOR* 31–33 (1987–88) I, SR.818, para. 35; Netherlands, (CCPR/C/42/Add.6), *HRCOR* 34–36 (1988–89) II, 141; Philippines, (CCPR/C/50/Add.1/Rev.1) *HRCOR* 34–36 (1988–89) II, 201; Norway, *HRCOR* 34–36 (1988–89) I, SR.844, para. 52; Tanzania, (CCPR/C/42/Add.12) *HRCOR* 46–48 (1992–93) II, 56; Egypt, (CCPR/C/51/Add.7) *HRCOR* 46–48 (1992–93) II, 173.

46 See Syria, CDDH/SR.36, 51; Qatar, ibid., 54; Iran, CDDH/SR.41, 152; Mozambique, ibid., 154.

47 Additional Protocol I 1977 to the Geneva Conventions of 12 August 1949, *ILM* 16 (1977): 1397.

The Court in the *Wall* Opinion also referred to bilateral agreements, in particular an exchange of letters on 9 September 1993 between Israeli Prime Minister Yitzhak Rabin and PLO President Yasser Arafat in which Israel recognised the PLO as, "... the representative of the Palestinian people." It also cited the Israeli-Palestinian Interim Agreement on the West Bank and Gaza Strip of 28 September 1995 which referred, "a number of times to the Palestinian people and its 'legitimate rights". The Court inferred that these rights included self-determination.[48]

Palestinian self-determination resembles the self-determination of colonial territories, which is well-established in international law in part from vigorous and successful promotion by the General Assembly. Nonetheless, there are connections but also differences between Palestinian and colonial self-determination. Palestine is not a non-self-governing or trust territory, which formed the focus on colonial self-determination in the UN era, but it was part of a mandate territory governed by the same principles. The ICJ in the *Wall* Opinion seemed to suggest that Palestinian self-determination, like the colonial variant, evolved from the principle of trusteeship. The Court recalled that Palestine was established as a class A mandate under Article 22 of the League of Nations Covenant. It also noted that in its *International Status of South West Africa* Opinion it identified two principles "of paramount importance" in the mandate: non-annexation and the sacred trust. Citing the *Namibia* opinion the Court considered that, "...the ultimate objective of the sacred trust' referred to in Article 22, paragraph 1, of the Covenant of the League of Nations 'was the self-determination ... of the peoples concerned".[49] The suggestion appeared to be that, although Britain abandoned its mandate over Palestine in 1948 and the General Assembly provided for its termination in GA Res. 181(III) of 1947,[50] Palestinian self-determination draws from the same principles as the colonial right.

The Court, though, did not specify the context and Judge Higgins in her separate opinion considered that Palestine represented a case of "self-determination beyond colonialism".[51] Palestine is often seen to fall into an ambiguous category of peoples subjected to alien or foreign domination

48 *Wall* Opinion, para. 118.

49 *Wall* Opinion, para. 88. See also Judge Koroma, Separate Opinion, para. 7; Judge Al-Khasawneh, Separate Opinion, para. 8; Judge Elaraby, Separate Opinion, paras. 21–3. See also James Crawford, "The Right of Self-Determination in International Law: Its Development and Future" in *Peoples' Rights* ed. Philip Alston (Oxford: Oxford University Press, 2001), 14.

50 GA Res. 181(III) (1947).

51 Judge Higgins, Separate Opinion, *Wall* Opinion, paras. 29–30.

and occupation that exists alongside the colonial right.[52] The right of peoples under alien domination to self-determination was recognised by the *Kosovo* Opinion 2010. The Court referred to a: "right to independence for the peoples of non-self-governing territories and peoples subject to alien subjugation, domination and exploitation".[53] The right of Palestinians to self-determination may be seen to run in parallel to that of colonial territories.[54]

The uniqueness or sui generis nature of Palestinian self-determination poses questions for how it should be exercised. Colonial self-determination was closely aligned with colonial territories. The Palestinian application seeks recognition of a state based on 1967 borders, which were defined by the 1949 Armistice Line or the "Green Line". The construction of Jewish settlements across this line in the West Bank was presented as frustrating the establishment of this state. But, there is a question as to why Palestinian self-determination should be defined by those borders.

The development of colonial self-determination proceeded with respect for the territorial integrity of a colonial territory. This coupling was reflected in Principles 2 and 6 of the Declaration on the Granting of Independence to Colonial Countries and Peoples, GA Res. 1514 (XV) 1960. The government in Guinea-Bisseau might not control large parts of its territory, but if in accordance with the Declaration it could extend its authority within a defined and protected territory. The protection of the territorial integrity was also extended to mandate territories in the case of the separation of Walvis Bay from Namibia by South Africa. Security Council and General Assembly resolutions condemned this separation as a violation of the principle of territorial integrity.[55] However, the equation of a colonial territory with a people was not evident in the early stages of decolonisation when the Palestinian mandate was terminated. The UN's support for the partition of Palestine in GA Res. 181 of 1947 undermines the proposition that its territorial integrity was inherently protected at that

---

[52] See Donald L. Horowitz, "Self-Determination: Politics, Philosophy, and Law" in *National Self-Determination and Secession* ed. Margaret Moore (Oxford: Oxford University Press, 1998), 201.

[53] *Accordance with International Law of the Unilateral Declaration of Independence in Respect to Kosovo* (Advisory Opinion), ICJ Rep. (2010), para. 79.

[54] On these connections see Catriona J. Drew, "Self-Determination, Population Transfer and the Middle East Peace Accords" in *Human Rights, Self-Determination and Political Change in the Occupied Palestinian Territories* ed. Stephen Bowen (The Hague: Martinus Nijhoff, 1997), 123–125.

[55] See GA Res. 32/9D (1977) and SC Res. 432 (1978).

time. Indeed, in the period from 1945 until the 1960 Declaration on the Granting of Independence to Colonial Countries and Peoples colonial territories were often divided.[56] The protection of territorial integrity for colonial territories cannot be easily extended to Palestine.

Decisions by the Badinter Commission in the break-up of Yugoslavia[57] and the ICJ in the *Burkina Faso/Mali Frontier Dispute* case[58] suggest that self-determination should be exercised consistently with *uti possidetis*, which upholds existing administrative frontiers. However, the application of *uti possidetis* to the Green Line is problematic as it represents a ceasefire line. A proposition that ceasefire lines should provide the presumed basis for international borders might be to stretch the principle too far. It would raise problems with Cyprus, China and Georgia and may be seen to legitimise the acquisition of territory by force.

Ultimately, the clearest connection between self-determination and the 1967 border stems from the status of Palestinian territory as under occupation. Self-determination often functions as a corollary for other principles. For example, the occupation of a state may not only constitute a denial of sovereignty, territorial integrity and the prohibition on the use of force, but also self-determination.[59] In the case of the occupied Palestinian territories self-determination can be seen to run parallel to the principle of the inadmissibility of the acquisition of territory by force.[60] This principle has been consistently applied in the occupied territory in regard to the construction of Jewish settlements[61] and Israeli measures to change the status of Jerusalem.[62] The principle of non-acquisition effectively defines and protects the Palestinian territory. It also creates a connection with self-determination, which was highlighted by the ICJ in the *Wall* Opinion

56 See Report of the United Nations Commission for Eritrea (1950) UN Doc. A/1285, paras. 161 and 176; GA Res. 1352 (XIV) (1959); GA Res. 1471 (XIV) (1959); GA Res. 1608(XV) (1960); J. S. Coleman, "Togoland," *International Conciliation* 509 (1956): 78–9.

57 Conference on Yugoslavia Arbitration Commission (Badinter Commission), Opinion No. 2, *ILM* 31 (1992): 1498.

58 *Case concerning the Frontier Dispute (Burkina Faso/Republic of Mali) (Judgment)* ICJ Rep. (1986), 567, para. 25.

59 See, e.g. the comments by Chile on Iraq's invasion of Kuwait: "The right of peoples to self-determination was one of the cornerstones of the United Nations. All countries were indissolubly bound by that guiding principle. The recent invasion of Kuwait by Iraqi military forces constituted a serious violation of that right, which was embodied in the Charter of the United Nations." UN Doc. A/C.3/45/SR.4, para. 9.

60 See Principle 1(10) of the Declaration on Principles of Friendly Relations, GA Res. 2625 (XXV) 1970; SC Res. 242 (1967). See also *Wall* Opinion, paras. 74, 87, 117.

61 SC Res. 446 (1979); SC Res. 452 (1979); SC Res. 465 (1980).

62 SC Res. 298 (1971); SC Res. 478 (1980).

in which *de facto* annexation and changes to demographics caused by the construction of the wall was seen to impede the exercise of self-determination.[63] Thus, it can be argued that Palestine as a people under occupation with a right to self-determination draws a significant element of its content from the law surrounding that occupation.

4. Recognition at the UN

According to the constitutive theory of recognition, the act of recognition by states endows a new state with its legal personality. Membership of international organisations provides evidence of collective recognition. However, the example of Palestine presents less a case of the simple acquisition of personality, rather a fragmented picture in which more particular rights and obligations are obtained from different organisations.

The Palestinian bid for recognition as a state in the UN creates two possible routes. The first is formal admission as a member state of the United Nations, but this is most difficult due to the United States stated position that they would vote against Palestinian membership. Article 4(2) contains a two stage procedure for the admission of members. Admission is "effected by a decision of the General Assembly upon the recommendation of the Security Council". A recommendation from the Council requires a positive vote by nine members and none of the five permanent members to exercise their veto. The significance of "recommendation" was examined by the International Court of Justice in the Second *Admissions* Opinion of 1950. The Court found that despite its apparent non-mandatory phrasing, a recommendation from the Security Council was the indispensable "condition precedent to the decision of the Assembly".[64] The context of the opinion was specifically the political use of the veto to prevent states joining the United Nations. In the Cold War the United States and Soviet Union vetoed the membership of states due to their opposed ideologies. There is no reason to believe that the interpretation of Article 4(2) has changed since then.

Article 4 also lays other conditions for member states. Under Article 4(1) membership is open to peace-loving states which accept the obligations contained in the Charter, and in the judgment of the organisation are

[63] *Wall* Opinion, paras. 121–122.

[64] *Competence of the General Assembly for the Admission of a State to the United Nations* (Advisory Opinion), ICJ Rep. (1950), 7–8.

able and willing to carry out those obligations. The Security Council and General Assembly, in fact, require applicants to make a declaration that they are peace-loving and accept and undertake to fulfil the obligations in the Charter.[65] The Palestinian application contained a Declaration to that effect.[66] Nonetheless, there are problems with this claim. The Palestinian authority does not control significant parts of its territory, notably Gaza, where Hamas denies the right to existence of Israel, a UN member, and from which there have been rocket attacks on Israel.[67] The question, though, of whether Palestine is peace-loving is a judgment for the United Nations expressed through the admissions procedure of the Security Council and General Assembly.

The second route is that the General Assembly could bypass the Security Council by awarding Palestine observer state status at the UN. It is believed that Palestinians have the two-thirds support in the Assembly to do this.[68] This status was used in the Cold War to ensure representation of states whose membership was objected to by Security Council permanent members. The number of observer states at the UN has, though, decreased as they have achieved full membership and the last remaining observer state is the Holy See. If the Assembly voted to accord Palestine this status it would be evidence of wide international recognition for its statehood, but in terms of its status within the organisation it may be less significant. The General Assembly has already gone as far as possible down the observer route without explicitly recognising Palestine as a state.

In 1974 the General Assembly invited the PLO as representative of the Palestinian people to participate as an observer.[69] Since then, the organisation's position has steadily increased both semantically and in the rights it enjoys in the Assembly. Following the 1988 independence declaration, the PLO representation was renamed as "Palestine", giving them a title that sounded just like that of a state.[70] In 1998 its right and privileges were further expanded to closely match those of an observer state.[71]

---

[65] Rule 58, Provisional Rules of Procedure of the Security Council 1983; Rule 134, Rules of Procedure of the General Assembly 1984.

[66] Declaration by Mahmoud Abbas, UN Doc. A/66/371-S/2011/592, 3.

[67] Israeli Strikes and Militant Rockets Test Gaza Truce, *BBC News*, 15 March 2012. Available at http://www.bbc.co.uk/news/world-middle-east-17380329. Accessed 27 April 2012.

[68] See Barak Ravid, "UN Envoy Prosor: Israel has no Chance of Stopping Recognition of Palestinian State," *Haaretz*, 28 August 2011.

[69] GA Res. 3210 (XXIX) (1974); GA Res. 3237 (XXIX) (1974).

[70] GA Res. 43/177 (1988).

[71] GA Res. 52/250 (1998).

A permanent observer state could be expected to enjoy certain rights and privileges. It can participate in the general debate in the General Assembly. It has the right of inscription on the list of speakers for agenda items in any plenary meeting after the member states. It has the right to make interventions and a right of reply. It has the right to have its communications relating to the work of the General Assembly issued and circulated as official documents of the General Assembly. The same is true for conferences under the auspices of the Assembly. It has the right to raise a point of order in matters relating to itself. It has the right to co-sponsor draft resolutions on matters that involve it, though these drafts can only be put to the vote at the request of a member state. It has the right to six seats in the General Assembly hall after the member states. However, it does not have voting rights and cannot put forward candidates for positions in the General Assembly.[72] These are rights, though, that Palestine already has.[73] Its principal gain from the title of observer state is recognition of its statehood from a body which represents almost all the world's states.

Recognition as a state may also bring other rights under the UN Charter. Article 2(4) prohibits the threat or use of force against the territorial integrity or political independence of "any state". The General Assembly in recognising the statehood of Guinea-Bissau in 1973 simultaneously condemned the illegal occupation and aggression of Portugal, the colonial power.[74] However, if a state or group of states were to draft a similar resolution in relation to Israel, it would certainly be highly divisive within the Assembly. Palestine as a state would also have a right of self-defence. Article 51 refers to self-defence by UN members, but the right is considered to be inherently held by states under custom.[75] However, if Palestine were a state this would also have implications for Israel's right of self-defence. Israel has been attacked by Palestinian militant groups and argued that it had a right of self-defence against such attacks. This argument was rejected by the ICJ in the *Wall* Opinion, which considered that armed attacks could not be made by non-state actors.[76] Practice on

[72] GA Res. 58/314 (2004).

[73] Note by the Secretary-General on Participation of Palestine in the Work of the United Nations, UN Doc. A/52/1002 (1998). See also GA Res. 43/160A (1988) and GA Res. 52/250 (1998).

[74] GA Res. 3061 (XXVIII) (1973).

[75] *Case Concerning Military and Paramilitary Activities in and Against Nicaragua (Nicaragua v. United States of America) (Merits)*, ICJ Rep. (1986), para. 176.

[76] *Wall* Opinion, para. 139.

whether self-defence requires an attack by a state is divided.[77] Nonetheless, if Palestine were a state and militant attacks of sufficient scale could be attributed to it, the exercise of a right of self-defence by Israel would certainly be more legally straightforward than it is currently. As an entity treated as a state by the UN, Palestine would be entitled to a range of rights under international law, including sovereignty, sovereign equality and non-intervention. However, while the framing of these rights may be different, their substance is arguably broadly similar to the right of self-determination which has already been extensively supported by the General Assembly.

Admission of Palestine as a non-member state might change the rhetoric of the General Assembly, but it may have less impact on the promotion of Palestinian rights, which are already institutionalised in the UN system. The General Assembly has since 1975 had a Committee on the Exercise of the Inalienable Rights of the Palestinian People[78] and the Secretariat a Division for Palestinian Rights since 1977.[79] Indeed, there is a danger that further entrenchment of Palestinian rights within the UN system may simply be seen to further politicise the organisation, potentially to the detriment of itself and by extension the Palestinians.[80]

There is also the issue of the relationship between Palestine and the International Court of Justice. The ICJ is the United Nations' judicial organ, but statehood not UN membership is the necessary condition of bringing cases before the court.[81] Palestine as a state could in principle become a party to the ICJ Statute without becoming a member state. Five non-member states became parties to the Statute, though they subsequently joined the UN.[82] However, as a UN organ, the ICJ is not a backdoor into the organisation. If Palestine attempted to accede to the Statute it would face the same obstacles as it would for UN membership. Article 93(2), UN Charter allows states to become parties to the Court's statute on the basis of the familiar process of a determination by the General Assembly on the

---

77 See, e.g. SC Res. 1368 (2001) and SC Res. 1373 (2001).

78 GA Res. 3376 (XXX) (1975).

79 GA Res. 32/40B (1977).

80 See Adam Roberts, "Prolonged Military Occupation: The Israeli-Occupied Territories Since 1967," *AJIL* 84 (1990): 100.

81 Article 34(1) Statute of the International Court of Justice 1945.

82 Switzerland, Liechtenstein, Japan, San Marino and Nauru. See Shabtai Rosenne, *The Law and Practice of the International Court 1920–2005* (4th Edition) (Leiden: Martinus Nijhoff, 2006) Volume II, 598.

recommendation of the Security Council.[83] Thus, an American veto could preclude this option.

Palestine has, however, been able to get support for its legal position, even without being a state through ICJ advisory opinions. With support from the General Assembly, the *Wall* Opinion 2004 allowed Palestine to bring a legal case against Israel over its construction of a security barrier in the West Bank. The Court found that the "wall" (a designation which itself represented a semantic victory for Palestine) violated international humanitarian and human rights law[84] and the prohibition of annexation of occupied territory.[85] It identified Palestinians as a people with a right of self-determination,[86] which had also been violated by the barrier.[87] This was non-binding but it bolstered Palestine's position in international law. If Palestine was party to the Statute it could, of course, initiate legally binding contentious proceedings against Israel but only with Israel's consent.

5. UNESCO

While the decision on UN membership was pending, Palestine successfully joined UNESCO, a specialised agency of the United Nations.[88] Admission to UNESCO presents less of an obstacle than the United Nations. States are admitted by a two-thirds majority by the General Conference upon the recommendation of the Executive Board, which crucially makes decisions by a simple majority without any veto privileges.[89] On 31 October 2011 the General Conference, following the recommendation of the Executive Board,[90] passed Resolution 36 C/ Res. 76 by 107 votes to 14, with

[83] See, e.g., SC Res. 600 (1987) and GA Res. 42/21 (1987) on Nauru.

[84] *Wall* Opinion, para. 137.

[85] *Wall* Opinion, paras. 121–122.

[86] *Wall* Opinion, para. 118.

[87] *Wall* Opinion, para. 122.

[88] An interesting argument on UNESCO membership is raised by Paul Eden who notes that under Article IX(5)(b)(4) of the Israeli-Palestinian Interim Agreement 1995 the Palestinian Authority has the power to conclude cultural scientific and educational agreements. Paul Eden, "Palestinian Statehood: Trapped between Rhetoric and *Realpolitik*" (Paper Presented at the SLS-BIICL Conference, London, 30 April 2012).

[89] Article II(2), Constitution of the United Nations Educational, Scientific and Cultural Organization 1945; Rule 50, Rules of Procedure of the Executive Board 2010.

[90] Executive Board Decision 187 EX/40. (Adopted by 40 to 4, with 14 abstentions). http://www.unesco.org/new/fileadmin/MULTIMEDIA/HQ/GBS/36GC/audio/36-VR-11-51-PrEXB-E.mp3. Accessed 20 April 2012.

52 abstentions,[91] admitting Palestine to the organisation. The decision took place against threats from the United States, which was legally obliged under national law to cut funding to the organisation if it admitted Palestine. Following the decision the US stopped its contributions.[92] Israel in response withheld the customs and VAT revenues that it collected for the Palestinian Authority, though it unfroze them a month later,[93] and accelerated the construction of 2, 230 settlements, mostly around East Jerusalem.[94] Moreover, while the vote was decisive, members raised concern about the impact of this unilateral step on future negotiations.[95] It was also considered that UNESCO should defer to the United Nations on the issue of statehood[96] and questioned whether it was useful to UNESCO's role as an educational and scientific organisation.[97]

Nonetheless, membership of UNESCO has enabled Palestine to obtain legal rights which directly relate to its status. Palestine has joined a range of conventions intended to protect its culture and heritage. In particular, Palestine on 16 January 2012 ratified the Convention concerning the

[91] http://www.unesco.org/new/fileadmin/MULTIMEDIA/HQ/GBS/36GC/audio/36-VR-11-60-Pres-E.mp3. Accessed 20 April 2012.

[92] BBC News, 31 October 2011, http://www.bbc.co.uk/news/world-middle-east-15530960. Accessed 18 April 2012.

[93] "Israel Unfreezes Palestinian Authority Tax Millions," *The Guardian*, 30 November 2011.

[94] Statement by Robert Serry, Special Coordinator for the Middle East Peace Process and Personal Representative of the Secretary-General, UN Doc. S/PV.6662, 2–3.

[95] See United States, http://www.unesco.org/new/fileadmin/MULTIMEDIA/HQ/GBS/36GC/audio/36-VR-11-62-Usa-E.mp3; Sweden, http://www.unesco.org/new/fileadmin/MULTIMEDIA/HQ/GBS/36GC/audio/36-VR-11-70-Suede-E.mp3; Germany, http://www.unesco.org/new/fileadmin/MULTIMEDIA/HQ/GBS/36GC/audio/36-VR-11-84-Allemagne-E.mp3; New Zealand, http://www.unesco.org/new/fileadmin/MULTIMEDIA/HQ/GBS/36GC/audio/36-VR-11-88-NouvelleZelande-E.mp3; Portugal, http://www.unesco.org/new/fileadmin/MULTIMEDIA/HQ/GBS/36GC/audio/36-VR-11-96-Portugal-E.mp3; Denmark, http://www.unesco.org/new/fileadmin/MULTIMEDIA/HQ/GBS/36GC/audio/36-VR-11-98-Danemark-E.mp3; Czech Republic, http://www.unesco.org/new/fileadmin/MULTIMEDIA/HQ/GBS/36GC/audio/36-VR-11-102-RepTcheque-E.mp3; United Kingdom, http://www.unesco.org/new/fileadmin/MULTIMEDIA/HQ/GBS/36GC/audio/36-VR-11-108-Uk-E.mp3; Netherlands, http://www.unesco.org/new/fileadmin/MULTIMEDIA/HQ/GBS/36GC/audio/36-VR-11-126-Pays-Bays-E.mp3; Australia, http://www.unesco.org/new/fileadmin/MULTIMEDIA/HQ/GBS/36GC/audio/36-VR-11-132-Australie-E.mp3. Accessed 20 April 2012; Thailand, http://www.unesco.org/new/fileadmin/MULTIMEDIA/HQ/GBS/36GC/audio/36-VR-11-142-Thailande-E.mp3 Accessed 20 April 2012.

[96] See, e.g., Japan, http://www.unesco.org/new/fileadmin/MULTIMEDIA/HQ/GBS/36GC/audio/36-VR-11-124-Japon-E.mp3. Accessed 20 April 2012.

[97] Singapore, http://www.unesco.org/new/fileadmin/MULTIMEDIA/HQ/GBS/36GC/audio/36-VR-11-112-Singapour-E.mp3. Accessed 20 April 2012.

Protection of the World Cultural and Natural Heritage,[98] which under Article 3 would allow the authority to designate sites of cultural heritage and natural heritage. Israel is also a party to the convention and has an obligation not to take deliberate measures that would directly or indirectly damage another party's cultural or natural heritage. However, the convention is about more than simply the protection of historic sites, it also allows Palestine to assert an ownership over the monuments, buildings and archaeology that form its disputed history with Israel. Palestine acceded on 26 April to the Convention for the Protection of Cultural Property in the Event of Armed Conflict 1954, to which Israel is again also a party.[99] Article 5 of the Convention provides that parties in occupation of the whole or part of the territory of another contracting party shall as far as possible support national authorities in safeguarding and preserving cultural property. Thus, UNESCO membership contributes more to Palestine's rights and obligations than simple evidence of statehood.

The admittance of Palestine into a UN specialised agency has significance for the UN system as whole and also for other organisations such as the International Criminal Court. Under Article 102 of the UN Charter the UN Secretariat functions as a depository for treaties. Some of these treaties may only be open to states and the Secretary-General may have the responsibility of determining whether an entity constitutes a "state". In practice, in areas of controversy the Secretary-General has deferred to the General Assembly and in that way the organisation's member states.[100]

There is also another practice, though, known as the "Vienna Formula". This emerged from the Vienna Convention on the Law of Treaties 1969, which in Article 81 was open for signature by member states of the UN. However, the experience in the Cold War period was that some states which were members of specialised agencies were not admitted into the United Nations due to the veto of a permanent member of the Security Council for political reasons. Thus, Article 81 also included members of specialised agencies, among other organisations, alongside the United Nations, and this has been taken as evidence of statehood in the UN system.[101] Entities which were not considered by the General Assembly to

[98] List of ratifications on UNESCO Website. http://www.unesco.org/eri/la/convention.asp?language=E&KO=13055. Accessed 26 April 2012.

[99] List of ratifications on UNESCO Website. http://www.unesco.org/eri/la/convention.asp?KO=13637&language=E&order=alpha. Accessed 26 April 2012.

[100] UN Office of Legal Affairs (OLA), Treaty Section, Summary of Practice of the Secretary-General as Depository of Multilateral Treaties, UN Doc. ST/LEG/7/Rev.1 (1999), para. 81.

[101] Ibid. paras. 79–80.

be states were, nonetheless, treated as states due to their membership of a specialised agency. In 1984 the Cook Islands which the Assembly did not recognise as independent applied for membership of the World Health Organisation. The Secretary-General accepted its deposit of an instrument of acceptance on the grounds that the composition of the organisation's World Health Assembly was essentially the same as the General Assembly, which he believed would have made the same decision. The same reasoning was applied to Niue in 1994.[102] Thus, recognition by specialised agencies within the UN family can provide evidence of statehood before UN organs, which itself may not require a decision from the General Assembly or the Security Council.

6. The International Criminal Court

In addition to the UN system Palestine has also sought recognition as a state before the International Criminal Court. Article 12(3) of the Rome Statute 1998 provides that a "State" which is not party to the ICC Statute may accept the jurisdiction of the Court in a declaration deposited with its Registrar. On 21 January 2009 the Palestinian National Authority's Minister of Justice submitted such a declaration.[103] Acceptance by the Court of Palestine's recognition of its jurisdiction would not only be evidence of its statehood, but would also open the possibility of Israeli officials being indicted by the Court for the construction of Jewish settlements on occupied land. Article 8(2)(b)(viii) of the Rome Statute defines as a war crime: "The transfer, directly or indirectly, by the Occupying Power of parts of its own civilian population into the territory it occupies, or the deportation or transfer of all or parts of the population of the occupied territory within or outside this territory".

Three years later, however, on 3 April 2012, the Officer of the Prosecutor issued a short statement which asserted that the prosecutor had "no authority" to determine whether Palestine was a state for that purpose.[104]

---

102 Ibid. paras. 85–86.

103 Available at http://www.icc-cpi.int/NR/rdonlyres/74EEE201-0FED-4481-95D4-C8071087102C/279777/20090122PalestinianDeclaration2.pdf. Accessed 18 April 2012.

104 The Officer of the Prosecutor, "Situation in Palestine", para. 6. Available at http://www.icc-cpi.int/NR/rdonlyres/C6162BBF-FEB9-4FAF-AFA9-836106D2694A/284387/SituationinPalestine030412ENG.pdf. Accessed 18 April 2012. See also Dapo Akande, "ICC Prosecutor Decides that He Can't Decide on the Statehood of Palestine. Is He Right?" *EJIL: Talk!*, 5 April 2012. Available at http://www.ejiltalk.org/icc-prosecutor-decides-that-he-cant-decide-on-the-statehood-of-palestine-is-he-right/. Accessed 18 April 2012.

Instead, the Prosecutor referred the role of the determination of a "state" for the Statute to the UN Secretary-General, who under Article 125(3) is the depository for applications by states to accede to the Statute. He further noted the practice that in areas of controversy the Secretary-General sought direction from the UN General Assembly.[105] The statement did not directly refer to UNESCO's decision, but noted that despite recognition as a state by "United Nations bodies", its status before the Assembly was currently that of an observer not a non-member state.[106] In addition to the Secretary-General advised by the General Assembly, the Prosecutor also considered that the Assembly of State Parties to the ICC Statute also had the authority to determine the issue of statehood under a catch-all provision relating to its powers, Article 112(2)(g).[107] The prosecutor like the Secretary-General, as an organ of an international organisation, saw the proper responsibility for determining controversial questions of membership residing with the state parties of the ICC or members of the UN. However, despite an indirect acknowledgment of UNESCO's decision, he also avoided the Vienna Formula which could allow Palestine's statehood to be recognised in the UN system outside of a formal decision by the General Assembly.

7. Conclusion

Palestine is far from a functioning independent state, but it has elements connected with statehood and a generally supported right to achieve a state. The rhetorical declaration of a state before it has been fully established is a normal procedure in the creation of states. Declarations of independence and the reaction of states to them are seen as largely political acts and this applies to Palestine. Recognition from states and membership of international organisations can be seen as an attempt to build an external framework of relations and rights around an emerging Palestinian state in which it can consolidate the internal aspects of its sovereignty. It reinforces a particular model of what a settlement between Israel and the Palestinians should be, giving expression to two states.

---

[105] Ibid. para. 5.

[106] Ibid. para. 7.

[107] Article 112(2)(g), Rome Statute of the International Criminal Court 1998: "The Assembly shall:... Perform any other function consistent with this Statute or the Rules of Procedure and Evidence."

Palestine certainly possesses some attributes of statehood, but lacks many attributes of a fully sovereign and independent state. In the absence of precise criteria for defining statehood in international law the question becomes one of whether the glass is half full or half empty. There is certainly no question that the glass is full.

The Palestinian position is similar to other declarations of independence, such as that of Kosovo. The Kosovo Declaration of Independence of 17 February 2008 was made in the context negotiations on its final status which failed and can be seen as a unilateral attempt to establish certain facts. Like Palestine, its attempt at recognition has gained significant support which strengthens its position. However, by this unilateral action a number of key issues relating to its sovereignty remain unresolved, notably Serbian areas which reject the government's authority. Ultimately, Kosovo is likely to need a negotiated settlement with Serbia to finalise its status and to gain membership of the UN, as is the case with Palestine. It can be remembered that the Palestinians are attempting to establish the independent state that the Roadmap planned that they would achieve in 2003. The unilateral acts of Palestine, while a backwards step from a negotiated settlement, do not actually move away from the planned direction of negotiations.

Palestinian statehood is fundamentally aspirational and grounded in rights as much as institutions. Indeed, Palestine stands out among entities seeking recognition of their statehood in having a well-established right to self-determination and independence. The problem is that the exercise of that right is at best incremental. By attempting to gain some elements associated with independent statehood: general recognition from and relations with states and a seat at the United Nations, the Palestinians hope to be in a stronger position to gain other substantive elements, in particular control of a defined territory and the population which lives on it. It is a state visibly being built piece by piece. By establishing external elements of statehood as "facts" no longer subject to negotiation, it seeks to strengthen its hand in possible future negotiations with Israel. As Sri Lanka argued in the debate in UNESCO, the admission to the organisation had shown that: "Palestine's independence is an idea whose time has come and that this has broad recognition in the world community".[108]

[108] Sri Lanka, http://www.unesco.org/new/fileadmin/MULTIMEDIA/HQ/GBS/36GC/audio/36-VR-11-90-SriLanka-E.mp3. Accessed 20 April 2012.

On the other hand, the Israeli acceleration of settlement building can be seen as a unilateral (and illegal) action to strengthen their position in an area where they are strong, namely their control of the territory that forms the basis for the proclaimed Palestinian state. Palestinians can build the external aspects of their sovereignty, but the weakness of their internal position still remains the critical flaw in their claim to statehood.

CHAPTER TWELVE

EGYPT'S COMPLICITY IN TORTURE AND EXTRAORDINARY RENDITIONS

Nirmala Pillay*

1. Introduction

Robert Baer, a CIA agent, exemplified the importance of the Mubarak government for US intelligence when he observed that "If you want serious interrogation you send a prisoner to Jordan, if you want them to be tortured, you send them to Syria. If you want someone to disappear... never to see them again... you send them to Egypt."[1] Hosni Mubarak enjoyed close ties with Western countries enabling the US, Canada, Britain, and Sweden to deport terrorist suspects to a regime that specialised in interrogation methods prohibited by international law.

This chapter examines the implications of the fall of the Egyptian regime of Hosni Mubarak for the prohibition against torture, a *jus cogens* norm of international law. Torture theorist Darius Rejali argued in a major study, published in 1997, that torture was never really eliminated from democratic countries, so a change of regime in Egypt in favour of a democratic form of governance is no guarantee that torture, an entrenched part of the Egyptian security regime, will necessarily abate. Rejali's thesis is probed in the light of the revelations of extraordinary renditions of terrorist suspects to Egypt and the implications of the Egyptian revolution for US and Egyptian collaboration in the "war on terror."

Extraordinary rendition is the practice of transferring terrorist suspects, "with the involvement of the US or its agents, to a foreign State in circumstances that make it more likely than not that the individual will be subjected to torture or cruel, inhuman, or degrading treatment."[2] This

* School of Law, Liverpool John Moores University, UK.

[1] Steven Macpherson Watt, "Torture, 'Stress and Duress' and Rendition as Counter-Terrorism Tools," in Rachel Meerpol (ed) *America's Disappeared: Secret Imprisonment, Detainees, and the 'War on Terror.'* (New York: Seven Stories Press, 2005), 82.

[2] "Torture by proxy: International law applicable to 'Extraordinary Renditions.'" Briefing Paper. The Centre for Human Rights and Global Justice. (New York University School of Law. December 2005), 6.

definition should be read together with Art 3(1) of the Convention against Torture and other Cruel, Inhuman and Degrading Treatment or Punishment (UNCAT): "(N)o State Party shall expel, return or extradite a person to another State where there are substantial grounds for believing that he would be in danger of being subjected to torture."[3] The Convention against Torture was an attempt to prohibit torture worldwide by eradicating it from every national judicial system. UNCAT explicitly embargoes the transfer of people to any other country suspected of engaging in torture. The US signed the Convention in October 1984 but since the 1990's has engaged in a programme of kidnappings, renditions and torture with the help of several Middle Eastern countries. After September 11, 2001 (until 2007)[4] three thousand individuals were detained, with US involvement, in detention centres in Egypt, Morocco, Syria and Jordan with arrests and detentions intensifying during the wars in Afghanistan and Iraq.[5] The US State department has repeatedly cited these countries for human rights violations and for torture[6] so suspects were sent there precisely because their methods were well known to US authorities. The US collaborated particularly closely with Egypt to extract information from suspected terrorists about the global terrorist threat and to share the intelligence gleaned. There seemed to be no difference in the belief of the utility of torture by the democratic government of America or the authoritarian regime of Egypt when it was judged that the situation necessitated it.

2. Torture in Egypt

On 25th January 2011, Egyptians took to the streets against their government. After 18 days of widespread public protests president Hosni Mubarak,

[3] Reprinted in Ian Brownlie (ed), *Basic Documents on Human Rights* 3rd Ed (Oxford: Clarendon Press, 1997) 38.

[4] Mayer, "Outsourcing Torture: The secret history of America's 'extraordinary rendition program'" (2005) 3 online: http://www.kuwaitifreedom.org/media/pdf/Outsourcing%20Torture.pdf.

[5] Saudi Arabia and Yemen are included in the list of the Parliamentary Briefing Paper. The American State Department accused these states as well for using torture in interrogation. The Briefing paper provides several examples: Ahmed Agiza and Mohammed al-Zari were transferred to Egypt; Hassan Osma Nasr to Cairo, Egypt; Khaled El Masri to Macedonia and then to Afghanistan; Jamal Quasim Aseed Mohammed to Pakistan and then to Jordan; Muhammad Saad Iqbal Madni to Egypt; Maher Arar to Syria and Mamdoudh Habib to Egypt. See "Torture by proxy: International law applicable to 'Extraordinary Renditions'," 6.

[6] Mayer, "Outsourcing Torture," 3.

stepped down. There are many underlying causes for the Egyptian mass movement but the proximate cause of the initial protest was the death of Khaled Said who was beaten and kicked fatally outside a Space Net internet Cafe in 2010 for exposing police corruption.[7] The incident outraged the Egyptian people weary of police brutality and Said's death was the spark that grew into a movement that eventually toppled the Mubarak regime.

Egypt is already a signatory to several multi-lateral treaties[8] that prohibit torture such as the International Covenant on Civil and Political Rights (1982) (ICCPR),[9] The Geneva Conventions (1952) and Additional Protocols (1992)[10] and UNCAT (1986).[11] UNCAT was incorporated into Egyptian law in July 1986 by Republican Decision No. 154 of 1986 and it is worth noting that it was in Cairo that the Organisation of Islamic Conference met in 1990 to address human rights. Art 20 of the Cairo Declaration of Human Rights not only expressly prohibits torture but, showed an awareness of the effect of emergency regulations on civil liberties, when the text included the following phrase "nor is it permitted to promulgate emergency laws that would provide executive authority for such actions."[12] Emergency regulations have been continuously in force in Egypt since 1986.[13] These

7 Associated Press in Cairo, "Anger in Egypt as police who killed Khaled Said get seven years," *The Guardian* Wed 26 Oct. 2011. Mohmoud Saleh and Awad Ismail Suleiman, the two policemen charged with killing Said, were never charged with murder.

8 Egypt is party to the following treaties: Additional Protocols 1 and 11 to the Geneva Conventions (1992); Convention against Torture (1986); African Charter on Human and Peoples Rights (1984); International Covenant on Economic, Social and Cultural Rights (1982); International Covenant on Civil and Political Rights (1982); Committee on the Elimination of Discrimination Against Women(CEDAW) (1981); Refugee Convention (1981); Committee on the Elimination of Racial Discrimination (CERD) (1967); Geneva Conventions (1952); Genocide Convention (1952).

9 Art 7 of the ICCPR prohibits "torture, cruel and inhuman or degrading treatment or punishment," International Covenant on Civil and Political Rights, opened for signature Dec 19 1966,999 U.N.T.S. 171,6 I.L.M. 368 (entered into force Mar. 23, 1976).

10 Art 3, 13, 14 and 17 of Geneva III prohibits "violence to life and person, in particular murder of all kinds, mutilation, and cruel treatment and torture...(c) outrages upon personal dignity, in particular humiliating and degrading treatment." Geneva Convention Relative to the Treatment of Prisoners of War, adopted on Aug. 12, 1949, 6 U.S.T. 3316, T.I.A.S. No.3364, 75 U.N.T.S. 135.

11 Opened for signature December 10, 1984, 1465 U.N.T.S. 85, 23 I.L.M. 1027 (entered into force June 26, 1987), in Brownlie, *Basic Documents on Human Rights*, 38.

12 Cairo declaration on Human Rights in Islam, adopted on Aug. 5, 1990, online: http://www.unhcr.org/refworrefworld/docid/3ae6b3822c.html (accessed 26 June 2012). Art 2(2) of UNCAT contains a similar provision "No exceptional circumstances whatsoever, whether a state of war or a threat of war, internal political stability, or any other public emergency may be invoked as a justification of torture, or other cruel or inhuman punishment."

13 "Of great importance to Egyptian society is the Emergency Law, which was implemented in 1967 during the Arab-Israeli War. The law dramatically expanded police powers,

treaties forbid torture, cruel and degrading punishment and *refoulment*—the transfer of individuals to states where they may face the risk of torture—and they permit no exceptions or derogations.

In addition to Egypt's international obligations to eradicate torture, Art 42 of the Egyptian Constitution provided that a detained person "will be treated in a manner concomitant with the preservation of his dignity." In addition, the penal code of Egypt prohibits a public official from participating in torture.[14] Despite these provisions, Egypt has been criticised for not defining torture clearly in either its Constitution or its Penal code and especially for not bringing its legislation in line with international standards.[15] Art 126 of the Egyptian Penal Code is very specific about when the law allows accusations of torture. It restricts the use of the word torture to cases of physical abuse; when a victim "is accused" and when officials employ torture to coerce a confession."[16] This narrow definition excludes the possibility that torture occurs in instances of intimidation and punishment and torture is not a category that applies to the treatment of witnesses or suspects.[17] Egypt's law also does not "fully criminalise torture" in the way laid down by the UNCAT. In February 2010, a MP of the Muslim Brotherhood submitted a proposal to the People's Assembly legislative committee seeking to bring the definition of torture in Egyptian law in line with international law. The government had promised as much to the UN Human Rights Council in November 2009. The proposal was rejected by the majority ruling National Democratic Party just before Egypt's Universal Periodic Review.[18]

---

suspended constitutional rights, and legalized censorship. The law is pertinent to NGO pushback as it gives the government the legal rights to act in any manner which it believes is needed for its national security." Nadine H. Abdalla, "Civil Society in Egypt: A Catalyst for Democratization?" *International Journal of Not-for-Profit Law* (August 2008) 10 (4).

[14] Egypt's law does not "fully criminalise torture in line with the international standard articulated in the UN Convention against Torture ... Art 126 of the Penal code restricts torture to cases of physical abuse and when a victim 'is accused' and when officials employ torture to coerce a confession." This narrow definition excludes instances when intimidation and punishment may constitute torture and torture does not apply to witnesses or suspects. Human Rights Watch. "Work on him until he Confesses." January 2011 3 online: http:/www.hrw.org.

[15] Egypt has long been criticised for not having a definition of torture in its legislation that is in line with Art 1 of UNCAT. *See* for example para 90 Committee Against Torture: Egypt, UN Doc. A/49/44, 12 June 1994.

[16] Human Rights Watch, "Work on him until he Confesses," 3.

[17] Human Rights Watch, "Work on him until he Confesses," 3.

[18] Human Rights Watch, "Work on Him until He Confesses," 3.

The Egyptian Penal Code is a weak deterrent to law enforcement authorities perpetrating torture or treating detainees in a degrading fashion. The Penal Code's guidelines for punishments are lenient and unfitted to the nature of the crimes. Even so Egyptian courts have been unwilling to punish perpetrators of torture to the full extent of the law. Moreover, courts repeatedly have recourse to Art 17[19] to reduce the punishment of an officer convicted of torture.[20] The vagueness and incompleteness of the constitutional and legal provisions against torture allowed enough room for torture to flourish under Hosni Mubarak.

In July 1996 the UN Special Rapporteur concluded that "torture is systematically practiced by the security forces in Egypt, in particular the state security intelligence ... (R)eported cases of torture are seen to be habitual, widespread and deliberate in at least a considerable part of the country."[21] In 2004 the Egyptian Organisation for Human Rights published disturbing figures documenting reported torture cases and deaths.[22] Between 2000 and April 2004 the organization recorded 108 victims of torture and 44 deaths under torture.

Evidence of torture in Egypt is also supplied by the various reports of Amnesty International and Egyptian Non-Government Organisations (NGOs). The latter include the Human Rights Centre for the Assistance of Prisoners (HRCPA) which monitored 1124 torture cases in prisons, and which alleged in 2004 that there were 20 000 Islamist detainees in Egyptian prisons and detention centres;[23] the Legal Aid Centre which recorded reports of torture in 1994 and 1995; the Egyptian Organisation for Human Rights and the Egyptian Association Against Torture (EAAT).[24] There have been allegations that as many as 5000 people have been incarcerated for years under emergency regulations with no charges proffered.[25]

19 In crimes requiring the sympathy of the court, the judge can reduce the penalty in the following way: in place of capital punishment, permanent or temporary hard labour.

20 Human Rights Watch, "Work on Him until He Confesses," 3.

21 Report of the Committee Against Torture, July 1996. United Nations. Supplement No. 44 (A/51/44).

22 Torture In Egypt—A phenomenon without restraint. The 12th report. The Egyptian Organisation for Human Rights, 2004 reproduced in Basma M. Abdel Aziz, "Torture in Egypt," *Torture* (2007): 17 (1).

23 The annual report of 2003. Human rights Centre for the Assistance of prisoners 2004, reported in Aziz, "Torture in Egypt," 52.

24 Figures and Organisations documented in Aziz, "Torture in Egypt," 49.

25 "Rights Groups Challenge detention without Charge or Trial in Egypt ... Case of Detainee Imprisoned for 15 years Reaches African Commission." The Egyptian Initiative for

Emergency laws were first introduced in Egypt in 1956 but since Hosni Mubarak became president in October 1981, these emergency regulations were never lifted.[26] The state of emergency suspends much of the ordinary law of the land allowing for extensive abridgement of civil liberties. Emergency rules give the security forces, including the State Security Investigations (SSI) unit unfettered authority by introducing a parallel system of law enforcement, security courts and prosecutors. This explains the large number of arbitrary arrests and detention.[27]

International law on torture requires states to investigate and prosecute instances of torture. Under Egyptian law the investigating body is authorised to inspect prisons and other official detention centres. It has no authority over unofficial detention centres. Yet many detainees reported that they were held incommunicado in illegal SSI detention cells, the existence of which Egypt had consistently denied. In her book on the revolution in Cairo, A. Soueif comments on the complete lack of due process accompanying arrests. People are usually sent to the State Security Intelligence Bureau in Lazoghli Square in Cairo. Families are not informed of the detainees' whereabouts. There they are held long enough to extract a confession by means of "insults, threats and beatings to fairly evolved methods of torture. Sometimes the person is not required to confess to anything; they are given a warning and let go. Sometimes the person dies. Mostly, they are sent to jail to await trial."[28]

The Human Rights Committee in 2002 noted that Egypt was in violation of Arts 6 and 7 of the ICCPR.[29] The committee accused the security services of displaying a systematic pattern of cruel and degrading treatment of prisoners and the state of not setting up an independent body to investigate and punish those responsible.[30] The Committee against Torture

---

Personal Rights and the Open Society Justice Initiative, December 14, 2010 online http://www.eipr.org/en/pressrelease/2010/12/14/1021.

[26] Nasser imposed a state of emergency from 1956–1964 and again in 1967. Anwar al-Sadat took over and continued with the emergency regulations which he lifted in 1980. Hosni Mubarak reinstated the state of emergency in 1981 and it has remained in force.

[27] Human Rights Watch, "Work on Him until He Confesses," 4.

[28] Ahdar Soueif *Cairo: My City, Our Revolution* (Bloomsbury: London: Bloomsbury, 2012), 45.

[29] Art 6 covers inherent right to life, amnesty, who may be sentenced to death and genocide. Art 7 provides "No one may be subject to cruel, inhuman or degrading treatment or punishment...," reprinted in Brownlie, *Basic Documents on Human Rights*, 127.

[30] Concluding Observations of the Human Rights Committee: Egypt,UN Doc. CCPR/CO/76/EGY, 28 November 2002, para. 13. This conclusion is repeated in the same words by Human Rights Watch in January 2011.

demanded that the Egyptian government set up such a body to enquire into the allegations of disappearances but the Egyptian government ignored the recommendation.[31] Enforced disappearances were again especially highlighted in Special Rapporteur Martin Scheinin's January 2010 report on Egypt.[32]

The Egyptian government maintained power through a combination of bribery and force and built up a standing security establishment of 1.5 million strong. Egypt has the largest security sector in the Middle East and spent more on internal security services than on its army. Reports show that "Egypt's national budget overwhelming emphasises internal security before other areas of public spending such as healthcare"[33] even though a good deal of the State's resources is foreign aid. There are several internal security agencies such as the General Intelligence and Security Service; the Military Security Service; the General Directorate of State Security Investigations and the State Security Service.[34] The security services investigation (SSI) unit is not the only body accused of torture. The Egyptian police force, the "*Mukhabarat*", had a reputation for brutality.[35] Police officers, especially those involved in criminal investigations (*mabahith*),[36] are also accused of being perpetrators of torture. The involvement of the police in torture automatically expands the range for which torture is used. Unsurprisingly Egyptian Human Rights Organisations reported that torture was being put to use in an increasing number of situations: to intimidate or recruit police informers; to punish those who do not accept the authority of the police, and even to intimidate those who demand proper procedures such as arrest warrants.[37] Endemic corruption in the police accounts for much of the brutality.[38] As Soueif reports, "police officers ran protection and drug rackets. People regularly fell out of windows

---

[31] Human Rights Watch, "Work on him until he Confesses," 40.

[32] A/HRC/13/37/Add.2. Available at http://www2.ohchr.org/english/issues/terrorism/rapporteur/docs/A_HRC_13_37_Add2.doc.

[33] Abdalla, "Civil Society in Egypt: A catalyst for Democratisation?" 39.

[34] Federation of American Scientists "Egypt: Intelligence Agencies." updated 10 June 2008 http://www.fas.org/irp/world/egypt/index.html.

[35] Mayer, "Outsourcing Torture," 5.

[36] Human Rights Watch, "Work on him Until he Confesses," 16.

[37] Human Rights Watch, "Work on him Until he Confesses," 16.

[38] Shambhavi V. M. Gopalkrishna, "Reflections of a Citizen Amidst Divided Lands on Reinventing Civil Society, Civil Liberties, and Governance in Post-Conflict Societies: Patterns, Potentials, and Challenges in the Globalized New Millennium." *International Journal of Not-for-Profit Law* (August 2008) 10 (4).

during questioning or had heart attacks in police custody."[39] The state also relied periodically on some 500 000 informal thugs or *baltagis*.[40] All the provisions safeguarding civil liberties in the 1971 Egyptian Constitution had been rendered completely ineffectual by the emergency regulations in force since 1986.

What did the Egyptian authorities hope to gain from the widespread practice of torture? It is impossible to analyse individual cases to assess whether torturers extract reliable information from victims to secure confessions for criminal trials since torturers habitually exaggerate the success of their practices. However, it has been shown in several other situations that torture has many uses. In Algeria, the French used torture to intimidate and subdue the native population. This was also the case in South Africa. Mysterious and sudden disappearances and covert violence in hidden detention centres has proved effective in forcing the majority of the population into compliance with the regime by instilling fear. Edward Behr concluded from his study of the use of torture in the Algerian conflict that its primary use was "to control the civil population."[41]

The Egyptian regime surveyed, controlled and intimidated communists, socialists, Islamists, human rights activists, protesters and criminals who were arrested, detained and tortured.[42] The range of victims who were watched and harassed exposes a lack of a coherent political philosophy or ideology in Egypt.[43] The Egyptian Constitution favours a socialist rather than a capitalist economic system, but Mubarak who assumed power after the assassination of Anwar Sadat, turned the economy towards privatization while maintaining a firm grip on political power.[44] Egypt is ostensibly a secular state but has Islamic social foundations that accommodate *Sharia* law.[45] The lack of coherence meant that the state survived by control and by suppressing criticism from any quarter. All non-government organisations were monitored closely. Law 84/2002 empowered the government to interfere in almost all NGO activities and to harass members

---

39 Soueif, *Cairo My City, Our Revolution*, 45.

40 Soueif, *Cairo My City, Our Revolution*, 67.

41 Edward Behr, *The Algerian Problem*. (London: Hodder and Stoughton, 1961) cited in D. Rejali, *Torture and Democracy* (Princeton: Princeton University Press, 2007), 487.

42 Aziz, "Torture in Egypt," 52.

43 Aziz, "Torture in Egypt," 52.

44 Arts 59 and 73 of the Egyptian Constitution. *See also* James Feuille "Reforming Egypt's Constitution: Hope for Egyptian Democracy," *Texas International Law Journal* (2012): 47 (1).

45 J. Feuille, "Reforming Egypt's Constitution: Hope for Egyptian Democracy," *Texas International Journal of Law*, 47:1 at 1.

of NGO's.[46] It is worth noting that the consistent focus of this harassment was the Muslim Brotherhood, though secular and liberal groupings and even students were also repeatedly targeted.[47]

The first multi-party elections in Egypt were held in 2005 but were undermined by the harassment of the government's political opponents, many of whom were restricted and some even imprisoned.[48] The Mubarak government was determined to maintain a grip on power by fair means or foul and to remain an ally of Western powers on whose aid Egypt relies. The US, in turn, values an ally that accepts its presence in the Gulf and supports its policies with respect to the Israel-Palestine conflict. The status and security of Israel is a major part of US policy in the Region. Egypt is a recipient of a great deal of US aid and after Israel, receives the largest amount of military aid from the US. The Egyptian army costs about a third of the GDP of the country.[49]

According to Abdalla in her study of civil society in Egypt, democracy activists "cite this close relationship as one of the major impediments" to the emergence of NGOs and the building of a more equitable and free Egyptian society."[50] The US was not unaware of the need for democratic reform in Egypt. In fact the US State Department has a genuinely fair record in cataloguing and reporting on human rights abuses in Egypt.[51] However, when western democracies faced serious threats from terrorist organisations, Egypt's record in torturing prisoners and their failure to abide by international obligations to reduce the incidence of torture was a welcome convenience to the West. Egypt could be relied on to interrogate

---

[46] *See* Abdalla, "Civil Society in Egypt: A catalyst for Democratisation?" 37 for an account of the arrest of Dr. Saad Eddin Ibrahim, director of the Ibn Khaldun Centre for Development Studies in Egypt.

[47] Abdalla, "Civil Society in Egypt: A catalyst for Democratisation?" 37.

[48] Abdalla, "Civil Society in Egypt: A catalyst for Democratisation?" 37.

[49] Abdalla, "Civil Society in Egypt: A catalyst for Democratisation?" 31.

[50] Abdalla, "Civil Society in Egypt: A catalyst for Democratisation?" 31.

[51] Steven C. Poe; Sabine C. Carey; Tanya C. Vazquez, "How are these pictures Different? A Quantitative Comparison of the US State Department and Amnesty International Human Rights Reports, 1976–1995," *Human Rights Quarterly* (2001) 23: 650–677, at 662.

Country Reports of the US State Department are the result of extensive work carried out by that Department. They are deemed to be the "most complete cataloguing of human rights practices around the world, in terms of the number of countries covered, and the range of rights". Writing in 2001 Poe, Carey and Vazquez concluded that the number of "times the reports of the Department were biased in favour of Egypt was 10 out of 20."

suspects in ways that were illegal in the domestic jurisdictions of western countries. Terrorist suspects were rendered to Egypt as early as 1995.[52]

2.1. *Extraordinary Rendition, the United States and Egypt*

Originally, overseas rendition was an occasional practice under President Reagan aimed at capturing people in "rogue" states such as Lebanon and rendering them either to the US or to foreign territories.[53] After the attack on the World Trade Centre in 2001 the practice of rendition accelerated into extraordinary rendition when terrorist suspects were captured and taken to destinations around the world. The purpose of such renditions was to subject those arrested "to aggressive methods of persuasion that are illegal in America—including torture."[54] Rendition is not illegal under American law. In an analysis of four leading cases DiMento and Geis point out that it did not matter, for the US judiciary, how the defendant was brought to justice, what mattered was "the physical appearance of the defendant before the court."[55] This practice of US law enforcement officers, developed into rendition to other countries and then to countries known to torture suspects.

Andrew Chang reporting for ABC news in August 2002 on people transferred to foreign detention centres observed that: "prisoners are subject to the law of the land where they're detained, which would permit more severe treatment than would be allowed under US law."[56] Also, according to Jane Mayer, in a landmark article for the New Yorker, rendition had expanded to "include a wide range and ill-defined population that the Administration terms "illegal enemy combatants."[57] Extraordinary rendition was a deliberate policy that sought to circumvent both US domestic

---

[52] Michael Scheuer, *Imperial Hubris: Why The West is Losing the War on Terror* (Washington, D.C.: Brassey's, 2004), in Mayer, "Outsourcing Torture," 5.

[53] *See* Gregor Noll, "Diplomatic Assurances and the silence of Human Rights Law," Melb. J. Int'l L (2006) 7: 108 for a discussion of individuals captured and rendered to Egypt at the behest of the US government.

[54] Mayer, "Outsourcing Torture," 7.

[55] *Ker v Illinois* (1886); *Frisbie v. Collins* (1962); *United States v. Toscanino* (1974); *United States v. Alvarez-Machain* (1992) in J.F.C. DiMento amd G.Geis, "The Extraordinary Condition of Extraordinary Rendition: The C.I.A., the D.E.A., Kidnaping, Torture, and the Law," *War Crimes, Genocide & Crimes Against Humanity* (2006) 2: 35–64, at 50–58.

[56] Andrew Chang, *Is torture a tool in the War on Terror? Has the war on terror changed attitudes on Torture?*, Aug. 13, 2002, at http://abcnews.go.com/International/story/id=79885&page=1.

[57] Mayer, "Outsourcing Torture." Mayer does not supply exact numbers of those rendered and the rough figure is 150.

legislation and international law by putting suspects beyond the Jurisdiction of US courts,[58] thus implicating the US and its allies in the torture of transferred suspects.[59]

According to Michael Scheuer, an American C.I.A. agent and counter terrorism expert, the focus of US intelligence in 1995 was Muslim political extremists, especially *Al Qaeda*. "Some of the senior people in *Al Qaeda* were Egyptian," and "it served American purposes to get these people arrested, and Egyptian purposes to get these people back, where they could be interrogated."[60] Between September 2001 and 2005 the Bush administration engaged in 60 to 70 episodes of rendition to Egypt alone.[61] Cultural affinity played a part in renditions to Muslim countries since it was considered easier to interrogate suspects if attention was paid to cultural and language issues.[62] Egypt was a favoured destination because the suspects were Muslim. Scheuer argues that Presidents Clinton and Bush preferred to render captives to third countries also to avoid giving them legitimacy by turning them into prisoners of war. They were uninterested in the treatment that would be meted out to the captives.[63]

The relationship between Egypt and the US facilitated the capture and transfer of a number of terrorist suspects without due process. None of the usual procedures for extradition were followed and some transferees remain unaccounted for.[64] Egyptian and US interrogators developed a close working relationship. "The Americans could give the Egyptian interrogators questions they wanted put to the detainees in the morning . . . and get answers by the evening."[65]

After the attacks on the Twin Towers in New York and on the Pentagon, Congress authorised the President to "use all necessary and appropriate force . . . to prevent any future acts of international terrorism against the United States by nations, organisations or persons."[66] The President was

---

58 DiMento amd Geis, "The Extraordinary Condition of Extraordinary Rendition,".

59 "Torture by Proxy: International Law Applicable to "Extraordinary Renditions," 6.

60 Scheuer, in Mayer, "Outsourcing Torture," 5.

61 DiMento and Geis, "The Extraordinary Condition of Extraordinary Rendition," 39.

62 Martin Rudner, "Hunters and Gatherers: The Intelligence Coalition against Islamic Terrorism," *International Journal of Intelligence and Counter Intelligence* (2004) 17: 193, 220.

63 Noll, "Diplomatic assurances and the silence of Human Rights Law," 105.

64 The details of names of terrorist suspects and where and why they were captured are chronicled in Mayer's article "Outsourcing Torture".

65 Scheuer, in Mayer "Outsourcing Torture," 5.

66 A Joint Resolution to Authorise the use of United States Armed Forces Against Those Responsible for the Recent Attacks Launched Against the United States. Pub. L. No. 107–40, 115 Stat. 224 (2001). For a full report on the legislative history of this resolution see Richard

also empowered by the Patriot Act which was passed in October 2001 to "arrest suspects and detain them almost indefinitely, deport them, hold them in solitary confinement, open their mail, tap their phones, monitor their emails and search their homes without a warrant."[67] The wide powers of the Patriot Act resulted in 600 people being held in prison by 2004 and a declared intention of the government to interrogate 5000 men from the Middle East on tourist visas to the US.[68]

While the new domestic legislation granted these powers to the United States government, international law is clear that no crisis or emergency allows derogation from the prohibition against torture. Apart from being a party to the main international instruments against torture, the US is party to the 1987 Inter-American Convention to Prevent and Punish Torture.[69] The way the US circumvented the jurisdiction of both regional and international law was to argue that UNCAT which bans "'cruel, inhuman and degrading treatment' of terrorist suspects does not apply to American interrogations of foreigners overseas."[70] This was the reasoning of Attorney General Gonzales who demonstrated a canny awareness of the scope of the international law on torture but also exposed the determination of the US to ensure that the actions of US officials remained technically within the bounds of legality. Gonzales must have been aware that shifting interrogations overseas was against the letter and spirit of UNCAT. The US position was that the provisions of international law would only apply to the US if suspects were interrogated at home.[71]

The C.I.A. acknowledged the link between the US administration and Egypt in their joint attempt to combat Islamic terrorism.[72] It is ironic that Western democracies worked closely with Egypt to prevent the rise of

F. Grimmett, CRS Report for Congress: Authorisation For Use of Military Force in Response to 9/11 Attacks (P.L. 107-40) online: http://www.fas.org/sgp/crs/natsec/R522357.pdf.

[67] Quoted in Stephanie L. Williams, "'Your Honour, I am here today requesting the Court's permission to torture Mr. Doe': The Legality of Torture as a Means to an End v. The Legality of Torture as a Violation of *Jus Cogens* Norms under Customary International Law," *12 U Miami Int'l & Comp.L. Rev.* (2004) 12: 301, 304.

[68] Williams, "Your Honour, I am here today requesting the Court's permission to torture Mr. Doe," 304.

[69] Inter-American Convention to Prevent and Punish Torture O.A.S.T.S. No. 67, I.L.M. 519 (entered into force Feb. 28, 1987) available at http://www.oas.org/juridico/english/treaties/a-51.html.

[70] Gonzales made this argument during his confirmation proceedings. Mayer, "Outsourcing Torture," 4.

[71] The Attorney general is also referring here to US interrogators in US prisons overseas such as Abu Graib and Guantanamo Bay.

[72] Scheuer, in Mayer, "Outsourcing Torture."

radical Muslim organisations since this collaboration produced the opposite effect. Chris Zambelis, in his consideration of the nexus between torture and the radicalisation of Muslims in the Middle East, argues that since regimes that torture its own citizens depend on US economic, military and diplomatic support, the US is seen to be complicit in these crimes. Islamists rejected the Middle Eastern regimes of Egypt, Jordan and Saudi Arabia as being corrupt, authoritarian and more accountable to the US than to their own people. The heavy handed methods, torture and rendition, used to prevent the consolidation of Islamist organisations had the effect of radicalising sections of Middle Eastern society and recruiting them to the Islamist cause. In Egypt, the torture of members of Islamist movements, emergency laws and the repression of NGOs, promoted the popularity of the Islamist opposition. "Even when governments have not purposely assisted the Islamists, they indirectly aided them through limitations and restraints on associational life."[73] The efforts made to contain members of Islamist groupings is revealed in a poignant description by Soeif of an incident at the height of the Revolution: "Word is coming through that the Dakheleyya is closing down selected jails and police stations across the country and letting—or even throwing- violent criminals out. In el-Wadi el-Gedeed prison all the cells were opened except for one which held thirty six newly detained Islamists, then the prison was set on fire. A group of convicted criminals risked their lives to break open the cell and set prisoners free."[74]

The suppression of Muslim Brotherhood activists began in the time of President Nasser. According to a prominent rights activist Nabil al-Hilaly, tortured in 1959, political detainees were tortured throughout the 1960's. These were mainly communists and Muslim Brotherhood members. Torture seemed to have abated in the 70's but became endemic again under Mubarak.[75] Members of the Al-Qaeda leadership Dr. Ayman al-Zawahiri and the late Abu Musab al-Zawahiri had both been captured and tortured by Egyptian and Jordanian authorities.[76] In a video released

[73] Augustus Richard Norton, "Civil Society in the Middle East," quoted in Abdalla, "Civil Society in Egypt," 40.

[74] Soueif, *Cairo My City, Our Revolution*, 35.

[75] Behind Closed Doors: Torture and Detention in Egypt (New York, 1992) in Human Rights Watch, "Work on him Until he Confesses."

[76] C. Zambelis, "Is There a Nexus between Torture and Radicalisation?" *Terrorism Monitor* (2008) 6 (13). *See also* James Toth, "Islamism in Southern Egypt: A case Study of a Radical Religious Movement," *Int. J.Middle East Studies*, (2003) 35: 547–572.

in 2007, Zawahiri explicitly mentioned torture.[77] The practice of systemic torture by Middle Eastern governments, especially in prisons, "receives a great deal of attention in militant literature, communiqués, and discussions on radical Islamist chat room forums." Torture is a repetitive theme in the rhetoric of Islamists. Even academic scholars have now begun to focus attention on the phenomenon of torture in Islamist rhetoric in an effort to better understand the "radicalisation process."[78]

2.2. *Torture as* Jus Cogens: *a Peremptory Norm of International Law*

The prohibition against torture in International Law is comprehensive and applies to every country because it enjoys an elevated status among human rights norms. After World War II international human rights expanded across the globe through a series of Conventions and enforceable multi-lateral treaties.[79] Each included an article prohibiting torture and allowing no derogation from its provisions even under states of emergency. The most important of these are the United Nations Declaration against Torture and the annex of 12 articles that prohibit torture (1975).[80] This was followed in 1984 by UNCAT. UNCAT defines torture as "any act by which severe pain or suffering, whether physical or mental, is intentionally inflicted on a person for such purposes as obtaining from her or a third party information or a confession, punishing for an act he or a third person has committed, or suspected of having committed, or intimidating or coercing him or a third person, or for any reason based on discrimination or any kind, when such pain or suffering is inflicted by or at the instigation of or with the consent or acquiescence of a public official or other person acting in an official capacity."[81] This definition not only

[77] Dr. Ayman al-Zawahiri, "The Advice of One Concerned," July 4, 2007 video.google.com/ videoplay.

[78] Zambelis, "Is There a Nexus between Torture and Radicalisation?".

[79] Michael Freeman, *Human Rights: An Interdisciplinary approach* (Cambridge: Polity Press, 2005).

[80] Declaration on the Protection of All persons from Being Subjected to Torture and Other Cruel, Inhuman, or degrading Treatment or Punishment, G.A. Res. 3452, U.N. GAOR, 30th Sess., Supp. No. 34, U.N. Doc. A/1034 (1975). The UN Declaration defines torture as "any act by which severe pain or suffering, whether physical or mental, is intentionally inflicted by or at the instigation of a public official on a person for such purposes as obtaining from him or a third person information or confession, punishing him for an act he has committed, or intimidating him or other persons."

[81] Convention against Torture and other Cruel, Inhuman Degrading Treatment or Punishment (UNCAT) Opened for signature December 10, 1984, 1465 U.N.T.S. 85, 23 I.L.M. 1027

holds State officials liable if they themselves torture but it places upon them a positive duty to stop the possibility of torture happening. The ICCPR and the Geneva Conventions also require States to punish officials responsible for torture.[82] Importantly, International law against torture proscribes the use of information extracted through torture in any judicial proceedings. In most democracies ordinary criminal law renders evidence or confessions extracted under duress inadmissible in court.[83] Art 12 of the Annex to the UN Declaration Against Torture also disqualifies the use of evidence obtained by torture in any court procedure.

The prohibition against torture is one of a small cluster of human rights that have the status of *jus cogens* or compelling law.[84] The broad category of customary International law includes norms, which in addition to being customary, possesses a certain moral force.[85] *Jus cogens* are norms of general international law without exception meaning that States may not contract treaties that conflict *or* derogate from them.[86] The recognised list of *jus cogens* offences are genocide, slavery and slave trading, murder or causing the disappearance of individuals, torture and other cruel, inhuman or degrading treatment or punishment, prolonged arbitrary detention, systematic racial discrimination, or a consistent pattern of gross violations of internationally recognised human rights."[87] All states, whether or not they are signatories to Anti-Torture Conventions

(entered into force June 26, 1987), in Brownlie, *Basic documents on Human Rights*, 38.

82 For a full account of the meaning of the "real risk" of torture faced by rendered suspects see "Torture by Proxy," 9–10.

83 Controversial methods of interrogation, such as water boarding, favoured by US interrogators, would run the risk of being dismissed as torture by US courts hence, any information extracted through these methods could not be led as evidence The US keen to use the information extracted from suspects not only as intelligence but also to secure convictions, got around the jurisprudential difficulty of Art 12 by trying suspects in military tribunals away from public scrutiny.

84 Vienna Convention on the Law of Treaties. Art 53 May 23, 1969, entered into force 27 Jan. 1980, United Nations *Treaty Series*, Vol 1155, p. 331 available at http://untreaty.un.org/ilc/texts/instruments/english/conventions/1_1_1969.pdf.

85 Pamela J. Stephens, "A Categorical Approach to Human Rights Claims: *Jus Cogens* as a limitation on Enforcement," *Wisconsin International Law Journal*, (2004) 22 (2): 250. *See also* John Dugard and Christine Van den Wyngaert, "Reconciling Extradition with Human Rights," 92 *Am.J.Int'l L.* (1998) 92: 187, 195.

86 Art 53 of the Vienna Convention on the Law of Treaties: "a treaty is void if, at the time of its conclusion, it conflicts with a peremptory norm of general international law." The Vienna Convention on the Laws on Treaties, opened for signature May 23, 1969, 1155 U.N.T.S. 331, 8 I.L.M. 679 (entered into force Jan. 27, 1970).

87 *See* Williams, "Your Honour, I am here today requesting the Court's permission to torture Mr. Doe," 323.

and Treaties, are obliged to eradicate torture in their own countries by investigating and prosecuting instances of torture by their own officials and, importantly, calling into question other States that torture.

Related to *jus cogens* is the principle of *erga omnes* or obligations flowing to all since "all States have a legal interest in the protection" of these norms.[88] The implication of a *jus cogens* norm is whether it places "*obligations erga omnes* upon states or whether states may exercise *an option* to proceed against those who violate the norm".[89] According to Bassiouni, a *jus a cogens* implies a duty not an option to enforce a jus cogens provision.[90] Indeed, international law jurisdiction, as regards peremptory norms, allows a foreign sovereign to refer another State to the international court if it fails to take action on a *jus cogens* obligation. This was certainly the language used when Belgium requested the International Court of Justice, in May 2009, to adjudge that the Republic of Senegal was *obliged* to bring charges against Mr. H. Habrè for the crime of torture when he was head of Chad. Alternately, Senegal was *obliged* to extradite Habrè to Belgium where he would stand trial.[91] International and regional courts have found against countries if charges are laid when there is evidence of torture.[92]

Jus cogens not only restrict the treaty making power of States but oblige States to align their domestic law with peremptory norms. In *Prosecuor v. Anto Furundzija*[93] the International Criminal Tribunal for the former

Restatement (Third) of Foreign Relations Law of the United States 702 (1987). The legal basis for the list derives from: I) international pronouncements that indicate that these norms are regarded as part of customary international law; 2) Language in preambles or elsewhere in treaties that give these norms a higher standing; 3) The number of States who have acceded to treaties related to theses norms; 4) international investigations and prosecutions of these crimes. See M. Cherif Bassiouni, 'International Crimes: Jus Cogens and Obligatio Erga Omnes," *Law and Contemporary Problems*, (59) 4: 63,68.

[88] Barcelona Traction, Light and Power Co. Ltd. (*Belgium v Spain*), 1970 I.C.J. 3, 32 (Feb 5).

[89] Bassiouni, "International Crimes: Jus Cogens and Obligatio Erga Omnes," 63, 66.

[90] Bassiouni, "International Crimes: Jus Cogens and Obligatio Erga Omnes," 65.

[91] Questions relating to the Obligation to Prosecute or Extradite (Belguim v Senegal) 28 May 2009 available at http://www.icj-cji.org/docket/files/144/15146.pdf.

[92] See *Republic of Ireland v United kingdom* 1978 Series A, No. 25 before the European court of Human Rights. http://lawofwar.org/Ireland_v_United Kingdom.htm. This is a landmark case invoking the prohibition against torture in the European Convention of Human Rights. The court ruled that the 5 interrogation techniques used by British forces on suspected IRA terrorists constituted torture. In September 1967 Denmark, Norway Sweden and the Netherlands filed a complaint to the Human Rights Commission of the Council of Europe against the military junta of Greece for acts of torture against thousands of Greek citizens. Greece withdrew from the council before a ruling was handed down.

[93] Case no. IT-95-17/1-T10, Trial Chamber, Judgement, 10 December 1998 available at www.icty.org.

Yugoslavia declared in an obiter that the prohibition of torture as a peremptory norm of international law has effects not only for inter-State relations but for individuals as well. "(I)t would be senseless to argue ... that on account of the jus cogens value of the prohibition against torture, treaties or customary rules providing for torture would be null and void *ab initio*, and then be unmindful of a State say, taking national measures authorising or condoning torture or absolving its perpetrators through an amnesty law ... at the individual level, that is of criminal liability." Where *jus cogens* norms are involved the court's view is that domestic laws in conflict with *jus cogens* norms could be ineffectual.

Multilateral human rights treaties and human rights international law seek to protect the rights and liberties of individuals in the national law of states. One of the most important provisions of UNCAT is Art 3(1) which prohibits *refoulment*. "No State Party shall expel, return ("refouler") or extradite a person to another State where there are *substantial* grounds for believing that he would be in danger of being subjected to Torture."[94] The *non-refoulment* provision applies to all individuals who entered the country, whether legally or illegally, and prohibits deportation to the country of origin and transfers to any country where the person may be at risk of torture.[95] The view taken by the court In *Prosecutor v. Anto Furundzija*[96] is that States enjoy "unfettered treaty making powers" and it would be inconsistent to prohibit torture to restrict such freedom while barring States from "prosecuting and punishing those torturers who have engaged in this odious practice abroad ..."[97]

The policy of extra-ordinary renditions pursued by the US and its allies to render terrorist suspects to countries where information would be extracted under painful duress violates this provision. The case law is unambiguously against torture in any jurisdiction. Arguments founded

---

94 Convention Against Torture and Other Cruel, Inhuman or Degrading Treatment or Punishment, *adopted* 10 Dec. 1984, G.A. Res. 39/46, U.N. GAOR 39th Sess., Supp. No. 51 at 197, U.N. Doc.A/39/51(1984) *(entered into force June 26 1987)*, in Brownlie, *Basic Documents on Human Rights*.

95 David Weissbrodt and Isabel Hörtreiter, "The Principle of Non-Refoulment: Art 3 of the Convention against Torture and Other Cruel, Inhuman or Degrading Punishment in Comparison with the Non-Refoulement Provisions of Other International Human Rights Treaties," *Buffalo Human Rights Law Review* (1999) 5 (1): 8. Art 22(8) of the American Convention also prohibits refoulment but Art 27 does allow a state to derogate from Art 22 if there is war or a state of emergency.

96 Case no. IT-95-17/1-T10, Trial Chamber, Judgement, 10 December 1998 available at www.icty.org.

97 Case no. IT-95-17/1-T10.

on jurisdiction, such as the one made by the US Attorney General, has no legal force. The non-*refoulment* provision covers instances when individuals are transferred to be tortured for information since it prohibits the transfer of individuals to jurisdictions where torture is practiced. It does not even permit the return of illegal immigrants, suspected terrorists or even dangerous criminals to jurisdictions that tortures even when the deporting authorities have no other interest than that some people should be returned. The point of anti torture provisions is to ensure that the criminal justice process in every country is fair and that prosecutions and punishments are according to the law.

Western governments have tried to get round the restriction in Art 3(1) by seeking diplomatic assurances that deported individuals will be safe from torture. This has not only proved unsatisfactory in practice because after receiving assurances transferred suspects were tortured, but seeking assurances from countries that torture violates Art 3(2) which requires that States make independent judgements by assessing whether there is a "consistent pattern of gross, flagrant or mass violations of human rights."[98]

In December 2001, Ahmed Agiza and Muhammed El Zary were removed from Sweden to Egypt aboard a US government plane. The Swedish Government requested assurances that "these persons will not be subjected to inhuman treatment or punishment of any kind by any authority of the Arab Republic of Egypt..." The Egyptian government responded that the human rights of these persons will be respected "according to what the Egyptian constitution and law stipulates."[99] The correspondence between Sweden and Egypt exposed the tension between the Egyptian National Constitution and Egypt's interpretation of international law.[100] According to Gregor Noll in his analysis of the aide-memoires between Egypt and Sweden, whenever the Egyptian authorities have claimed to act in accordance with their constitution, they are really signalling a reservation to the norms of international law. The Nordic states have always interpreted the phrase "according to what the Egyptian... law stipulates" as a qualification to international law and have routinely objected. In January 2005 the Swedish Minister stated to his parliament that "(t)he Egyptian Constitution prohibits torture, but we are well aware of the methods employed in

98 UN Convention Against Torture Art 3(2).

99 Excerpts of the aide-memoires are reprinted in Noll, "Diplomatic Assurances and the silence of Human," 108.

100 Noll, "Diplomatic Assurances and the silence of Human Rights Law," 108.

prisons and detention centres in Egypt."[101] The Swedish authorities knew that Egypt's emergency regulations had had the effect of suspending the legal and institutional inhibitions to torture of the Egyptian constitution. Yet Sweden was prepared to accept Egypt's diplomatic assurances and agreed to the rendition of the men. Agiza later proceeded against the Swedish government contending that Sweden had breached Art 3 of UNCAT since Sweden could have foreseen that he would be tortured. Part of Agiza's contention was that the monitoring arrangements that were agreed between Sweden and Egypt fell far short of those implemented by the International Committee of the Red Cross.[102]

The Committee Against Torture found that Sweden was in breach of Art 3 of UNCAT when it agreed to yield Mr Agiza to the US authorities for rendition to Egypt.[103] Their finding was based not on the fact that Agiza was tortured but that the guarantees by the Egyptian authorities "did not suffice to protect against the manifest risk of torture."[104] Noll's criticism of Sweden is trenchant: Sweden "deferred to Egypt's reading of human rights norms" interpreted in terms of Egypt's own constitution when Nordic states were aware and had repeatedly objected to Egypt's use of vague Constitutional Law provisions to avoid being bound by international law.[105]

3. The Persistence of Torture in Democratic Societies

The phenomenon of extra-ordinary rendition to Egypt is best examined in conjunction with the apparent failure of international law to eradicate the practice of torture worldwide.

Despite the rapid development of an international human rights regime that not only lists and defines torture and cruel punishments but also monitors countries compliance with multilateral human rights treaties, torture does not seem to have abated. The revelations that Egypt colluded

---

101 Reported in Noll, "Diplomatic Assurances and the silence of Human Rights Law," 109.

102 Reported in Joseph, "Rendering Terrorists and the Convention against Torture," *HRLR* (2005) 5: 339, 342.

103 *Agiza v Sweden*, Committee Against Torture, Communication No 233/03, UN Doc CAT/C/34/D/233/2003, in Noll, "Diplomatic Assurances and the silence of Human Rights Law," 119. Agiza claimed that his rendition to Egypt breached Art 3 of the C.A.T. which prohibits the extradition of an individual to a state where the person may be tortured. *See* Joseph, "Rendering Terrorists and the Convention Against Torture," 339.

104 Joseph, "Rendering Terrorists and the Convention Against Torture," 342.

105 Noll, "Diplomatic Assurances and the Silence of Human Rights Law," 118.

with Western democracies to torture suspected terrorists seems to prove that global monitoring failed to eradicate torture and that the only effect of torture monitoring has been to push torture underground by making it invisible.

After the attacks in New York, London and Madrid the case against the prohibition of torture seemed to be softening. Several factors contributed to this. There was a strong feeling that the world was unsafe, that terrorists have the upper hand, and that conventional methods to apprehend and try them have failed. Television programmes popularised the idea that torture worked and that there would be no time for moral niceties in a "ticking bomb situation."[106] Even some legal scholars promoted the idea that torture, in rare instances, is unavoidable.[107] Suddenly detention and 'enhanced interrogation' of captured detainees appeared both reasonable and necessary. That this was a dangerous compromise of the very rationale of democratic states founded on a commitment to the rule of law seemed less important when faced with a threat to the 'life of the nation.'

Justifications of torture proceed on the assumption that it is possible to keep a society safe by torturing a few suspects who can be made to yield crucial information vital to the security of the nation. It is not the purpose of this analysis to examine whether torture works or to engage with the various philosophical debates about the immorality of torture. These ideas have been discussed at length elsewhere.[108] The main purpose of torture today is neither to punish nor to obtain confessions but to extract

---

[106] *24*, American TV series produced for FOX about a Counter Terrorist Unit (CTU) agent. Over a period of nine years the drama depicted the effectiveness of torture.

[107] See Michael Ignatieff, *The Lesser Evil: Political Ethics in the Age of Terror*. (Princeton: Princeton University Press, 2004) and Alan M. Dershkowitz, *Why Terrorism Works: Understanding the Threat, Responding to the Challenge*. (New Haven: Yale University Press, 2003).

Karen J. Greenberg and Joshua l. Dratel (eds.), *The Torture Papers: The Road to Abu Graib* (Cambridge: Cambridge University Press, 2005) and Karen J. Greenberg *The Torture Debate in America* (Cambridge: Cambridge University Press, 2006) discuss the infamous torture memos between John Yoo, former Assistant Attorney General in the Bush Administration, and Jay Bybee authorising enhanced interrogation.

One of the first accounts against torture is the essay by the Italian philosopher Cesare Beccaria entitled "On crimes and Punishments" (1763), re-printed in: Micheline R. Ishay, *Human Rights Reader: Major Political Essays, Speeches and Documents from the Bible to the Present* (New York: Routledge, 2007).

[108] See Rejali, *Torture and Democracy*; Dershkowitz *Why Terrorism Works: Understanding the Threat*, Ignatieff, *The Lesser Evil: Political Ethics in the Age of Terror*; Jeremy Waldron "Torture and Positive Law: Jurisprudence for the White House," August 29, 2004 Public Lecture: Victoria University of Wellington, New Zealand http://www.columbia.edu/cu/law/fed-soc/otherfiles/waldron.pdf.

information and to intimidate. All the available evidence is against the conclusion that tortured suspects generate reliable and accurate information. In fact moving interrogations abroad and relying on uncorroborated information obtained through torture has proved fatal for US policy in the region. The information that persuaded the US to launch an attack on Iraq was the evidence supplied by a kidnapped trainer of an Al-Qaeda training camp Ibn Sheikh al-Libi.[109] Al- Libi was captured in Afghanistan by American soldiers. He claimed he was tortured in Egypt.[110] Under torture he alleged to his interrogators that Iraq supplied and trained *al Qaeda* operatives in the use of chemical and biological weapons.[111] This information, which was yielded under torture and on which so much depended, was subsequently proved false.[112] In his comment on the efficacy of rendition Rejali observes that "(e)xtraordinary renditions violate two cardinal rules for gathering human intelligence: Do not surrender your assets and resources to others, and do not depend on intelligence from allied agencies without independent corroboration. Failing to recognise these important warnings makes intelligence agencies even more susceptible to false information ... Cultural familiarity and linguistic skill are not substitutes for professionalism."[113] The experience of many intelligence officials is that torture is inimical to good intelligence gathering and no substitute for traditional police work, trust and cooperation which are more effective *modus operandi.* Yet torture persists.

Darius Rejali, in his majestic study of torture in early and modern times offers the grim verdict that democratic societies are just as likely to torture as authoritarian ones. So democracy is not, of itself, a good predictor of reduced incidences of torture. The difference between democratic governments and authoritarian regimes is the manner in which torture is practiced. Democratic societies quickly developed a stealth style of torture which was only later imitated by authoritarian states. During the 1970's and 1980's clean techniques of torture surged as monitoring of human rights abuses by NGOs and other international bodies matured.[114]

---

109 Rejali, *Torture and Democracy*, 505.

110 Mayer, "Outsourcing Torture," 20; Dana Priest "Wrongful imprisonment: Anatomy of a CIA mistake," Washington Post, Dec. 4, 2005, cited in Rejali, *Torture and Democracy*, 504.

111 Rejali, *Torture and Democracy*, 504.

112 "When the FBI later asked him why he lied, he blamed the brutality of the Egyptian intelligence service," Nat Hentoff, "Longtime U.S. Ally Mubarak Also CIA Torture Partner," http://www.cato.org Feb. 10, 2011.

113 Rejali, *Torture and Democracy*, 507.

114 Rejali, *Torture and Democracy*, 13.

Robust international and domestic monitoring of both democratic and authoritarian regimes encouraged experimentation with torture techniques that leaves few physical traces so evidence of torture becomes difficult to detect: "stealth torture appears to be a perverse effect of the growing robustness of international monitoring."[115] It is difficult in democratic societies which pride themselves on their openness and willingness to let observers "monitor specific behaviours" to explain why monitors should be denied access to prisons or to records. No law and order institution in a democracy whether the police, the military or the secret service is free from supervision by independent official bodies, informal organisations such as human rights NGOs or other democratic institutions such as a free press.[116] It is precisely the freedom enjoyed by citizens of democratic nations to "review public power or name violent injustice" that encourages interrogators to develop clean techniques refined to produce no scars.[117] The unintended consequence was that "observers changed the behaviour they sought to document."[118] Torturers in the West could inflict pain but leave few traces of their work. For example, electro torture, which leaves little scarring is an invention of the American and French police.[119] Electro torture was a technique common in the West but absent from communist States.[120]

Authoritarian regimes were more careful about giving *carte blanche* to observers so treatment meted out to dissenters was often rougher and if scars were left this served as a warning to the general population. However, it was not long before the international monitoring of rights changed the behaviour of authoritarian States as well as the human rights record of States began to play an increasing role in decisions on foreign policy and aid.[121]

Most states sign up to torture prohibiting treaties because of the political significance of human rights. Rejali suggests that this was especially evident during the cold war when human rights played a part in the ideology of both sides. In the West human rights became part of the definition of a liberal democracy which had to be supportive of the auditing of political violence by the State in terms of international human rights norms. A

---

115 Rejali, *Torture and Democracy*, 418.
116 Rejali, *Torture and Democracy*, 2.
117 Rejali, *Torture and Democracy*, 2.
118 Rejali, *Torture and Democracy*, 572.
119 Rejali, *Torture and Democracy*, xvii.
120 Rejali, *Torture and Democracy*, 17.
121 Rejali, *Torture and Democracy*, 571.

good human rights record was important for political legitimacy, foreign aid or even membership of the community.[122] The US and the Soviet Union both felt a compulsion to comply with international human rights norms because each side "claimed a superior morality, a commitment to human rights in terms of their own political and ideological traditions."[123] Governments avoid the appearance of hypocrisy and even authoritarian governments function with a modicum of public trust. Hence, it is important to create a plausible gloss over the ruthless suppression of any opposition. Brutality occurs stealthily, sneakily and with more refinement.

Rejali's thesis is persuasive and the evidence he provides for his main argument is compelling. He demonstrated the affinity public monitoring has with "stealth torture" and shows that "where free elections have gone, where monitoring agencies have set up shop, and journalists have taken to the streets and airwaves, they have been followed by electric prods and electroshockers, tortures by water and ice, drugs of sinister variety, sonic devices—and by methods that are less technical, but no less sophisticated or painful: the modern democratic torturer knows how to beat a suspect senseless without leaving a mark."[124]

He provides a long list of clean methods that have their genesis in Britain, America and France: relay interrogation and sleep deprivation; beatings with blunt objects which because they possess no sharp edges will leave no marks; illegal and painful uses of light and electricity; and endurance and position torture such as standing for long periods; exposure to hypo—and hyperthermia (cold rooms and sweat boxes).[125]

The El Nadeem Centre for Psychological Management and Rehabilitation of Victims in Egypt described in their 2003 report the mixed methods of torture recorded by victims of Egyptian interrogators between 1993 and 2001 in detention centres in Egypt.[126] These were beatings, suspension, spraying icy water on the body, sexual abuse and rape, sensory deprivation, humiliation and insults, electric shock, unsanitary conditions, threats of harm to the victims' families, watching the torture of other victims, dragging on the floor, scalding hands, breaking bones and burning.[127] This

---

122 Each time the inclusion of Turkey in the EU is discussed, for example, Turkey's human rights record is part of the conversation.

123 Rejali, *Torture and Democracy*, 439.

124 Rejali, *Torture and Democracy*, 3.

125 Rejali, *Torture and Democracy*, 571.

126 Torture in Egypt, facts and testimonie, El Nadeem Centre for Psychological Management and Rehabilitation of Victims of Violence, 2003, in Aziz, "Torture in Egypt," 49.

127 Torture in Egypt, facts and testimonies, in Aziz, "Torture in Egypt," 49.

list seems to be mainly non-scarring torture techniques such as electric shocks but some scarring techniques such as burning and scalding appear as well. It is not possible to provide an analysis of the techniques used on different categories of prisoners but it is noteworthy that the Iocobucci inquiry in Canada into the actions of Canadian CSIS officials in the torture in Egypt of El Maati, a Canadian citizen, revealed that the torture techniques used on him were mainly non-scarring—electric shock to hands, back and genitals, sleep deprivation, painful stress torture.[128] There was clearly enough independent monitoring in Egypt to account for both the preponderance of non-scarring techniques that were used on certain prisoners and the presence of secret, illegal detention centres as well.

The evidence shows that active monitoring of law and order forces encourages covert torture. Overt torture is usually more readily detectable during the chaos of war and in rural areas.[129] Another significant reason for covert torture in democracies is that torturers have no legal protection if they are exposed. Non-scarring torture techniques develop to make it difficult to furnish proof that there has been illegal, physically damaging violence. If victims could prove torture perpetrators would face criminal prosecution or at least the loss of position. Covert, non-marking torture has the effect of destroying the credibility of the claims of the victim both in the community and before the courts.

Monitoring tries to shame governments into compliance with international norms and states violating *jus cogens* may be tried before the international court of justice. If Rejali is correct to assert that stealth torture is a consequence of torture monitoring, the imperative for liberal democracies was simply not to get caught. This is perhaps the answer to the question why the need for extraordinary rendition in the first place? The US and its Western allies tried to keep their own hands clean and their own official's safe from prosecution by employing the expertise of torturers in other jurisdictions. Rendering suspects to foreign jurisdictions was a further refinement of the policy of democratic states to hide illegal methods of extracting information.

[128] Kerry Pither, "Iacobucci Inquiry exposes new information about how CSIS contributed to the torture of Canadian Ahmad El Maati in Egypt," Tuesday, 23rd February available at http://kerrypither.com/tag/iacobucci-inquiry/

[129] Rejali, *Torture and Democracy*, 11.

3.1. *The Effectiveness of Torture Monitoring*

The prevalence of numerous treaties and enforcement bodies prohibiting torture has failed to eliminate it even among democratic Western nations. The photographic evidence of the torture of detainees by US personnel at US detention centres abroad and the phenomenon of extraordinary renditions to Egypt and other countries seems only to furnish further proof that democratic countries do have recourse to torture in certain circumstances. Authoritarian States that are allies of the West, instead of being encouraged to eradicate torture, simply learnt cleaner techniques of torture which explains why "clean techniques tend to cluster around authoritarian states most closely allied with the main democratic states" of the US, the UK and France.[130]

This is a damning indictment of international efforts to stop people being tortured. Apart from monitoring there are few means available to enforce the provisions of human rights treaties. However, considered in a different light, the necessity of foreign detention centres and extraordinary renditions to Egypt and other countries as a means of combating terrorism may actually be proof that scrutinising States for their compliance with torture treaties is working and international prohibitions against torture are worthwhile after all. The US and its allies wanted the use of enhanced methods of interrogation but they knew that their own domestic law and their international obligations had made this impossible. Indeed it is possible to reach the optimistic conclusion that even the development of covert, non-scarring torture techniques would not ultimately escape public scrutiny. For this reason torture had to be outsourced. Extraordinary renditions to Egypt were clearly a response to the effectiveness of robust public monitoring. The recent revolution in Egypt is therefore, extremely significant for US policy on terrorism. Egyptians have rejected a regime dependent on torture thus removing a key ally in the fight against terrorism by prohibited means.

If human rights monitoring served to make torture covert, it has also made torture increasingly more difficult to practice in democratic countries, hence the curious necessity to outsource torture to foreign jurisdictions. Extraordinary rendition became necessary when the line separating interrogation from torture reached its legal limit and efforts at shielding enhanced interrogation methods from public scrutiny failed. Extraordinary

130 Rejali, *Torture and Democracy*, 13.

rendition has itself failed as a policy to keep torture covert. The ways and means countries colluded with willing partners, such as Egypt, to torture on their behalf, has been exposed and governments complicit in extraordinary rendition, censured. The cases of Ahmad Agiza and Muhammad al-Zari, mentioned earlier, are cases in point. Even though the government of Sweden had procured from the Egyptian authorities assurances that the detainees would not be tortured, the UN human Rights Committee concluded that Sweden had breached a *jus cogens* norm by allowing the Egyptians to be removed and that the assurances given to Sweden were not enough.

Similarly, in July 2005, an Italian court issued arrest warrants charging thirteen CIA operatives of kidnapping Omar Moustafa Hassan Nasr or Abu Omar, a Muslim Imam from Milan, who had been granted political asylum in Italy and rendering him to Egypt.[131] Omar was an Egyptian and a member of a radical Islamic Organisation, *Jamaat al Islamiya*. The Italian courts charged the Americans and attempted to extradite Omar from Egypt. On his release Omar alleged that he was tortured in Egypt. In November 2009, 23 CIA agents were convicted of kidnapping *in abstentia*.[132]

Public outrage at the involvement of Canadian CSIS officials in extraordinary rendition of Canadian citizens to Egypt and Syria forced the Canadian government to set up the independent O'Connor Inquiry. The Report on the 'events relating to Maher Arar' revealed that Arar was rendered by the US, acting on information supplied by Canadian officials (RCMP), to Syria where he was held and tortured for a year.[133] Arar received an apology from the Canadian government and $10 million in compensation in 2006.[134] The Iacobucci Inquiry of 2008 also found Canadian officials complicit in the torture of three Arab Canadian men in Syria. Justice Iacobucci found that when CSIS officials informed the Egyptian authorities that El Maati, who was in detention in Egypt, may have been involved in a terrorist plot in Canada, their information was not based on evidence but on confessions extracted from the Syrian authorities. The judge concluded that CSIS should have known that such a confession was

---

131 DiMento and Geis, "The Extraordinary Condition of Extraordinary Rendition," 42.

132 Human Rights Watch, "Work on him until he confesses," 16.

133 Report on the Events Relating to Maher Arar: Analysis and Recommendations, Commission of Inquiry into the Actions of Canadian officials in Relation to Maher Arar, http://www.pch.gc.ca/cs-kc/arar/Arar_e.pdf.

134 Audrey Macklin, "From Cooperation, to Complicity, to Compensation: The War on Terror, Extraordinary Rendition and the Cost of Torture," *European Journal of Migration and Law*, (2008) 10 (1): 11–30.

the result of torture and that communicating this to the Egyptian authorities contributed to their mistreatment there. The UN Committee against torture has condemned Canada's complicity in torture and human right violations. The Committee accused Canada of participating in the extraordinary rendition of Abdulla Almalki, Ahmed Abou Elmaati and Myayyed Nureddin to Syria and Egypt where they were subject to illegal forms of interrogation.[135]

In Britain sustained questioning by MP's, NGO's, victims of extraordinary rendition and even soldiers has revealed the extent of British involvement in the rendition of terrorist suspects.[136] After first denying any involvement in rendition, Foreign Secretary David Miliband, in a statement to the House of Commons on 21st February 2008, admitted that Britain was involved in two cases of extraordinary rendition when planes transporting detainees refuelled in Deigo Garcia, a British Indian Ocean Territory.[137] It has since emerged that over 240 rendition flights may have occurred dating back to 2001. In August 2008 the high court found that British authorities were actively involved in the rendition of Binyam Mohammed. Their "involvement was far beyond that of a bystander or witness to the alleged wrongdoing."[138] Mohammed was British resident, who had been subject to torture in several countries in the Middle East including Egypt.

---

135 Terry Milewski, "Canada accused of 'complicity' in torture in UN report," CBS news, 1 June 2012, available at http://www.cbc.ca/news/politics/story/2012/06/01 pol-un-report-torture-canada-milewski.html. *See also* Frank Iacobucci, "Internal Inquiry into the Actions of Canadian Officials in Relation to Abdulla Almalki, Ahmad Abou- Elmaati and Muayyed Nureddin," published by government of Canada, Oct. 2008, Supplement to Public Report, online at: http://dsp-psd.pwgsc.gc.ca/collection2010/bcp-pco/CP32-90-1-2010-eng.pdf. CANADA Briefing to the UN Committee Against Torture 48th Session, May 2012, Amnesty International, online at http://www.amnesty.org/en/library/asset/AMR20/004/2012/en/b46d9371-1b2c-414b-90e9-b97c3953cb48/amr200042012en.pdf.

136 See the efforts to obtain full disclosure by the All Party Parliamentary Group on Extra Ordinary Rendition and The Information Commissioner and Ministry of Defence 2011 UKUT 153 (ACC) online: http://www.judiciary.gov.uk/ResourcesJCO/Documents/judgements/appger-v-ic-judgement.pdf. See also Press statement of Ben Griffen ex soldier Special Air Service (SAS), read in London 25 February 2008, online: http://www.spokesmanbooks.com/Spokesman/PDF/griffen99.pdf. On 28 February the Ministry of Defence obtained an injunction against Griffen from the High Court.

137 Richard Norton-Taylor, "UK's role in the rendition of terror suspects under fresh scrutiny," The Guardian Thursday 19 April 2012.

138 R (Binyam Mohamed) v Secretary of State for the Foreign and Commonwealth Office. [2009] 1 WLR 2653 and Mohamed, R (on the application of) v Secretary of State for Foreign & Commonwealth Affairs [2010] EWCA Civ 65 [2011] QB 218.

4. Torture and the Egyptian Revolution

Torture by Western democracies had not stopped; it simply shifted elsewhere. There were no examples of the torture of suspected terrorists in US, Britain or Canadian prisons. These administrations were careful not to breach domestic law or international provisions that banned torture. Also, Western democracies did not deport suspects to each other for interrogation. For torture to be eradicated States must recognise the enhanced status of *jus cogens* norms in their domestic jurisdictions. The example set by Switzerland and the recent revolution in Egypt may promise an end to the era of states finding partners in torture.

Switzerland's interpretation of UNCAT Art 3 (1) on the absolute ban on *refoulment* may be a precursor of things to come. The Federal Constitution of Switzerland binds national law to *jus cogens.*[139] In July 1992, The People's Initiative submitted to the Federal authorities included a constitutional amendment that sought to deport, without the possibility of appeal, asylum seekers entering the country illegally. This was invalidated by both chambers of the Swiss Federal Parliament on the grounds that people who were fleeing persecution should not be deported back to a state where they could be subjected to torture or cruel and degrading treatment. "This would constitute a violation of the peremptory prohibition of *refoulment* and thus one of the most elementary norms of international law." This is a striking example of how "peremptory norms of international law gained explicit constitutional recognition as a material limitation to the legislative process."[140]

The fall of Hosni Mubarak in January 2011 was a demand by the Egyptian people for a less coercive more accountable government. One of the slogans of protesters in the square was 'Eish! Horreya! Karama insaneyya' (Bread, Freedom, Human Dignity).[141] However, even before the revolution, statements on torture made by Egyptian public officials revealed a shift in attitude. In 1999 Egyptian prosecutors dismissed allegations of torture as "exaggerations." By 2010 the minister of the Interior Habib al-Adly was prepared to admit on television cautiously that torture would harm the reputation of the ministry but he explained the torture allegations

---

139 Erika de Wet, "The Prohibition of Torture as an International Norm of jus cogens and Its Implications for National and Customary Law," *European Journal of International Law*,(2004) 15 (1): 97–121, 101.

140 de Wet, "The Prohibition of Torture as an International Norm of jus cogens," 101.

141 Soueif, *Cairo My City, Our Revolution*, 18.

away by insisting that where there were incidences of torture it was the normal rate of "infractions" one would expect in any public institution.[142] The January 2011 Human Rights Watch Report on Egypt attributes this shift in rhetoric to "greater media freedom and information dissemination in Egypt in recent years." The report stated that it had become impossible for the government to deny the repeated allegations of torture "when disturbing images of its results are widely available on the internet, social networking sites and other media."[143] New technologies have made secret torture more difficult by exposing the coercive methods employed by the regime. The state had shown a willingness to investigate and prosecute more allegations of torture but this was not enough of an indication that torture practices would cease.

The almost four million people involved in the demonstrations in Cairo and elsewhere in Egypt were protesting deep social political problems that included unemployment, housing and education.[144] But the slogans of the crowds also revealed an unequivocal rejection of the violence and control the State had exerted. When it became clear that Mubarak had lost support the US urged that the government be handed to Omar Suleiman, Vice-president and former head of intelligence. The Egyptians rejected this as evidenced by the shouts of the crowd in the Midan: "No Mubarak/No Suleiman/No more umala amrikan (agents for America).[145] Suleiman was closely identified with Egyptian intelligence and torture and with US intelligence. According to Mayer, Suleiman was involved in renditions authorized at the top levels of both governments.[146] Soueif adds that the history of the personal involvement of Vice-president Suleiman in "rendition and torture" was well known in the Midan.[147] Soueif's report of the impression Suleiman created when he was interviewed by Christiane Amanpour for CNN describes a man Egyptians regarded as synonymous with torture. "We watched the old torturer, stiff with formality and self-belief, clinging onto his simple conspiratorial concepts, holding himself rigid against the tide, the tsunami of us in the Midan and in the streets, his thumbscrews and cattle prods for the moment useless."[148]

---

142 Human Rights Watch, "Work on him until he confesses," 16.
143 Human Rights Watch, "Work on him until he confesses," 31.
144 Soueif, *Cairo My City, Our Revolution*, 55.
145 Soueif, *Cairo My City, Our Revolution*, 51.
146 Mayer, "Who is Omar Suleiman"? *New Yorker.com* Jan. 29, 2011.
147 Soueif, *Cairo My City, Our Revolution*, 150.
148 Soueif, *Cairo My City, Our Revolution*, 160.

Democracy by itself is no guarantee that a society would respect the rule of law and be free of covert and illicit violence. Egypt's neighbour, Israel, has deemed it necessary to accomodate highly suspect methods of interrogation as the only way to curb Palestinian terrorism and Israel is the only recognised democracy in the region.[149] Extraordinary rendition proves that torture is still part of the security establishment of democratic countries but effective torture monitoring in the West drove it abroad: the sophistry of legal argumentation over definitions of torture was limited and efforts to keep torture hidden had become unwieldy.

If the new Egyptian constitution entrenches human rights with a clear and unequivocal provision prohibiting torture there will be fewer places for democratic countries to go if they wish to continue to subject people to torture. This is enormously significant not only for the political changes so sorely needed within Egypt but for the effort to eradicate torture globally. Governments having banned torture in their own jurisdictions will have to abandon illegal methods of interrogation altogether if they no longer have willing allies.[150] As the New York Association of the Bar declared: "Far from being an acceptable tool in the "War on Terror," extraordinary renditions are illegal and constitute a perversion of justice and must be prosecuted."[151]

[149] For an analysis of torture in Israel and of the high court decision on torture see Williams, "Your Honour, I am here today requesting the Court's permission to torture Mr. Doe," 350–360.

[150] "Human Rights cannot be regional. The rule of law cannot be selective. Guantanomo, Belmarsh, Lazoghli and Facility 1391 in Israel are part of the same configuration; they stand together or one hopes fall together," A. Souief, *The Guardian*, 9 March 2006.

[151] Association of the Bar of the City of New York & Center for Human Rights and Justice, N.Y.U. School of Law, "Torture by Proxy: International and Domestic Law Applicable to 'Extraordinary Rendition'," *The Record* (2005) 60 (13).

INDEX

www.ingramcontent.com/pod-product-compliance
Lightning Source LLC
Chambersburg PA
CBHW031321230926
51848CB00001B/37
9789004230415